Carthage at War

Carthage at War

Punic Armies c. 814–146 BC

Joshua R. Hall

Pen & Sword
MILITARY

First published in Great Britain in 2023 by
Pen & Sword Military
An imprint of Pen & Sword Books Limited
Yorkshire – Philadelphia

Copyright © Joshua R. Hall 2023

ISBN 978 1 47388 538 7

The right of Joshua R. Hall to be identified as Author of this work has been asserted by him in accordance with the Copyright, Designs and Patents Act 1988.

A CIP catalogue record for this book is
available from the British Library.

All rights reserved. No part of this book may be reproduced or transmitted in any form or by any means, electronic or mechanical including photocopying, recording or by any information storage and retrieval system, without permission from the Publisher in writing.

Typeset by Mac Style
Printed in the UK by CPI Group (UK) Ltd, Croydon, CR0 4YY.

Pen & Sword Books Limited incorporates the imprints of After the Battle, Atlas, Archaeology, Aviation, Discovery, Family History, Fiction, History, Maritime, Military, Military Classics, Politics, Select, Transport, True Crime, Air World, Frontline Publishing, Leo Cooper, Remember When, Seaforth Publishing, The Praetorian Press, Wharncliffe Local History, Wharncliffe Transport, Wharncliffe True Crime and White Owl.

For a complete list of Pen & Sword titles please contact

PEN & SWORD BOOKS LIMITED
47 Church Street, Barnsley, South Yorkshire, S70 2AS, England
E-mail: enquiries@pen-and-sword.co.uk
Website: www.pen-and-sword.co.uk
or
PEN AND SWORD BOOKS
1950 Lawrence Rd, Havertown, PA 19083, USA
E-mail: Uspen-and-sword@casematepublishers.com
Website: www.penandswordbooks.com

To my parents,
Curtiss and Patricia Hall

Contents

Acknowledgements		viii
Chapter 1	General Introduction	1
Chapter 2	Warfare and Imperialism in Early Carthage	7
Chapter 3	Armies Against Syracuse	27
Chapter 4	The Wars with Dionysius I of Syracuse	50
Chapter 5	Timoleon, Agathocles, and Pyrrhus	75
Chapter 6	The First War with Rome	120
Chapter 7	The Truceless War	166
Chapter 8	The Second War with Rome	178
Chapter 9	Killing a Phoenix: The End of Carthage	225
Chapter 10	Punic Warfare: Conclusions	245
Notes		253
Bibliography		305
Index		316

Acknowledgements

This book owes its existence to a number of things. The first, and certainly most important, is the coursework and research which constituted my MA degree at Cardiff University. I was guided to this topic by my masters, and then doctoral, supervisor, Dr. Louis Rawlings, without whom this book would never have come to be. Louis helped to guide my development as an historian for more than half a decade, and I cannot adequately express my indebtedness to him. Many others at Cardiff are owed debts of gratitude regarding this monograph. Foremost amongst them is Dr. Kate Gilliver, whose passionate interest in the Roman army drove my own. I am also very thankful for the time I was able to spend talking with Dr. Richard Evans, whether about Cicero or Syracuse. I would like to thank all the rest of the amazing faculty at Cardiff, even those who I only got to know during my years as a doctoral candidate, as you all helped to shape my thinking about the ancient world.

The idea for this book has bounced around in my mind for quite some time, but it was only realized in the current form thanks to a conversation with Philip Sidnell, editor at Pen & Sword. It was through this contact that I finalized my aims and the discussion, as it is set out here, was organized. One of these aims was to write a book which looked at Punic armies and appealed to a wide audience of enthusiasts, undergraduates, and academics. Because of this wide-ranging audience, readers should find this to be a readable, yet informative, take on Punic war making. I use a combination of narrative and analysis to elucidate for all of those who pick up this book a better vision of how the Carthaginians fought against their neighbours.

Most of the work for this book has been undertaken with the support of my parents, whose encouragement and generosity are directly responsible for it having been finished. I also need to thank those who unknowingly helped me complete it, especially the University of Oregon's Knight Library, Western Oregon University's Hamersly Library, and

Willamette University's Hatfield Library, all of which are open to the public and contain works referenced in this book that I would not have been able to otherwise access. And as always, I should remind everyone that all omissions and errors to be found in this book are mine, and mine alone, and none of those who have been acknowledged should be held responsible!

Chapter 1

General Introduction

Carthage occupies a special place in the study of the ancient world. On one hand, we know that its civilization was one of the most important and powerful in the central Mediterranean, but on the other we know relatively little about the city, its empire, and its people. This latter fact is based primarily on the almost complete destruction of Punic literature. The problem is compounded by the loss of many of the Greek and Latin historical texts which specifically documented Carthage. We are not left in the dark completely, however, and from the evidence which remains we know enough to corroborate its position of importance and can rank Carthage amongst the greatest civilizations of the ancient world. From its foundation through to the period of the wars with Rome, Carthage grew into one of the largest cities in the Mediterranean basin, growing rich through both its intrepid traders and expansive territory. Her ships plied the sea from the Atlantic coast of North Africa to the Levant in the east.

From a military perspective, Carthage was no less powerful than it was wealthy. It was a major power from at least the early fifth century BC. Their earliest invasion of Sicily, for which we have any real knowledge, was forceful enough to have been compared to the Persian invasion of Greece which occurred in the same period. As we shall see, at least one element which led to this judgment was propagandistic, but there was reason for the Western Greeks to fear Carthage. Their strength continued to grow throughout the fifth and fourth centuries, allowing for the creation of the central Mediterranean's first 'overseas' empire. It was at the apex of Punic expansion and power that they came into conflict with the other rising power in the region, Rome. Through three bitter wars, these two civilizations battered one another until Carthage finally gave, resulting in the destruction of the city and her empire.

Carthage's position as one of the great civilizations of the ancient world has created a lasting interest in the minds of scholars, philosophers, and writers. Like the study of most aspects of Mediterranean history, there has been a steady development of scholarship from the nineteenth century to the present day. Many older works relied almost entirely on the evidence for Carthage's civilization which can be found in ancient texts. The real progress in Punic studies, though, has happened thanks in part to the expansive archaeological projects in and around Carthage, as well as its hinterland and parts of the empire outside of Africa, all of which have shed unprecedented light on Carthaginian culture. Since the turn of the last century, there has been a considerable rise in the city's popularity in Anglophone literature, with the publication of a number of accessible and comprehensive surveys of the history and archaeology of Carthage based in the modern scholarly outlook.[1] Although there has been more attention paid to the details of Punic culture and society, there have been few attempts to get to grips with their armies and warfare in a serious way. There have, of course, been books and articles published on the topic, though those in English tend to be targeted at the most casual of audiences. Readers of other languages have been more fortunate, with the most interesting recent monograph on the subject being in German, with many insightful scholarly articles having been recently produced in Spain.[2]

This work aims to fill this gap partially and provide readers with a critical narrative of the wars fought by Punic soldiers and generals. Its structure has been designed to guide enthusiasts of ancient history and warfare through the history of their wars and provide insight along the way, along with a brief tidying up at the end. Some readers may ask 'why another book on the Punic Wars?' While this is a fair question to level against other works, this book was purposefully written to not emphasize the period of the wars with Rome. All periods of Carthaginian history are given weight in the analysis of Punic warfare. Because of my approach in writing this book, I focus on the Carthaginian sides of the wars against Rome and do not provide as full of an account as the many works which focus specifically on that subject. For any reader hoping for in-depth discussions of Scipio or of internal Roman affairs, I do apologize, but there are many, many other well-written accounts which deal only with the Punic Wars.[3] Although this book was written primarily for a general audience, I hope that readers of all interest-levels in the ancient world, from the novice to the scholar, will find in it something of value. If it encourages even one person to conduct their own research on Punic history, I will feel that it has been worthwhile.

We begin in this chapter with a survey of the sources used in this book, as well as the prehistory and early history of Carthage, starting with the Phoenicians in the eastern Mediterranean. This introduction also looks at the foundation of Punic international strategy. Chapter 2 moves into the fifth and fourth centuries and examines the wars between Carthage and the Greeks in Sicily. This theme is carried into the third chapter which extends our discussion into the Hellenistic period. Chapters 5 to 9 deal with the period of the wars against Rome, commonly known as the 'Punic Wars.' This is both a well-trodden period in historical scholarship, but also the richest period in terms of our knowledge of Carthaginian affairs. The final chapter is an analytical examination of Punic armies and war-making which provides a clear answer to some of the pressing questions about these, notably on the service of Carthaginian citizens and the motivations for the state to go to war.

Throughout this book, readers will encounter places with which they are unfamiliar, and possibly some terms as well. I will admit that I have not been consistent in my use of Latinized, Hellenized, or modern renderings of place names. For instance, I use the Greek 'Akragas' rather than Agrigentum (modern Agrigento on Sicily), but I use modern English 'Syracuse' rather than Greek Syrakousai or modern Italian Siracusa. I have typically used Latinized personal names, especially for the Carthaginians. While I believe that it is interesting and would do justice to an otherwise historically oppressed people to spell these as they would be in the Punic language, I think that it would do a disservice to my readers, many (if not most) of whom will not be professional historians. I hope that these choices do not cause considerable confusion, and one of the benefits of living in the information age is that readers confounded by any place or word they find in my text can easily search for it on the internet, which will doubtlessly provide a better answer and description than I could ever hope to.

Our Sources

No Punic historical texts survive. Our knowledge of the history of Carthage comes primarily from Greek and Roman writers, most of who wrote much later than the events which they discuss. This is one of the great tragedies of history, as we know that the Carthaginians were a literate people and it is almost certain that their own historians would have given a much different, and more detailed, version of events than that with which we are left. Amongst the sources which are extant, we do not have a continuous narrative of the city's history. The closest to this could be Diodorus Siculus, although his universal history is of a form which does not fit this description. What we have, then, is a number of authors in whose works episodes and short continuous narratives of Punic history exist. Each of these authors must be dealt with on their own terms and all of the evidence that they provide us with must be examined alongside our knowledge of their biases or the biases of the sources which they exploited. These are introduced below in the order in which they are encountered in the main text of this book, with those whose works only make casual references to Carthaginian history coming after those who provide more information and something closer to a narrative.

Diodorus Siculus is an author with whom the reader will become well acquainted throughout the first four chapters of this book. His surviving work is known alternatively as the *Bibliotheke* or *Library of History*. This is the only extant history written by a Western Greek; he originally came from Agyrium, a town on Sicily. We know relatively little of his life, except that he was likely resident in Rome in 46 or 45 BC and that he remained there for quite some time.[4] He composed his history over the course of the first century BC and it was published around 30 BC, considerably later than most of the events for which it enlightens us.[5] The *Bibliotheke* is our principal source of knowledge for the earliest wars fought between Carthage and the Sicilian Greeks and thus provides us with the earliest long narrative of Punic history. But this means that it was written 450 years after the Battle of Himera and 393 years after the sack of Motya. Diodorus' uses of previous historical works, and his references to them, however place at least some of his information all the way back to the late fifth and early fourth centuries.

The historical value of Diodorus' work has regularly been questioned in modern scholarship. Judgment has been passed that he was incompetent and at best a mere copyist. Although these were the conclusions of a considerable number of scholars throughout the previous century, opinion has swayed, to some extent, in the other direction. A number of recent scholars have shown that rather than being a poorly assembled series of stories and miscopied histories, Diodorus actually provides us with a well thought out and even carefully written work.[6] For events concerning Carthage, he followed a number of earlier historians, such as Philistus of Syracuse and Timaeus of Tauromenium, both Greeks from Sicily, or Ephorus, a Greek historian from Cyme, in what is modern Turkey. Most of the works which Diodorus used are all but lost to us, with his *Bibliotheke* representing much of what we know of them. It is helpful that he occasionally signalled from which earlier historian he was taking information, as this allows us to better inquire into details of these passages. Later sections of this book touch on historiographical issues such as this.

Perhaps the best-known source of Carthaginian history to the average reader, and especially to the armchair general, is Polybius. Born in Megalopolis, a town in Arcadia, to a prominent family sometime around 200 BC, he lived considerably closer in time to the events about which he wrote. His early life was probably spent being groomed as a young elite male in his homeland, and we know that he was elected to the second highest office in the hierarchy of the Aechaean League, that of Hipparchos. Polybius' political ambitions, however, came to an abrupt end when, in 167, he was selected as one of 1,000 hostages sent to Rome by Aemilius Paullus in the aftermath of the Third Macedonian War. Here, he developed a friendship with Scipio Africanus and a detailed understanding of Rome and the processes which were rapidly making her the master of the Mediterranean world.[7]

Polybius' *Histories* are useful for the present book as they cover the period of the First and Second Punic Wars, those between Rome and Carthage for domination of the central and western Mediterranean. Much of his information on these events must have come from Roman sources. For both of these, he would have been able to use historical accounts already circulating in the city, such as that by Fabius Pictor, although the bias of this author in particular, a contemporary of the Second Punic War, was noted by Polybius.[8] It is also probable that he would have been able to speak directly with veterans of that war, who would have been still living, though quite elderly. Polybius' account does exhibit a Roman bias in places, as well as a number of other systemic issues from a modern 'objective' historian's position.[9] Spectacularly, though, he was present at the destruction of Carthage during the Third Punic War and wrote a heart-wrenching account thereof.

For Punic history during the period of the wars with Rome we also have much of the account written by Livy. He was born in Patavium (modern Padua) in the middle of the first century BC and lived until the second decade of the first century AD. He wrote an extensive history of Rome from its foundation to his own day known as *Ab Urbe Condita*. It is one of our main sources for the early Roman Republic, and is an invaluable source for the Second Punic War. For the period after the Battle of Cannae, we lose Polybius' continuous narrative of the war. Additionally, Livy drew on many earlier historians to compile his work, and on occasion cites different accounts that preserve variant traditions of certain events. His historical judgment may be questionable sometimes, but he provides generally reasonable sounding accounts of the periods for which we need him. It is true that his account of certain years of the Second Punic War is hard to follow, sometimes nonsensical, but he is better than nothing. We should note, however, that a degree of pro-Roman bias is detectable in his work, though this is perhaps to be expected.

A second-century AD writer known to us usually as Justin preserves snippets from early Carthaginian history not recorded elsewhere. It is on his work that we must rely for the very earliest period of Punic military history, though his account is so brief that there is not much in it. This is because his surviving work is actually an epitome – that is, a summary – of the presumably much more thorough history written by Pompeius Trogus, who was active during the reign of Augustus. While Justin's work is important for us, like many later epitomizers it lacks much of what we as modern historians would desire to know.

The final ancient author I wish to highlight for readers – as his works provide extensive coverage of our topic – is Appian of Alexandria. He also flourished in the second century AD and wrote a 24-book history of Rome. It does not survive in its entirety, but some of the portions that do are invaluable to us. This is particularly true for the third war between Carthage and Rome, for which he is our main source. But there is a problem with Appian's coverage of the Punic Wars. Where we can test his information, it often differs from our other sources: Polybius and Livy. Many times, the version of events preserved in Appian are implausible or downright impossible. Thus, we must tread with caution when using him as a source, but again, there are times that he is the only reason we know particular details.

Chapter 2

Warfare and Imperialism in Early Carthage

The early history of Carthaginian warfare is very hard to present as a coherent narrative. Unlike in the later chapters, this one is roughly divided into thematic sections, rather than proceeding in a chronological fashion. Each section examines a particular strand of history. It first looks at the foundation myth of Carthage and discusses the possible early conflicts with indigenous groups in North Africa, as well as the spread of Punic power from Libya to the Atlantic coast. The second examines the evidence for Carthaginian interest in islands, ranging from the Balearics to those of the central Mediterranean. The third traces the stories of some of the earliest Punic leaders we know by name, such as Malchus and Mago and his descendants. The fourth discusses the series of conflicts which pitted Carthage against various Phocaean Greek colonies in the north Tyrrhenian Sea. The fifth looks at the stories of a Greek adventurer/colonist, Dorieus of Sparta, and their conflicts with the Phoenicians, Elymians, Macae, and possibly Carthaginians. In the concluding section of this chapter, all of this evidence will be examined to try to piece together an idea of what kind of wars Carthage may have been fighting before the start of the ongoing conflicts with the Sicilian Greeks and address the question of early Punic imperialism.

As can be gleaned from the first chapter of this book, the events discussed in this chapter are only known from much later historical sources. Some, such as the Battle of Alalia, were recorded in earlier historians, such as Herodotus, but even then, this occurred over 100 years before he wrote his *Histories*. This causes a problem in interpretation and makes us question whether what we read is historically reliable. It is impossible to definitively answer the question of 'is this true?' when confronted with wayward historical 'facts' like those upon which we must build any history of Carthage's early ambitions and wars. As Richard Miles put so eruditely, 'researching a history of the city is rather like reading a transcript of a conversation in which one participant's contribution has been deleted.'[1] He was speaking specifically about the almost complete loss of Punic literature, but it is an apt metaphor for the sources with which we are left. Even within the Greek and Roman *corpi*, we are confronted by major historical lacunae. Thus, although the evidence used in this section is treated critically, it is important to keep in mind that for many Greeks and Romans, the Carthaginians, and Phoenicians more broadly, were useful antagonists and that much of what we read of them may be exaggerations based on biases held by ancient authors.

The Foundation of Carthage and Conflicts in Africa

Carthage was founded by settlers who canonically originated in the Levantine city of Tyre. It was one of many cities to which we refer collectively as 'Phoenician'. However, this is a loaded term, as are so many ethnic nomenclatures, as those it describes would never have called themselves this. It is questionable if all of the different groups of 'Phoenicians' would have identified as a single ethnicity – or race – in the ancient period. The case has been strongly made recently that the communal identities of these peoples was complex.[2] Their identities may have been focused more on individual cities or city-states than in any wider way. It is clear, however, that these peoples who originated on the coast of what is now Syria, Lebanon, and Israel began to emigrate throughout the Mediterranean basin in the early Iron Age.[3]

Emigrants from this region, almost certainly from Tyre, began to settle on a small peninsula on the North African coast by the middle of the eighth century BC. Here they would go on to found the city of Carthage, or *Qart-Hadasht*. The meaning of the city's name in its own language was 'New City', an indication that it was a purposeful foundation and not an accidental conglomeration of traders and adventurers. Foundation stories abound regarding how it came to be, but how much truth there is in any of them remains to be see. Whether or not a late ninth-century princess named Elissa fled her evil brother Pygmalion and founded the city can never be known, while the shameful love affair between an alternative mother-queen, Dido, and the Romano-Trojan hero Aeneas is almost certainly a later fabrication. What we can say about the foundation of the city, though, is that it happened, and that the eighth-century immigrants to this corner of ancient Libya set in motion the development of one of the greatest cities of antiquity.[4]

The early relations with native peoples may have been relatively peaceful, and the stories about the city's foundation make it sound as though they were happy to have the new settlers as long as they paid them tribute. A yearly dispensation was given to the local tribe.[5] If this is historical, the fact that it wasn't thrown off until the fifth century BC may mean that Carthage did not look to expand at the expense of its most immediate neighbours for the first three hundred years of its existence. But successful campaigns against unspecified Africans were carried out by the earliest known *rab*, or general, in the city's history: Mazeus (discussed in more detail below).[6] These early wars may have been directed at native African peoples who were otherwise hostile to Carthage, i.e. not those to whom the city was paying tribute. But the ruling clan which followed Mazeus, known as the Magonids, waged much wider campaigns. Although the founder of this dynasty, Mago, is said to have greatly increased the city's territorial possessions, we do not have details of his campaign(s). His sons, Hasdrubal and Hamilcar (who was killed at Himera in 480 BC), would fight against the Africans to whom the city paid tribute, but were unsuccessful and the conflict only ended after a sum was paid by Carthage. However, the sons of this generation, six in number (though one was exiled), would establish the Carthaginians as the pre-eminent power in this part of Africa. After another war against the Libyans that collected Punic tributes, this time ending in a victory, the payments were brought to an end. They also campaigned against the Numidians, whose lands existed on the fringes of Carthaginian and Libyan territories. Mago's grandsons were also supposed to have fought against the Mauri, a tribe who lived in what is today Morocco. The latter conflict could have been in defence of trading interests in the west.[7]

Where exactly these conquests are to be located is a hard question to answer. There were certainly areas of Libya that Carthage controlled by the sixth century BC, including the Syrtis Major – perhaps stemming from the conflict against Dorieus (see below) – and this may be land claimed by them in the first treaty with Rome in c. 509 BC. But there is archaeological evidence that the Carthaginians were investing heavily in protecting the area around Cape Bon and the Syrtis Minor in the fifth century, and this may be related to the Magonid campaigning we hear about in Justin. Kerkouane, a Punic colony, already had been settled on the cape in about 550 BC.[8] But this was followed up in the fifth century by a defensive position at Kelibia on the south coast of the peninsula.[9] This would have helped guard against ships sailing around Cape Bon. Numerous other colonies or fortresses dot the landscape.[10] These settlements, large and small, were probably meant to secure the hinterland for Carthage. Ancient states throughout the Mediterranean practised this type of policy by sending out defensive settlements, with Rome being one of the most prominent.[11]

How exactly Carthage maintained their possessions in Africa is unknown. As we do not have texts that describe their policies, we can only assume that it was through the usual combination in the ancient world: alliances and force. Of the former we know more in later periods. During the second war with Rome, for instance, the Carthaginians were allied to a Numidian king named Syphax. Although he would eventually lose his kingdom, while he was a friend of Carthage he ensured that his people did not harass those of the city. Likewise, the Libyan tribe to whom the Carthaginians at first paid tribute may be viewed in a similar light. A system of alliances and dependent states was an important aspect of how Rome maintained control of Italy.[12] Maintaining control through force of arms, for instance by installing garrisons or taking hostages, was also a widely used tactic in the Mediterranean. Carthage was certainly doing this on Sicily throughout its period of dominating much of the island, and there is no reason to think that Punic garrisons were not scattered throughout Libya. But, however they maintained their hold, it was always tenuous. We find rebellions by native peoples, generally just referred to as Libyans, all through Carthaginian history. Numidians, as well, would revolt and cause chaos in North Africa. In this way, Carthage was less successful than Rome, who seemed able to maintain control in areas for longer periods between rebellions. Nevertheless, it appears that early in the city's history its hinterland in North Africa was conquered to some degree. While there would be campaigning throughout the next few centuries, we know relatively little about it compared to Carthage's wars with the Greeks and the Romans.

Carthage, Sicily, and Two Failed Colonies: Pentathlus and Dorieus

Dominating the horizon in northwest Sicily, near Trapani (ancient Drepana), is a mountain peak known today as Mount Erice, but to the ancients as Mount Eryx.[13] On its peak was a celebrated temple dedicated to Astarte, Venus, and on its slope was a town which bore the mountain's name. The original settlement was ethnically Elymian. The Elymians were an indigenous population of western Sicily in the period before Phoenician and Greek colonization. Little is known of their civilization and language, with its place in linguistic history even in dispute. From at least the sixth century BC, they interacted in a friendly manner with the Phoenicians who resided on this coast of Sicily, but had a mixed relationship with the Hellenes of the island. Eventually, though, Elymian culture became rather Hellenized. This is despite constantly coming into conflict with the Greek city of Selinus with whom Segesta, one of the principal Elymian cities, shared a border.

Sometime around 580 BC, an expedition set out from Cnidus and Rhodes, the former a Greek city in Asia Minor, to found a settlement in the west.[14] This was, perhaps, driven by the poor treatment of the Cnidians at the hands of unnamed 'kings of Asia', as Diodorus relates.[15] The voyage was led by a man named Pentathlus, noted as being from Cnidus. They sailed from the eastern Mediterranean to Sicily, where they intended to settle. Rather than landing and attempting to found a colony on the ever more crowded eastern side of the island, they went to the area around which would become the Phoenician settlement of Lilybaeum.[16]

The proposed placement of this colony was not haphazard. It was a strategic point which separated the Phoenician settlement of Motya from the cities of their kinsmen to the north, as well as from the Elymians, with whom the Phoenicians maintained good relations, and probably something like an alliance.[17] As A. J. Graham put it, 'this colony plainly threatened Motya's existence as a port and the symbiotic relationship of Phoenicians and Elymians in western Sicily.'[18] This location was also along the sea-route between North Africa, Sardinia-Corsica, and Italy, which was heavily trafficked by Carthaginians, Phoenicians, Greeks, and those with whom they traded.[19] Pentathlus and his companions may have been directed to this spot by some of the Greeks already inhabiting Sicily, perhaps those of Selinus, who often found themselves in conflict with the Elymians. Cutting off Motya would have been in their interest.[20] Even if this was the case, we should not conclude, as some commentators have, that this was the beginning of a Greek bloc which aimed to 'drive them [the Phoenicians] out from the island'.[21] Certainly, trade and other peaceful interactions occurred between Phoenician and Hellene on Sicily and abroad.

Regardless of whether or not they were sent to Lilybaeum by Sicilian Greeks, Pentathlus' group eventually found itself in the middle of a war between Selinus and an alliance of Phoenicians and the Elymian city of Segesta. Of the two version of the story we possess, that by Diodorus and the other by Pausanias, there is discord on this conflict. According to the former, when the would-be colonists arrived on Sicily, they found themselves in the middle of an ongoing war, and he only mentions the Selinuntes and Segestans.[22] The latter, however, relates that once Pentathlus had founded his new settlement, they 'were hard pressed in a war with the Elymians and Phoenicians, and driven out.'[23] I am inclined to believe that they had founded their new settlement, though it was probably not very developed by the time they were expelled. The war between Selinus and Segesta had probably been raging, on and off, for a number of years before Pentathlus' arrival, with the former having expanded its territory to Poggioreale.[24] The Cnidian and Rhodian interlopers may have been the catalyst for bringing the Phoenicians into the conflict. Pentathlus was killed in the war, and his companions expelled from the island. They were not discouraged, though, and founded a successful community on Lipara.[25]

Although the Carthaginians are not mentioned in our sources as having participated in this conflict, it may have been enough to draw their attention.[26] While they did not send troops to Sicily, discussions may have begun between Punic officials and representatives of the Phoenician and Elymian cities about some sort of alliance. Lilybaeum's proximity to Motya, the primary Phoenician settlement on the island at the time, would have been enough to set this in motion. Pentathlus' expedition's proximity to Motya, and the war more generally, probably spurred on the construction of that city's first fortification wall, which is dated to the second quarter of the sixth century BC.[27] This would have been a major project, drawing further attention to the potential for violence in western Sicily.

These rumblings may have deepened Carthaginian interest in the Phoenician colonies of Sicily, and, probably at their request, Punic leaders eventually took action. The earliest known military commander to go to Sicily is known to us through Justin as Mazeus.[28] He seems to have begun his career campaigning in Africa, presumably against indigenous peoples. But he then went on to wage war on Sicily. Both of our sources for his life consider this to have been a failure, saying that the Carthaginians had 'long fought unsuccessfully in Sicily'.[29] This, however, seems to be contradicted one line later in Justin's account, as he claims that under Mazeus the Carthaginians 'conquered a part of Sicily'.[30] Additionally, his son Carthalo had been sent to Tyre with some of the spoils from Sicily to make a tithe to Melqart.[31] Only successful attacks would result in plunder, so something must have been accomplished on the island. Mazeus later went on to campaign on Sardinia (discussed below), where he got most of his army killed. He and the survivors of this force were exiled but returned and supposedly laid siege to Carthage until the leaders capitulated and allowed them to return.[32] Although accepted back temporarily, he was eventually tried for crucifying his son and planning a coup to become king, and was executed.[33]

We do not possess a precise chronology for the exploits of Mazeus. Orosius claims that he was active during the reign of Cyrus the Great, which places him between 559 and 529 BC.[34] Various dates have been proposed by modern scholars, though none of them are unquestionably convincing.[35] It must have been sometime during the sixth century BC, and certainly before 509 BC when Carthage claimed authority in Sicily. I am unconvinced that Mazeus' campaigns were a direct response to Pentathlus, though it was the period after his attempt to settle in western Sicily that makes sense to me, even if the dating provided by Orosius puts him later in the century. After the threat of new arrivals to western Sicily was realized in Carthage, they could have begun to make plans.

There is also no indication of against whom Mazeus campaigned. Many scholars propose that it was directed against the Phoenician colonies in an effort to bring them under Carthaginian control.[36] David Asheri, for instance, argues that 'the striking prosperity of sixth-century Selinus and Acragas [sic] speaks eloquently against the assumption that [Mazeus'] "long wars" in Sicily were waged against the Greeks. For this reason it has been very plausibly argued that his enemy may in fact have been Punics from Motya and elsewhere.'[37] E. A. Freeman came to the same conclusion, though perhaps more simplistically, pointing to the eventual leadership of Carthage over the Phoenician cities on Sicily in the sixth century, and concluded that 'it is hard to avoid the inference that Panormus, Solus, and Motya were brought under the power of Carthage by the arms of [Mazeus].'[38] Against this conclusion, though, can be brought two arguments. The first is that a tithe was dedicated to Melqart in Tyre from the loot taken from Sicily. It is improbable that the Carthaginians would have celebrated victory over fellow Phoenicians by making a dedication such as this. Several scholars have pointed to this problem.[39] This, to me, is almost insurmountable in arguing that Mazeus conquered the Phoenician settlements on the island. The second argument against this is that the materialization of Carthaginian hegemony in western Sicily does not have to have come about through warfare. The Romans, for instance, relied heavily on diplomacy in the formation of their empire, and there is no reason to reject the idea of Punic leaders peacefully forging a pan-Phoenician alliance on Sicily.[40] Because of these two problems, and the absence of specific targets mentioned in our sources, I am inclined to believe that Mazeus' campaign was primarily one of raiding and plundering, which would help to explain the loyalty of his soldiers, despite his later failure in Sardinia; if they lost no battles, and suffered few casualties on Sicily, they would have been heavily indebted to their general. This does not necessarily preclude this expedition's role in bringing the Phoenicians of Sicily under the sway of Carthage. It could have also functioned as what a modern strategist may call 'force projection', using a display of power to help stabilize a region or accomplish a similar goal, while not necessarily engaging in actual warfare.

Following Mazeus' actions in Sicily, we hear even fewer details about Carthaginian actions on the island. It is possible that Mago and his sons, whom we have read about in the preceding section, campaigned there in the aftermath of Mazeus' rebellion and death, but which of these men commanded there is unknown. Justin is vague in the extreme, saying only that, in the wake of Hasdrubal's death in Sardinia, 'the people of Sicily, therefore, applying, in consequence of the perpetual depredations of the Carthaginians, to Leonidas, the brother of the king of Sparta, for aid, a grievous war broke out, which continued, with various success, for a long period.'⁴¹ While the inclusion of Leonidas of Sparta is an error, probably for his brother, Dorieus, the rest of this line should not be rejected outright.⁴² If this is correct, Carthaginian armies were campaigning on Sicily during the time of Mago and his sons. While some authors maintain that this was against the Phoenician cities of the island, as with the campaigns of Mazeus, I find this unlikely, especially in light of Justin's notice.⁴³ His source, Trogus, implies that the Punic campaigns of this period were against the Greeks, hence the calling for Spartan aid, as it seems improbable that the Phoenician cities would have done this. Even if we reject a connection to Sparta, and thus to the Dorieus incident, as suggested by scholars such as Véronique Krings, this does not mean that we can dismiss the Punic depredations, despite the description of them being 'vague et conventionnel'.⁴⁴ It is undeniable that some sort of misinterpretation occurred on the part of Trogus and/or Justin, but we should not discount the presence of Punic soldiers on Sicilian soil in the lead up to their confident claims to part of the island in their c. 509 BC treaty with Rome.

The final thing we hear from Sicily before, or right around, this agreement is the return of Dorieus (discussed in the next section), who, rather than attempting to found another colony in North Africa, sought new fortunes in the area of Mt. Eryx.⁴⁵ Upon his return to the Peloponnese after having been driven from the River Cinyps, he was convinced to embark on this new venture by a man named Antichares. He told the prince that the territory around Eryx belonged to Herakles who won it as his own, thus it belonged to his descendants.⁴⁶ As the Spartan royal lines claimed descent from him, this gave Dorieus a good reason to claim the land in western Sicily. He then went to Delphi to consult the oracle, who gave him a positive answer. Returning to Sparta, the prince collected a group of Spartiates and their followers: Thessalus, Paraebates, Celeës, and Euryleon.⁴⁷

This force set out from the Peloponnese and sailed to the west. Their next move is disputed. According to a Sybarite legend, Dorieus and his companions, before going to Sicily, came to Italy and joined in the war with Croton. The Spartans sided with the Crotonians, and helped in the destruction of Sybaris. The Crotonian version of the war, however, claimed that this was wrong, and the only foreign assistance they had was an exiled Sybarite seer named Callias of Elis.⁴⁸ Scholarly views on which version is correct, and whether or not Dorieus intervened in Italy, are divided, though most believe that the Spartans did participate in the conflict. There are still doubts, however. The presence of Philippos of Croton, who had been exiled from his homeland because he had married a woman from Sybaris, is problematic for both interpretations.[49]

For those who support that the expedition went to Italy, we must ask: would the Crotonians be open to help from a group which included one of their exiled citizens? It is possible that his participation would have been an act of contrition for marrying a Sybarite, though this would force us to presume that he had no political enemies amongst the city's leadership. If his participation was approved of, and he and Dorieus did indeed help Croton, then Philippos not staying in the city, but rather travelling on with the Spartans to Sicily, must be explained.[50] It is plausible that they accepted their help and then refused to accept Philippos back, which would be another good reason for the Crotonians to deny any participation at all from the expedition. Luring Dorieus into the war with the false promise of welcoming his friend back into the city would not look good.

But Philippos' death on Sicily, and its aftermath, raises questions about this theorized problem. According to Herodotus, the Segestans developed a hero cult which worshipped him sometime after his death, and they offered sacrifices at his tomb and erected there a shrine.[51] This was supposedly because of his good looks. This is a bizarre notice. The Segestans, as we shall see below, were involved in the war against Dorieus and his followers. Why, despite his beauty, would they then worship one of their slain enemies? It could have simply been the reason given by Herodotus, as rephrased by Freeman:

> 'to him were given honours which fell to the lot of no other among his comrades. It shows the deep impression which manly beauty made on the minds of barbarians as well as Greeks that the men of Segesta – it must have been when they came to strip the slain – were overcome by the majestic form, noble even in death, of the victor of Olympia, most beautiful of all the Greeks.'[52]

This is an explanation based on a way of thinking alien to many modern readers, though that is not a good reason to dismiss it. Despite this, I find the entire passage to be unlikely. Segestan seduction by the beauty of a dead man is dubious, as well, the position of this passage in Herodotus' text furthers my doubt. Philippos is not mentioned in the main narrative passages for the Dorieus incident but is rather mentioned as an aside. It is possible that Herodotus, or more likely his informant, confused the Segestan worship of a Crotonian named Philippos with the expedition of Dorieus. It is not inconceivable that such a story could have erroneously coalesced around the hero cult of a Greek amongst the Elymians who inhabited the area around Mt. Eryx.

Whether or not they stopped in Italy, eventually Dorieus and his companions made their way to western Sicily. Here, they attempted to settle. Diodorus is our only source which claims they actually founded a city, but his version is problematic. He claims that their settlement grew quickly and that it made the Carthaginians jealous and they worried that it would soon eclipse their own power.[53] This is a massive exaggeration, and there is no way that a newly settled town could eclipse one of its neighbours on Sicily that quickly, let alone Carthage.[54] It is more likely that the Lacedaemonians had landed in the neighbourhood of Eryx and were attacked in a temporary camp where they had planned to found their city. According to Herodotus, they were defeated in battle by a combined army of Phoenicians and Segestans, while Pausanias only mentions the latter.[55] Were the Carthaginians involved at all?

The answer to this question is probably yes, though certainly not to the extent claimed by Diodorus, who says that they brought against the new settlement 'a great army.' Some authors, such as Dexter Hoyos, see the probable confusion of Phoenicians and Carthaginians in the army which marched against Himera in 480 BC (see next chapter) as evidence that the language used by Herodotus was, to some extent, fluid; thus 'Phoenicians' could be used to describe both those of the western Sicilian cities and also the Carthaginians.[56] The problem of interpreting Herodotus' word-choice, however, is more complex than this, as has been exhaustively shown by Véronique Krings.[57] It is difficult to say, based solely on linguistic grounds, that the Carthaginians 'massively intervened in Sicily at the time of the Dorieus expedition' but this evidence also does not rule it out completely.[58]

There is historical support, though, to think that the Carthaginians were probably involved in some way. Near contemporary to Dorieus coming to Sicily, the Carthaginians negotiated a treaty with Rome in which they claimed hegemony over part of Sicily.[59] It is inconceivable that they would be claiming any part of the island besides that of the western corner, wherein existed the Phoenician cities, and perhaps extending to the Elymian communities. More will be said about this treaty in the concluding section of this chapter, but it is important in our interpretation of Punic participation in the Dorieus affair. If their claim to power in this part of Sicily was true, which it seems like it must have been for them to include it in their treaty with Rome, then they had good reason to not want a Greek interloper founding a new city here. Therefore, I am certain that they participated in some way, though sending an army from Carthage is probably out of the question. In light of the significant role which the Elymians seem to have played, it is quite possible that the Punic role was to finance the campaign, and perhaps to provide a leader or to send supporting troops from the Phoenician cities of Sicily.[60] Any conclusion which sees the Carthaginians as having not participated at all must reconcile this with the implication of the Roman treaty.[61]

Although Punic participation in the short war against Dorieus is a complex subject, there is a perplexing element of the story which must be addressed. That is, the non-participation of the Sicilian Greek cities. No one came to their aid before they were attacked, and only later in the early fifth century BC was a campaign seeking vengeance launched, almost certainly using the story simply as a propaganda tool by Gelon of Syracuse. In fact, after the defeat of Dorieus and his companions, one of the Spartans, Euryleon, the only of them to survive, went on to capture the Selinuntine colony of Minoa, and eventually deposed Peithagoras, the tyrant of Selinus. At this point, the Spartan then took power and ruled, presumably as a tyrant, for a short while before himself being ousted by a popular uprising.[62] Selinus could have been allied, in some way, to Carthage for most of the sixth century BC, and it was probably trade which drove this.[63] This could be part of the explanation as to why Euryleon attacked them specifically. Though the absence of any Greek support of the expedition is telling that the confused memory preserved in Justin, of a Hellenic call for aid to Sparta, is either false or at least does not belong to this era. It is also indicative that the idea of bloc politics, in which Carthaginians, Phoenicians, and Elymians were politically aligned against the Greek city-states *en masse* is incorrect and should only be seen, with significant caveats, in a later period.

Carthaginian Intervention in Sardinia

Sicily was not the only island important to the new powers of the central Mediterranean. Sardinia, though perhaps more obscure than its larger neighbour, was full of resources sought by Phoenicians, Carthaginians, Etruscans, and Greeks. Precolonial contact between the eastern Mediterranean and the island are evidence of its richness.[64] From the eighth century BC onward, Phoenician interest in the island turned into a permanent presence. Although the original draw of the colonists to the island may have been metals, only one of their colonies, Sulcis, was settled in such a spot to principally take advantage of mining territory.[65] Its territorial holdings quickly grew, and from the seventh century BC the people of Sulcis began a programme of building fortifications in the hinterland. This has been interpreted as 'ensuring direct territorial control of a hinterland rich in lead and silver'.[66] These fortifications, as well as those of the major Phoenician centres and elsewhere on the island, have been pointed to as more complex than those of the native population and evidence of 'Phoenician expertise' in defensive architecture.[67] Coupled with the primary settlement's position on an islet, and its fortifications, it is not to be doubted that its protection was important. This was probably because considerable wealth was created and passed through the city. The wealth of most of the Phoenician cities on Sardinia was likely impressive; notable evidence is the abundance and quality of gold jewellery found there, especially at Tharros.[68] This is also suggested by the diversity of imports found in the sites through modern archaeological excavation.[69]

Establishing themselves on Sardinia may have been seen as important by the early colonists. This is if we are to believe that the high concentration of colonial foundations in the south-west part of the island was part of 'a genuine territorial strategy', as some scholars believe.[70] This is not a universally accepted idea, and the apparently peaceful process of settlement detected here must be contended with. For instance, Tronchetti has pointed out that we cannot say for sure whether the Phoenicians settled wherever they pleased or if there was a process which involved the local peoples.[71]

By the middle of the sixth century BC, Carthage became involved with affairs in Sardinia. As with Sicily, our earliest evidence comes from one of our later sources, Justin's epitome of Pompeius Trogus.[72] The same

Mazeus that we have seen above active on the larger of the two islands led a fateful, unsuccessful, campaign on Sardinia. Having met with enough success on Sicily to send tribute to Tyre, Mazeus and his army sailed to Sardinia where they campaigned against someone. Who this was, though, is unclear. Serge Lancel believed that it was 'doubtless' he was 'grappling with the natives whose pressure on the coastal settlements had to be weakened'.[73] This conclusion leads to the hypothesis that Mazeus, or perhaps Carthaginian assistance more generally, was called in by the Phoenician settlements. If we accept that he was primarily plundering in Sicily, as argued above, then his army may have campaigned in the same manner once they reached Sardinia.

Just like Mazeus, the early Magonids are also said to have followed a similar, though reversed programme of warfare. They first campaigned in Sardinia, and then later in Sicily. On the former, the sons of Mago, Hasdrubal and Hamilcar, went to war. Hasdrubal was mortally wounded in battle there, and would take his last breath on the island. Before his death he is said to have held the 'dictatorship' eleven times, and celebrated four triumphs.[74] These are later Latin interpretations of both the office and the celebration, which would have already been translated, at best transliterated, into Greek by the time Pompeius Trogus read about them. Both are to be viewed with scepticism, but probably had some basis in historical truth.

In Rome, a dictator was an office of the Republic in which a man was appointed with supreme authority for a short term in order to deal with a specific crisis. This was in contrast to the typical election of two annual magistrates, the consuls, at the head of the government, who shared power and executive duties. We do not know if Carthage had a similar political position, and the paucity of other evidence as to Hasdrubal's true position within the Punic government does not help us. Both he and his brother are elsewhere described simply as generals by Justin (Mazeus as well), and perhaps the implication of Hasdrubal's eleven supposed dictatorships was that he held both a generalship as well as another, higher, political office. The interpretation of the four triumphs may be more straightforward if we assume that it simply means he won four great victories. There may have been a ritual procession, like in Rome or elsewhere in the Mediterranean, as attested in Carthage after the Truceless War in 237.[75] Hoyos has proposed that the path of these parades may have gone from the

Agora to the Byrsa and the temple of Eshmun, a wholly plausible, if only theoretical, reconstruction.[76] If this was a common practice in Carthage, we do not hear of it often, but there is no reason to doubt its existence in some form, based on the commonness of celebratory parades and festivals across the Mediterranean world. Some of these may have been celebrated by Hasdrubal after victories in Sardinia, as it does not seem he and his brother were very effective against the Africans (see above).

Despite the failure of Mazeus in Sardinia, and the death of Hasdrubal while there campaigning, it was probably during his wars, or perhaps more rightly those of his brother Hamilcar, that the Carthaginians won control of the island. They drove all of the hostile peoples of the island into its mountainous interior. Amongst these are numbered some Libyan or Iberian mercenaries, who disagreed with the partition of booty after the, presumably, final campaign. Carthage, apparently, at this juncture settled a number of colonies directly under its control around Sardinia. This, at least, is the picture we get from a single passage in Pausanius.[77] Archaeologically, there is evidence for violence on the island in the sixth century BC, such as the violent destruction of Cuccureddus, a Phoenician settlement, the partial abandonment of the settlement at Monte Sirai, again Phoenician, and the destruction of Su Nuraxi, an indigenous settlement. Changes in imports, notably the cessation of the import of Ionian pottery and the new importing of Attic pottery, has also been pointed to as an indication of the Carthaginian conquest.[78] The problem is, however, none of this is definitive. We have no reason to think the destroyed settlements were because of Punic intervention, just as we cannot say that the Attic imports were due to this rather than shifts in market trends.[79] Both positions, that this evidence does and does not indicate a Carthaginian presence, though, are dependent on any particular scholar's interpretation of Punic ambitions in this period. The vast number of diverging opinions can be seen in the discussion in a recent work by Andrea Roppa.[80] Regardless of the position we take here, it cannot be seen as definitive.

It is likely that Carthage was involved in some way in Sardinia in the second half of the sixth century BC. This was almost certainly not a sweeping military conquest; although we have some sites with evidence of destruction during this period, the vast majority of Phoenician and native settlements do not. But this should not be taken as a complete rejection of the campaigns of Mazeus and the Magonids. Except for large-scale 'total war', we should not expect it to have left a considerable mark in the archaeological record. Raids, pillaging, and punitive actions which only saw pitched battles, or at least battles in the field, will not (generally) be detectable. There is no reason for us to discount the effectiveness that this small-scale warfare could have had in spreading Punic influence on the island,[81] and thus, though they are suspicious, the stories presented by Justin should not be thrown out simply on the grounds that the archaeology does not entirely support them. That Carthage does claim some authority over at least a portion of the island in its first treaty with Rome around 509 BC, still supports their presence.

Wars with the Phocaeans

Amongst the stories of early Carthage, conflicts with one group of Greeks are consistent. The sixth century saw them clash with various groups of Phocaean Greeks who had immigrated to the central Mediterranean. Phocaea, their home town, sat on the coast of Anatolia, in modern Turkey. Its inhabitants were Ionian Greeks. The Phocaeans were supposedly the earliest Hellenes to make long voyages, and Herodotus tells us that they were the first to sail the Adriatic and the first to reach Tyrrhenia (probably Central Italy), Iberia and Tartessus.[82] They had established such amicable relations with the king of Tartessus, Arganthonius, that he funded a wall for their home town after hearing about the aggression of the Persians.[83] In general, Phocaeans seem to have carried on amicably with the native populations of the central and western Mediterranean where they founded their colonies.[84]

The principal Phocaean settlement in the central Mediterranean was Massalia, modern Marseilles in southern France. It was founded around 600 BC, perhaps in an effort to dominate the tin trade from further north.[85] Although it began rather small, it expanded relatively rapidly.[86] Although the settlement may have existed somewhat peacefully alongside its native neighbours, this was not the case regarding those with whom their ships shared the sea.[87] According to Justin, the city was made rich through fishing and trading, but most of all through piracy.[88] If the notice of their ships sailing up the Tiber to Rome during the time of one of the Tarquin kings has any truth to it, this is perhaps an example of one of their piratical raids.⁸⁹ It is behaviour reminiscent of the Viking river raids of much later times. Its absence from the Roman tradition, though, such as that presented by Livy, makes it rather suspect. The behaviour of their sailors, however, did bring them into conflict with the Carthaginians at an unknown date. We could possibly see this as the same clash mentioned around the time of Massalia's foundation, though this latter notice is usually dated to the influx of Phocaeans to the west after the destruction of their city in 545 BC.⁹⁰ At issue in Justin's narrative was the capture of a number of fishing boats, presumably by the Massaliotes, although the quarrel could have resulted from Punic piracy – our source is not clear.⁹¹ The Greeks were victorious and eventually made peace with Carthage, the latter accepting their defeat.⁹²

It is unclear if this conflict was actually between Carthage and Massalia, though. For much of their early history, the two were separated both by a great distance as well as numerous intervening peoples. Although Justin does describe the Massaliotes' opponents as Carthaginians (*Karthaginiensium*), and Thucydides calls those fought at the foundation of the city in the same way (καρχηδόνιοι), the proximity of Phoenician colonies on Sardinia to Massalia is enough to make us consider that they may have been the Hellenes' true adversaries. Regardless, our sources are unanimous that the first clash with the Massaliotes ended in a Greek victory.

In 565 BC a Phocaean colony was established at Alalia, on Corsica.⁹³ Twenty years after its foundation, its population was bolstered by a group who fled the destruction of their hometown by the Persians. These new arrivals began pillaging the settlements of their neighbours and almost certainly preyed on commercial shipping.⁹⁴ As Herodotus portrays them as primarily antagonizing the Etruscans and Carthaginians, and that the latter responded with naval action, this implies that the Phocaean depredations were being carried out via the sea. After five years of this behaviour, their victims responded. Carthage and the Etruscan city-state of Caere sent a combined fleet of sixty ships coming from each, sailing against the Phocaean fleet of sixty ships total.⁹⁵ The two groups met somewhere in the Sea of Sardinia, a vague reference made by Herodotus. It has been convincingly argued that this is meant to designate the sea between Sardinia and the Italian peninsula, which would have been the main route connecting the Etruscans and the Phoenicians to the island.⁹⁶

When the fleets found one another, a fierce battle ensued, known typically as the Battle of Alalia.[97] Despite their numerical advantage, the combined Punic and Etruscan fleet was defeated. We do not hear of their losses, but as the Phocaeans lost forty ships and still 'won' the battle, the allied fleet must have suffered considerable casualties; this led Herodotus to describe it as a Cadmean victory. Of the twenty Greek ships which survived the battle, they all had bent rams and were unable to fight, showing the intensity of the struggle.[98] These limped back to their port at Alalia, but, in light of their losses, the Phocaeans decided their best course of action would be to abandon their settlement. They loaded women, children, and moveable wealth into what of their ships they had left, and sailed for the Greek colony at Rhegium. From there, they chose a new home and settled a new town called Hyele, known from the Roman period onward as Velia.[99]

Although the conflicts mentioned above appear as discrete events in our sources, modern scholars have argued that they all are rooted in what became a mangled memory of the Battle of Alalia. Various pieces of literary evidence, and archaeological evidence at Delphi which may indicate the building of a treasury by Massalia around the same time as the battle, have been pointed to as indicating that the references to clashes between the Carthaginians and the Massaliotes all stem from this one event.[100] The argument is generally appealing, and the participation of Massalia in the struggle against Carthage and the Etruscans in the seas off Sardinia, standing alongside their Phocaean kinsmen, is sensible. I am reticent, however, to concede that all the notices of conflicts between Carthage and Massalia relate to this one battle. The strongest objection I have is that the absence of Alalia, or even Corsica more generally, from Thucydides and Justin is problematic. Both of them relate their battles to just Massalia.[101] It is right to dismiss the importance of Thucydides and Pausanias assigning victories to the Massaliotes over the Carthaginians at the 'foundation' of the colony, especially Thucydides appears to use the phrase Φωκαῆς τε Μασσαλίαν οἰκίζοντες to remind his readers, or to educate them on the fact, that Massalia was a Phocaean foundation.[102] It could be that the Athenian historian specifically ignored the Battle of Alalia found in Herodotus because it 'ends with them [the Phocaeans] suffering such losses in battle that they end up abandoning' the settlement.[103]

Any interpretation which suggests all of these notices relate to a single battle is also doing an injustice to the evidence and to Massalia. It turns what was probably a series of clashes between the Phocaean settlers and the Carthaginians into a single, epic, battle. If we read the sources as they are presented to us, we hear of at least one naval victory of Massalia over Carthage (Thucydides, Justin, and Pausanias) and a separate Cadmean victory (or simply a defeat) by the Phocaeans of Alalia, possibly with Massaliote assistance, against both Carthage and an unknown Etruscan power (Herodotus). It is possible, as well, that Massalia is to be credited with two victories over Punic fleets, as Pausanias does mention two different monuments that they deposited at Delphi, though it is unclear if they are meant to commemorate the same or different events.[104]

Viewed in this light, there were a number of naval engagements fought between the Carthaginians and Phocaean settlers in the north-central Mediterranean around the middle of the sixth century BC. This was caused by two simultaneous, though perhaps not directly related, phenomena. The first was developing Punic interest in the island of Sardinia, as shown above by the campaigns of Mazeus and the Magonids, and the colonisation of at least two settlements by Carthage. This would lead them into contact with the second phenomenon, which probably began before a strong Punic presence in the ancient Sea of Sardinia, which was Phocaean piracy. While we do not know if there was a response from the otherwise independent Phoenician cities of Sardinia, once Carthaginian shipping was threatened the problem became personal for the budding imperial city-state. This new player in the region then colluded with their allies in Etruria to bring a strong fleet against the sea-borne raiders, targeting the problematic colony on Corsica, and chased them out of the area. I am partial to seeing the Battle of Alalia ending in a Greek defeat, despite Herodotus calling it a Cadmean victory, which would mean that this was the first naval victory won by Carthage, of which we hear.[105] This battle, and the clash(es) between Carthage and Massalia, however, should not be seen as part of a conflict between ethno-political blocs of Phoenicans and Etruscans versus Greeks. As Véronique Krings concluded, we need to see a 'Mediterranean "in motion", in which we do not see well-constituted blocs, but rather groups of individuals acting on the basis of personal interests and occasional circumstances', and that we should not see in these events a 'framework of grand designs'.[106]

Conclusions: Early Punic Ambitions

Thus, we see that early on in the history of Carthage, territorial ambitions existed. While we must always be wary of how much confidence we put in the stories related by Justin and the other sources, there is a regular theme of early Punic expansion. Interestingly, alongside this we hear about the development of military institutions. The typical thinking that Carthaginians were averse to military service may have in the past made historians doubt these notices, but there are no solid grounds for dismissing them outright. We know that at least in the fourth century BC (as noted in Chapter 10) Punic citizens took considerable pride in serving in the army. It could very well be that this value of martial skill dates all the way back to the early periods of the city's history. To the extent that an empire was being forged, though, we must concede that there is little strong evidence for this.

Chapter 3

Armies Against Syracuse

The Origins of the Conflicts against Sicily

The greatest adversary of Carthage, before Rome, was the Sicilian Greek city of Syracuse. That these two states would come into conflict was probably inevitable, as they were the largest, and wealthiest, in the central Mediterranean until the rise of Rome. The legacy of Syracuse as the greatest of the Hellenic *poleis* is well cemented in ancient and modern thought. For many years it was the seat of a great hegemony, if not actual empire, which spanned much of eastern Sicily and parts of southern Italy. Carthage, on the other hand, controlled much, if not most, of north Africa west of the altars of the Philaeni. When this western border with Cyrene was established is impossible to know, though scholars have proposed dates from the late sixth century to the last third of the fourth century BC.[1] It was also the centre of a lucrative trading network, with ties to Spain, Italy, and the Aegean. This chapter examines the history of the first two major conflicts between Carthage and the Sicilian Greeks.

Phoenicians had been present on Sicily for some time before the coming of the Greeks, as we have seen above. From what we can glean from the literary sources, they were forced out of many of their original settlements by the so-called Hellenic colonists. Though the Greeks were to establish the most significant settlements on the island, the Phoenicians still held the west of Sicily with principal settlements at Motya, Panormus and Soluntum. Before the late fifth century, it is unclear what exactly the relationship between Carthage and the Phoenicians of Sicily was like. It could be that there was some form of hegemonic control between the great city and the Phoenician diaspora in the central Mediterranean, but it is also possible that there was little to no formal relationship at all.[2] By the late fifth century, it is apparent that Carthage held considerable sway, if not direct control, over much of western Sicily.

The Armies

The events of this chapter fall over the course of the fifth century. Throughout much of the Mediterranean, the combat of this period is identified with 'hoplite warfare'.[3] This mode of combat originated in Greece and spread throughout the Mediterranean during the seventh century.[4] The most basic version of this transmission is that as non-Hellenic cultures came into contact with the Greeks, and met them in battle, the superiority of hoplite warfare became apparent and was adopted by them.[5] It is certain that the equipment typically associated with the hoplite spread throughout the central Mediterranean, but it is a leap to simply assume that 'hoplite warfare' itself did.[6] Hoplite arms are readily evident in early Rome, for example, but it has been pointed out that 'hoplite warfare' did not likely follow.[7]

Traditionally, hoplite combat is described to revolve around the phalanx, a tightly packed infantry formation that is seen by some scholars as virtually impregnable. The soldiers were armed with a large, heavy, shield and a long spear. Occasionally, wealthier hoplites would have worn bronze armour, such as cuirasses and greaves.[8] The burden of the shield, in particular, is often noted by modern scholars.[9] Because of this, hoplites were supposedly forced to fight in the phalanx, a closely packed mass of soldiers. The shield was too heavy to fight in a looser formation.[10] The evidence, however, does not support the idea that hoplite arms were so burdensome to require this. In reality, the hoplite could be fairly mobile, and the protection offered by the large shield made him a formidable opponent in almost any situation.[11] That said, they were still vulnerable to mobile and ranged troops.[12]

At least some of the soldiers in the Greek armies which Carthage fought during this period were armed as hoplites. Diodorus does not use the term when describing Western Greek soldiers.[13] Though, in the description of Gelon's forces offered to the Aegean Greeks, we hear of hoplites.[14] These, however, were part of a larger force which included archers, slingers, and light horsemen. This was not purely a 'hoplite' army. As we see below, the Greek armies of the second Puno-Syracusan war also included light infantry, with Dionysius' army at Gela having at least 2,000. It seems safest, then, not to describe the Greek armies as 'hoplite' armies, but as mixed forces which included hoplites.

The Carthaginian armies, of course, were somewhat more complex as they included many different ethnic groups. The Carthaginians themselves, and their Phoenician kinsmen, were likely heavily armed, perhaps like their Greek hoplite counterparts. Scarabs from Carthage and Phoenician Sardinia depict warriors armed with large shields and spears.[15] In later wars, they are said to have fought as a phalanx and with iron breastplates, bronze helmets, and large shields.[16] If this is how Carthaginian citizens were armed in the fifth century, then we should clearly consider them to have been 'heavy infantry'. There is little evidence to not engender a conclusion such as Daly's, that they fought 'something like a Greek phalanx'.[17]

Their Libyan allies were likely drawn from subject peoples in the hinterland of Carthage. The exact nature of the relationship is unclear. Libyan troops' manner of fighting is also not well known. We hear of Libyans fighting in the Persian army, and they are described as wearing leather garments and being armed with javelins.[18] We also hear of Libyan charioteers who fought at range with javelins.[19] The latter may never have been part of Carthaginian armies. Libyans were most likely used as infantry, especially light infantry as they were by the Persians. Missile troops would have been very valuable in the sieges during the campaigns of Hannibal and Himilco discussed in this chapter, and we hear of archers and slingers being used at Selinus, though we do not know to which ethnic group they belonged. Even if Libyans typically operated as skirmishers and missile infantry, there is no reason that they could not also have fought as spearmen, as was the case with Archaic Greek soldiers.[20]

The Iberian mercenaries in the Carthaginian armies likely came from the southern coast, the area in which Phoenician colonies had been established from at least the ninth century. In the fifth century, the primary offensive weapon of the Iberians was the long spear with a large blade. Swords were also an important part of their kit. The presence of javelins in Iberian contexts indicates that their typical mode of combat included showering the enemy with missiles before charging into close combat.[21] This is similar to the later practice of the Roman legions. It is likely that they fought as 'heavy infantry' in the Carthaginian armies.

Of the Campanian mercenaries we have few details from the literary evidence as to how they were armed or operated. During the conflict between Segesta and Selinus we hear that the Carthaginians secured horses for them, indicating that they may have been a unit of cavalry.[22] Artistic evidence from Campania shows that they were likely armed with large round shields and spears, again much like the Greek hoplite. Whether they fought on foot or on horseback, the Campanians were likely heavy troops, much like the Carthaginians and the Iberians.

The Balearic islanders that we hear of in the campaign of 406 were almost certainly slingers.[23] They would have operated as skirmishers in the Punic armies. During sieges, and the defence of the Carthaginian camps, Balearic slingers would have been very valuable as missile troops, inflicting heavy losses on the Greeks in both situations.[24] Slings have been shown to have been extremely dangerous weapons in the hands of skilled soldiers.[25] According to Strabo they would have also been armed with javelins and a small skin shield.[26]

How all of these different peoples worked together to form a coherent fighting force is not revealed by our sources. It is clear that ethnic groups fought together as units, rather than being separated throughout the army, typically. This was a fundamental practice in the ancient world, with the earliest person to advise such an organization being Nestor in the *Iliad*.[27] As we see later in this chapter, the Greeks also practised this type of organization. Keeping ethnic groups together would have increased the horizontal unit cohesion of the Punic armies by unknowingly exploiting effects like the 'buddy principle', by which peers with some level of familiarity fight better together. There is little evidence, however, of the vertical structure of the Carthaginian forces in this period, as in how command and control worked. It is probable that the mercenary units would have reported directly to Punic officers, which would have helped the generals control individual units.[28] But later evidence indicates that mercenary units were directly commanded by their own officers.

The First Puno-Syracusan War

The first major conflict between Carthage and Syracuse, for which we have any details, was caused by an alliance between the state, or possibly just the Magonid family, and the *tyrannos* of Himera, Terillus. The latter was close enough for Herodotus to describe him as a 'guest-friend' of Hamilcar, who was a prominent leader of the Carthaginians at this time.[29]

This alliance proved to be a costly one for Carthage. The trouble began in 483 BC when Terillus was driven out of Himera by Theron, the tyrant of Akragas.[30] Together with his son-in-law Anaxilaus, tyrant of Rhegium in southern Italy, he appealed to Hamilcar and Carthage to restore him to power.[31] In order to show their loyalty and dedication to this endeavour, Anaxilaus sent his children to the Carthaginians as hostages. The Punic state was moved to action.

What may have been a simple, and smaller scale, conflict between the Punic-Terillus alliance and Akragas was made more complex, and deadlier, because of the alliance between Theron and Gelon of Syracuse. The latter was an important figure in Sicilian history. The first we hear of Gelon in the historical record is as a cavalry commander in the army of Hippocrates, tyrant of Gela. He earned this place through valorous deeds in sieges against Callipolis and Naxos, Zancle, and Leontini, and in other battles against the Syracusans and against many barbarians.[32] Herodotus records that he fought with the highest distinction in all the campaigns engaged upon by Hippocrates. Gelon rose to power in the aftermath of Hippocrates' death, which may have come in battle near Hybla during a war against the Siceli.[33] The late tyrant's sons, Euclides and Cleander, were not popular amongst their countrymen and a revolution against the tyranny ensued. Gelon at first took the side of the brothers and defeated the Geloans in a civil war. We know nothing about the details of this conflict, though the brief treatment by Herodotus may imply that it was short. In the wake of this victory, Gelon ousted Euclides and Cleander and made himself tyrant in their place (c. 491–490 BC).[34]

Having taken power in Gela, Gelon looked to expand his dominion. Fortunately for him, a revolution was brewing in Syracuse. The ruling class, known as the *gamoroi* (meaning 'landowners'), was expelled by the people and the slaves.[35] Making a base at Casmene, the *gamoroi* and Gelon marched on Syracuse. The city was taken without a battle being fought and the people surrendered themselves to Gelon. Syracuse was now under his control. He left his brother, Hiero, in control of Gela and shifted his attention almost exclusively to Syracuse (c. 485 BC).[36] Under Gelon's leadership, the city began to flourish. He razed Camarina and removed its population to Syracuse. Half of the population of Gela was also moved thusly. He continued this strategy of bolstering the city's population throughout the early part of his reign.[37] Some modern scholars have described these actions as 'ruthless', though the feelings of those displaced are unknown to us.[38] Through this practice, Gelon brought one-time enemies under his direct control and enlarged the body from which he could enrol soldiers. By doing this he became, in the words of Herodotus, a tyrant of great importance.[39]

The power of Gelon and his newly created empire in eastern Sicily is apparent from an event which occurred in 481 BC. On the cusp of Xerxes' invasion of Greece, the allied council of the Hellenes appealed to Gelon to bolster the strength of their army and navy. According to the version of their speeches preserved by Herodotus, the embassy referred to the tyrant's position as one of great power and claimed that he controlled much of the Greek world.[40] In response to this, Gelon offered a large force and grain for the entire Hellenic expedition on the grounds that he would be the supreme commander of the army.[41] Assistance under these conditions was rejected by the Aegean Greeks. As it turns out, it was fortuitous that his troops were still on Sicily as the Carthaginians invaded a year later.[42]

From the expulsion of Terillus from Himera until 480 BC, the Carthaginians had been preparing for an invasion. Three years seems like a rather long time but considering the preparations we hear of it is possible. According to both Herodotus and Diodorus, the Punic forces numbered 300,000 men and 200 ships.[43] The figure given for the size of this expedition is obviously exaggerated. There was a tendency in Greek historiography to inflate the size of barbarian armies.[44] It is impossible to know exactly how many soldiers made up this force, although 30,000 would not be out of place with the numbers attributed to other armies of the period.[45] Although this is a number arrived at by simply reducing the original figure to one-tenth, it is certainly closer to reality than the 300,000 given by our sources.[46] All of those brought over seem to have been infantry. Diodorus preserves a story in which a storm destroyed the ships which were carrying the horses and chariots to Sicily.[47] While this is possible, it seems odd that these were the only ships that sank. We know that Selinus, allied to the Carthaginians, was going to provide some cavalry, thus it is possible that the force which set sail from Carthage did not actually contain any horses with the expectation that allies would supply them.[48] Whatever the size and composition, this army was commanded by Hamilcar, the ally of Terillus.

The soldiers which made up this force were diverse.[49] Herodotus tells us that they consisted of Phoenicians, Libyans, Iberians, Ligurians, Elisyces, Sardinians, and Corsicans. Diodorus differs slightly, saying that they recruited mercenaries from Italy, Liguria, Gaul, and Iberia, and recruited 'men of their own race' from all of Libya and Carthage.[50] It has been suggested that he mistakenly added Italians and Gauls in this list, and that the Carthaginians were not yet recruiting from these regions.[51] This is probably correct. The 'Phoenicians' are certainly Carthaginians (and perhaps inhabitants of other settlements such as Motya), while the Libyans, Sardinians, and Corsicans likely subject peoples.[52]

The Punic forces landed at Panormus, in western Sicily. After resting for three days, Hamilcar marched his army towards Himera, with the fleet following them along the coast.[53] They encamped to the west of the city. Having established his base of operations, the Carthaginian general marched his best troops up to Himera and engaged the city's defenders in a fight outside their walls.[54] The Punic troops were victorious, and supposedly killed many of the Greeks. It is unclear who exactly Hamilcar's 'best troops' were, but as he appears to have been in personal command, I believe that they were probably the Carthaginian citizen soldiers. Whether or not inspired by this defeat, or simply the enemy presence, Theron, who had brought an army from Akragas to help defend Himera, sent word to Gelon in Syracuse, asking for assistance.

Gelon set out from Syracuse with an army of 50,000 infantry and 5,000 cavalry.[55] These numbers, like those attributed to the Carthaginian army, may be inflated.[56] When the mainland Greeks had sought Gelon's help against the Persians, we hear that he offered to supply 20,000 hoplites, 2,000 cavalry, 2,000 bowmen, and 2,000 slingers.[57] It has been suggested that this probably reflected the largest army that he could raise.[58] Using the figures given in the context of the embassy, Gelon would have had access to 24,000 infantry (counting the skirmishers in this category) and 2,000 cavalry. This closely maintains the ratio of infantry to cavalry (ten to one) that we see in the earlier numbers for the army. It is possible, though, that the figures given to the Greek embassy only included citizen and subject troops. We know that Gelon settled 10,000 mercenaries in Syracuse, who could have served as additional troops during the Himera campaign.[59] We may be able to substantiate the numbers of 50,000 foot and 5,000 horse, though, if we consider this to be the entire force of the anti-Carthaginian alliance. If Gelon brought with him an army of 34,000 infantry and 2,000 cavalry, for instance, this would mean that his allies provided 16,000 foot and 3,000 horse, which are both reasonable numbers. Comparing the numbers of this army and that of the Carthaginians, it is possible that the latter were outnumbered rather than being at a considerable numeric advantage.

We know little about the details of the battle when these two armies finally met outside the walls of Himera. It appears that it began early in the day, as Gelon drew up his army at daybreak.[60] The fight was bloody and long and lasted late into the evening.[61] Gelon led the Greek army into battle, but Hamilcar left the leadership of the Carthaginians up to his subordinates.[62] Throughout the day the battle swayed back and forth, with both sides fighting well. Neither side was prevailing. The flow of the battle, however, turned when a group of Syracusan cavalrymen set fire to the Punic ships and camp. They had been able to infiltrate their enemies because Gelon had intercepted a letter from Selinus to Hamilcar detailing their plans to send a group of cavalry to bolster the Punic army. He sent his own men to the camp on the appointed day.[63] Upon seeing the flames, the Carthaginian army panicked and broke, allowing the Greeks to slaughter many of them.[64]

The chaos amongst the Punic troops was supposedly exacerbated by news that Hamilcar had been killed in the raid on the camp. This, at least, was the version preserved by Diodorus. The Syracusan horsemen who had torched the ships had also killed him as he was performing sacrifices.[65] Hamilcar's death, however, is not that straightforward and it is one of the most intriguing controversies in the study of the ancient world. Herodotus preserves two different versions of events from Diodorus. The first, provided to him by his Sicilian sources, was that when defeat of his army was obvious, Hamilcar vanished. Gelon exhaustively tried to find him, but to no avail.[66] The other story known to Herodotus originated from the Carthaginians themselves, who believed that their general threw himself onto the pyre as he was performing sacrifices and whose body was thus rendered irrecoverable.[67] A fourth version of his death is preserved by Polyaenus, who also attributes it to a stratagem of Gelon's conception, but rather than involving infiltration, used a more complicated bit of subterfuge. The Greek leader sent out a group of archers disguised as priests, including one who looked like him.

They hid their bows underneath myrtle branches. They marched out of the camp feigning to make a sacrifice. The Carthaginian general, whom Polyaenus names as Himilco, then came out of his own camp to do the same. Upon seeing him, the disguised archers shot him down.[68]

All of these stories are possible, though they cannot all be correct. That preserved by Polyaenus is certainly a fiction. The stratagem is, *a priori*, too fantastic and complicated and the error in name of the Punic general engenders further suspicion. Additionally, the late date of Polyaenus (second century AD) does not make me any more confident. The other three versions of Hamilcar's death, though, all seem plausible. The account of Diodorus, however, clashes with the first story preserved by Herodotus. If Gelon's cavalry had killed him then there is no reason for him to have searched fruitlessly all over Sicily. This leaves us with the Carthaginian version of events, by which Hamilcar sacrificed himself. If this version of events is correct it makes sense why Gelon's troops were unable to find him or his corpse thus making the two explanations in Herodotus logically coherent. As well, this show of devotion, if that is what it is to be called, is reflected in the hero worship of Hamilcar after his death, throughout the Phoenician colonies and Carthage.[69] Whatever his manner of demise, two basic facts are apparent: his body was never recovered, and he died a hero in the eyes of his people.

The Carthaginian defeat was total. Diodorus describes the slaughter as being great, although the supposed 150,000 dead is certainly an exaggeration.[70] A saying developed in the aftermath of the battle that not a single person made it back to Carthage to deliver the bad news, although this was false.[71] Twenty ships made their way from the Sicilian coast, but on their journey back to Libya were all but destroyed in a violent storm.[72] A single small boat made it through and informed their people of the defeat at Himera. The city went into a panic. Punic concern was twofold: for those who were lost and fear of a Greek invasion of Africa.[73] Because of this, they, and their allies, immediately sued for peace. Through the aid of Gelon's wife, Demaretê, peace was achieved at the price of two thousand talents of silver; that is perhaps 52,000kg of silver.[74] They were also to construct two temples, in which would be housed copies of the peace treaty. In thanks for her help in ending the hostilities, the Carthaginians gave Demaretê a gold crown made from one hundred talents of the precious metal.[75]

The aftermath of this war saw the first demarcation of Punic and Greek zones in Sicily, split somewhat down the middle of the island. It was considered a great victory by both Theron and Gelon. In Akragas, sculpted figures representing Carthaginian captives were added to the columns supporting the architrave of the Olympieum.[76] Gelon used the triumph as the centrepiece of a great propaganda campaign, which included relatively mundane endeavours such as the construction of a temple to Victory at Himera and more complicated cultural tactics such as promoting his accomplishment in the Pan-Hellenic sanctuaries.[77] In order to further promote the significance of the battle, a synchronism was developed which linked it with the Greek victory at Salamis, and later with Thermopylae.[78] Although this was certainly an image which Gelon and his successors wanted to establish, it was not universally accepted.[79] This was despite concerted effort.[80] Despite the propaganda being disseminated, though, this was not a war between the valiant Hellenes, led by Gelon, and the evil barbarian Carthaginians. The latter entered the conflict at the behest of other Greeks. Thus, from a critical point of view, the image that Gelon – and later his brother Hiero – presented to other Greeks was a complete fabrication.

Even though Himera was a great defeat for Carthage, it did not have a catastrophic effect on the city-state. It is true that a Punic army would not be sent against the Sicilian Greeks for over fifty years, but there was growth at home.[81] They did, however, wage war on their native neighbours in Africa, eventually bringing much of the area around Carthage under their control.[82] This could have been brought on, in part, by the loss of so many ships during and after the Himera campaign and the partial isolation of Carthage. The conquests in Africa were undertaken by Hamilcar's son, Hanno, who is said to have made the Carthaginians into Africans, rather than Tyrians.[83] It is unfortunate, but we know almost nothing about these campaigns.[84]

The Second Puno-Syracusan War

The Carthaginians were to return to Sicily late in the fifth century BC because of another call for help from allies on the island. This time, however, they did not send an army to aid a Greek tyrant but one in support of an Elymian city, Segesta. In 410 a conflict broke out between

Segesta and the Greek settlement of Selinus over a land dispute. This was not the first time that these two towns had come into conflict, and the earliest war that we know of between the two of them occurred over a century before (c. 580 BC).⁸⁵ We lack a detailed description of the war which broke out in 410. It may have consisted of a series of cross-border raids, as we hear of the Selinuntes pillaging the land nearest their border, scattering far and wide and collecting loot.⁸⁶ However combat was occurring, the conflict appears to have been a rather desperate struggle for the Segestans, as they offered their city to the Carthaginians in exchange for assistance against the Selinuntes. Personal reasons may have played a part in swaying Punic support, as the eventual general of the army, Hannibal, was the grandson of Hamilcar, who died outside of Himera in 480.⁸⁷ This was accepted and aid came in the form of an expeditionary force of 5,000 Libyans and 800 Campanian mercenaries.⁸⁸ With their forces bolstered by these troops, the Segestans were able to overcome the army from Selinus in a battle, killing around 1,000 of their soldiers. In the wake of this engagement, both sides envisioned a larger war and thus sent embassies to Carthage and Syracuse, respectively, asking them to join. Both sides accepted.⁸⁹

The Carthaginian invasion of Sicily was to come in 409 BC. They had amassed an army which numbered either 200,000 or 100,000 soldiers.⁹⁰ As with the figures given for the army of 480, this is almost certainly an exaggerated number. Reducing it to one tenth would give the Punic strength at either 20,000 or 10,000. The first of these two figures is more likely, although it feels small. Regardless of its size, this was a diverse force, consisting of recruits from the citizen population of Carthage, Libyans, and mercenaries hired from Iberia.⁹¹ They were to be led by a general named Hannibal. It is important to note the three different forms of recruitment recorded by Diodorus. The citizens were enrolled (καταγράφω), meaning one of a number of things. This verb could imply that they were formally summoned by a written notice, or perhaps they were called up based on a register of military-aged men. Regardless of how exactly the system functioned, this is certainly an official means of recruitment. Of the Libyans, we are told that Hannibal selected (ἐπιλέγω) the strongest amongst them. The verb used here implies a 'hand-picking' from the population. In contrast with the last group who we hear of as being hired foreigners, it is likely that the Libyans came into

Carthaginian service through treaty obligations, or something similar. The final group, Iberians, were enlisted (ξενολογέω), with Diodorus' choice of words implying that they were done so as mercenaries.⁹² This army was transported to Sicily from North Africa aboard 1,500 transports, along with missiles and siege engines. They were escorted by a fleet of sixty warships.⁹³

The Punic force landed near what would be in the future the Phoenician settlement of Lilybaeum. Cavalrymen from Selinus were operating in the area at the time of the landing and were able to ride back home and inform their countrymen of the forces arrayed against them.⁹⁴ Upon hearing this news, they sent for aid from Syracuse. At this point, the Carthaginian army was bolstered by troops coming from Segesta and 'the other allies'. We do not hear who these were, specifically, but it is safe to assume the Phoenician towns of Sicily, and perhaps the other Elymians, sent aid. We also know that the expeditionary force sent around a year earlier joined with the main body, thus we can count the Campanian mercenaries as part of this army. There were also an unknown number of Greeks who served as allied troops.⁹⁵

Quickly after landing on Sicily, Hannibal broke camp and marched towards Selinus. He took a trading station on the River Mazarus with one assault. The Punic army then invested Selinus. The forces were divided into two parts. Hannibal sent against the walls six siege towers described by Diodorus as 'exceptional' in their size as well as six metal-plated battering rams.⁹⁶ This could have been the first time a Greek city had to deal with the threat of siege towers.⁹⁷ He employed his archers and slingers to keep the city's battlements clear of defenders, allowing his engines to proceed unimpeded. The defenders' situation was dire. They had gone for many years without a war, and their defences had fallen into a state of disrepair. But, they took advantage of all the city's inhabitants, with women delivering aid to those fighting from the walls.⁹⁸ Eventually, a hole in the wall opened up and the Campanian mercenaries, looking to win glory for themselves, burst through. Though they were at first successful, this initial assault was repulsed resulting in heavy losses to the Campanians.⁹⁹ When night came, Hannibal was forced to call off the attack on the town.

Early the next morning, the Carthaginians renewed their attack on the walls. They moved on the city from every direction. Hannibal targeted the place in the wall which had fallen the previous day, sending his best troops against it in waves. Although the losses were heavy on both sides, no decisive moment was to be found. The siege lasted for nine days, the Carthaginians continually inflicting losses against the defenders. Eventually, the part of the fortifications which had already been compromised was breached by some of the Iberian mercenaries. Seeing this, and hearing the panicked screams of the civilians, the defenders retreated from the walls and formed small groups throughout the city. They barred access to streets and alleyways in a last-ditch attempt to defend their hometown. Those Selinuntes who had retreated to the roofs of their houses were hurling down roof tiles and rocks upon the heads of the Carthaginian troops. Although the assailants took heavy losses, they were not repulsed. The defenders were continually pushed towards the agora, where they made their last stand, dying to a man.[100]

After eliminating the remaining resistance, the Punic forces began looting Selinus. They took everything of value from the homes. What Selinuntes were left alive did not fare well. Some were burned alive in their homes, others were dragged into the streets and killed: men and women, old and young. They mutilated the dead, some even carrying severed hands on their spears.[101] The only persons who were spared were those that fled into the temples. Diodorus claimed that this was only done in order to prevent them from setting the sanctuaries alight, thus destroying their wealth, which the plundering army wanted to extract. It is claimed that only the Carthaginians were so cruel as to disrespect suppliants. This is meant to contrast with the piety of Greek soldiers. While there is no reason to presume that incredibly cruel acts were not committed against the people and gods of Selinus, the implication that only Carthaginian armies would do such things is resolutely anti-Punic hyperbole.[102]

Many of the inhabitants were killed during the sacking of the city. We hear of at least 16,000 dead and 5,000 taken captive.[103] The sight of this must have been horrifying. If each of the dead lost even one-third of their blood through their wounds, 8,000 gallons of sanguine gore would have flowed through the streets of Selinus.[104] While this may not have been an uncommon sight for veterans, the remaining civilian population would certainly have been shocked to see their city streets running red with torrents of blood.[105] The survivors were further terrorized by the soldiers of the Carthaginian army, who raped their female captives during the nights following the capture of the city. Only 2,600 residents escaped, fleeing to Akragas for safety. Hannibal razed the walls of Selinus and then marched his army on to Himera.[106]

Upon reaching their new target, the Carthaginian army split into two forces. One was encamped in the hills near Himera, while the other group invested the walls. Here they were joined by fresh soldiers from the Siceli and the Sicani.[107] These supposedly numbered 20,000, although, as we have seen above, this would be about the size of the original army (not counting the allies who joined after Hannibal landed on Sicily). It would be more reasonable that they would have sent 2,000 troops, perhaps 1,000 from each ethnic group. Not counting losses occurred at Selinus, the Carthaginians' optimal paper strength was probably somewhere around 27,800 men.[108]

The assault on Himera began when Hannibal advanced against the walls with his siege engines. His troops, still energized from their victory at Selinus, were very successful and steadily wore down the defenders' spirit. Although the machines were having an impact, Carthaginian mining operations met with the most success.[109] Miners tunnelled under the Himeraean walls, supporting their shafts with timbers. When all was ready, these were set alight, collapsing the tunnels and bringing down a section of the wall. Where it fell, a great struggle ensued. The defenders fought well, eventually driving the Punic troops out of this small foothold.[110] Whatever damage the mines did to the fortifications, it was quickly patched up and the breach was sealed.

The attackers broke off their assault at nightfall. Coinciding with this, a relieving force arrived, consisting of 4,000 soldiers from Syracuse and Akragas, and led by Diocles, a Syracusan. The next morning, not satisfied to stay within their walls and be slowly killed off, as had happened at Selinus, the defenders sallied forth 10,000 strong. This caught the Carthaginians off guard, and the Greeks initially met with success. They killed a significant number of the besiegers, although the numbers given by Diodorus, either 6,000 or 20,000, are too high.[111] Although the Punic forces which were closest to the city were routed, Hannibal brought up his reserve force that was still camped in the hills and repulsed the Greeks.[112] The figure given for their dead, 3,000, is more plausible than the figures given for the Carthaginian casualties, and is more likely to have been known to Diodorus' sources.[113]

After the sortie had retreated back within the walls of Himera, twenty-five triremes arrived in its port. These had just returned from the Aegean, where they had been fighting on the side of the Spartans. After their arrival, a rumour spread throughout the settlement that a select group of Carthaginian troops were preparing to break camp and sail for Syracuse, whose entire army was supposedly on the march towards Himera.[114] Believing this to be true, Diocles and the other leaders inside the besieged city decided that their best course of action was to abandon it and return to Syracuse. They evacuated as many women and children as they could on the triremes. Those who would not fit set out with Diocles and his troops, on foot.

A skeleton crew, of sorts, was left behind. They remained under arms on the walls, likely to keep the Carthaginians' attention so that the evacuees would not be pursued. The plan was for the Syracusan ships to return and rescue those who remained behind, but this would not happen.[115] The Punic attack on the walls that day were too swift and devastating. Their siege engines quickly brought down a section of the walls. The Iberian mercenaries were again the first troops through the breach. They successfully withstood a number of Himeraean counterattacks, and eventually took control of the walls.[116] As at Selinus, the Punic troops slaughtered many of the inhabitants, except those who were found after Hannibal had ordered for prisoners to be taken. His soldiers captured 3,000 Himeraean men, who were marched out to where Hannibal's grandfather, Hamilcar, had died during the battle against Gelon, tortured them, and then put them all to death. They also began looting the city's wealth.[117] After this victory, Hannibal dismissed his army. Ambassadors were sent to Carthage by Syracuse, censuring them for the war and requesting that they refrain from doing the same in the future, to which no clear answer was given.[118]

This phase of the war had a remarkable impact. Carthage's large army of mercenaries spurred on the minting of coins for the first time in the city's history. This initial issue was a tetradrachma based on the Attic standard. They bore the inscriptions of 'QRTHDŠT' and 'MHNT', translating, respectively, as 'Carthage' and 'the camp'.[119] The latter is an obvious reference to their origination from the military camp during the invasion of Sicily.[120] Although this may have been something of a burden to the city, the great wealth that we hear of Hannibal bringing back certainly made up for this.¹²¹ He was celebrated upon his arrival as one of the greatest generals in the history of his people.

The war was renewed between Carthage and the Sicilian Greeks two years after Hannibal's return. This was due, in part, to the actions of a wayward Syracusan general named Hermocrates. He was the admiral in charge of the triremes which arrived at Himera, having come from the Aegean. Upon his return to Syracuse, he found that his political rivals had conspired against him and he was exiled. He went to Messene where he commissioned the construction of five triremes and recruited 1,000 mercenaries. Moving westward, Hermocrates recruited an additional 1,000 men, survivors from Himera and an unknown number from Selinus and elsewhere, eventually assembling a force of 6,000 troops. Having seen that his situation in Syracuse was, for the moment, unrecoverable, he seized what was left of Selinus, fortifying a portion of the town with a wall.¹²² From here, he and his assemblage of troops raided lands controlled by Phoenician settlements, notably Motya and Panormus. A pitched battle was fought against the latter, in which the Greeks were victorious, killing as many as 500 of the Phoenicians. From these raids he accumulated a great amount of booty. These actions helped restore him to his position in Syracuse.¹²³

Diodorus claims that the reason for the second expedition, in 407, was not the aggression of Hermocrates, but rather out of a desire to conquer the entire island. While there may have been an interest in establishing more concrete control on Sicily, corroborated by the Punic colonization of Therma the year before, they do not appear to have wanted to completely dominate it.¹²⁴ It is possible that one of the reasons for the new campaign was some sort of alliance between Carthage and Athens.¹²⁵

Hannibal was again chosen as general but given a subordinate to assist in his duties, named Himilco, who was a relative. The two generals enrolled (καταγράφω) soldiers from Libyan and Phoenician settlements in Africa. Wealthy and respected Carthaginians were sent to Iberia and the Balearic Islands with great sums of money to recruit mercenaries from these areas. Allied kings and peoples also contributed soldiers to the growing army. New mercenaries from Campania were sought, as those who had been left behind on Sicily after the last campaign were now in the employ of the Sicilian Greeks.¹²⁶ Gathering these troops at Carthage, the strength of the army is said to have numbered either 120,000 or

300,000.¹²⁷ Thus, using the basic methodology outlined above, the true strength may have been between 12,000 and 30,000 infantry and cavalry, with the latter figure probably closer to the truth.

Before sending their transports towards Sicily, the Carthaginians dispatched an advanced fleet of forty triremes to ensure the security of the sea. The Syracusans were made aware of this flotilla and responded with a similarly sized group of ships. After a long battle, the Greeks emerged triumphant, having sank fifteen Punic ships and driving the rest back into the open sea. Hearing of the defeat, Hannibal personally led a group of fifty ships to prevent the Syracusans from taking advantage of their triumph and blocking his ground forces from crossing over to the island.¹²⁸

With dominance of the sea re-established, the Punic army crossed over to Sicily. After landing, they immediately marched towards Akragas, where they made two camps. One was in the hills near the city, while the other not far from the walls.¹²⁹ The Carthaginians first attempted to bring the Akragantini over to their side, but this offer was resolutely rejected. They had, in fact, been preparing for the war for some time. Everything from the countryside had been brought into the city in anticipation of a siege, and they had recruited the Spartan *condottiero*, Dexippus, who commanded 1,500 mercenaries.¹³⁰ Eight hundred of these were the Campanians who had served the Carthaginians in the previous phase of the war.

When it became obvious that the people of Akragas would not become their allies, Hannibal and Himilco initiated their siege. Identifying a part of the wall which they believed to be the most vulnerable, they brought forward two large towers and began assaulting the defenders who were stationed on the battlements. Greek casualties were high, but the defence never faltered. As the sun went down, the Carthaginians recalled their troops. Not willing to stand by as Punic soldiers broke against their walls like waves on a rock, the Akragantini launched a night sortie against the siege towers, torching both of them.¹³¹

Because of this, when Hannibal renewed his assault on the walls, he was forced to figure out a new manner of attack. Troops were sent against the fortifications in multiple places, instead of the concentrated effort of the towers. Their general ordered them to tear down the monuments and tombs around the city and use the debris as fill for siege mounds. The intention was to make these high enough for the Carthaginian soldiers to assault the defenders on top of the walls. Before the plan could come to fruition, a plague broke out within the attacking army, killing many of them, including Hannibal.[132] In response to this, Himilco supposedly sacrificed a boy and a large number of cattle to a selection of deities in order to check their wrath.[133]

Whether or not these sacrifices actually happened, it appears that the plague either subsided rather quickly or was not as severe as Diodorus implies, as Himilco was not forced to abandon the siege. He did not even take a break from attacking the walls, although he did alter the methodology. The remaining siege engines were advanced against the fortifications. Himilco must have identified a new weak point, as he ordered his troops to fill a part of the river which ran by the city in order to bring the machines against a specific place.[134] We do not hear of what kind of siege engines remained after the siege towers were set alight, and the term used by Diodorus (μηχανή) is too generic to give us any indication and simply means 'machine' or 'engine of war.'[135]

At the same time that Himilco was trying new methods of breaching the walls of Akragas, a relieving force led by Syracuse was moving towards the city. Daphnaeus was elected general of this army and led a mixed force of Syracusans and allied troops from Messene, Italy, Camarina, Gela, and some from the interior of the island, although we do not hear of their origins. In total, he had 30,000 infantry and 5,000 cavalry under his command.[136] While the army marched along the coast, a small fleet of thirty ships followed them, likely carrying supplies and protecting them from the threat of the Punic navy.

Learning of the approaching Greek army, Himilco sent his Iberian and Campanian contingents to meet them. The two forces met after the Greeks had crossed the Himera river. A pitched battle was fought which lasted for much of the day. In the end, Daphnaeus was victorious, his troops having killed many of the enemy. The remainder of the Punic units retreated back to the main camp which sat near the city walls. The Syracusans were restrained in their pursuit, their general being worried that they would be caught in a state of disorder by the main body of Himilco's army. The commanders within Akragas held their troops back as well, allowing the Carthaginian army to reform itself at their main camp.

Daphnaeus led his men to the secondary Punic camp and settled in, using it as his army's headquarters. They were joined by the Akragantini as well as Dexippus and his mercenaries. Accusations were brought against the leaders that they had been bribed to not attack the retreating Punic detachment. Four of the five generals from Akragas were stoned to death by their soldiers, with Argeius, the only of them named, spared because of his youth. Dexippus and Daphnaeus were spared, despite the former being accused of collusion. Command of the allied army was then given over to Menes of Camarina.[137]

The decision was made to contain the besiegers within their camp. Daphnaeus led out the troops under his command and proceeded to blockade the Carthaginians. He deployed his cavalry in the hinterland around Akragas, taking care to block all of the roads. The horsemen also scoured the countryside, capturing all the Punic foragers that they came across. This strategy was working. Within the Carthaginian camp, resources began to run out. After some of the soldiers began dying of hunger, a group of Campanians pushed their way into the tent of Himilco and demanded that rations be increased. They threatened desertion if their demands were not met.[138]

The Carthaginian cause was saved thanks to a piece of intelligence reaching Himilco as his troops were starving. He was informed of a flotilla of Syracusan ships bringing supplies to the Greek forces. The Punic general sent word to Panormus and Motya to send their ships against them. These caught the Syracusan fleet by surprise, sinking eight of their ships and driving the rest to shore, where the Carthaginian ground forces were able to capture the supplies. Clearly, whatever means by which Daphnaeus was attempting to keep his enemies penned up in their camp were not working. This saved the Punic army and affected a reversal of fortune for the Greeks. Not only were they deprived of much needed food, the Campanian mercenaries serving with them defected to the Carthaginians, thinking that the Hellenes' cause was now hopeless.[139]

As the supplies ran out in both Daphnaeus' camp and the city, the Greeks were forced to abandon both. There may have been an element of treachery involved in the decision, and we hear that Dexippus was supposedly bought off by the Carthaginians for fifteen talents.[140] He was responsible for convincing the leaders of the allied troops from Italy that the war should be continued elsewhere. The population was evacuated to

Gela, where they arrived safely thanks to the remaining soldiers guarding their column.[141]

There were some people left behind in Akragas. We hear of the sick and feeble being left behind, and that many of those who evacuated acted out of self-interest. Others stayed in the city because of their nostalgia for their ancestral home.[142] After the evacuation, Himilco took Akragas without opposition. His troops ran rampant throughout, dragging suppliants from the temples, looting the wealth of the entire city. Amongst the booty taken by the Carthaginians was the infamous Bull of Phalaris.[143] Much of the booty was sent back to Carthage.[144] Spectacularly, an inscription survives which commemorates the victory of both Hannibal and Himilco over Akragas.[145] Altogether, the siege of Akragas lasted for eight months, ending just before the winter solstice.[146]

Although the city was taken, the fallout from the Akragas campaign was not over. With the transfer of survivors to Syracuse, tensions once again rose between the people and the leaders of the failed defence. They accused the Syracusan generals of treachery and blamed them for the fall of their city. The other Sicilian Greeks who were present joined in the protests.[147] The loudest voice amongst the accusers was Dionysius, the son of Hermocrates. He continually spoke out about the rumoured treachery of the generals, so much so that he was fined by the archons.[148] Through a series of public harangues, subterfuges, and political moves, Dionysius seized supreme power in Syracuse, becoming its newest tyrant.[149] An interesting element to his ascension was that he reminded his countrymen that under Gelon, a tyrant, they had previously triumphed over the Carthaginians and that the present situation called for an equally independent and powerful leader.[150]

While Dionysius was seizing power at Syracuse, the Punic army was wintering in Akragas, unmolested. They used this time to prepare new siege engines and replenish the supply of missiles for their troops with the intention of marching on Gela in the coming campaigning season.[151] When summer came, Himilco invaded the territory of both Gela and Camarina, pillaging the countryside, taking booty and presumably what food supplies they could find. The Punic army set up their camp alongside the Gela river, not far from the city.[152] They proceeded to strip the land of its trees to fortify their position, and entrenched their encampment. This was in preparation for Greek attacks on their position. Before this occurred, a number of skirmishes were fought between Carthaginian foragers and Geloan troops who ranged over their hinterland in order to harass the enemy.[153]

While they were losing many from their foraging parties to the Greeks, the Punic army was also launching repeated assaults against the city's walls. Coming in waves, and continually bringing up siege engines, they steadily beat down the defences of the Geloans. Although their battering rams breached the walls in a number of places, the defenders did not give way. While the youth of the city were under arms, as would be the norm when a Greek city came under siege, all the inhabitants of the city helped in the defence, including the women and children. Unlike during the defence of Selinus, we hear nothing of this supposedly bringing shame on them.[154]

Dionysius finally set out from Syracuse after having received troops from his Greek allies in Italy, as well as those on Sicily. His army consisted of 30,000 infantry and 1,000 cavalry.[155] They were accompanied by a small fleet of fifty ships. The allied army made their camp by the sea, keeping the army and the ships together in one protected place. Dionysius' strategy was similar to that of Daphnaeus in the Akragas campaign, to use his light infantry, cavalry, and fleet to prevent the Carthaginians from foraging or bringing supplies in from the western portion of Sicily, which was under their control.[156] This tactic was not as successful as it was previously, though it did delay any significant engagement for twenty days.

Seeing that his army was unable to starve out the enemy, Dionysius resolved to attack their camp directly. His assault came as the Carthaginians were making another attempt at the Geloan fortifications. He divided his infantry into three parts based on the origin of the soldiers. The first, which consisted of the Sicilian Greeks, he advanced against the Punic camp. The second group, made up of allied troops, moved forward along the shore. The third division, the mercenaries led by Dionysius himself, moved into the city and reinforced the position on the wall where the Carthaginian siege engines were battering away. His cavalry was to overrun the plain and clear it of enemies, while the fleet was to sail into the enemy camp.[157] The cavalry was to join the main combat if they saw the allies winning, but if there was a retreat to cover them.

The Greek ships were the first to move against the Punic camp. They sailed around the fortifications and attempted a landing. Carthaginian contingents moved to block their disembarkation, depriving the palisades of defenders. The Italian division of Dionysius' army took advantage of this and forced their way into the camp successfully. When the defenders realized that they were being attacked on two fronts, however, they turned *en masse* against the Italiotes and routed them. The two other Greek infantry divisions were delayed and could not support them or take advantage of the break in the Punic camp. The Iberians and Campanians pursued the Italian Greeks, killing around 1,000 of them. They were saved from utter destruction only by the archers on their allied ships showering their pursuers with arrows. When the Sicilians finally reached the fight, they routed the Libyan division which confronted them, driving them all the way back to their camp. This success was short lived, countered by a push from Iberian, Campanian, and Carthaginian units. They drove the Sicilian division behind the city's walls. The cavalry quickly followed, themselves being pressed hard by the Punic army.[158]

Dionysius and his mercenaries do not seem to have even made it through the city by the time the other divisions had been beaten back. Seeing that his plan had failed, he resigned to take up a defensive position within Gela. After meeting with a council of his advisors, Dionysius resolved that the city could not be defended, and withdrew the population and his troops to Camarina. He left behind 2,000 of his light troops with orders to keep fires burning and make as much noise as possible, so as to make the Carthaginians believe the city was still garrisoned by the entire allied army. This stratagem worked, and the Greeks were able to successfully withdraw. Himilco's army then moved into the city unopposed and looted it.[159]

Once reaching Camarina, the Greek cause was made no better. Factional strife between Dionysius and his adversaries caused the breakdown of the allied army. After accusations that he was allowing the Carthaginians to devastate Gela and Camarina as part of a strategy for Dionysius to become lord over all the Sicilian Greeks, it splintered. The Italian allies returned to the peninsula. The Syracusan cavalry deserted the main body of the army, returning to Syracuse in hopes of sparking a revolution against Dionysius. Although they looted his house and ravaged his wife, they were ultimately unsuccessful. Dionysius had now secured his position.¹⁶⁰

After these victories, the Carthaginians were forced to sue for peace. Although there is a lacuna in Diodorus at this point, it is generally assumed that Himilco's army was devastated by another plague after the Gela and Camarina campaigns.¹⁶¹ They took this back to Libya with them, and it ravaged their home country and those of their allies. The terms of the treaty clearly indicate that the war was a 'victory' for Carthage. The Phoenician, Elymian, and Sican cities were all to belong to them. The survivors from Selinus, Akragas, Himera, Gela, and Camarina were allowed to return to their cities, so long as they did not rebuild the fortifications and paid a tribute to their new overlords. Leontini, Messene, and the Sicel towns were all to live under their own laws, but Syracuse was to be ruled over by Dionysius. All of the spoils of war, including captives, that the Greeks had taken were to be turned over to the Carthaginians.¹⁶² This peace was not to last long, and as we shall see in the next chapter, helping to legitimate Dionysius' power in Syracuse would come to haunt the Carthaginians.

Conclusions

We have seen that the first two conflicts for which we know any real details in Carthaginian history were against the Greek cities of Sicily. These two wars prompted Carthage to recruit large mercenary forces, but also included considerable citizen components. This is best seen in the wake of Hamilcar's defeat in 480 when the entire city went into mourning over the loss of their fighting-aged men. The defeats inflicted upon the Greeks in these two wars were significant but did not break their spirits. Over the course of the early fourth century, as discussed in the next chapter, new conflicts would rage between these two belligerent groups, but now with Dionysius of Syracuse firmly at the head of the Greek allies.

Chapter 4

The Wars with Dionysius I of Syracuse

As we left the situation in Sicily, the Carthaginian invasion had been stopped by a plague. Before this happened, Dionysius I had taken power in Syracuse. In the period after the Battle of Gela, he secured himself as sole ruler in the city.[1] Part of his political strategy was to invoke 'ethnic prejudice' against the Carthaginians.[2] This led to him arguing for a pre-emptive war against Punic positions in Sicily, as he argued that they were plotting against the Greeks, even though they were forced to evacuate their army after the last war.[3] He went so far as to say that 'they were most hostile to all Greeks generally and that they had designs at every opportunity on the Greeks of Sicily in particular.' Singling out the Carthaginians may have been a direct response to the humiliating peace treaty that he was forced to agree to in the wake of the last war.[4] Whether or not Dionysius and his countrymen actually believed a Punic invasion was imminent, this rhetoric set in motion a series of events which brought Syracuse, her allies, and her tyrant, back into war with Carthage.

The First War

Preparations for the first of Dionysius' wars against the Carthaginians were substantial. His first action was to engage the services of skilled workmen from all the territories under his control, using the vast wealth he had acquired through consolidating his power to hire them from Italy, Greece, and even areas under Punic control.[5] Part of his strategy to win the coming war was using these workers to design and create new weapons of war, superior to those used by his enemies. These included various types of missiles, as well as both quadriremes and quinqueremes.[6] The other great innovation of this push to arm Syracuse was the invention of the catapult.[7] Scholars typically assume that these resembled mechanical versions of more ordinary bows of the time.[8] They were, perhaps, modelled on the *gastraphetēs*, a type of crossbow which was fired with its stock braced against the shooter's stomach.⁹ These would prove useful for the coming campaign, which culminated in a great siege. Amongst the more mundane preparations were the creation of 140,000 shields, daggers, and helmets and a little over 14,000 corselets.¹⁰ Dionysius ordered that a number of different types were to be created to accommodate the tastes and experiences of his mercenaries who came from various places.¹¹ He wanted all of his soldiers to be able to fight as effectively as possible.

In contrast to the preparations undertaken by Dionysius, those of Carthage were less grand. It was only after the Syracusan army began to move on the Punic controlled part of Sicily that they began assembling one of their own. Diodorus' sources explained this as a result of the plague which devastated the Carthaginians in the last war. It made them apprehensive of a new one – though there may be more to it than this. The nature of Dionysius' war meant that a defeat would probably result in his removal from power. By launching a surprise attack, he would help stack the odds in his favour. Thus, what seems like a delayed response to a growing threat from Syracuse was actually a scrambled reaction. If this is correct, then the embassy sent by Dionysius (mentioned below) was surely meant to be rejected and was probably sent as his army mobilized. Carthage began its preparations by sending members of its government to recruit mercenaries from 'Europe' (Εὐρώπη).¹² It is unclear exactly where they went in search of soldiers of fortune, but later in Diodorus we hear of them recruiting in Iberia.¹³ The rest of the army was recruited throughout Libya. Despite these troops being gathered, they did not arrive in Sicily for the opening stage of Dionysius' war, leaving Carthage's allies and subjects to defend themselves against the Greek onslaught.

It is probably right to trace the beginning of the conflict to the tyrant seizing all property which belonged to Phoenicians living in Syracuse. A great number of Carthaginians had settled in the city, and at the time that Dionysius began his move against their kinsmen there were many Punic merchant ships in the harbour.¹⁴ All of these were impounded, and the wealth gained by Syracuse through these actions must have been great. Other Greek cities on Sicily followed suit and did the same.¹⁵ Dionysius then sent an ultimatum to the Punic government, threatening to declare war unless they withdrew their garrisons and claims to the Greek cities they had conquered on the island.¹⁶ As we have seen above, though, he had already made his preparations and this embassy, if it was actually sent, was surely fully expected to be rejected.

When all was ready, Dionysius marched on the Phoenician city of Motya. This was the most important of their settlements on Sicily and had been occupied continuously since the eighth century. It sat on an island just off the coast, with a small lagoon separating them.[17] Motya was formidably defended. Not only was it situated on an island, connected to the land by only a small causeway, but it was encircled by stout defensive walls. These dated back to at least the sixth century and reached a thickness of around two metres in places. All around the island, towers were set at regular intervals, adding additional protection.[18] Despite all of this, Dionysius was undaunted and determined to sack this icon of Phoenician power on the island.

On the march between Syracuse and Motya, Dionysius' army was supplemented by levies from the Greek cities that it passed by. Men came from Camarina, Gela, Akragas, and Selinus. All told, his army is said to have numbered 80,000 infantry, over 3,000 cavalry, and just fewer than 200 warships.[19] The figure of the infantry must have included the rowing crews from the ships, a supposition supported by the fact that Dionysius had ordered his ships drawn up on the shore.[20] Triremes carried crews of around 200 men, meaning that 40,000 of the infantry mentioned at Motya probably came from the navy.[21] This would mean that the 'regular' infantry numbered around 40,000, according better with the sizes of the armies of earlier campaigns we have discussed in the last chapter.[22] Regardless, this was still a massive army, and the ratio between infantry and cavalry (26.7:1), which is considerably off balance from other Sicilian Greek armies which had higher proportions of cavalry, indicates that troops were sought from sources not previously exploited.[23]

Dionysius ordered his engineers to build a mole to reach the island the city sat upon, which had been cut off from the mainland when its inhabitants destroyed their causeway.[24] While this was happening, though, the tyrant set out with his infantry, pillaging the territories of Solus, Panormus, and Halicyae, cutting down the trees of the latter. He then laid siege to Segesta and Entella, launching regular sorties against them.[25] Himilco, who had been chosen to lead the Carthaginian response, hearing that the Syracusan ships were drawn up on shore, resolved to send a naval squadron to destroy them.[26] He thus set out with 100 of the best Punic triremes to seize the Greek ships.[27] This force arrived at daybreak and took the Greeks by surprise. At first the Punic squadron was successful, disabling a number of the enemy's ships by ramming them or setting them alight.[28] Dionysius, having returned from his pillaging expedition, led the defences. As Himilco was in position to attack ships as they left the harbour, the tyrant ordered his vast forces to haul their triremes overland so that they could be launched into the open sea. The first ships they launched were attacked by the Carthaginians, who they repulsed thanks to a stratagem of Dionysius. He had ordered that they be manned by his archers and slingers, whose missiles warded off the attacks of the Punic ships. They were also aided by the crews of the new catapult weapons which hurled deadly sharp bolts at the attackers.[29] These supposedly instilled fear in the Carthaginians as they were a previously unknown device.

Himilco's raid was foiled. He was forced to retreat to Carthage, realizing that he was outnumbered almost two to one, even after the initial victories of the dawn sorties. This would prove disastrous for Motya. By not crippling Dionysius' fleet, and thus making it easier for Punic aid to arrive, the opportunity was given him to complete the mole and cross the lagoon. When this was done, he moved a number of siege engines across it, including battering rams and six-storey siege towers. The latter were wheeled and were built to be equal in height to the tall houses of the city. Rams continually battered the wall's towers, and catapults were brought up to keep the battlements clear of defenders.[30]

Despite this, the Motyans put up a stout defence, resisting 'with all the fire for which Phoenicians… were famous'.[31] They constructed platforms upon beams which gave them a height advantage over the attackers. From these, the defenders were able to throw firebrands and textiles covered in pitch down upon the siege engines.[32] Although they were quick to catch fire, the besiegers were even quicker in dousing the flames. As the attack wore on, a part of the wall finally succumbed to the force of the rams.[33] The resulting combat was fierce, with the defenders realizing they had no chance of escape, and the attackers wanting to exact revenge for the Carthaginian treatment of Greek cities in the previous two conflicts. The latter were to find that the city was less easily taken than they presumed.

Once inside the walls, Dionysius' troops found themselves fighting in narrow streets which had been barricaded by the Motyans. Aiding the defenders were their tall homes. These functioned almost as walls themselves, providing high bastions from which Phoenician missiles rained down upon the invaders.[34] The rather unusual architecture of the city led to what must have been an even more unusual sight in the ancient world, a battle fought six storeys high. In order to combat the defenders in the houses, the Greeks advanced their siege towers to the first set of them and used gangways to cross to their roofs.[35] After this, the battle was primarily fought hand-to-hand.

Although they had taken the fight to the heights of the houses, the Greeks were still held back by a fierce resistance. The Phoenicians defenders were encouraged by the pleas of their parents, wives, and children.[36] Many of the attackers were killed in this phase of the struggle, being cut down by the weapons of the Motyans or, perhaps more horrifically, being forced from the gangways and roofs, falling six storeys to their deaths.[37] This must have been demoralizing for both the other troops fighting on the rooftops and those at street level, who would have been able to see with great detail the gruesome fate of their comrades who tumbled this far. Although the gore of a more typical battle would have inculcated them against this to some degree, the sight of those who fell would have been new and likely traumatizing.

This pattern of fighting house to house, and alley to alley, lasted for days. Dionysius employed a stratagem to try to break through and finish the fight. He regularly recalled his troops close to nightfall and got the Motyans accustomed to a schedule of combat. After he was sure that his enemies had fallen into a cycle, he ordered one of his commanders, Archylus of Thurii, to take a group of picked troops on a night attack against the fallen houses being used as a defensive position by the Phoenicians. Establishing themselves here, the Greeks were able to open a gap in the defences whence the bulk of their forces were able to finally overpower the will of the defenders.[38]

After Dionysius' forces burst into the city, they ran rampant. They killed all those unfortunate enough to be caught out, including women, children, and the elderly. This slaughter was supposedly a repayment of the cruelty shown by the Carthaginians when they had conquered the Greek cities in the previous conflict. It is hard to see how these experiences would not have affected the behaviour of Motya's attackers.[39] Their leader, however, had other plans for the inhabitants of the city; he wanted to sell them into slavery. Enslaving a defeated settlement's population was common practice in Greek warfare.⁴⁰ He sent criers throughout the city, imploring the Motyans to shelter in temples, as they would not be killed by the Greeks in such places, as this was considered sacrilegious.⁴¹ The soldiers, now without a population to massacre, turned their rage on the property of their victims, looting all that they could. Motya yielded to the victors large amounts of both silver and gold, as well as considerable quantities of unnamed luxuries. Dionysius allowed this looting to help cultivate the loyalty of his troops, which he needed to carry out his future plans.⁴² In the aftermath of the sack, he sold the surviving population into bondage but crucified all the Greeks who had been fighting on the side of the Phoenicians and were still alive after the battle. The final actions of this phase of the war saw the garrisoning of what was left of Motya by Dionysius' Sicel troops, led by Biton of Syracuse, and the besieging of both Segesta and Entella by Leptines, the Syracusan admiral.⁴³

Dionysius then engaged in a campaign similar to that of Hermocrates in the late 400s. His army ravaged the territories of settlements loyal to Carthage and continued the sieges begun after the sack of Motya. Although the bulk of the army had originally marched back to Syracuse, the tyrant brought it back into the field in this fresh attack on the Punic sphere of influence. It was only now that the Carthaginians mobilized the troops they had mustered and transported them to Sicily.⁴⁴ Again, the numbers we hear of for the size of this force are far too large, being given as 300,000 infantry, 4,000 cavalry, 400 chariots, and 400 warships by Ephorus, or 100,000 total troops with 30,000 allies joining them on Sicily by Timaeus.⁴⁵ If we reduce the number of infantry provided by Ephorus, as we have done previously, then it would put the total strength of the Punic army at 30,000 infantry, without changing the other figures, as they do not seem exaggerated. In fact, the slightly higher ratio of cavalry to infantry than we have seen in previous wars can be explained by the problems the Carthaginians faced in the campaigns against Akragas, for example, during which Syracusan horsemen and infantry easily overran their scavenging parties. If we add in the 30,000 additional troops who came from the Sicilian allies (or possibly as mercenaries), then the Punic infantry was somewhere around 60,000 in number.⁴⁶ This is a plausible, if rather large, army.

The cavalry and chariot figures do not need to be adjusted. The number of warships noted, 400, however, is suspect. Even during the first war with Rome, the larger fleets numbered only around 330–350.[47] Although an argument can be made that we should accept fleet numbers in our sources, and that it is perhaps fruitless to try to guess at different figures, 400 warships is simply too many.[48] It is more reasonable that the entire fleet, including transports, numbered this many ships.[49] The Punic war fleet numbered, perhaps, around 200 ships. This is, of course, a guess, but it accords better with the other figures from the period and still leaves the Carthaginians with an advantage over the Syracusans at sea.

In crossing his army to Sicily, Himilco used a clever strategy. Rather than issuing orders to the ship's pilots before the fleet launched, he gave each of them a sealed document, only to be opened once they were at sea. These detailed the sailing plans, which were to make for Panormus.[50] To further conceal the movements of his fleet, Himilco may have had it launch in the dark of night.[51] The warships and the transports were to sail in two different groups, and it has been suggested that he was using the war fleet to lure away the ships of Leptines, who had been left in command of the Syracusan navy.[52] Regardless of his carefully laid plans, Himilco's transports were attacked by the Greek ships, which sank fifty of them, killing five thousand soldiers and sending two hundred chariots to the bottom of the Mediterranean.[53]

Nevertheless, the bulk of the Punic army made it safely across to Sicily and landed, as planned, at Panormus. Himilco marched his army towards Motya, but made a stop at Eryx en route. Dionysius had seized this Elymian town during his campaign.[54] This was an important strategic point between Panormus and Motya. Interestingly, neither Dionysius nor Himilco had to use force to take the hilltop town. The former was given control because the inhabitants were in awe of his army, while the latter took control back through treachery.[55] This was a surprisingly common occurrence in the ancient world, and many of the precautions advised by Aeneas Tacticus for cities under siege included measures to prevent traitors from betraying their countrymen. Many of the other settlements which belonged to Sicily's native peoples were also caught in the crossfire of this war. Dionysius' plan was to retreat towards the eastern end of Sicily. On the way, he 'suggested' to the Sicani that they should abandon their settlements and join his army, promising that after the war they would be given richer lands than they currently controlled. Not many of them took him up on this offer, but those that did seem to have done so only because they feared his army would loot their properties if they refused.[56] Some of Dionysius' erstwhile allies abandoned him while he was on the move, with Halicyae making an alliance with the Carthaginians. The fears of the Sicani were realized when the Syracusan army left a path of destruction in its wake while executing their strategic retreat.[57]

After gaining control of Eryx, Himilco marched his army to Motya and laid siege to the garrison left there by Dionysius. We do not hear of any details for how this was carried out, but it is probable that few, if any, of the Greeks survived. The siege does not seem to have carried on very long, although Diodorus does not give us the duration.[58] What seems clear, however, is that the Greek garrison had rebuilt, to some extent, the fortifications that they had previously destroyed, or at least shored them up enough for the Carthaginian army to have to lay siege.

Retaking Motya was only the beginning of Himilco's strategy and the war on Sicily. His first goal was to secure the straits around Messene, which is the strip of water between Sicily and the Italian peninsula. According to Diodorus, this was to prevent the Greeks of Italy and the Peloponnesus from sending aid to Dionysius.[59] Before this could be accomplished, however, the Carthaginians had to make their way through erstwhile hostile territory. To avoid being bogged down in fighting, Himilco entered into an alliance or non-aggression pact with the inhabitants of Himera and Cephaloedium, which seemed to guarantee his army easy passage across the north coast of Sicily. He also had to contend with the Liparians, who exercised considerable power on the sea along the south west coast of Italy.[60] The Punic fleet, and possibly army, took control of the settlement, and extorted thirty talents from its population.[61] As the army made its way across northern Sicily, the fleet joined it and sailed alongside, ensuring that their supply lines were not cut and that they would not be harassed by the Greeks from the sea.[62]

The Punic general did not march directly on Messene. He led his army to Pelorias, where they established themselves. This put them around eighteen kilometres from their ultimate target. When word reached the Messenians of the position of the Carthaginians, they deliberated what to do. There were sensible reasons to try to prevent the conflict from coming to blows. Messene's walls had fallen into dire disrepair and there was not time enough to rebuild them before Himilco arrived. In addition to this, their cavalrymen were at Syracuse, serving as hostages to secure the city's loyalty to Dionysius, thus depriving them of an essential element of any Greek army.[63] Despite these problems, some of the citizens believed that they should try to fight off the invaders, thanks in part to an oracle which had said 'Carthaginians must be bearers of water in Messene.'[64] They believed this to mean they had divine support against the Punic threat. Rallying the rest of the population, they sent their best troops towards Pelorias in order to prevent Himilco from entering their territory.[65] Regardless of whether or not they thought there was a chance at driving them back, support of the gods or not, the Messenians sent the women and children to Syracuse.

But the strategy of trying to fight at Pelorias would prove disastrous. When the select body of troops arrived from Messene, Himilco sent his own advanced force up the coast in 200 ships to attack the city directly.[66] The main body kept the Messenian troops occupied long enough, and the Punic ships easily sailed into the harbour at Messene, aided by a strong wind. Carthaginian troops then began attacking the dilapidated defences of the city, making their way through the useless fortifications, becoming masters of the city.[67] Although some of the inhabitants put up a resistance, it was evidently not long lived, and they were slain in the streets. Those who chose not to fight, but rather to flee, made their way either to nearby towns or into the mountains and to the strongholds therein. Remarkably, some fifty Messenians are said to have taken to the sea and swam safely to the other side of the strait, although 150 others died attempting this.[68] Himilco took what forts he could in the hinterland, although most were too strongly built and defended. When he had accomplished all that he believed possible, he ordered his army to raze Messene, tearing down what was left of the walls, sundering homes, and burning or breaking every other timber, tile, or stone.[69]

Seeing that the Carthaginian cause was the strongest at this point, the Siceli revolted against Dionysius and, with the exception of the town of Assorus, allied themselves to Himilco. It also appears that Dionysius was experiencing a manpower shortage. He freed a considerable number of slaves, perhaps 10,000, and used them to man sixty warships and sent for 1,000 mercenaries from the Lacedaemonians.[70] Although we do not hear of a reason for this shortage, it has been explained by assuming many of the rowers from Dionysius' previous campaign were mercenaries, who had already returned to their homes, and that he had garrisoned a considerable number of men in the defences scattered throughout Syracusan lands.⁷¹ In addition to this, it is also possible that the revolt of the Siceli and fear of the large Punic army could have helped shrink the pool from which he could draw soldiers.⁷² Using what troops he had, Dionysius began fortifying the countryside around Syracuse, stocking them thoroughly, and taking special care to supply those in the country of Leontini.⁷³

Having secured his defences as best as possible, Dionysius marched his army out of Syracuse. This force was made up of 30,000 infantry, 3,000 cavalry, and 180 ships, few of which were triremes.⁷⁴ This was a considerably smaller army than that with which he took Motya. The defection of the Siceli and the Himerans, and likely other smaller settlements as well, over to the Carthaginians deprived Dionysius of many troops, and if we are right to think that a large number of mercenaries had been released from service after the previous campaign there is no mystery as to why the current army was smaller.

Himilco's army began moving at about the same time. Their destination was Tauromenium, which was at that time a Sicel stronghold.⁷⁵ The Syracusans, on the other hand, marched towards a peak called Taurus, near which was a suitable harbour.⁷⁶ The two armies were separated by both a distance as well as the aftermath of an eruption of Mt. Aetna, which had left lava blocking the coastal route between them.⁷⁷ The ultimate destination of the Carthaginians was Catane, where the Punic and Syracusan fleets would actually come to blows. This settlement had been evacuated by its Campanian inhabitants at the behest of Dionysius.⁷⁸ Thus, the situation was that the Punic fleet sailed towards a mostly abandoned Catane while the army marched all the way around Mt. Aetna, and Dionysius' combined forces were making their way to the city, unimpeded by volcanic malefaction.

Whether because of information from his scouts or just by chance, Dionysius arrived with both his army and his fleet around the same time or just before Mago – the leader of the Carthaginian ships – did with the Punic fleet.⁷⁹ Leptines was put in charge of the Greek ships and sailed out to meet the Carthaginians. He had under his command 180 vessels, while the Punic fleet numbered at least 500, including both warships with oars and rams as well as the merchant ships.⁸⁰ The Syracusan land forces lined up along the shore to cheer on the navy, as well as to prevent the enemy from making landfall.⁸¹ Seeing that the Carthaginians could not land, Leptines advanced against them. In the van were his thirty best ships, who engaged the Punic fleet well ahead of the rest.[82] Although this charge is portrayed as being valorous, our sources acknowledged that it was not a prudent decision.[83] Mago's ships swarmed this squadron, surrounding them. Because of the number of ships, there was no room to manoeuvre and engage in the usual tactic of ramming. Instead, the ships came alongside one another and the embarked soldiers engaged in hand-to-hand combat, described as resembling a battle on land.[84] Troops crossed to enemy ships, attempting to slay their crews; some of these did not make it across, falling into the unforgiving sea, drowning, and possibly being crushed as the mass of ships swayed upon the waves.

Locked in this melee, Mago's numerical superiority was enough to crush Leptines' fleet. As the latter began to flee, realising the day was lost, the Carthaginians pursued them, destroying every ship that they could. Syracusan losses amounted to 100 ships, well over half of the fleet. Using their small, swift craft, the victors patrolled the shore in order to kill any Greek sailors who attempted to swim to land.[85] Between this tactic and the battle itself, at least 20,000 of Dionysius' men were slain.[86] This defeat demoralized the Syracusan army, in front of whose helpless eyes the seaborne slaughter was wrought. Mago took a number of ships as prizes, and towed them into the harbour at Catane, which he occupied without resistance. These would serve as a reminder of their victory and encourage the Punic army to push their cause to Syracuse itself.[87]

Dionysius was now faced with a very difficult decision: how to proceed. His Sicilian Greek allies encouraged him to attack Himilco's army as it was marching towards Catane, thus still taking advantage of its separation from the fleet.[88] Although this presented Dionysius with an attractive plan, his Syracusan friends pointed out that it would leave Syracuse open to being attacked by the Punic fleet. Taking into account Mago's success in a similar manoeuvre, he settled on marching the army back to Syracuse. This decision infuriated many of his Sicilian allies who deserted him and returned home or fled to the nearby fortresses. Dionysius' retreat enabled Himilco to join with the fleet in Catane.[89] It is evident that the defeat at sea was a major setback for Dionysius' cause, but not everyone abandoned him. Himilco attempted to turn the Campanians in Aetna against Syracuse, but they did not capitulate, due in part to their hostages held by Dionysius.[90]

While Himilco was attempting this, Dionysius sent Polyxenus, his brother-in-law, to Italy, Lacedaemon and Corinth seeking allies to come to his aid. Additionally, he sent recruiters to the Peloponnesus to hire mercenaries as a means of supplementing the Syracusan army.[91] As his enemies searched for more troops, Himilco moved his army into position to besiege Syracuse. He ordered the fleet to conspicuously display the loot taken in their previous victories on the decks of their ships and sail into the Great Harbour, flaunting their successes to the whole of the city. There were so many vessels that the harbour was clogged. The army advanced around the city, joining up with the fleet near the temple of Olympian Zeus.[92] After making camp, the Carthaginians drew up in battle lines at the city's walls, offering a fight, as 100 of their most impressive ships sailed towards the harbours. The Syracusans did not come out to accept the challenge, and Himilco recalled his forces.[93]

The Punic army then began preparing for a long siege. They covered the countryside, harvesting timber and laying waste to anything that they did not need.[94] Carthaginian troops overran Achradine, the portion of the city which connects to Ortygia. At this point they also ransacked the temples of Demeter and Core. The Syracusans did not sit by idly and won a number of skirmishes against Himilco's raiding parties.[95] The Carthaginians continued to dig in, and built three forts along the Great Harbour. Into these were imported wine, grain, and everything else needed to maintain the siege. They used all available materials, going so far as tearing down tombs in the area, including that of Gelon and his wife Demarete.[96]

Although the war appeared to be going in the Carthaginians' favour, they were hindered by a ruthless enemy, more deadly than the Syracusans. While they were digging in around the city, a plague broke out. Diodorus blamed it on their sacking of the temples to Demeter and Core, his sources believing that the sacrilege was to blame.[97] The Carthaginians themselves may have believed this, as we hear of them importing the cults of these goddesses into the city in 396 in an attempt to appease them.[98] Although this notice is striking, it has been pointed out that Phoenicians on Sicily had already been worshipping these deities, and that the spread of their cult to Carthage more likely came through them.[99] It is possible that the deities were already being worshipped before 396, but after the disaster outside of Syracuse, and the subsequent rebellion in North Africa (discussed below), the city's elites devoted more attention, and perhaps resources, to the cult.

As Himilco was fortifying his position, Dionysius' brother-in-law returned from Greece, bringing with him thirty ships from their allies, as well as a Lacedaemonian admiral, Pharacidas.[100] During the journey from the Peloponnese to Sicily, they fell in with a group of Punic ships, fought an engagement, and captured nine of them.[101] The Greeks used these captured vessels on their return to Syracuse in order to slip past the Carthaginian blockade of the harbour. They made it appear as though the Phoenician ships were towing the Greek ships as if they had been the ones captured. This allowed them to pass unhindered.

After the triumphal arrival of the new ships, the Syracusans engaged in an active defence at sea. Much as they had been launching sorties against scavenging parties, they now attempted to hinder supplies coming to the Carthaginian camp from the sea. We hear of one successful attack in which the Syracusans used a squadron of five ships to seize a supply ship which was heading for the enemy encampment. Himilco was not ready to remain inactive, and sent out a number of ships against the Greeks, but the Carthaginians were defeated, even losing their flagship.[102] Dionysius, and his brother Leptines, were away from the city during this engagement, escorting supply ships of their own to Syracuse. This particular episode is complicated by the events which supposedly followed. The populace was thrown into a state of elation by the victory because it was carried out not by Dionysius or one of his cronies, but by regular citizens. The tyrant tried to quell the crowd's excitement by bringing them together and praising their deeds and promising to win the war quickly.[103] Before the assembly could be dispersed by Dionysius, though, an elite Syracusan named Theodorus stood and delivered a rousing speech in favour of liberty. He decried the tyrant's behaviour in both war and peace, and advocated for power to be restored to the citizens, or alternatively to the Corinthians, the mother-city of Syracuse, or Lacedaemon, to whom he ascribes the status of first city amongst the Greeks.[104]

The authenticity of this speech has been questioned, and it has been suggested to have come from Timaeus, the anti-tyrant historian who flourished during the third century BC.[105] Many of the arguments against the speech being authentic are sound, and it does read as though it was written by a later author railing against tyranny. But this does not mean that the entire episode was a later construction, and there is no reason to dismiss it entirely, as Caven does.[106] It is interesting that Dionysius and his brother were out of the city, but we should not, as Caven does, presume that no loyalist had been left in command.[107] The narrative does not preclude this, and may substantiate it. When the citizens first sallied out to capture the Punic supply ship, they only had five vessels in their squadron, obviously not the entire Syracusan fleet and plausibly an endeavour led by a small group operating outside of the control of whomever was officially in command. The small size points to this being the case. Towards the end of the siege, we hear of the populace, not being able to hold themselves back, manning small vessels and looting burnt out enemy ships, even while Dionysius was just outside the city.[108] Once the Carthaginians came out in force, the entirety of the Greek fleet was launched, possibly commanded by whomever Dionysius had left in charge. Even if it was led by this person, the citizens may have still been able to claim the victory for themselves, as it had been their initiative which ultimately caused it to happen. Regardless of whether or not one views the details of the Theodorus episode as historical, whatever effort was made to get rid of Dionysius was unfruitful and resulted in Pharacidas reaffirming his, and the Lacedaemonians', allegiance to the tyrant.[109]

The remainder of the Punic siege was benign. We do not hear of any major assaults on the walls, or sorties against Greek positions. The explanation for this probably lies in the plague which we mentioned earlier. It appears that the disease hindered any plans Himilco may have had to press his attack. Libyans in the Carthaginian army were supposedly the first to be stricken by the disease. At first they buried their dead and nursed those who were sick, but as more and more of the army was afflicted both of these became impractical. Corpses began stacking up quicker than they could be interred, and those who gave care to the ill contracted the sickness. Because of the former, a stench and miasma began to hang over the camp, which could have done nothing but further demoralise the army.[110]

We hear details of the symptoms thanks to Diodorus' sources.[111] It began with a build-up of mucus in the nose and throat. Next came a swollen throat, followed by burning sensations and pain, especially in the back, as well as heaviness in the victim's arms and legs. The final symptoms were dysentery and pustules covering the entire body.[112] Death came on the fifth or sixth day.¹¹³ Some of the infected succumbed to a madness, being bereft even of their memories, and surrounded the camp, attacking others at random.¹¹⁴ It is unclear what pathogen brought on this epidemic, and any attempt to identify it is very difficult.¹¹⁵ If it was the same disease which affected Athens from 430, as has been proposed by Littman, it could have been smallpox.¹¹⁶ The identification of the Athenian plague, however, is not settled, and as a recent scholar has pointed out, the possible mutation of pathogens between the ancient period and modern occurrences may have resulted in symptoms changing over time thus complicating any modern efforts to identify it.¹¹⁷

Regardless of what caused it, the epidemic in the Carthaginian camp was the beginning of the end of Himilco's campaign. Deserters and prisoners taken from his forces brought the situation to Dionysius' attention and he resolved to take the offensive. He concocted a relatively complex plan, which modern scholars have pointed out as similar to his strategy in the Battle of Gela.¹¹⁸ Under the cover of darkness, on a moonless night, Dionysius marched his army out of Syracuse and far enough around the Punic camp so as not to be detected. At daybreak, he was in place and began sending forth his forces.¹¹⁹ His first move was a feint, sending his cavalry and 1,000 of the mercenary infantry against a part of the Carthaginian camp which extended towards the interior. As soon as they engaged, the cavalry was ordered to retreat, leaving the infantry to be slaughtered to a man. This both eliminated these particular mercenaries, who had been disruptive and mutinous, and put the defenders on the wrong foot.¹²⁰

Dionysius then moved the rest of his army against the Punic camp and laid siege. He led in person the main body of the infantry against the fortifications at Polichne, while the cavalry attacked Dascon, which appears to have been the main anchorage for the Punic transports as well as the primary supply depot.¹²¹ Both of these attacks were aided by the Syracusan fleet, commanded by Pharacidas and Leptines. A squadron detached from the main body helped the cavalry take Dascon. Eventually, the rest of the ships attacked en masse. Both of the army groups were successful in their initial objectives, and both the forts of Polichne and Dascon were captured. The Carthaginian resistance was handled incompetently. When their commanders realised that the forts had been captured, they haphazardly sent their troops against them. But when they realised that they were also being attacked from the seaward side, panic took hold and they incautiously tried to wheel their troops around. This was unsuccessful.

The Greek ships rammed the Carthaginian fleet while it was anchored. Unsatisfied with simply damaging the ships, or making them unusable, the captains ordered their men to reverse and continually ram their targets, breaking them asunder. This caused such a great noise that none of the men, either on land or on the ships, could ignore it, and it struck fear into the Carthaginian ranks. Their vessels were broken, and the shoreline of the camp was littered with corpses of their fallen comrades.[122] The Syracusans eagerly boarded the sundered ships, slaughtering all the crews upon whom they came.[123] Those troops who attacked from the land met with no less success. They breached the defences of the Punic camp, being able to reach as far as the ships anchored at the naval depot near Dascon. Dionysius personally took command of the contingent here, ordering that the enemy ships be set alight. An inferno quickly spread amongst the vessels, burning warship and merchantman alike. Fearing suffocation and immolation, the crews began jumping overboard, but because of the rough sea many were crushed as their ships swayed and crashed into each other. The scene was so violent and dire that Diodorus' source compared it to that of 'men struck by lightning from heaven for their impiety.'[124] The image of divine punishment is repeated when described from the city, we hear that 'from a distance the sight resembled a battle with the gods, such a number of ships going up in fire'.[125] This has been described as Dionysius' 'greatest victory' by at least one scholar.[126] It was such a total defeat that civilians, observing it from Syracuse, rowed out to the husks of the Punic fleet and began looting anything that was left undamaged, while the rest of the city cheered from the wall.[127]

Himilco's army was broken. What remained of it was holed up in their camp, though unable to commit any significant actions against the Syracusans and unable to affect an escape. Out of desperation, Himilco petitioned Dionysius to allow his army to evacuate and return to Libya, offering the tyrant three hundred talents in exchange. The latter replied that he could not allow the entire army to withdraw, but would consent to Himilco and the Punic citizens returning safely to Carthage. This was a unilateral decision, and it is probable that the notice in Diodorus, that Dionysius hid this decision from his allies and the Syracusans, is accurate.[128] He would not have wanted them to be alerted to the vast sum of silver he was about to have in his possession. The decision to allow Himilco and the citizen troops to withdraw should also be seen as a prudent and cautious move by Dionysius, as it all but guaranteed that he was to be victorious, as the remaining mercenary troops were left leaderless.[129] Allowing some of the army to escape also preserved the 'Punic threat', which was part of the foundation for Dionysius' hold on power in Syracuse.[130] The abandonment of the mercenaries, as well, undermined Carthaginian credibility and weakened their ability to wage future wars.[131]

After concluding this deal, the Greek army withdrew into the city. On the fourth night thereafter, the Carthaginians transported the silver to Ortygia and gave it to the agents of Dionysius. Himilco and the citizen soldiers then boarded forty triremes under the cover of night and sailed out of the harbour. A squadron of Corinthian ships, not waiting for Dionysius' command, as it was slow coming, launched a sortie against the fleeing Punic vessels, sinking a number of those at the back of the line. Dionysius, eventually, led his army out of Syracuse and marched against the remaining mercenaries. The Sicels who had served Himilco escaped before the Greeks could set up proper guard stations, and almost all of them made it to their homes safely. Most of the remaining troops threw down their weapons and surrendered to the tyrant, begging for their lives. They were taken as captives. A contingent of Iberian mercenaries, however, banded together, ready to fight for their freedom, and sent a proposal to Dionysius to be taken into his service. This he accepted.[132]

This disastrous end of the war in Sicily had repercussions for the Carthaginians in Libya. Native peoples who lived under Punic rule, upon hearing of the defeat, revolted. Rebellious sentiment had been brewing for some time because of oppressive Carthaginian policies, and the abandonment of the army at Syracuse, which included Libyan troops, pushed them into open conflict. According to Diodorus, they assembled an army of 200,000 men and marched on Carthage, seizing Tunis, not far from the city. This figure is certainly exaggerated, and is perhaps better rendered as 20,000 using the methodology discussed in the previous chapter, but that is simply a guess.[133] They defeated the Carthaginians in the field and forced them within their walls. They sought the help of the gods to save the city, and it was perhaps at this point that they redoubled their worship of Demeter and Kore. The siege was doomed from the start, and divine intervention was not needed to save Carthage.

The rebels lacked strong leaders, and many of their fighting aged men had probably been taken captive on Sicily in the aftermath of the siege of Syracuse. Additionally, Carthage was supplied with provisions from the sea, especially from Sardinia, which prevented the Libyans from starving its inhabitants into submission. In the end, a number of the rebels were bought off with Punic gold, and the revolt fizzled, with the remaining freedom fighters scattering and returning to their homes.[134]

Himilco's fate was far drearier than that of the city. He faced continual abuse from his countrymen who blamed him for the defeat in Sicily. The general seemed to acknowledge his guilt. Going around to the temples of the city, dressed in rags, he admitted to impiety and offered restitution to the gods for his crimes. If he succeeded in anything, it was to make his fellow citizens more pious. But they were never to forgive him. As his melancholy closed in on him, he locked himself in his house and starved himself to death.[135]

A peace of sorts followed between Carthage and Dionysius, and for two years nothing of consequence was undertaken by the former in Sicily. Mago, admiral under Himilco, was put in command of Punic forces on the island. We hear very little detail of the preparations, but he recruited an army large enough to be functional and set out on a campaign against Messene. This city had been resettled by Dionysius in the intervening years with a number of colonists from Locri, Medma and the Peloponnese, who also refortified it.[136] This was part of a wider programme of consolidating his power. We know little about the army with which Mago marched, although it is probable that it consisted of a mixture of Carthaginian citizens, allied troops from the Phoenician areas of Sicily, Sicel troops who were again allied with Carthage, and refugees from Dionysius' power grab.[137]

Mago was unable to take the city, but laid waste and pillaged its hinterland. After this, he marched his army into a camp near the allied city of Abacaene.[138] It was here that Dionysius caught up with the Punic army. The two generals marshalled their troops and committed to a pitched battle which ended in a Carthaginian defeat and the loss of as many as 800 soldiers. They were forced into the allied city, after which Dionysius withdrew from the area back to Syracuse. He took advantage of the Punic defeat to launch a surprise assault against Rhegium.[139] Mago withdrew his forces and returned to Carthage.

A year later, Mago returned to Sicily, this time with a more carefully prepared army.[140] This was made up of troops from Libya, Sardinia, as well as Italians. Himilco's abandonment of the mercenaries outside of Syracuse obviously had not discouraged every group from serving with the Carthaginian army, but the absence of Iberian mercenaries is conspicuous. This army numbered 80,000 according to Diodorus' unnamed source, but this is certainly an exaggeration, although not nearly as much so as in previous instances.[141] If we use our simple methodology of reducing the size to ten per cent, it would leave Mago with an army only numbering 8,000, which is too small. Fred Ray postulates a strength of around 40,000 for the Punic army, which may be closer to the truth.[142] As this looks like an 'economy expedition', for instance it was only accompanied by a few ships, a figure closer to that of Dionysius' army of 20,000 may be better.[143] Again, though, this is only a guess. The reason to assume that Mago had a smaller army than in previous campaigns is because Carthage was almost certainly running low on money at this point, between the disaster at Syracuse and the Libyan revolt.

The Carthaginian army marched across the Sicel lands, whose settlements all went over to them as they had in the past. It is unclear if they sent troops to join Mago's forces, but it seems likely. The march continued until they entered the territory of Agyrium, a Sicel city which did not go over to the Punic cause.[144] It was, at the time, one of the most powerful cities on Sicily, and its military strength was second only to that of Dionysius. Hearing that the Carthaginian army had encamped near to Agyrium, the Syracusan tyrant set out with his army of 20,000 and made for the Sicel settlement. His army set up camp near to Mago's, and immediately sent an embassy to Agyris, the tyrant of Agyrium. The two entered into an alliance, and the latter supplied the Syracusan army with food while also mustering his own forces.[145]

The two factions remained in the hinterland of Agyrium for some time. Mago attempted a campaign of raiding and pillaging, probably similar to Himilco's strategy at Gela. He was, however, less successful. His foragers were continually ambushed by troops for Agyrium thanks to their familiarity with the terrain. Dionysius and his ally also cut off supply lines which stretched back through the Punic allied territories. The Syracusan contingent of the army grew anxious and demanded that Dionysius lead them into battle against the Carthaginians. He was unwilling, though, and believed that starving them out was a better course of action. Accordingly, they abandoned him and marched back to Syracuse. The strategy worked, though, and Mago was eventually forced to sue for peace. The resultant treaty brought an end to the first war between Dionysius and Carthage. In it, all of the Sicel territories were ceded to the Syracusan, as well as Tauromenium, much of whose population was banished and the site resettled by some of Dionysius' most loyal mercenaries.[146] Carthage remained in control of much of western Sicily, including the Phoenician towns, and the Elymian and Sican settlements.[147]

The Second War

After Mago made peace and retreated from Sicily, Dionysius continued expanding his empire. He consolidated his power throughout Sicily and Southern Italy. Dionysius forged what is rightfully described as an 'empire', even if it wasn't as large as those of Persia, Alexander, or Rome.[148] After he had secured the territories now under his control, he decided to go to war with Carthage. In preparation for this, he led a piratical raid against the coastal Etruscan cities, notably looting Caere's port, Pyrgi. These raids yielded at least five hundred talents, a sizable war chest. With this, Dionysius recruited a large group of mercenaries from many different peoples.[149] All he needed now was an excuse to start a war. This he found in the subject cities of Carthage, many of which were unhappy with Punic rule and were close to rebellion. These Dionysius brought into an alliance in 383/2 BC, which prompted the Carthaginians to send ambassadors in protest. When they were refused, war was inevitable.[150]

Carthage sought new allies and entered into friendship with the Greeks of Italy. This would enable them to open a two-fronted war against the Syracusan tyrant. Punic preparations began immediately, but we do not possess the level of detail that we have for previous campaigns.[151] They enrolled citizens from the city's 'capable youth' and hired a large force of mercenaries, although whence we do not know. The size of the army is also a mystery, perhaps more so than usual. All that we are told is that the Carthaginians moved 'tens of thousands of soldiers across to Sicily and Italy.'[152] Mago was chosen to the lead the expedition.[153]

The deficiencies of the text continue into the description of the war itself. We know it was fought on two fronts, in Sicily and in Italy. In the opening phases there 'were many battles here and there between groups of soldiers and minor and continuous engagements' but they were of no consequence, at least to Diodorus, his source, or his epitomiser. The outcome of the conflict was apparently determined by two major pitched battles, a rarity in the conflicts we have seen. The first of these took place near Cabala, an unknown site. Dionysius was victorious and killed as many as 10,000 soldiers from the Carthaginian army, capturing an additional 5,000. Amongst the dead was Mago, who was struck down whilst in the midst of the melee. The remaining army retreated to a fortified hilltop and regrouped. Unfortunately for them, however, their bastion did not have a source of water.[154]

Trapped on a hilltop with no fresh water, the Carthaginian army's situation was desperate. They elected Mago's son to command and had to settle on a strategy. Initially, peace was sought, but the conditions offered by Dionysius were too extreme to be accepted. It would have seen Carthage giving up all holdings in Sicily and paying an indemnity to Dionysius to cover the entire cost of the war. Cleverly, either Mago's son or perhaps the remaining Punic commanders together, devised a means of escaping by replying to Dionysius that they were willing to accept his terms but had to get approval from Carthage. This led to both sides agreeing to a truce of a few days. During this time Mago was given a fitting funeral and his son drilled and trained his troops, emboldening them with inspiring speeches. After the truce expired, no definitive answer was given to Dionysius.[155] Another version of this story recorded that the Carthaginians claimed to need the approval of 'the admiral' before they could conclude a treaty, and thus were given permission to move their camp to where their fleet was anchored.[156] This gave them time to regroup and eventually confront the tyrant's army.

Which of these versions we should accept, if either, is unclear. Caven has reconstructed the situation as follows. He rejects both of the stories about a Carthaginian trick, saying that 'it is perfectly clear that neither of these accounts is acceptable as it stands.'[157] The basis of the 'accustomed knavery' (τῇ συνήθει πανουργίᾳ) may be in Ephorus' attitude towards Carthaginians and barbarians more generally, as suggested by Stylianou.[158] This, of course, requires Ephorus to be the source of this passage.[159] But does this mean we have to completely reject the idea of a Carthaginian trick? I think not, but the details of it may not be recorded entirely accurately by either Diodorus or Polyaenus. The former's version of events is the least believable. This is especially true of the proposition that the new Punic commander exercised and drilled his troops in front of the enemy, and it did not draw any suspicion. It is more likely that they would have withdrawn to the coast and connected with their fleet. Dionysius' cautionary approach to attacking armies in fortified positions, such as at Agyrium, is well documented and probably the real reason that the defeated Carthaginian army was able to escape total destruction.[160] And it is plausible that the truce we hear of as a trick was actually the customary ceasefire after a battle to retrieve and bury the dead.[161]

However it was accomplished, Mago's son was able to remove his army from harm's way and reconnect with the Punic fleet. It is unclear how much time passed before they were ready to march against Dionysius. During this period, we are probably right to place the drilling and exercising of the troops by Mago's son that we heard of earlier. He may have also been reinforced with fresh troops, citizen, dependant, or mercenary.[162] If a multi-ethnic relieving force was sent, this would explain why he had to train them so hard.[163] When the army was ready, it was marched against Dionysius and the two came to blows near the settlement of Cronium.[164]

Both Dionysius and his brother, Leptines, commanded contingents during this battle. They each led their forces on one of the wings, although we are not told which. Whichever side Leptines commanded saw heavy fighting, and many casualties were suffered on both sides. In the midst of this, Leptines could be seen valiantly standing against his enemies, but eventually he succumbed to the Carthaginians and was slain on the field. After his death, the emboldened contingents on this wing of the Punic army pushed their opponents dearly and put them to flight, thus turning Dionysius' flank. As his line collapsed, the picked band around the tyrant on the opposite wing lost heart and broke as well, which caused the entire Syracusan line to rout. The Punic army pursued, killing as many as 14,000 Sicilian Greeks. After their victory, Mago's son marched his army to Panormus and retired to Carthage.[165]

This is perhaps the last major engagement of the war. But thanks to the preservation of Diodorus, a peace may not have been reached after Cronium. In 379/8 BC, Carthage re-established an independent polity at Hipponium, a town which Dionysius had earlier conquered. They restored the exiles and refugees. This is placed after the description of the peace treaty in Diodorus' narrative, but some scholars do include it in their narrative of this war. Others have pointed out, though, that we have no reason to believe that the peace prevented Carthage from meddling in the affairs at the edge of Dionysius' empire, as Hipponium was in southern Italy and thus not in the hotbed of Greco-Punic conflict, Sicily.[166] Whenever the peace was concluded, we know the details. It maintained the previous possessions of both Dionysius and Carthage, but added to the latter's holdings the territories of both Selinus and Akragas. While these two cities had been paying tribute to Carthage, they now came under direct Punic control. Dionysius was also required to pay an indemnity of 1,000 talents.[167]

After the war, and the re-establishment of an independent Hipponium, a plague broke out in Carthage. It killed enough of the population to threaten Punic hegemony. The peoples of Libya and Sardinia, seeing that their overlords were vulnerable, revolted. Direct control was lost over Sardinia, and presumably much of the North African holdings. While the Carthaginians were besieged by the rebels within their walls, a divine madness supposedly took hold, causing a number of hallucinations and leading to conflicts within the population. This was dealt with by appeasing the gods. Of course, the divine nature of these symptoms is nonsense, but they could have been related to whatever illness caused the plague. Regardless, Carthage recovered and subdued the rebellions in Africa and Sardinia, retaking complete control of the island.[168]

The Third War

Carthage and Dionysius were to come to blows one final time, in the year before the tyrant's death in 367 BC. Like the previous war, we know less about this conflict than we may like, thanks to the deficiency of our sources. The origins of the war can be found in another rebellion of the Libyan natives against Carthage, presumably in 370 or 369 BC, and yet another plague. This encouraged Dionysius to make a play for their lands in Sicily. He used as his case for a 'just war' the excuse that Phoenicians had violated his territory.[169] An alternative cause of the war points to the Carthaginians as the aggressors, but as the war was fought within their sphere of influence in Sicily it is probable that Dionysius had made the first move.[170]

Dionysius assembled a large army. It consisted of 30,000 infantry, 3,000 cavalry, and 300 triremes.[171] Although he had recruited larger forces than this in the past, the navy was the largest he had ever fielded, and probably the largest in Syracusan history.[172] As in previous campaigns, he launched a surprise attack on Punic Sicily. His first targets were Selinus, given to Carthage after the last war, and Entella. These he took quickly, possibly through treachery; unfortunately, we do not know the details. Dionysius' army then settled into a programme of pillaging and raiding the territory under Carthaginian control. Eryx was his next target, which seems to have been taken by force. He then besieged Lilybaeum. Carthage, however, had made it into an impregnable fortress and manned it with a strong garrison, an action certainly influenced by the loss of Motya at the beginning of the century. The Greek army was unable to take the city, and their advance broke upon its walls.[173]

The Syracusans were forced to retreat to Eryx.[174] Carthage may have prepared a small force to be transported to Sicily, under the leadership of Hanno 'the Great', although the evidence is not very strong. Diodorus does not mention an army being sent over, but Justin recorded an invasion (although names it as the cause of the war), and Polyaenus knew a story of Hanno outrunning the Syracusan fleet while in the waters around Sicily.[175] If any troops were sent to Sicily, they could not have been great in number and they did not engage in a campaign against Dionysius.[176] What is clear, however, is that a fleet did arrive and attacked the 130 triremes that the tyrant had garrisoned in Drepanum. He had divided his fleet, sending 170 ships back to Syracuse, having received news that the military shipyards in Carthage had been burnt, presumably meaning the fleet was destroyed, but it had not been.[177] It is possible that Punic military leadership had orchestrated a campaign of disinformation, using a network of Syracusan informants at the head of which sat one of their own aristocrats, named Eshmuniaton.[178] Thanks to this piece of poor intelligence, a fleet of 200 Punic ships was able to win a skirmish against the fleet at Drepanum, and captured many of Dionysius' triremes stationed there.[179] This loss, and the onset of winter, led the two belligerent states to agree to an armistice, thus ending hostilities but not concluding a formal peace, which would not happen until the reign of Dionysius' heir, Dionysius II.[180]

There should be little doubt that Dionysius was planning to reignite his offensive in the coming year.[181] His death, however, prevented this from happening. It was in Carthage's favour for this to have happened, as Dionysius had recently gained a new and powerful ally, Athens. Her power had waned considerably since the end of the fifth century, but it was none the less an important event. The text of the treaty is fairly well preserved in an inscription that was found on the Acropolis.[182] Through this treaty, Athens and Syracuse entered into a compact of mutual defence; if one is attacked then the other would send aid.[183] This means that if any 'Phoenicians' violated the territory of Dionysius' empire, as was the excuse for his final war with Carthage, the Athenians would send military aid to him. The importance of this may be underlined by the size of his army in this last war, which was smaller than those of the past, which may be evidence that Dionysius was having problems recruiting soldiers by 368 BC. This would not be the first time that help came to him from the Aegean, in such a form as the Lacedaemonian admiral, Pharacidas. It was also a triumph in messaging for him, and helped to legitimise his position.[184] Athens benefited as well, gaining a powerful ally in a tumultuous time in the Greek mainland between the battles of Leuktra (371 BC) and Mantinea (362 BC).[185] It could have even been brought about at the instigation of the Athenians, who had declared that they were going to look for friends besides the king of Persia.[186]

The war, though, was essentially over in the winter of 367 BC. And with the passing of Dionysius I in that same season, hostilities between Carthage and Syracuse would wind down for a short time.[187]

Conclusions

The period of wars between Carthage and Dionysius lasted for almost fifty years. During this time, Motya was destroyed, one amongst numerous Greek cities meeting a similar fate, though not always because of the conflicts between Punic and Syracusan interests. Both Carthage and Dionysius followed patterns of war which are familiar from the events discussed in Chapter 3, preferring sieges to pitched battles. But the stage was now set for further hostilities between Carthage and the inhabitants of Sicily, though the nature of some of their enemies would change. In the next chapter, we discuss wars against three individuals, two of whom came from outside the island yet waged war on it.

Chapter 5

Timoleon, Agathocles, and Pyrrhus

Punic conflict with Greeks in Sicily did not end with the death of Dionysius I. The island would play host to their armies all the way through first war with Rome. In the period between these, Carthage would struggle against three principal threats: a Corinthian liberator, another Syracusan tyrant, and a marauding Epirate king. Timoleon came to Sicily to remove the tyrants and 'restore' some sort of representative government to Hellenic politics there, a quest which would lead him into war with Carthage. Agathocles, the tyrant of a resurgent Syracuse, styled himself as King of Sicily, an action which predictably provoked war. It was during his reign that Punic fortunes would fall to their lowest point before they came to blows with the Romans. Pyrrhus, King of Epirus, came to Sicily at the request of a besieged, and discordant, Syracuse, only to retreat from the island without effecting a lasting change. This chapter examines the wars which raged between Carthage and these figures, and this will take our discussion up to the period of the First Punic War.

Carthage and Sicily in the Age of Timoleon

The death of Dionysius I ushered in a chaotic period in Syracuse. His son took up the tyranny, but not with the skill or charm of his father. Dionysius II was a licentious hedonist who lost the support of his countrymen. Some of his incompetence can be blamed on receiving a rather poor education, but that certainly should not account entirely for his failure to hold on to power. One of the major figures in his downfall was Dion, the brother of one of Dionysius I's wives, Aristomache. He was an admired figure by later Greeks, appearing as one of the figures of Plutarch's *Parallel Lives* and even featuring in Cornelius Nepos' biographies. He was also friendly with a number of Carthaginians. Dion was responsible for driving Dionysius II from Syracuse, but was subsequently murdered, opening the door for the tyrant's return. Soon after this occurred, a Punic fleet was spotted off Sicily, sending some of its inhabitants into a panic. A plea was sent to Corinth, the traditional mother-city of Syracuse, to ask for help. Timoleon, a well-known figure in the city at the time, accepted the call, recruited a small army, and sailed for the island.

While he was making his way there, the ruler of Leontini, Hicetas, entered into an alliance with the Carthaginians. They had brought to Sicily a large army under the command of Hanno, numbering perhaps as many as 50,000 infantry, 300 chariots, and 2,000 horses (perhaps to be read as cavalry). This force marched on Entella, a city which was still occupied by Campanians who had been installed years earlier by the Carthaginians. A small relieving force from the city of Galeria was intercepted and destroyed. After a brief battle outside Syracuse, he was able to take possession of much of the city, save Ortygia. The stage was set for Timoleon to arrive. A small Carthaginian squadron of twenty triremes attempted to stop him from reaching land, but they were unable to do so. He moved first against Hicetas, taking his camp outside of Adranum – which was being besieged – and then was able to storm portions of Syracuse.[1]

By this point, the Punic army had made its way to Syracuse. It was camped on the Great Harbour, now joined by a fleet of some 150 triremes. After being augmented by an army from Catana, Timoleon's forces were considerably bolstered, and seemed to grow at a regular pace from new allies. Whether it was because of the presence of new enemies, or for some other reason, the Punic forces which were encamped near the city in support of Hicetas suddenly pulled up stakes and sailed off. Without their support, Syracuse was occupied by Timoleon, who then recovered Messana which had declared for the Carthaginians. He then dislodged Dionysius II from Ortygia and took full control of Syracuse, implementing new laws and practices.[2]

Although Carthaginian ambition can be seen in their intervention in Syracusan affairs, open warfare between them and the Greeks would not erupt until after Timoleon secured himself as leader of Syracuse. In 342 BC, he began a programme of expelling minor tyrants from their seats of power, such as Leptines from Engyum. Maintaining his power, however, meant keeping his mercenaries happy. This required significant resources which were not immediately at his disposal. Perhaps taking a page out of

Dionysius I's playbook, Timoleon decided to plunder the territory of his enemies to come up with the money he needed. He sent two of his most trusted commanders, Deinarchus and Demaretus, into Punic Sicily on a grand campaign of pillaging, carrying back all the wealth that they could manage.[3] Entella was taken from the Carthaginians, and fifteen of the leading men who supported Punic control were executed.[4] The success of these campaigns, and Timoleon's apparent power, encouraged a number of the Sicel and Sican cities subject to Carthage to defect to him.

Punic commanders in Sicily were unable, or unwilling, to counter the Corinthian. It could have been that his tactics of raiding, rather than marching his entire army, into enemy territory made this difficult. Alternatively, there may not have been a strong or wilful leader amongst the Carthaginian garrison commanders. The leaders of the state in Libya resolved to send an expeditionary force under the command of Hasdrubal and Hamilcar to deal with the situation.[5] They took their time recruiting an army of 80,000, including 70,000 infantry and 10,000 cavalry and chariots, as well as 200 warships.[6] They levied soldiers from the Punic aristocracy and drafted soldiers from their Libyan subjects, as was common. Mercenaries were sought from the Iberians, Celts, and Ligurians.[7] While none of these groups are entirely unexpected, this army is often claimed to have contained an inordinate number of Carthaginian citizens, including the so-called Sacred Band.

This army landed at Lilybaeum in 341 BC, an accomplishment which did not go unnoticed. Word reached Timoleon and the Syracusans that their forays into Carthaginian territory had finally elicited a response.[8] The Corinthian decided that he would make his stand in enemy territory, rather than letting the large Punic army march to the eastern side of the island and pillage the lands of his allies.[9] This strategy was not well received by all of the soldiers in his command, and caused at least 1,000 of them to return to Syracuse.[10] This left him with either 11,000 troops, as Diodorus records, or 6,000, as Plutarch writes.[11] The larger figure is preferable, and I find it unlikely that even with favourable conditions Timoleon would have emerged victorious with only 6,000 men under his command.[12]

The Greek army marched across the island and camped on hills near the banks of the River Crimisus. Timoleon used these to hide his troops from the Carthaginians, who were marching towards them. It seems that the Greeks reached the river first and had evaded any enemy scouts which may have been deployed in the area.[13] Their own lookouts, however, were more effective and spotted the Punic army as it prepared to cross the river.[14] Unknowingly stepping into a trap, Hasdrubal and Hamilcar ordered their army to begin crossing. Aided by a thick fog, Timoleon led his army down from the hills and pounced on those Punic troops which had first come across the river.[15] These were the chariots and 10,000 infantry, amongst whom were the 2,500 members of the Sacred Band, a cadre of wealthy citizen-soldiers.[16]

Hasdrubal and Hamilcar must have been surprised to see the Greek army approaching from the hills. Although sudden, a cavalry charge led by Demaretus, which was directed towards the Punic citizen infantry, was thwarted by the Carthaginian chariots that were deployed between them and Timoleon.[17] Skirmishing between the chariots and the Greek cavalry continued for some time until Timoleon decided to deploy his infantry. He sent his Sicilian Greek allies to the wings of his formation and concentrated the Syracusan citizens and his best mercenaries under his own command in the centre.[18] His ranks tightened and they marched forward against the Carthaginians. Demaretus took the cavalry around the chariots and attacked the Punic line on its flank, although we are not told which, although it could have been both.[19] Despite being attacked on the flank as well as from the front, the Carthaginian line held fast, thanks in part to their heavy armour.[20] The two lines battered one another until their spears shattered. As the melee continued, it turned into a contest of swords, with which the Greeks were said to have been more skilled.[21] Punic fortunes were at their lowest, and their army was being cut down rapidly. Most of the initial force which had crossed the river was killed. During this time, more and more of the Carthaginian army had made its way across the Crimisus, threatening to overwhelm Timoleon's army simply by strength of numbers.[22]

The Punic advantage was quickly undermined when a storm blew in over the hills whence Timoleon's army had descended. Flashes of lightning and the crack of thunder overwhelmed the din of the battle. A violent rain broke out, accompanied by hailstones and a strong wind. All of this was blowing into the backs of the Greeks, but into the faces of the Carthaginian troops. Blinded and otherwise hindered by the storm, the Punic army began to crumble. The rain was coming down so ferociously that it weighed down the heavily armoured amongst Hasdrubal and Hamilcar's troops, impeding their movement and preventing them from fighting effectively. As the Greeks took advantage of this, Punic casualties began to mount; their compatriots who were still crossing the river, and those still fighting, lost heart and their line broke. They attempted to flee back towards their camp but were slowed by the torrents beginning to flood the plain between the hills and the Crimisus. The corpses of their fallen colleagues were so thickly strewn in the sodden mud that they acted like a roadblock. Timoleon's light troops and cavalry took advantage of the hindered movement of their opponents and chased down all of those who fled from the battlefield. Many of those who had not been killed by the Greeks were trampled by their fleeing allies, stamped upon by human feet and crushed beneath the weight of the chariots.[23]

Lying lifeless at the feet of the Greek army were 10,000 soldiers of the Carthaginian expeditionary force. Amongst these were the 2,500 members of the Sacred Band.[24] It is possible that all the dead were Carthaginian citizens, as we heard from Plutarch that the initial 10,000 infantry to cross the river were all Carthaginian citizens, and that the Sacred Band was an element of this group.[25] We do not know for sure, however, that this was the case and some of the dead could have come from the subject or mercenary contingents. We hear only that 3,000 of the killed were Carthaginian citizens in Plutarch's account.[26] This was supposedly the most citizens killed in any battle to-date. Surely some, if not most, of those who crossed after the initial collision must have been non-citizens. In addition to the soldiers killed, 15,000 were taken prisoner.

We do not hear of any Greek casualties, but they must have existed. When we hear that the Carthaginians 'resisted his first attack courageously' it would be unthinkable to imagine that none of Timoleon's soldiers fell.[27] They may have suffered considerable losses, as it took them a long time to loot the bodies of the enemy's dead because 'there was only a small number of men' to do this.[28] As Timoleon had started out with 11,000 troops, 1,000 more than the Carthaginians lost dead, the lack of manpower to strip the dead implies that the Greeks suffered considerable losses. It is true that some of them would have been needed to guard the captives they had taken, but the noted shortage of looters is important.

The remnants of the Punic army made their way back to Lilybaeum.[29] We do not hear about Hasdrubal or Hamilcar again, but our sources do not explicitly say they were killed.³⁰ Timoleon sent a considerable amount of booty to Corinth, including captured armour.³¹ A monument erected in the city commemorating the Battle of the Crimisus, and naming the cities which gave their support, partially survives.³² This victory was used as propaganda, with the message being that 'the Corinthians and their general Timoleon freed the Greeks living in Sicily from the yoke of Carthage.'³³ This is reminiscent of the Deinomenids' use of victories over the Carthaginians to promote their dynasty and legitimize their power in the wider Hellenic Mediterranean.

Despite the setback at the Crimisus, the Carthaginians were not driven out of Sicily, despite what the Corinthians may have told their compatriots in the Aegean. The remnants of the army had made it to Lilybaeum and must still be considered a threat, even if they were lacking in legitimate leadership. The news of the defeat created havoc in Carthage and fear spread that Timoleon would cross over to North Africa and conquer them.³⁴ This is probably Greek hyperbole, but there is little reason to doubt that the disaster at the Crimisus did have a demoralizing effect on the city.

A feeling of desperation makes the recall of Gisco, one of the sons of Hanno the Great, sensible. He had a reputation as a capable soldier and general, and was appointed commander of Punic forces in Sicily. After arriving back in Carthage from his exile, he sailed to the island with a fleet of seventy ships. He also recruited a force of mercenaries, including Greeks, which both Diodorus and Plutarch claim as being a first in Carthaginian history. These troops were probably added to what remained of the expeditionary force under Hasdrubal and Hamilcar that had sought refuge at Lilybaeum.

Gisco's first objective must have been to evict those of Timoleon's mercenaries which had been left in Punic territory after the Battle of the Crimisus to pillage the enemy's lands.³⁵ At least some of the Carthaginian troops were sent to aid the tyrants Hicetas and Mamercus, with whom they were now allied. The combined forces of the triple alliance won two victories over mercenary armies loyal to Timoleon. The first was near Messene, where 400 of the mercenaries were killed. The second took place at Ietae, a town just south of modern Palermo, which was in the Punic-controlled part of Sicily. These were the last of Timoleon's pillaging forces we hear of in Carthaginian territory and may have been those who remained after the clash at the Crimisus.[36]

Punic troops continued to operate in support of the allies, but we do not hear of a unified army. At some point Hicetus may have been cut out of the triumvirate as there is no reference to Carthaginian troops amongst those killed in his final battle against Timoleon.[37] Gisco was still providing assistance to Mamercus when Timoleon attacked him at Catana. The former's army was routed in a pitched battle at the river Abolus, losing 2,000 killed. Many of these were soldiers sent to him by the Carthaginians.[38] By this point, 339/338 BC, Gisco may have dismissed most of his mercenaries, having ousted the Greek raiding parties in the Punic zone. There is nothing in our sources about the end of the expeditionary force but, according to Plutarch, the defeat at the Abolus caused the Carthaginians to sue for peace, which may mean that their loss of just under 2,000 soldiers was significant.[39] It is possible that peace was sought because Gisco had accomplished his primary objective, removing the Greek mercenary presence from the Punic area of Sicily.[40]

The resultant treaty was similar to the previous two. It re-established the border between the Carthaginian zone and the Greek territories at the River Halycus. It also stipulated that the Hellenic cities were to remain free, an obvious attempt to prevent another powerful entity such as Dionysius' Syracusan empire from appearing, thus threatening Punic power.[41]

Agathocles at the Gates

After concluding a treaty with Timoleon in 339/338 BC, Carthaginian military activities quieted down. They sent a force to the aid of Cyrene in its war against Thibron, a Spartan mercenary captain who had invaded their territory in 324 BC. He had taken command of the mercenary company he was a part of by murdering his commander, Harpalus. There were 7,000 under his command. Two years of fighting ensued after Thibron seized the harbour at Cyrene. Carthage's role in fighting against his troops was probably minimal, but their willingness to send some sort of support to the Cyrenians should not be doubted. We have seen other examples of them aiding cities by sending small mercenary forces. A desire to protect their African possessions from a rogue Greek polity next door was a sufficient reason to send help in this case. Thibron's attempt to forge a territorial state in North Africa was unsuccessful; he was defeated and killed by Ophellas, a general of Ptolemy, who annexed Cyrene.[42]

This would turn out to be a minor episode in a landscape of more dire events for Carthage in the last quarter of the fourth century. The year of Thibron's defeat, 322 BC, was important in the events which would see Punic North Africa attacked, as this was the year in which Agathocles returned to Syracuse from his exile in southern Italy. This man was brought up in a humble household. He was trained as a potter by his father, according to Diodorus at least, although it is more likely that he was taught how to run a lucrative family business, which may have been a large pottery operation.[43] He was exiled on multiple occasions for attempting to overthrow the established government in Syracuse. This did not stop him from eventually seizing power, however, and in 317 BC he took over the government and installed himself as sole ruler. As many tyrants in history have done, he resorted to war early in his reign as a means of legitimizing his position. In this regard, for a Sicilian tyrant, there was no better enemy with which to pick a fight than the Carthaginians.

Agathocles' opening movements against Punic Sicily were not directed at the Phoenician cities, but rather towards Akragas. His goal was to bring the city over to him, perhaps through peaceful negotiations. The Carthaginians either received news of his movements or simply got lucky, and sixty of their ships entered the harbour there as the tyrant was marching on it. Agathocles may have begun a siege, but our sources do not explicitly state this.[44] The arrival of the Punic fleet caused him to abandon the enterprise and instead begin a campaign of pillaging the hinterland of the city. He took a number of the rural forts by force and others through negotiation.[45]

While Agathocles was busy plundering Punic Sicily, exiles from Syracuse were trying to forge an alliance with the Carthaginians. Before the two sides could unite, the exiles marched on Centoripini. It was garrisoned by troops loyal to Agathocles, but a member of the city's aristocracy was ready to betray it. As the rebel troops entered the city, however, the garrison commander realised what was happening and rallied his men to beat back the stealthy assault. The infiltrators were killed, including their commander, Nymphodorus. As this was happening, a fleet of fifty Punic ships entered the Great Harbour at Syracuse. They were unable to do anything of consequence, although they did seize two merchant ships from Athens, sank them, and cut off the hands of the crew. Some of their ships were later seized by a squadron loyal to Agathocles off the coast of southern Italy.[46]

Part of Agathocles' army was then sent to Galeria to put down an uprising led by Deinocrates and Philonides, more Syracusan exiles. Agathocles dispatched Pasiphilus and Demophilus with 5,000 soldiers to deal with the rebel force of just over 3,000. They fought a pitched battle in which the tyrant's agents were to prevail. Philonides was killed and Deinocrates was forced to retreat.[47] The Carthaginians took up a defensive position and marched an army to Mt. Ecnomus, near Gela. It was a strategic point and allowed them to stop Agathocles from easily marching into Punic territory and would have limited him to the interior of the island. He besieged this force and tried to draw them into a pitched battle, which their commander repeatedly refused. Unable to dislodge his enemies, Agathocles again pillaged the countryside, the spoils from which he dedicated in the major temples at Syracuse.[48]

In the coming year, the Carthaginian government decided to take a more aggressive stance against Agathocles and his ever-growing domain. They appointed Hamilcar son of Gisco as the leader of a new expeditionary force.[49] We have a very detailed accounting of the troops under his command. There were 2,000 citizen soldiers, including many aristocrats, 10,000 Libyans, 1,000 infantry and 200 horsemen from Etruria, and 1,000 slingers from the Balearic Islands.[50] The citizen contingent is likely to be interpreted as the Sacred Band. This army of around 14,200 soldiers set sail for Sicily with a sizable fleet. Before they got very far across the strait, a storm hit it, sinking sixty triremes and 200 supply ships. Many of the land-troops lost were from the Punic nobility, which caused the city to go into a period of mourning, displaying the traditional black cloths on their walls. Hamilcar survived, as well as much of the army. To his surviving forces, the general added mercenaries and allied troops from Sicily. In total, he fielded an army of around 40,000 infantry and almost 5,000 cavalry.[51]

After setting the army ashore, the fleet sailed around to the Straits of Messene and there inflicted the first losses upon Agathocles. The

Punic and Syracusan fleets came to blows, with the former capturing twenty ships from the latter, including their crews. While this happened, Agathocles determined to make Gela into the headquarters for his army. Diodorus preserves a version of events in which he slowly sent soldiers into the city in small detachments, not wanting the Geloans to be made aware of his plan to occupy their city and use it as a command post. This was because he was suspicious of their loyalty, even though they had not given any sign of disloyalty since 316 BC.[52] The real series of events was probably simpler: either the citizens of Gela rebelled and he took the city by force (perhaps in a surprise attack), or rebellious feeling started to spread after he occupied the town without resistance.[53]

The troops which Hamilcar had brought to Sicily, and those which he collected upon arrival, marched to Mt. Ecnomus and joined with the Punic garrison already in that fort. Agathocles ordered his army to occupy a fortress nearby called Phalarium. Separating the two forces was the River Himeras. The enemies were satisfied to 'stare down' one another for some time, engaging in the common practice of raiding the area around the camps, trying to prevent foragers from keeping their comrades supplied.[54] For this, Hamilcar seems to have been using his Libyan troops. During one of the Greek raids into Punic held territory, they attempted to herd off some cattle back towards their own camp. Troops began to pursue from the Carthaginian position. Agathocles was not going to let them follow his men all the way back to their own ramparts, so he sent a number of picked troops to set up an ambush at the ford both sides had been using. When the Punic troops crossed the Himeras, they sprang the trap on them, easily routing them, killing many. As their corpses began falling in the river, Agathocles decided that this was an opportunity to draw the bulk of his enemy into a battle.[55]

As a body, the Greek army marched out of their stronghold, following in the footsteps of their ambush party. They quickly marched up Mt. Ecnomus, reaching Hamilcar's camp while his army was unaware. Agathocles ordered his men to begin filling in part of the moat which protected the Punic position. This was executed briskly and allowed them to break a hole in the enemy's palisade. At first, the resistance was haphazard, with any soldiers who were near the breach contributing. Though they were without direction, the troops put up a fierce defence. The Carthaginians organised themselves without much haste, after the alarm had been sounded, and the aristocratic citizen troops (probably the Sacred Band) made their way to the breach. Unwilling to relent, the Greek onslaught continued with vigour.[56]

Hamilcar, by this time, had taken command of the situation. He saw that the soldiers resisting Agathocles' advance were slowly being overwhelmed and resolved to take the initiative. He ordered the contingent of slingers from the Balearic Islands to move forward and engage the Greeks.[57] They must have had the advantage of an elevated position in order to be most effective. Immediately, they showered the enemy with a tempest of deadly stones, shattering their armour and rending their flesh.[58] With the arrival of these new troops, the attack was halted and those who had made their way inside the fort were driven out. Agathocles' army, however, had been attacking other points of the palisade, thus creating small breaches in a number of places. Hamilcar's defences were holding, but only just. It was with the arrival of fresh soldiers from the beaches that the Carthaginians were emboldened and had the strength and willpower to force out the rest of the Greeks from their camp. These came either in the form of a relieving force sent by Carthage (as Diodorus reports) or were perhaps the soldiers already standing guard over the fleet while it was beached.[59]

Surrounded, Agathocles was forced to order a retreat. Most of the army made its way back to the Himeras, attempting to cross back over whence they had come. The distance between the two camps was enough that the Carthaginian cavalry were able to ride rampant over the fleeing Greek troops. Punic horsemen pursued them closely and slaughtered all whom they caught. Those lucky enough to escape the riders' blades found themselves exhausted and dehydrated, owing to the oppressive summer heat. Some of these stopped to drink from the Himeras when they reached it, not knowing of its high salinity, and were later found to have fallen without wounds near the banks of the river.[60] Agathocles' losses were far higher than those of Hamilcar's, with the former losing 7,000 dead and the latter 500.[61]

In the aftermath of the battle, Agathocles gathered what remained of his army and retreated inside the walls of Gela, abandoning and burning their field camp. The tyrant was now pressed to decide on a new strategy, having not defeated Hamilcar in the field. While he was mulling over his options, the Carthaginian cavalry spread out through the territory, harassing all those Greek soldiers who were still in the area. A group of

300 horsemen captured a number of Agathocles' troops who told them that he had set out with the army back towards Syracuse. Thinking that the city was now in friendly hands, they rode in to reconnoitre the situation. Once they were admitted into Gela, however, they were shot down by the tyrant's men. None of the Punic riders survived. Being made aware that the enemy was still in the city, Hamilcar marched his army from their fortress and laid siege. He soon discovered that this was a fruitless endeavour, and that Agathocles had supplied himself well enough to holdout. Rather than pushing the issue and directly assaulting Gela's defences, the Punic commander decided to begin stripping his enemy of his allies.[62]

Hamilcar ordered the army to march throughout Sicily, visiting the fortified settlements and the cities throughout. His objective was to win their inhabitants over through kindness, and a promise to keep them free from Agathocles' tyranny. Many towns went over to Hamilcar, including Camarina, Leontini, Catana, Tauromenium, Messene, and Abacaenum. His message of freedom and goodwill was appealing to many, but there were other reasons why they may have defected from the cause of the tyrant.[63] It is interesting to note that we hear of the 'common people' as being a driving force behind this, when throughout the narrative of Agathocles' career they were his supporters, and oligarchs were his adversaries. As Tillyard explained, this is not 'hard to understand. As long as tyranny meant ease and plunder it was welcome, but when the loans and levies of a long war were impending, the allegiance of the people was bound to waver. It is also likely that the cruel treatment of Gela by Agathocles had opened men's eyes to the real nature of his rule.'[64] While Hamilcar was thus engaged, Agathocles marshalled the remainder of his army and marched them quickly back to Syracuse, evading any Punic troops who may have still been in the area.[65]

Agathocles was now bottled up in Syracuse. His allies had abandoned him for the more stable-looking Hamilcar. The Carthaginians were now in possession, either through direct control or alliance, of the entire island, except for the city which was their perpetual enemy. Knowing that he had to do something drastic, Agathocles began preparing an expeditionary force to take the offensive and shift the theatre and momentum of the war. Most of his infantry had been killed at the Himeras, so he had to find a new source of manpower. His solution was to conscript some of the Syracusan citizens, separating family members from one another by choosing some for his field army and the others for the defence of the city. In need of money, he seized the wealth which belonged to orphans, looted the temples, and absconded with the jewels of the wealthy matrons. Agathocles also killed off a number of the wealthiest men of the city, confiscating their property and freeing those of their slaves whom he deemed fit for military service.[66] In total he had around 13,500 soldiers, 3,500 of whom were Syracusan citizens.[67]

The army thus assembled, and what resources were at hand gathered, they boarded sixty ships and waited for the perfect opportunity to evade the Punic blockade. They stayed sequestered on the vessels for a number of days, until some grain ships were spotted sailing towards the Syracusan harbour. The entire Carthaginian squadron maintaining the blockade broke off from their positions to pursue the merchantmen. At this, Agathocles ordered his small fleet to set sail. At first, the enemy thought that they were coming to the rescue of the grain ships, and thus positioned themselves for a battle. The tyrant had other plans, though, and his vessels continued on their course. The Punic commander ordered a pursuit, granting safety to the supply ships who made it safely to Syracuse. Agathocles' group, however, had too much of a lead and made an escape from their pursuers 'with a heroism which is almost unparalleled in warfare.'[68] Up to this point, not even his soldiers knew their destination, but it eventually became apparent: they were launching an invasion of Punic Africa.[69] Meister poignantly describes this attack as a 'course of action that in audacity was on a par with the boldest ventures of the Diadochi'.[70]

The expedition began with a dramatic portent. On the day after breaking out from the harbour at Syracuse, Agathocles' fleet observed a total solar eclipse.[71] His soldiers believed this to be a sign of their coming failure, but he convinced them otherwise. He delivered a short speech, according to Justin: 'If it had happened before they set out, he should have thought it a portent unfavourable to their departure, but since it had occurred after they had set sail, its signification was directed against those to whom they were going. Besides, the eclipses of the heavenly bodies always presaged a change in the present state of things, and it was therefore certain that an alteration was foretold in the flourishing condition of the Carthaginians and in their own adverse circumstances.'[72]

It was important for him to quell any fears, as they had another four days of sailing ahead of them.

After six days and nights of travel, they finally made landfall in Africa. At the final daybreak of their journey, they spotted land and a fleet of Carthaginian ships. Knowing that it would be easier to stop the invaders at sea, the Punic captains urged their rowers on to beat the Greeks to the shore. Although the latter had a significant lead, their foes moved quickly enough to catch up and begin biting at their heels. The Punic ships in the van began launching missiles at their prey as both groups raced for the beach. The rear of Agathocles' squadron responded in turn with their own weapons, coming to close quarters with some of the Punic ships, driving them off thanks to the strong complement of soldiers on board. His ships were thus able to safely beach at Latomiae, on Cape Bon, and after disembarkation the soldiers quickly built a palisade to protect their position.[73]

After making sure that his camp was secure, Agathocles called a meeting of his soldiers to make a speech. In this, he declared that during their crossing, when the Carthaginian ships were closing in and threatening their entire endeavour, he vowed a massive burnt offering of all of the Greek ships to Demeter and Kore in return for their protection. The captains burned their vessels, creating an inferno which reached high into the heavens. The real reasons for this act of pyromania were twofold. Firstly, Agathocles knew that he did not have enough men to guard the ships and to wage a successful campaign against the Carthaginians and their holdings. If left unguarded, the ships would fall into enemy hands and give the Punic cause an even greater advantage at sea. Secondly, by destroying their means of escape his soldiers were further incentivized to fight hard against the enemy.[74] There could have been a third motive. Although the dedication to Demeter and Kore may simply have been a way of explaining his decision to burn the ships, this could have been a deliberate attempt at propagandising the campaign as 'Greek revenge' for the deeds carried out by Carthage on Sicily.[75]

Seeing that no army had marched out to confront him, Agathocles ordered his army to begin moving through the African countryside, towards the Punic city of Megalepolis. Between their landing site and this settlement, the soldiers saw first-hand the wealth accumulated by the Punic elite. Gardens and plantations of innumerable crops covered the landscape, fed by streams and irrigation channels throughout. There were vines, olives, and other fruit-bearing trees. Cattle, sheep, and horses grazed in the plains. Many homes were found, luxurious in construction, the wealth of their owners shown, in part, by their stucco decoration. These, as well as the farm buildings, were filled with all the luxuries of a wealthy society, safely tucked away out of the path of war and destruction for many years.[76] The great wealth that they saw before them, ripe for the taking, lifted the spirits of Agathocles' soldiers, who had begun to despair at being so far from home.[77]

This new enthusiasm spread to the army's commander, and he was emboldened to make an audacious decision. Agathocles ordered his army to assault Megalepolis' walls directly, not engaging in a safer, yet more time consuming, siege. It is unclear what, if any, equipment the Greeks had to use to breach the walls of the city, but they made quick work of it.[78] The inhabitants held out for a short time. Once inside, the soldiers ran rampant, with the support of their commander. He let his men pillage all that they could, and they accumulated a great amount of booty.[79] It appears that Agathocles was able to take Megalepolis by surprise, which shows a glaring strategic error made by the commander of the Punic fleet which pursued him to the shore of Cape Bon. He did not send word to the settlements in the countryside that a hostile army had landed. Instead, he ordered his men to seize the bronze prows of the Greek ships (which survived the fire), which he sent to Carthage.[80]

Agathocles then moved against Tunis. Again, his army was able to take the settlement by storm. No response had yet come from Carthage, and we have no evidence of much resistance coming from the rural inhabitants. In the case of Tunis, word may have reached them of an approaching army, but that obviously did not help them prepare an adequate defence. The invaders were forced to decide on where to camp now that they had captured two major settlements between their landing site and Carthage itself. Some of the soldiers suggested that they occupy both towns and use them as bases of operation. Agathocles, however, did not believe this to be a good strategy, and instead pulled down their walls and buildings, and ordered his army to build a camp in a new position, near Carthage.[81] From here, they continued to pillage the countryside, laying waste to farms and fortresses alike.[82]

Inside Carthage, the atmosphere was tense. Refugees came from the countryside and told of the enemy's conduct. Many within the city thought that Agathocles' presence in Africa meant that their army and its commander, Hamilcar, had been destroyed outside of Syracuse, reasoning that this was the only explanation as to why the tyrant would risk transporting so many of his soldiers off the island. This caused a panic, and even led to public displays of mourning. The deliberative bodies of the government were called together to come up with a solution to the seemingly dire situation. There were few, if any, veteran soldiers in the city, which made the inhabitants even more anxious. Some suggested suing for peace, but a more tempered option prevailed, which was to delay and wait to learn what exactly had happened on Sicily. Messengers from the fleet arrived not long after who were able to explain the actual situation, and that the army was still encamped outside Syracuse.[83] Hearing that their expeditionary force was still intact, the people of Carthage gained heart, and resolved to put an army into the field against Agathocles in Africa.

First, they elected two generals from amongst their political elite: Hanno and Bomilcar.[84] Their families were rivals and may have represented the two dominant political factions in Carthage at that time. This dual appointment was meant to prevent either party from attempting a coup d'état or betraying the city to Agathocles.[85] Because of the imminent threat posed by the Greek army, the newly appointed generals decided not to wait for reinforcements from abroad, and instead raised an army of Punic citizens. They were able to recruit 40,000 infantry, 1,000 cavalry, and 2,000 chariots. Although the number of infantry seems rather large for a single city to muster, given the direness of their situation it is probable that all military-aged males were conscripted into service.[86]

With the army assembled, they marched directly against Agathocles. They did not take the time to drill or train the soldiers, which would prove to be a problem. Hanno and Bomilcar moved their forces onto a small hill not far from the enemy's camp and arrayed them for battle. On the right wing was Hanno, with those citizens who served in the Sacred Band. Bomilcar commanded the left wing and marshalled his men into a deep formation on account of rough terrain on his left. The chariots and the cavalry were in front of the infantry and were to be used to prod the front ranks of the Greek army. Upon seeing the Carthaginians' deployment, Agathocles moved his own army into a position to offer battle. On the right wing was Archagathus, the tyrant's son, along with 2,500 infantry. Moving from right to left, he then deployed the 3,500 Syracusan citizen infantry, 3,000 Greek mercenaries and 3,000 infantry made up of mercenaries from Samnium, Etruria, and a group of Celts, and finally his own bodyguard of 1,000 picked hoplites. Agathocles took command of the left wing, aiming to personally confront Hanno and the Sacred Band, who were likely conspicuous because of their shields. The Greek army also had 500 archers and slingers who were divided between each wing.[87]

Agathocles supposedly attempted two tricks to help ensure a victory. The first was to deceive the Carthaginians into thinking he had more heavily armed troops than he really did. To do this, he ordered the rowers from the ships, who were otherwise not armed for heavy combat, to stretch the shield covers of the infantrymen with sticks to make them appear as though they were properly armed soldiers.[88] Tillyard doubted that this would have actually happened, pointing out that 'it is also unlikely that any large number of men lacked arms; Agathocles must have known that every oarsman would have to be a land-fighter' once they arrived in Africa.[89] While this is a fair argument, there is no reason to think that at least some of the shields originally loaded onto the sixty ships in Syracuse were not lost in the skirmish at sea as the Greeks raced against the Carthaginians to the beach, or during the storming of Megalepolis and Tunis.[90] Giving the illusion of having a larger force of heavy infantry than he really did may have made the Carthaginians more cautious in their attack, and thus make it a useful tactic. The second trick was to release a number of owls which he had brought on the expedition for just such on occasion amongst his men, to give the impression that Athena gave her blessing to them in the coming battle.[91] Most historians question this supposed stratagem, and it seems very improbable. It is impossible to see why Agathocles would have gone through the effort that it would have required to keep a significant number of owls with his army, and, more importantly, to keep them secret from the majority of his army.[92] Tillyard tried to rationalise the episode, hypothesising that 'the truth underlying the [owl] story may be that a few of Agathocles' men happened to start some owls not long before a battle. The birds, being half blinded by the daylight, flew about aimlessly in the camp.'⁹³ Even this is unlikely, and from an historical perspective it is best to dismiss this story.

The battle opened with a charge by the Punic chariots. Some of the charioteers and their vehicles were destroyed, while others were allowed to pass through gaps in the Greek line. Hanno and Bomilcar then ordered their cavalry to charge but they were repelled and, after suffering many losses, fled the field. By the time they had broken, though, the main body of infantry had reached the fighting. Quickly, the two lines entered into a fierce melee. The most severe struggle we hear of during the battle was fought on the Carthaginians' right wing, where Hanno and the Sacred Band crashed into Agathocles and his picked soldiers. At first the Punic troops had the upper hand, and the general was cutting a path through the enemy, slaying many himself. Agathocles' missile troops, however, began to take their toll. Arrows and sling bullets continually rained down upon Hanno and his men, and after suffering a number of wounds, the general was felled.⁹⁴ His death became known, and the Sacred Band began to waver. Seeing their enemies begin to falter, Agathocles' bodyguard pressed their attack, but were still held fast by their stalwart adversaries.⁹⁵

Bomilcar received word of his colleague's death, and ordered a general retreat. The army did so in an orderly fashion, maintaining their formations, and headed for the hill whence they had earlier descended. The last unit to begin a withdrawal was the Sacred Band, who stood for some time as the rest of the army had left. Despite beginning in a constructive manner, eventually the Punic army broke into a full retreat, and, rather than heading for their camp, made for Carthage. Still, because of their great number, Agathocles did not risk a full pursuit, and instead directed his army towards the enemy's now abandoned camp.⁹⁶ Only 200 of the Greek army were killed, while between 1,000 and 6,000 of the Carthaginians were killed, including Hanno.⁹⁷ The majority of the Punic army, however, made it safely back into the city. They were now penned up inside.

This defeat led to one of the most infamous occurrences in Punic history, as far as we know it. The aristocracy, fearing that the defeat in the Battle of Tunis was because they had angered the gods, began an extensive programme of child sacrifice. Their fear was based in the perceived sacrilegious behaviour of many of the elite families substituting slave children for their own when making sacrifices. Investigations proved that a number of these clans had, indeed, been cheating the gods. A decision was made to give up 200 children from the most noble lines to the gods and the sacrifices were made publicly. An additional 300 families sacrificed children, fearing rumours which were circulating which accused them of having only sent purchased children to the pyre. Less spectacularly, the Carthaginians also sent a tithe dedicated to Melqart in Tyre, which consisted of a considerable sum of money as well as unnamed decadent offerings. This was a practice that had been interrupted after Alexander the Great's conquest of Tyre in 332 BC.[98]

Practical decisions were also made within Carthage. Seeing as their best general was currently laying siege to Syracuse, the government sent messengers to his camp to inform him of the situation in Africa. Along with their news, they brought with them the prows which had been taken from the burnt remains of Agathocles' ships.[99] When the couriers reached Hamilcar's camp and informed him of what had happened at Tunis, the commander quickly came up with a clever plan of disinformation. He ordered that they not spread word to the rest of the army of the Punic defeat. Instead, they were to tell the soldiers a fabricated story about how Agathocles had lost both his army and his fleet. Some of the messengers from Africa were sent into Syracuse, carrying with them the ship prows, and demanded the surrender of the city in light of the supposed defeat of their tyrant.[100]

This caused discord within the city. Many of the common people believed the reports, and began agitating. The tyrant's opponents within the elite also moved to negotiate with the Carthaginians. Those whom Agathocles had left in charge were not convinced, or perhaps believed that they would be in more danger if they handed the city over rather than resist. Having all of the power, they were able to force out those who advocated for Syracuse's surrender. No fewer than 8,000 people were exiled from the city. These found refuge in the camp of Hamilcar, who took them in and offered them safety. But those left behind in the city were in a panic, with an enemy army camped just outside their walls and their leader supposedly killed.[101]

Hamilcar sent another message into the city, offering safety to Antander, Agathocles' brother who was in charge of the garrison, as well as anyone else who would surrender the city.[102] A heated debate ensued in the Syracusan assembly. There were clearly some factions that wanted to surrender the city, the most outspoken of whom was a man named Diognetus. Antander, perhaps at the instigation of Erymnon, an Aetolian mercenary leader, refused to concede the city and instead resolved to wait for word from his brother.[103] All the while, Hamilcar was making his assault preparations visible to the Syracusans, and likely began assembling his siege engines in full sight of the defenders.[104] Unfortunately for the Carthaginians, it was at this time that two small, fast, ships made their way from Africa to Syracuse, bringing news from Agathocles' camp. These vessels had been constructed by his army in the wake of the Battle of Tunis. They each had thirty oars and were crewed by his most talented rowers. Although the Punic fleet was blockading the harbour at Syracuse, the smaller craft slipped by their picket.[105]

The population of Syracuse now flocked to the boats which just arrived as their crews were decked in garlands and singing songs of victory. Carthaginian observers saw the crowds gathering at the port and Hamilcar believed that the time to attack the city was now, while at least some of the defenders were absent from their posts. He ordered his most skilled troops to move against the walls with scaling ladders, attacking a point between two towers. This would allow him to establish a bridgehead in the enemy's defences. The attackers began mounting the wall unnoticed, as the guards from this portion were not in their posts. A patrol of Syracusan soldiers, walking on their regular path, however, stumbled upon the assault and raised the alarm. Together with soldiers who quickly returned from further inside the walls, they began pushing the Carthaginians back. Some of the attackers were killed by the spear, others were thrown from the battlements. Seeing that the thrust into the fortifications was being thwarted, Hamilcar ordered a retreat. After regrouping, he ordered his army to break camp and withdraw from Syracuse. He subsequently sent 5,000 troops to Carthage, as had been requested.[106] The defeat on the walls may have had less to do with Hamilcar breaking the siege than the troops which were sent to Africa, as this amounted to just over one-third of his strength when he first invaded Sicily. This almost certainly weakened his position more than the losses on the walls.

In Africa, with the Punic forces now bottled up in the city, Agathocles began a sensible campaign of devastating the hinterland. He first strongly fortified his camp outside of Tunis, providing him with a safe haven in case anything was to go awry in the field. Much as we have seen Carthaginian armies doing in Sicily, Agathocles first took by force the fortified settlements around the city. He then moved on a number of larger cities: first Neapolis, modern Nabeul, and then Hadrumetum, modern Sousse. The first was taken by storm, seemingly quickly as Diodorus gives us no detail except that the Syracusan treated the inhabitants humanely. The second, however, withstood his initial attacks and he was forced to lay siege.[107]

While encamped at Hadrumetum, a Libyan king by the name of Aelymas came to the tyrant and the two leaders formed an alliance. News of this reached Carthage, and the city leaders resolved to prevent the army of the latter from being brought into play. In order to do this, they ordered that the army attack Agathocles' camp outside of Tunis, which was taken by force. Those of the Greek troops who survived the attack retreated into what was left of Tunis, forcing the Punic army to bring siege engines against its fortifications. Messengers were sent to the tyrant's camp outside of Hadrumetum who apprised him of the setback outside of Tunis. Understanding that this reversal of fortune could undo his entire invasion, Agathocles concocted a stratagem by which he would force the Carthaginian army to retreat from Tunis and make the inhabitants of Hadrumetum surrender. He left the bulk of his army in the siege camp, but ordered his bodyguard, as well as a number of additional troops, to follow him into the hills back towards Carthage. Here, they lit fires over a large swathe of territory, making it look as though a massive army was encamped here. As this was visible to both groups of enemies, the joint goals were achieved. The army at Tunis retreated back into Carthage and the people of Hadrumetum surrendered.[108]

This stratagem, while clever if true, is not accepted by all historians. George Grote, for instance, believed that the distance between Hadrumetum, identified with modern Sousse, and Tunis was too great for this to have been possible. He suggested that the narrative of Diodorus was untrue or that he misnamed the second town, and that it could have instead been visible if Agathocles' army was besieging Neapolis, modern Nabel, instead.[109] Tillyard echoed the problem of the distance between Tunis and Hadrumetum, claiming that 'at all events there would have been nothing more than a faint glow in the sky', not enough to instil fear in anyone.¹¹⁰ This is, though, perhaps less of a problem than these authors have made it sound. As Champion has pointed out, 'all that would be needed is a hill somewhat greater in height than 200m. There are a number of these, some over 1,000m, between Tunis and Hadrumetum and widespread campfires on their slopes could be recognised as such.'¹¹¹ Indeed, Diodorus tells us that Agathocles had ordered his men to light fires over a large area (πολύς τόπος) and not just a large fire in one place. We do not have to imagine that all of the soldiers that he took up the hill stayed close to the tyrant, and it is possible that some travelled quite a long distance to continue kindling fires.

Further questions have been raised about why the stratagem would have worked had it actually taken place, and had the fires been visible to both forces. Schubert and Tillyard both questioned why the Carthaginian army outside of Tunis or the defenders inside Hadrumetum would have thought this was a Greek army.¹¹² Both presume that the Hadrumetans would have 'just as well have thought that a Punic and not a Greek army was coming'.¹¹³ This criticism, though, ignores the situation which those loyal to Carthage were experiencing. News of the defeat of the large Punic army at the Battle of Tunis had spread throughout the region, and so surely had news of the capture of numerous settlements, such as Neapolis.¹¹⁴ For the defenders at Hadrumetum, what would have made them think a Carthaginian army still existed or whether it was in a state to bring aid? Surely, they were unaware of the 5,000 soldiers being sent back to Africa by Hamilcar as well as the army that had marched out of Carthage and was currently besieging the Greeks in the ruins of Tunis. It seems more likely, especially in a city under siege, where tension was already high, that despair would have been guiding many judgments, including any debate over which side this approaching (phantom) army belonged to. Assuming that it was a Carthaginian army would have been far less likely given the circumstances than being confident that it was another force coming to join with Agathocles. Thus, while this stratagem is out of the ordinary, we do not need to read it as a flight of fancy such as the owls in the line of battle at Tunis.¹¹⁵

In the aftermath of Tunis being relieved and Hadrumetum being taken, Agathocles continued to capture settlements loyal to Carthage. He first took Thapsus by force, and then began storming smaller towns throughout the area. As Hamilcar had been able to do on Sicily, Agathocles won over some of settlements through persuasion, or more likely, by simply being an alternative to the Carthaginians.[116] He may have captured as many as 200 settlements, as we hear from Diodorus. The Punic leaders were no longer going to accept a Greek tyrant running rampant throughout their territory, and again put an army in the field. This time, it was bolstered by the 5,000 soldiers who had been sent to Africa by Hamilcar. Rather than sending a single force against the camp outside of Tunis, they separated their forces and began to pacify the smaller centres which had fallen to Agathocles.[117] As well, they effectively cut the lines of communication between the tyrant and Neapolis, overrunning all of the roads.[118]

After accomplishing this, a large Punic force once again besieged the Greek army left in Tunis. A message got through to Agathocles, however, and he marched with the main body of his army to counter this threat. He made a night march towards the Carthaginian camp, using a stratagem of forbidding that his men light fires, as they would give away their position. At dawn, his army pounced on the Punic troops who were sent out as foragers as well as all those who were milling about outside of the camp. A battle may have been fought, although we do not hear of one with the Carthaginian army. Diodorus, though, says that while attacking foragers and those outside of the camp, Agathocles killed 2,000 and captured a great number of others. If this figure is to be trusted, it sounds more like a battle than capturing a few scattered troops out collecting supplies.[119] In a separate battle, Agathocles defeated Aelymas, the Libyan king who had been his one-time ally but subsequently defected back to the Carthaginian side. The king was killed in this encounter, along with many of his soldiers.[120]

Agathocles was once again in a good position in Africa when he went into winter quarters. In the following year, 309 BC, Carthage was to suffer another setback, this time in Sicily. As we saw above, after an aborted assault on Syracuse, Hamilcar had taken his army into camp further into the island. With the coming of the new campaigning season, however, he again moved on the city. We do not hear much about the army. One detail we do hear is that he had appointed Deinocrates commander of the cavalry.[121] The figures given by Diodorus for the size of the force, however, are unreliable. He says that there were 120,000 infantry and 5,000 cavalry.[122] The latter of these, while large, is not inconceivable. The 120,000 foot soldiers, however, is far too high, unless perhaps it included the rowers from the fleet as well as the camp followers.[123] It is possible that many troops came from the allies, as most of the island was loyal to the Punic cause at this point, but even then the figure seems quite large.[124] There is no reason to think that this army, in fact, numbered much higher than that of the previous year, which consisted of about 40,000 infantry and 5,000 cavalry.[125]

Whatever the true size of the army, Hamilcar led it against the territory of the Syracusans. He first captured the fortified centres which he or his allies did not already control. With possession of the hinterland, his forces then laid waste the crops in the area. This (coupled with having for some time maintained a naval blockade of the city) Hamilcar hoped, would help starve out the defenders.[126] To press his advantage, the general decided to march his army close to Syracuse's defences, settling on taking the area of the Olympieum, where previous camps had been established while trying to take the city. This required his army to march down the valley of the River Anapus, which he decided to undertake at night. During this night march, Hamilcar also endeavoured to capture the Euryalus fortress, on the Epipolae. His plan was betrayed, however, and the Syracusans quietly stationed there an extra garrison of 3,000 infantry and 400 cavalry.[127] As the Punic army was marching, some of it on the way to the Olympieum, while some marched against the Euryalus, the Syracusan troops attacked. Hamilcar's soldiers were not ready for battle. They were also encumbered by the presence of the baggage train and camp followers within their ranks. All of these men, carts, and animals were hemmed in by the narrowness of the path. While they were experiencing these problems, the troops who had been garrisoned on the Epipolae descended upon the Carthaginian army, which was thrown into much confusion because of the darkness compounded by their already unruly state.[128] Missiles rained down on them from those Syracusans who remained on the hilltop, who easily repulsed those Punic troops sent to capture it.[129]

Hamilcar and his retinue stood fast. He tried to rally the rest of his troops that were near, but to no avail. Quickly, the general was abandoned by the few that fought alongside him. Many fled in panic because of the confused state of the army and an ignorance of the strength of their enemy. Once Hamilcar was abandoned, and whatever bodyguards he may have had were killed, he was captured by the Syracusans.[130] They also managed to bring into the city considerable plunder, probably from taking the baggage train of the enemy. After parading Hamilcar around through the city, he was tortured in horrific ways, although we do not know the details. He was put to death in an ignominious way, and his head cut from his corpse. This was then sent to Agathocles, in Africa.[131] Thus, Carthage lost one of its most talented commanders to-date. This also meant that the Punic government lost its only bargaining chip and would not likely be able to negotiate a peace in which Agathocles left Africa.

In the wake of this setback, the grand alliance between the Carthaginians and the Greek exiles dissolved. The Punic army was now leaderless, but it did coalesce back into a whole after the rout. They elected those who commanded under Hamilcar as their new leaders, although we are not given any names. The Greek exiles elected Deinocrates as their general, which is of no surprise.[132] The situation on Sicily was now turned upside down. The power of both Carthage and Syracuse was at its lowest point in more than a century. This vacuum was filled by the Akragantines, led by a man named Xenodicus.

Akragas was ascendant. Xenodicus was given a sizeable army and marched to Gela. There, traitors inside the city allowed him in and he easily cleared Agathocles' garrison and brought most of the inhabitants over to his cause. From here, the new Greek alliance continued to free cities throughout the island. Enna came over to them willingly. Xenodicus had to take Erbessus by force, battling a Carthaginian garrison stationed there. The fighting was fierce, but the Greeks managed to force 500 of the garrison to surrender. The new Akragantine League, as some modern scholars call it, continued to grow, adding Leontini, Camarina, and Echetla to their ranks, and driving out the garrisons of Agathocles in those places. Xenodicus also made advances into Carthaginian territory, and we are told that he liberated a number of strongholds and cities therein.[133] Thus, on Sicily a state of warfare existed between three parties simultaneously: Carthage, Syracuse, and Akragas.[134]

Carthage was left with little to do on the island but defend their territories. At sea, however, they still held supreme power and maintained a blockade of Syracuse. The city was on the brink of starvation, when a number of grain ships were dispatched to relieve it. The inhabitants manned twenty triremes in an attempt to run the blockade. They were successful in breaking out of the harbour and made it all the way to Megara Hyblaea. Here they awaited the relief ships. On their return to the city, though, a squadron of thirty Punic warships sailed against them. The two groups came to blows at sea, and the ships from Syracuse were driven to the shore. The fighting then continued over the beached ships. Using grappling hooks, the Carthaginians were able to capture ten of the enemy vessels. A sally of troops from Syracuse were able to beat back the Punic ships and save the other Greek ships from capture.[135] Tillyard is probably correct in his assessment that this was just one of a number of minor skirmishes fought during this time, but we do not hear of others.[136]

Back in Africa, Agathocles experienced a setback within his own camp.[137] Sedition began brewing after a dinner which involved heavy drinking, at least by Lyciscus, one of the senior officers. He began prodding the tyrant with insults after he had become drunk. While Agathocles ignored it, valuing him as he did for his skills in warfare, Archagathus took the slight to his father more seriously. He chastised and threatened Lyciscus. At the end of the night, Archagathus himself was insulted by the man, who taunted him for a supposed impropriety with his stepmother. The tyrant's son was unable to contain his anger at this, and impaled the intoxicated man with one of the guard's spears. After this act became known, a number of soldiers throughout the army took it upon themselves to push for justice, arming themselves as if for battle. They used this occasion to also demand their wages which had not been paid. Some of them ascended the walls and thus besieged the leaders within their own camp.[138]

News of this sedition spread to nearby Carthage, whose leaders wanted to take advantage of it. They sent emissaries to the disillusioned soldiers, urging them to change their allegiance. Carthage was able to offer them better pay, as well as bonuses for coming under their flag. Some of the leaders of the revolt were amenable to this offer, but only around 200 actually defected. Agathocles pleaded for his soldiers to remain loyal, and eventually won them over. We then hear a story that the Carthaginian army was coming to meet the deserters, or perhaps assault the Greek camp, but the tyrant took them by surprise as they were not expecting an attack. This allowed him to easily rout them and drove the army back into its camp. It is improbable that this was the entire body of the Punic army, and we should probably read this as a repulse of the Carthaginian negotiators who were trying to turn the Greek soldiers.[139]

As the campaigning season of 308 BC opened, Agathocles found himself in a better position. His army was squarely back under his control and his opponents were still hemmed in around Carthage. The Punic leadership decided to take a more proactive approach to the war. Their first goal was to bring back into alliance some of the nomadic tribes who had defected to the Greeks. Thus, the Carthaginian army marched out from their camp into the Libyan interior. They were pursued by the enemy. Agathocles took with him 8,000 infantry, 800 cavalry, and fifteen Libyan chariots.[140] The Punic force was able to reach a tribe known as the Zouphones, who came back to their side. With their troops united, they set up camp on top of a hill, surrounded by a number of deep streams. They did this knowing that Agathocles was on their heels, and that a defensive position such as this would give them the advantage.[141]

The Carthaginian commander directed the Zouphones to harass the Greek column as it marched towards the camp in an effort to slow them down, or prevent them from attacking all together. They were countered by Agathocles' archers and slingers and successfully driven off. The tyrant then marched the rest of his army against the Punic position. The commander of this army saw that the enemy was closing and drew his own troops up for battle. He launched his attack as Agathocles was fording one of the rivers which protected the hill. In the initial shock, many in the Greeks' front line were cut down. Despite this setback, the Hellenes stood fast. The battle lasted for a considerable time, and eventually the Carthaginians' nomad allies were driven from the field. The portion of the line at which Agathocles was in command was the first to rout their opponents, driving them back towards their camp. The only Punic cavalry to remain on the field until the end were Greek mercenaries led by a man named Clinon, who stood up to Agathocles' most heavily armed troops.[142]

What was left of the Carthaginian army after the battle retreated inside their camp. The tyrant did not let them escape, and spurred his force on to mount the hill on which the enemy was encamped. They suffered no fewer losses than they had at the river, as the terrain was rough and made them easy targets for the Punic troops above them. As Agathocles got close to the camp, the nomads who had fled the field led a charge against the Greek baggage train. There, they killed what defenders were left, and took numerous prisoners, presumably from the camp followers. The Zouphones also captured a considerable amount of plunder from the baggage of the Hellenic troops. The tyrant only realised what was happening when it was too late to save his own camp. He allowed his men to plunder the enemy's belongings and divide them equally to make up for their losses. Agathocles' army captured some of the enemy, including 1,000 Greeks who had served Carthage, amongst whom were 500 Syracusans. After being sent into a fortress doubling as a prison, they realised what their fate was to be, and attempted to fight their way out. Although they were able to take over the fort they were in, they were tricked into leaving under a flag of truce and subsequently slaughtered by Agathocles' army.[143]

Despite his repeated victories, Agathocles came to the conclusion, in the wake of this battle, that his army was not up to the grand task of bringing Carthage to its knees. It is unclear what would have made him think this, and it is possible that we do not have all of the details of the campaign of 308 BC. The tyrant's solution was to forge an alliance with Ophellas, the Ptolemaic general who ruled Cyrene, whose rise to power there we have seen above.[144] In return for his friendship and dedication of his army to fighting Carthage, Agathocles was willing to let him rule Libya, saying that Sicily was plenty for himself. Reaching the decision that this would be beneficial, Ophellas committed to the campaign. He sent word to Athens and the other cities of mainland Greece, and drew from there many new soldiers into his service.[145] Many of these were eager to colonise in North Africa, presuming that they would defeat the Carthaginians.[146]

When his forces were ready, Ophellas marched towards Libya with an army of 10,000 infantry, 600 cavalry, and 100 chariots, along with 300 charioteers and men to fight alongside them. Along with these were around 10,000 camp followers, as many of the Greeks had brought their wives and children with them, as they aimed to settle in Africa after their victory.[147] The march took over two months to complete and was very treacherous. They ran extremely low on food and water, and had to suffer venomous snakes and other natural impediments.[148]

Eventually, the host made its way to where Agathocles was camped, and established their own nearby. The tyrant brought some supplies to Ophellas' camp, but encouraged the Cyrenean leader to secure his own food sources. Over the next few days, most of Ophellas' soldiers scattered throughout the countryside foraging for whatever they could find. Seeing this, Agathocles accused the Cyrenean leader of plotting to betray him, summoned his troops and led them, fully armed, against the new arrivals. Few soldiers remained in their camp, and Ophellas was quickly overwhelmed. He died fighting off Agathocles' surprise attack. After their leader was killed, the rest of the army laid down their weapons and were won over by the Syracusan.[149]

This is the version of events as Diodorus tells us, but Justin preserved a different tradition. In his telling, Ophellas was actively seeking ways of conquering a larger swathe of North Africa than was currently under his power. To do this, he exchanged a number of embassies with Agathocles, negotiating the terms of an alliance by which the latter would control Sicily and the former Africa, after they defeated Carthage. Once Ophellas had come to Libya, he and the Syracusan tyrant became friends, dined together often, and the former even adopted the latter as a son. The friendship was not to last, however, as Agathocles murdered him not long afterward.[150]

There is a third version of the betrayal of Ophellas, which is preserved by Polyaenus. In this telling, the Cyrenean was advancing against Agathocles with his army, rather than having made an alliance with him and coming as a friend. In order to stall this attack, the Syracusan decided to send his son, Heracleides, to the approaching enemy and seduce him. This is because the son supposedly possessed an extraordinary beauty and because Ophellas was supposedly addicted to attractive young boys. Heracleides was ordered to lead his target on for a number of days, and to repulse all of his approaches, but to tease him and keep him interested. On a day when Ophellas was sufficiently distracted by the wiles of his son, Agathocles launched an attack on his army, defeated it, and killed the duped would-be lover.[151]

The true details of this event are unclear. Tillyard suggested that amongst the details 'certain facts are plain. Agathocles welcomed Ophellas very friendly, dined with him and very likely gave him his son to adopt.'[152] These certainly seem to be the most likely of all the events described. We should also add that the hopeful colonists from Greece were shipped off to Syracuse, with most dying en route.[153] The adoption of Agathocles' son was probably meant to solidify the relationship between the two leaders without a formal exchange of hostages. What remains to be solved is the question of what brought on the hostilities between the two. There is no reason to presume treachery from one and not the other.[154] Agathocles has been seen to want power at all costs, and Ophellas would have been exposed to the intrigue and infighting in the army of Alexander and his successors. Some sort of disagreement seems to have developed between the two of them, perhaps regarding leadership of the proposed combined army or what was to happen in the aftermath of their defeat of Carthage. It was, perhaps, simply luck that Agathocles struck first, and with deadly force.[155]

After uniting the two armies, Agathocles was forced to turn his attention back to the war with Carthage. The Punic army had sallied out in force against the Greeks and forced them into battle.[156] They had, perhaps, observed what was happening between the Syracusan and Ophellas and thought that the time was right to strike. It was, however, a mistake. We know none of the details of the battle, but it was a magnificent defeat for the Carthaginians.[157] Both armies suffered heavy losses, but the victory was ascribed to Agathocles. Once driven back inside their walls, tensions rose amongst the Carthaginians and Bomilcar, the traitorous general, used the chaos to launch an insurrection against his fellow countrymen.[158]

> Be that as it may, when Bomilcar had reviewed the soldiers in what was called the New City, which is a short distance from Old Carthage, he dismissed the rest, but holding those who were his confederates in the plot, five hundred citizens and about a thousand mercenaries, he declared himself tyrant. Dividing his soldiers into five bands, he attacked, slaughtering those who opposed him in the streets. Since an extraordinary tumult broke out everywhere in the city, the Carthaginians at first supposed that the enemy had made his way in and that the city was being betrayed; when, however, the true situation became known, the young men ran together, formed companies, and advanced against the tyrant. But Bomilcar, killing those in the streets, moved swiftly in the market place; and finding there many of the citizens unarmed, he slaughtered them. The Carthaginians, however, after occupying the buildings about the market place, which were tall, hurled missiles thick and fast, and the participants in the uprising began to be struck down since the whole place was within range. Therefore, since they were suffering severely,

they closed ranks and forced their way out through the narrow streets into the New City, being continuously struck with missiles from whatever houses they chanced at any time to be near. After these had occupied a certain elevation, the Carthaginians, now that all the citizens had assembled in arms, drew up their forces against those who had taken part in the uprising. Finally, sending as envoys such of the oldest men as were qualified and offering amnesty, they came to terms. Against the rest they invoked no penalty on account of the dangers that surrounded the city, but they cruelly tortured Bomilcar himself and put him to death, paying no heed to the oaths which had been given. In this way, then, the Carthaginians, after having been in the gravest danger, preserved the constitution of their fathers.[159]

Bomilcar's execution was colourful. He was crucified in the middle of the Carthaginian forum. From his cross, as he was bleeding and suffering unimaginable pain, he cursed his countrymen. The dying man highlighted what he believed to be the city's recent sins, such as the punishment, or at least condemnation, of earlier generals who happened to be his relatives, such as the Hamilcar who negotiated with Agathocles, rather than wage war against him. While this heroic version of his death makes for an interesting story, it is probably just that. Undoubtedly, he had some choice words for his fellow citizens, and may have even been able to shout some of them out as he was being nailed to his cross, though the historically relevant, and rather specific, things cited by Justin should not be accepted without question.[160]

With the Carthaginians behind their walls sorting out their internal problems, Agathocles renewed his campaigning in Africa. His first target was Utica, one of the last major settlements still loyal to Carthage.[161] The Greek army took the inhabitants by surprise and took prisoner 300 citizens whom they found outside of the city walls. These Agathocles used as hostages and demanded the surrender of the city in return for the safe release of his prisoners. The leaders refused this proposal, however, and Agathocles began an aggressive siege. He ordered a siege tower to be built, sufficiently large to threaten Utica's fortifications, whatever they may have been. Upon this engine, the Greeks hung the Utican captives, using them as a human shield. While their fellows inside the city pitied them, 'the liberty of all' was 'of more account than the safety' of these poor prisoners. Seeing that this was still not enough to make the city capitulate, Agathocles ordered a full assault. Atop this single siege tower, he stationed his slingers, archers, and catapults, all of whom rained their missiles down on the defenders. The Uticans, after a brief hesitation, began to attack the engine, being forced to kill many of their countrymen who were dangling from it.[162]

The Greek army began assaulting the walls at points all around the circuit. Eventually, they found a weak spot in the fortifications and exploited it, breaking into the city. The battle then became a street fight, with Uticans resisting as they retreated into their houses or into the temples. Many of the citizens were cut down in hand-to-hand fighting. Those who fled to the temples, seeking asylum and invoking divine protection, were not granted it by Agathocles, and he ordered his men to hang anyone they took prisoner.[163] The army looted the town of its movable wealth. Agathocles intended to move against further settlements loyal to Carthage, and thus marched out of Utica with most of his army, leaving behind enough soldiers to safely maintain the garrison.[164]

His next target was Hippou Acra, modern Bizerta. This was an important settlement as it possessed the best harbour in the area.[165] Before the city was a great marshland which acted as a natural fortification. Agathocles laid siege to this, as well as he could. The decisive move in taking Hippou Acra, however, seems to have been a naval victory which the Greeks won over the inhabitants. After this, they were able to take the city by storm.[166] Now in possession of such a useful port, Agathocles set upon a construction programme to improve it, probably intending it to be a sort of capital city in his new North African holdings. He had walls, a fortress, a harbour, and dockyards built, all to a high standard.[167]

Agathocles was now in possession of most of Libya, and the lands which were previously loyal to Carthage. The only exception to this was the interior, where the nomadic peoples reigned, only some of whom were allied to the tyrant. With his position secure, Agathocles resolved to return to Sicily, where the situation was continuing to deteriorate. Along with 2,000 troops, he sailed for the island on a number of small ships and pentecontars which had been built in his new port. He left his son, Archagathus, in charge of his troops in Africa.[168] Not long before Agathocles arrived, his generals, Leptines and Demophilus, had defeated Xenodicus in a pitched battle and forced him to retreat back to the safety of Akragas. Agathocles landed at Selinus and brought Heraclea under his power immediately. He then crossed to the other side of Sicily and made an alliance with the citizens of Therma, which included granting safe passage out of the area for the Carthaginian garrison which had been resident there.[169] Granting the garrison a peaceful departure is interesting and may indicate that Agathocles had made some sort of pact or agreed to a ceasefire with the Carthaginians before leaving North Africa.

After his father's departure, regardless of any agreements which may have been made with Carthage, Archagathus ordered one of his commanders, Eumachus, to campaign south of the region they had already captured. This was likely the campaigning season of 306 BC. He captured a number of cities: Tocae, Phelline, Meschela, a different Hippou Acra, and Acris.[170] By taking these cities, the Greeks were able to bring the neighbouring tribes into submission. Unlike the other four, Eumachus allowed his soldiers to pillage Acris and he enslaved the population.[171] He then returned to Hippou Acra only to be given new orders for another campaign to the south. He marched through the territory that he had just conquered and attacked a city called Miltine. The Greek army took the inhabitants by surprise and easily breached its defences. Once inside the city, a running street battle developed. Although initially successful, Eumachus' army was eventually driven out, having suffered many casualties during the assault.[172]

He then marched his army through twenty miles of mountains which were swarming with wild cats. They then came upon three cities which were teaming with apes. These settlements were named for the animals, as were the children of their inhabitants. Apes were sacred to the peoples living here, and to kill one was an offence worthy of death. They lived amongst the population and took from the storehouses as they pleased. Of these cities, Eumachus took one, after which he won the other two over through persuasion. His position seemed secure, until he learned that a large army was being assembled to counter his campaign. Learning this, he ordered his troops to march back to the region by the sea.[173]

The Carthaginians, having finally recovered from Bomilcar's attempted coup and straightening out their internal affairs, organised an actual resistance. The city's leadership decided to form three armies which would all be directed at different parts of the lands conquered by Agathocles and his commanders. The first was to march on the coastal cities, the second would move into the middle regions, while the third was to remove the lingering Greek power, and restore Punic hegemony, in the interior. Each of these forces was 10,000 men strong, while a suitable garrison was maintained in Carthage itself. Besides the military goals they hoped to achieve, these expeditions were organised to help relieve the strain on supplies currently afflicting the city.[174]

This three-pronged strategy forced Archagathus to follow a similar plan, even though he had fewer troops at his disposal. Thus, he sent three armies to pursue the Carthaginian columns, leaving only a small garrison in Tunis. The first armies we hear of finding one another were those in the midland region. An otherwise unheard-of Hanno commanded the Punic troops, while Aeschrion was the commander of the Greeks. The former, knowing where his enemy was marching, presumably through superior scouting, laid an ambush. When it was sprung, the Carthaginians slaughtered their enemy, killing 4,000 infantry and 200 cavalry; amongst the latter was Aeschrion. Some of the soldiers made it back to Archagathus' army, while others were taken prisoner. The campaign which was sent to the interior of the south was led by a Carthaginian named Himilco; sensibly, as he already had campaigned in the area and thus knew the terrain, Eumachus had been appointed to lead the Greek army. Another Punic trap was laid, this time more elaborate. Himilco had marched his army into an unnamed city. He left part of his army therein, while he mustered the rest for a pitched battle. When this force engaged Eumachus' men, they feigned a rout and fled back towards the town. The Greeks, as was common practice in the ancient world, broke their formations in pursuit of their enemy, and were thus more vulnerable. The Carthaginian troops still in the city, upon seeing their comrades retreating and the enemy in disorder, charged forward and forced the Greeks into a panic. It appears that Himilco's unit must have retreated at an angle to the city, and those laying in ambush only launched their attack after Eumachus' troops had followed their comrades far enough that they could be cut off from their camp. After they routed, this meant that the Greeks could not return to their own camp, and were forced to flee to a nearby hill which lacked a reliable supply of water. Himilco's army then encircled them. Of the 8,800 men Eumachus had under his command at the beginning of the campaign, only thirty infantrymen and forty cavalrymen escaped.[175]

Word got to Archagathus about the defeat of two of his armies, which forced him to retreat behind the walls of Tunis. All of the survivors from the renewed Carthaginian offensives made their way back to him as well, though there could not have been many of them.[176] The Greek commander also sent word to his father, asking him to return to Libya in haste with reinforcements. The Punic campaigns achieved another objective besides containing and reversing the Greek expansion: many of the allies that Agathocles and his men had won over abandoned them. The Carthaginian armies collapsed in on Tunis and shut Archagathus off from the rest of North Africa. Himilco occupied the passes in the higher terrain, denying the enemy from communicating with the interior. Atarbas, another Punic commander, encamped his army near Tunis, preventing the Greeks from making any moves in secret. The Carthaginian fleet also maintained a blockade of the coast. Through these measures, Archagathus and his army were being slowly starved.[177]

In Sicily, Agathocles was being hard pressed by one of the factions, the Syracusan exiles led by Deinocrates, who had been part of Hamilcar's army. Nevertheless, he was resolved to sail to Africa and relieve his besieged son. Seventeen ships were made ready for the crossing, but they were still blockaded in the harbour by a Carthaginian squadron of thirty ships. Agathocles came up with a strategy, by which he sailed his ships past the Punic fleet, drawing them into a chase. This was the signal for eighteen Etruscan ships, recently arrived allies, to row out from the harbour at Syracuse. Agathocles' ships turned as if to ram the Carthaginians, who saw that they were now trapped between the two squadrons. The Carthaginians withdrew, but five of their ships were captured and the Punic commander committed suicide in the face of defeat.[178] This also seems to have broken the blockade of Syracuse, allowing supplies to be brought into the city. This had been halted for some time and the city was experiencing food shortages.[179]

His fleet then sailed for Libya. He was able to unite with his forces in Tunis, where he found an army distraught. They protested over having not been paid what they were owed, a concern which was relieved when the tyrant told them to seek it from their enemies and not from him, as the sacking of Carthage would surely bring them enough loot.[180] To relieve their stress, Agathocles resolved to lead them into battle. All together his troops numbered 6,000 Greeks, 6,000 mercenaries (Celts, Samnites, and Etruscans), 10,000 Libyans (who were unreliable), 1,500 cavalry, and a very unbelievable 6,000 Libyan chariots. This last number is almost certainly incorrect or has been corrupted. He marched this army towards the Carthaginian camp, and arrayed them for battle. Seeing that they still had the Greeks surrounded and did not have to offer battle, the Punic commanders ordered their forces to remain in camp. Agathocles then made a bold decision, to attack the enemy's camp. This was a dangerous assault and would prove costly. The Carthaginian army countered the Greek move and came out in full force against them. For a while the battle was a stalemate, but eventually Agathocles' men were beaten back. The first to rout were the mercenaries, although we are not told which group in particular. His Libyan allies do not seem to have been making much of an effort against the Punic host, and may have even switched sides during the battle, as we hear during the rout the Carthaginians did not make an effort to kill them. By the time the Greeks made it back to their camp, they had lost 3,000 soldiers.[181]

That night, the Carthaginians prepared a great bonfire on which to sacrifice the fairest of the prisoners from the battle. A strong wind came up as they were getting ready to begin the ceremony, however, and blew the flames into the nearby sacred building. The ceremonial area was adjacent to the commander's tent, which quickly caught fire. From here, the blaze spread throughout the camp, burning the tents and huts, which were made of reeds and straw. The soldiers were unable to quench the flames, and it engulfed everything in its path. It just so happened that 5,000 of the Libyans who had defected from Agathocles' army were coming to the Carthaginian camp that night. When the Punic scouts saw them, they reported to their comrades that the entire Greek host was advancing on them. This made the escape from the fire even more chaotic. Panicked soldiers ran amok, most ran for Carthage. In the darkness, allies didn't recognise one another, and thus a great slaughter occurred. As many as 5,000 Carthaginian troops were killed in this debacle.[182]

Agathocles' troops experienced a similar disaster. The group of Libyans who had marched towards the Carthaginian camp, seeing the inferno ahead of them, turned around and headed back towards the Greeks. The latter believed that this was the entire Punic army marching against them. When this reached the camp, it caused a stir. Agathocles ordered his troops to prepare for battle, which increased the anxiety of his men.

A panic ensued which was compounded when the Libyans reached the camp and mixed in with the army. People bumping into each other in the darkness led to outbreaks of violence, which escalated into a general slaughter. More than 4,000 of Agathocles' soldiers were killed during the disturbance of this night.[183]

It is an unlikely coincidence that these two disasters happened on the same night. But there is no reason to reject them out of hand. Tensions must have been running high in both camps in the wake of the battle outside the Punic position. A large force approaching in the night would have likely been enough to set off a panic, thus the story of the roaming Libyan troops being the cause of the chaos is not impossible. The most improbable part of the night, however, is thinking that it was the same group of 5,000 Libyans who had wandered back and forth between the camps. What seems more probable is that the force of around 10,000 Libyans who had come to the battle with Agathocles had splintered into two groups, one which remained loyal to the Greeks and the other which sought to defect to the Carthaginians.

Agathocles' position was now untenable. All of his Libyan allies had deserted him and his army was now at a significant disadvantage to the Carthaginians. The tyrant decided that his best option was to flee. He knew, though, that the Punic fleet would notice and sail against a large group of ships trying to leave Africa. Because of this, he planned on evacuating only a small group of followers and the younger of his sons, Heracleides. Archagathus, however, got word of the planned escape and made it known to the other leaders in the army. By doing this, he stopped his father who was arrested by his own commanders, bound in chains, and his treachery broadcast throughout the army. Internal divisions, however, eventually led to Agathocles' release. It appears that he had considerable support amongst the common soldiers. Despite many of his men still being loyal, Agathocles decided to abandon the army. He sneaked away, leaving behind both his sons. Diodorus sets this in October or November of 307 BC.[184]

The army was now left on its own. The soldiers seized Archagathus and Heracleides and put them to death. Thus, two sons were made to pay for the failings of their father. Unwilling to be slowly killed off by the superior army of Carthage, the Greek army sued for peace. Punic hopes to end the war in Africa were realised, and they agreed to the following terms. The invaders were to give up all of the cities that they had captured in return for 300 talents. Carthage offered to employ as many of the soldiers as were willing to come over to them at their regular rate of pay. All of those who did not wish to work for the Carthaginians were given safe passage to Sicily and allowed to settle at Solus, on the north coast of the island. Some of the soldiers, however, refused to agree to either of these offers and fortified the positions they currently held. Punic armies were dispatched to these settlements and were able to take them by storm. The leaders of these units were crucified while the rank and file were enslaved and used to rebuild and replant the countryside that Agathocles had destroyed.[185]

Agathocles went on a rampage when he arrived back on Sicily. He first went to Segesta, a city to which he was allied. Some of his soldiers rendezvoused with him there, and they extracted considerable resources from the population by force. They tortured and murdered most of the wealthier citizens. Agathocles ordered that the sons and daughters were to be carried off to Italy and sold to the Bruttians. When word reached the tyrant of his sons' murder at the hands of the army in Africa, he became enraged. He sent some of his loyalists into Syracuse who ordered his brother, Antander, to slaughter all of the relatives of the soldiers who took part in the Libyan campaign. They took them down to the sea and butchered them, throwing their corpses into the Mediterranean. So many were slain on that day that the waves turned red with their blood.[186] He was then forced to deal with the army of Deinocrates.[187]

The tyrant sued Carthage for peace in 306 BC. Ambassadors negotiated the terms of a treaty, by which the Carthaginians would pay Agathocles 300 talents and 200,000 bushels of wheat.[188] In exchange for this, they were again given control of Sicily beyond the Halycus.[189] There may have been a fresh Carthaginian army in Sicily at this point, which would have helped force Agathocles' hand, but it is more likely that he sought peace with them because of the threat still posed by the exiled oligarchic faction.[190]

Agathocles' warlike character did not end with the conclusion of the Carthaginian war. He continued to fight with his neighbours throughout the rest of his life.[191] In his final years, Agathocles planned one final war with Carthage. He would die before this plan could come to fruition. It was an ambitious idea, though. The campaign would have opened with another invasion of Libya. Unlike in the previous war, Agathocles planned to establish domination of the sea in order to prevent Punic ships bringing grain from Sardinia and Sicily. This would allow him to successfully execute a siege and starve the city into submission. To do this, he commissioned the construction of 200 ships, consisting of an unknown combination of quadriremes and sexremes ('fours' and 'sixes'). Agathocles, who had by this time made himself 'king', rather than tyrant, was murdered by his servant Menon before anything beyond planning could be accomplished.[192]

The king's assassin sought refuge with the man who convinced him to carry out the deed, Archagathus, Agathocles' grandson and the eponymous son of the man who was killed in Libya. He was encamped at Aetna with the Syracusan army. Menon won over the troops and assumed command. He resolved to go to war against Syracuse, probably to install himself as tyrant. The citizens, however, were not defenceless. They elected a man named Hicetas as general and sent him, with an army, against Menon. The two armies engaged in a game of cat and mouse, without coming to blows. The Carthaginians sent an army in support of Menon, which turned the tide of the war. Syracuse was forced to capitulate to Punic demands. They were required to send 400 hostages to the Carthaginians to guarantee peace. The exiles were also to be welcomed back into the citizen body. Renewed hostilities began between the mercenaries in the city and the Syracusans, as the former were denied suffrage. A peaceful solution was negotiated, however, and the mercenaries were to leave Sicily. They did not abide by these terms. When they reached Messene, rather than cross the straits, they occupied the town, killed many of its citizens, and renamed it Mamertina.[193] This was an action which was to have far reaching consequences, as we shall see below.

On reflection, Carthage's war against Agathocles was a warning of things to come. He was the first enemy to bring an army into Africa and threaten the city itself. The vulnerability of the hinterland was now obvious and probably made well-known throughout the Mediterranean.

Pyrrhus comes West

The last great upheaval in the central Mediterranean before the commencement of the great wars between Carthage and Rome occurred when Pyrrhus, King of Epirus, answered a call for help from Tarentum.[194] In the centuries prior to this, the Romans had been slowly bringing much of the Italian peninsula under their power through a series of wars and diplomatic strategies.[195] As they moved in towards Tarentum, a treaty was struck by which the Romans would not venture past a certain part of the coast; they supposedly violated this, and conflict erupted. The Tarentines, fearing the strength of their Latin adversaries, called in help from the east. Pyrrhus responded and brought an army and fleet to their assistance. Through a series of bitter battles against the Romans, he managed to stave off their advance for a while, but in the end would fail to protect Tarentine autonomy. While he was in southern Italy, however, the Epirote king was called to Sicily to aid the Greeks in a renewed struggle against Carthage.

This call for help came at a time of tumult on the island. After the death of Agathocles and the upheaval that followed in its wake, a number of tyrants took power in the Hellenic cities. Hicetas was in power at Syracuse, Phintias at Akragas, and Tyndarion at Tauromenium. As had been the case in the past, this assortment of absolute rulers eventually came into conflict. A war broke out between Hicetas and Phintias. It began with raids on the territories of both Syracuse and Akragas, with Diodorus saying that they 'pillaged the estates and made the area a wasteland'.[196] Eventually, the two armies met in a pitched battle, with the Akragantines suffering a crushing defeat. This so enlivened Hicetas that he felt confident in attacking the Carthaginian-held part of Sicily. The tyrant soon learned that this was a mistake, however, and he was defeated in battle at the river Terias.

We know nothing about this battle, nor what the Carthaginian army may have looked like. Hicetas' defeat, however, may not have caused his fall from power, though he was eventually overthrown by two men, Thoenon and Sosistratus. They ruled Syracuse, though not cooperatively.[197] According to Diodorus, once the tyrant was ousted, the two revolutionaries came to blows. Before this, they may have jointly sent word to Pyrrhus to come to Sicily and chase out the Carthaginians who had been agitated by Hicetas, but he did not answer their plea. Having around 10,000 men total, Thoenon and Sosistratus turned Syracuse into a battleground.[198] The former was in control of Ortygia, while the latter controlled the part of the city on the Sicilian mainland, as well as Akragas and a number of other settlements which he had previously taken.

While all of this was going on inside the city, a Carthaginian fleet of about 100 ships was blockading Syracuse by sea, with a land army of 50,000 blockading it by land.[199] A call for help went out to Pyrrhus at about the same time that the king learned of the death of Ptolemy Ceraunus, king of Macedonia. This forced the Epirote King to decide which direction to take his army. If he went to Greece, there was the possibility of securing control over all of Macedonia. However, we are led to believe that the appeals of the Sicilian Greeks were more seductive as Pyrrhus had his eyes set on conquering Libya.[200] This, to me, feels like a fabricated ambition, created by an unknown Hellenic historian to add a bit more flair to the story. We also hear that the king was married to Lanassa, who was a daughter of Agathocles, and thus he had a claim of sorts to the leadership of Syracuse.[201] Whatever drove his decision, Pyrrhus sent his deputy Cineas to the cities of Sicily to negotiate his arrival on the island.[202]

As Pyrrhus was tarrying in Italy, Carthage forged a new treaty with Rome. This was likely struck by a Punic admiral, Mago, who sailed to Ostia with 120 ships, offering his city's assistance in the war against the Epirote interloper.[203] The terms of the agreement were thus: 'If they make a treaty of alliance with Pyrrhus, the Romans or Carthaginians shall make it on such terms as not to preclude the one giving aid to the other, if that one's territory is attacked. If one or the other stand in need of help, the Carthaginians shall supply the ships, whether for transport or war; but each people shall supply the pay for its own men employed on them. The Carthaginians shall also give aid by sea to the Romans if need be; but no one shall compel the crews to disembark against their will.'[204] Although some modern historians have suggested that Carthage paid Rome to agree to this treaty, there is no strong evidence for this and the theory should be rejected. The benefits to both states were advantageous enough that there would have been little need for further incentives.[205] Carthage also made an alliance with the Mamertines, who had occupied Messana.[206] All of this, seemingly, was in an effort to stop Pyrrhus from crossing the Straights and onto Sicily. This is further evidenced by the Punic transport of 500 Roman soldiers to Rhegium, where they destroyed timbers intended for use in ship construction, and continued to watch the waters there.²⁰⁷

Regardless of the Straights being watched, Pyrrhus crossed to Sicily with about 8,000 troops, landing at Tauromenium and bringing its tyrant Tyndarion into an alliance.²⁰⁸ He then sailed to Catana, which honoured him with wreaths of gold. From here, his army marched on land towards Syracuse, with the fleet guarding them on the seaward side. Seeing his approach, the Carthaginians broke their blockade of the city, with both army and fleet fleeing upon Pyrrhus' arrival.²⁰⁹ On the surface, this is bewildering. With their army supposedly numbering 50,000 men, and their fleet about 100 ships, they should have been a match for the newcomer. It could have been fear of Pyrrhus himself, having been the victor recently over the Romans, or perhaps it was a fear of his army and that within Syracuse uniting in one large sortie? We could also accuse our sources of inflating the size of the Punic force, although I am reticent to believe that any Carthaginian leader would have invested Syracuse with a small army. Pierre Lévèque also suggested that the Punic commander could have been wary of pitting an army of mercenaries against the veterans under Pyrrhus, which is also a viable explanation.²¹⁰ Jeff Champion points to the withdrawal of the Carthaginian fleet as a possible cause for the complete abandonment of the siege, saying that without their ships the siege would be 'fruitless'.²¹¹ Whatever the real reason, which we will probably never know, thanks to the retreat, Pyrrhus was now in control of Syracuse.

With the Carthaginians abandoning eastern Sicily and marching their army back into the area directly under their control, and presumably sailing the fleet to a home-harbour, Pyrrhus began concentrating his power on the island. He settled the quarrel between Thoenon and Sosistratus. With this, he seems to have taken power in Syracuse and took possession of the armoury, including siege engines and 140 ships, as well as the royal 'nine'.²¹² This gave him a fleet of over 200 vessels, a formidable force. While this was going on, the master of Leontini, Heracleides, sent word that he would give his territory to Pyrrhus, as well as 4,000 infantry and 500 cavalry.²¹³ He proceeded to Akragas, being given control of the city and being handed its 8,000 infantry and 800 cavalry. These were said to all be 'picked men' and equals to the Epirotes in Pyrrhus' army. In addition, handed over to him was Enna, which had expelled its Punic garrison, and thirty other towns (probably some small fortresses) which had previously been ruled by Sosistratus. He was now ready to march against the Carthaginian territories in the west.

Pyrrhus summoned the siege engines from Syracuse and set out from Akragas with an army of 30,000 infantry and 1,500–2,500 cavalry.[214] His army is also said to have included a number of elephants. It was now spring 277, and Pyrrhus made his move. He took Heraclea Minoa and Azones, with Selinus, Halicyae, Segesta, and others coming over to him willingly.[215] We do not possess details about his march west through Sicily, but it appears that the majority of the fighting was in the form of sieges. Justin tells us that Pyrrhus fought 'many successful battles with the Carthaginians', but he is the only source to claim this.[216] Regardless of how he made his way to it, the Epirote king eventually reached Eryx and decided to lay siege to the fortress upon it.

His motivation for taking this place was partially driven by the same factor which supposedly drew Dorieus and others there: its association with Heracles.[217] Pyrrhus, like the others, claimed lineage from the hero. The town was garrisoned by a large force of Carthaginian troops, though who exactly they were we do not know. Engines were brought against the walls, thus beginning a long siege. In an attempt to win personal glory, Pyrrhus led the final assault against the fortress. As Plutarch retold it, 'he put on his armour, went out to battle, and made a vow to Heracles that he would institute games and a sacrifice in his honour' if he would help win the day.[218] According to the same narrative, after a barrage of missiles cleared the walls of defenders, scaling ladders were brought against them, with Pyrrhus being the first to mount the walls. By all accounts, he slew many enemies, either throwing them from the ramparts or killing them with his sword.[219]

Now in control of Mt. Eryx, Pyrrhus would have been able to survey much of what remained of the Carthaginian presence on the island. Only two significant places were still in their hands, Panormus and Lilybaeum. He first moved against the former. As his army marched towards Iaetia, a fort which was well-positioned for an attack against Panormus, the citizens surrendered rather than enduring a siege. Panormus was then taken by storm, although a siege perhaps preceded this. Lilybaeum, the last Punic position on Sicily, was now in Pyrrhus' aim. He took the stronghold of Herctae, intending for this to be his base of operations again the larger city. This fortress was on the coast between Eryx and Panormus, with Polybius concluding that it 'was obviously a particularly good spot for establishing a long-lasting and defensible camp'.[220] Although this was said in the context of the First Punic War, its defensibility was probably what attracted Pyrrhus to the site.

While the king's army was readying itself for the attack on Lilybaeum, the Carthaginians were able to organize a relief effort. They shipped over a large army, grain, and war engines. These troops strengthened the fortifications of the city on the land side, building new walls and towers, as well as digging a large defensive ditch. This was all accomplished because Carthage had become master of the seas. We hear nothing of Pyrrhus' fleet at this point, and when he returned to Italy after abandoning Sicily it had been reduced to 110 ships. It is possible that he had been defeated in a naval battle unknown to us, or perhaps lost a large part of his armada to a storm, but we do not know for sure.[221] Whatever the reason, the situation was now completely opposite to how it had been when Pyrrhus first landed on Sicily. The Carthaginians were now besieged within their last foothold on the island, but dominant at sea.[222]

They dug in deep at Lilybaeum, but did not necessarily want to have to fight it out with Pyrrhus. After shoring up the city's fortifications, the Carthaginians sent an embassy to the king, asking for peace. They were willing to pay a large war-indemnity in return for not being forced off the island. Pyrrhus was convinced not to accept this, as his allies saw Lilybaeum as too dangerous of a foothold on Sicily and continued Punic control would leave it open to attack. Seeking peace was clearly against the treaty that Carthage had made with Rome and is an important indicator of the state of affairs. Based on this betrayal, it seems likely that the earlier alliance was simply one of expedience and was not part of a long-term Punic strategy.

As these talks went nowhere, Pyrrhus put the city under siege. Unlike the smaller centres throughout Sicily which had either been taken by storm or capitulated, Lilybaeum was too well fortified to be captured easily. The large force which Carthage had transported there meant that the walls were always manned, even after suffering casualties. The armaments that they had brought over included so many catapults, capable of launching both stones and missiles, that there were too many to all be mounted on the fortifications. Repeated attacks by the Greek forces were repelled, costing them many troops. Although they attempted to undermine the walls and build larger siege engines, they were ultimately unsuccessful in taking the city. After two months of this, Pyrrhus broke the siege and settled on a new strategy: build a fleet and invade Libya.[223]

This was not to happen. He went about gathering resources for this venture in an impudent manner, eventually alienating his allies in Sicily. Pyrrhus was accused of acting like a tyrant, seizing private property, replacing local magistrates with his own men, and garrisoning otherwise friendly cities. His behaviour was so offensive that some of the Greek cities which had been allied with the king defected to the Carthaginians.[224] This seems to have given the Punic commanders hope for retaking what they had lost, and they mounted an offensive eastward from their bastion at Lilybaeum. They pursued the war vigorously, and though they lost a pitched battle against Pyrrhus, continued to push into Greek territory.[225] In the end, he was forced to abandon the island. Pleas from his allies in Italy gave him a reason to leave which was perhaps better than truly admitting defeat. The Carthaginians would have one last swipe at the Epirote king, however, with their fleet falling upon his as it tried to cross the straights. Although they sank or captured a number of his ships, Pyrrhus himself made it through and would go on to further adventures. The quote attributed to him while he was leaving the island, that he was leaving behind 'a wrestling ground for Carthaginians and Romans' was certainly inserted into the historical tradition sometimes after the major wars between Carthage and Rome.

Conclusions

By looking at the history of Punic warfare between the three leaders in this chapter we learn some important things about Carthaginian armies and their approach to war. Their determination to hold power in western Sicily was strong, and even when they were driven to the farthest reaches of that domain they invested significant resources to recapture anything that was lost. We see in all three periods that the Punic part of the island was taken somewhat easily, but then retaken with relative ease. Although garrisons were maintained throughout their holdings, these were easily destroyed, readily betrayed, or quick to flee in the face of invading armies.

Chapter 6

The First War with Rome

Carthage's entanglement in Sicilian affairs not only led to continual wars against the Greek inhabitants of the island, but also would be the most basic cause of the first war against Rome. Although the two, great, central Mediterranean powers had been allies against Pyrrhus, this temporary friendship was not to last long. What would result from a seemingly minor confrontation in 264 BC was a twenty-four-year long war which would end with Carthage finally forced off Sicily, something that centuries of Greek efforts could not do. This was the first of three destructive conflicts between these two powers. To understand this war, we must begin by looking at its cause.

We must trace the origin of the first war between Carthage and Rome to the reign of Agathocles. A group of Campanian mercenaries in his service had seized the Sicilian city of Messana, which was strategically important in the control of the eastern part of the island and traffic through the straights. This group called themselves Mamertines, or the sons of Mamers/Mars. When they came into the city, they killed or exiled the male citizens, seized their property, and took for themselves their wives and children. Once they had seized the city, around 288 BC, they used it as a base for raiding the lands of their neighbours, being a particularly annoying nuisance for Syracuse. Over the course of about twenty years, they established a small territorial state. They were allied to the Romans through the precariously held city of Rhegium, whose one-time Roman garrison had betrayed their hosts in an act which was probably inspired by the Mamertine's success in Messana.[1]

Mamertine power continued to grow until the ascendant ruler of Syracuse, Hiero II, took action against them.[2] His first campaign ended in the Battle of the Cyamosorus River, sometime around 269 BC. Although this resulted in a defeat for the Syracusan, it showed that he was willing to test the resolve of the state based in Messana.[3] Hiero was not discouraged and brought a new army against the Mamertines sometime around 264 BC, decisively defeating them at the Battle of the Longanus River.⁴ Pursuing them to Messana, the Syracusan commander laid siege, perhaps hoping to resolve the Mamertine problem once and for all. Hemmed in within their walls, the besieged Campanians sent embassies to both the Carthaginians and the Romans asking for help.⁵

Carthage was the first to respond. Hannibal, a Punic admiral stationed with a fleet at Lipara, responded to the Mamertine appeal. He went first to Hiero's camp to congratulate the Syracusan on his victory. While this was happening, the Greek army was idle; during this lull, Punic soldiers made their way into Messana, thus bolstering the defences of the city. Seeing that continuing the war against the Mamertines would mean entering into a war against Carthage, Hiero abandoned his siege and returned, triumphantly, to Syracuse, where he was proclaimed king.⁶ For the time being, it was Carthaginian protection which preserved Mamertine independence. But their saviours were not to savour having some type of control over the city for long. Though a Punic garrison had been placed in the city, it was removed by the Mamertines, perhaps with knowledge that the Romans had accepted their call for aid. Whether this was accepted because of a Roman fear of Punic domination of Sicily or for another reason, it does not appear that neither they nor the Carthaginians expected intervention at Messana to lead to a major war.⁷ Pursuant to accepting their call for help, Rome sent the consul Appius Claudius Caudex, with an army of probably around 20,000 men, to their relief.⁸ He evaded a Carthaginian fleet which attempted to block his passage from Italy to Sicily, and made his way into Messana.

The Opening Moves

With Appius Claudius' army now across the straights, the stage was set for the first major clash of the war. As H. G. Wells was to write: 'so began the first of the most wasteful and disastrous series of wars that has ever darkened the history of mankind.'⁹ A Carthaginian army laid siege to Messana, and were joined in this endeavour by Hiero and an army from Syracuse. The consul attempted to negotiate a solution, reaching out to both the Punic and the Syracusan camps. This went nowhere. Claudius saw that his situation was perilous; the enemy controlled both land and sea. He decided on forcing the issue, rather than remaining blockaded in Messana. Hiero was the target, perhaps because Claudius thought that he had the weaker army, or perhaps it was simply smaller than that of the Carthaginians. The Roman army marched out against the Syracusans, offering battle, which was accepted. We do not know many of the details of this engagement, but according to Zonaras the Roman cavalry was defeated but the infantry held on and won the day. There is no reason to reject this notice, with the possible exception that we do not find it in Polybius, but his sparse narrative for these opening events should make this a moot point. Adrian Goldsworthy has suggested two sensible reasons for the defeat of the Roman cavalry: 'given the difficulties of transporting horses by sea... [and] it is also worth recalling that historically the Syracusan cavalry had a good reputation.'[10] Regardless of why the infantry won the day, it was a Roman victory. Claudius' men stripped the corpses of their enemies and returned to Messana for the night. The next day, having found out that the Syracusans had retreated from the siege, the consul decided to attack the Carthaginians. He marched his army out at first light and found a Punic army willing to fight. Once again, the Romans came out victorious, inflicting serious losses on the Carthaginians and sending the survivors fleeing throughout the countryside.[11]

With Messana relieved, Claudius turned his attention towards Syracuse. He marched his army southward towards the city, ravaging the land as he went. The Romans raided and pillaged the territories controlled by both the Syracusans and their allies. No doubt, this added considerably to the coffers of the army. Upon reaching Syracuse itself, Claudius encamped near to the walls and began a siege. Hiero sent a number of sorties against them, winning some of the engagements, losing others. Claudius himself was almost captured during one of these small engagements, only extricating himself by feigning the desire to negotiate with Hiero. The objective of this campaign from the Roman perspective is difficult to discern. Even if Claudius had a typical consular army with him, consisting of two legions plus allied troops, numbering about 20,000 men, this would probably not have been a large enough force to do any significant damage to well-fortified Syracuse. Additionally, the Romans did not have a substantial fleet with which to blockade the harbours. Even with larger armies and huge numbers of ships, the Carthaginians were never able to force the city into submission, although we should not presume that Claudius was intimately aware of the history of wars between Carthage and Syracuse. That the consul was not awarded a triumph upon his return is confirmation that little of consequence was achieved either outside of Syracuse or in the engagements at Messana.[12] Regardless of what he was trying to do, Claudius was eventually forced to retire from the siege because of want for supplies. After this he returned to Messana, left a garrison there, and returned to Rome.[13]

The actions of both Carthage and Rome at Messana help us understand what their purposes were in getting involved with the Mamertines. The original Carthaginian response, sending a fleet and small garrison and driving off Hiero, seems as though it was done out of sympathy for the besieged. However, their attack on the city soon after reveals the true purpose of their efforts. While the Mamertines were in control of the city, straights, and north-eastern Sicily, they were valuable for Carthage as a check on Syracusan power. They stood between Hiero and absolute control of eastern Sicily. As soon as Roman troops arrived, however, and it was clear that the Mamertines were now in their camp, Carthage was presented with the problem of a third major power on Sicily, something that they could not tolerate. For about a century and a half, Punic policy on the island was to maintain the status quo, protect Phoenician and allied settlements in the west, and to do their best to check the undulating power of Syracuse. The arrival of Rome signalled a change to existing power structures. The temporary alliance between Carthage and Syracuse, and their siege of Claudius' army and Messana, was an effort to prevent a Roman beachhead from being established.[14] The campaigns of Claudius and the consuls of 263 BC (as we shall see below) make it obvious that the Roman objective was Syracuse, and not a war with Carthage. Interestingly, in the *Periochae* of Livy we find only that during these years 'for the first time Roman troops crossed the sea, and they fought several times against Hiero with success.'[15] This corroborates our conclusions above, that when the Romans decided upon war in Sicily it was against Syracuse and, probably, meant as a means for Claudius and his men to win glory and plunder considerable wealth.

The year after Claudius' expedition to Sicily, both consular armies were dispatched to the island under the command of the consuls of 263 BC, Manius Otacilius Crassus and Manius Valerius Maximus. With the considerable forces at their disposal, they began capturing and laying siege to Sicilian cities. Hadranum, Ilarus, Tyrittus, and Ascelus were taken by storm and Centuripa, Macella, and Hadranon were besieged.[16] These are the only cities that we hear of, specifically, being attacked. Many cities appear to have defected to the Romans voluntarily, betraying their existing alliances with Carthage and Syracuse. In total, sixty-seven towns may have come over to them in this way, including Halaesa and Segesta. The foray towards the west which saw a number of these cities captured or capitulate may have been led only by Valerius.[17] The lack of a Carthaginian military response indicates that they either did not have a large field army on Sicily or did not view the Roman threat as a lasting one. It could also be that they had planned to join with Hiero's army before engaging the enemy. With much of the countryside subdued, and troops from these new allies added to the armies of the consuls, the Romans marched against Syracuse. Seeing the successes of Otacilius and Valerius, and the massive army they led, Hiero was driven to seek peace. Before the Roman army was able to besiege Syracuse, his envoys reached the consuls and negotiated a fifteen-year peace. The price of this was steep, with Hiero having to pay 100 silver talents to Rome.[18] This sum, though seemingly large, may have been less than the Romans originally wanted, and it may have been agreed because the consuls heard news of a coming Carthaginian relief force for Hiero.[19]

Although it may have seemed like it, Syracuse had not yet been abandoned by their Carthaginian allies. Not long after their king had made peace with the Romans, a Punic fleet landed at Xiphonia, somewhat north of the city. We do not hear what kind of forces were at his disposal, but the leader of this expedition, Hannibal, had been dispatched to give aid to Hiero. Upon hearing that the king had given in to Roman demands, he immediately left, certainly knowing that attacking two consular armies, supplemented by their new allies, would be suicidal.[20]

The last major city loyal to Carthage in the traditionally Greek part of the island was Akragas. It was decided that a stand against Rome would be made here. They gathered here considerable stores and a large army. Mercenaries were recruited from amongst the Ligurians, Celts, and Iberians.[21] As many as 50,000 people were crowded into the city, which would make their gathered supplies less than adequate. How many of these were of fighting-age and equipped with arms and armour is unknown, but it appears to have been a relatively small number. In command of what garrison troops were in the city was Hannibal, the son of Gisco. The Romans were not ignorant of the importance of Akragas, and the consuls of 262, Lucius Postumius Megellus and Quintus Mamilius Vitulus, advanced directly against it when they reached the island with fresh armies. Their first action was to blockade the city from the rest of Sicily with a siege wall. It was probably not coincidental that they arrived at the usual time for the grain harvest, and once encamped the consuls ordered their men to forage through the farmland. By bringing the local crops into their camp it would alleviate their need for supplies as well as deny them to the enemy. Unfortunately for the Romans, however, Hannibal was keeping a watchful eye on the besiegers. When they fanned out to begin harvesting grain, the Carthaginian launched an attack from Akragas, routing the Roman foragers. At this point, the Punic sortie split into two groups, one attacked the troops covering the foraging parties and the other marched on the enemy camp. We hear nothing of what happened in the field, but we know that Hannibal's troops were repulsed at the Roman camp, pursued back to the city, suffering many casualties in the affair. Polybius attributes Roman discipline and institutions to the victory, noting especially that the defenders at the camp were inclined to fight to the death as abandoning their posts would have resulted in the same.[22]

In the aftermath of the Carthaginian sally, Postumius and Mamilius decided to separate their armies: one remained in the original camp while the other build a new camp west of the city.[23] They then dug two defensive trenches, in front and behind the camps, in order to protect against further attacks from the garrison as well as against any armies elsewhere on Sicily. This siege camp kept Hannibal penned up inside Akragas, and only a few small skirmishes were fought. The Romans kept up their blockade for five months, by which time a fresh army was sent to Sicily from Carthage. Doubtlessly, messages had advised the Punic leadership of the situation at Akragas. The newly arrived troops were put under the command of Hanno, perhaps the same Hanno who failed outside of Messana. His new army consisted of 50,000 infantry, 6,000 cavalry, and sixty elephants.[24] They landed at Lilybaeum, but he mustered his newly arrived troops at Heraclea and planned an attack against Herbessus, the town being used as a supply depot by the Romans and their allies. This he took by surprise, facing little resistance if the lack of a battle in our sources is to be trusted. Herbessus may have been betrayed to him by dissidents within, as reported by Diodorus.[25]

Having seized the enemy's supplies, Hanno then moved his army into a position where he was besieging the Roman camps, who were, in turn, still besieging Akragas. This was a situation not uncommon in ancient warfare. Despite the halting of fresh supplies coming to them, the Roman refused to give up the siege. Hunger began to set in, followed shortly by disease. We do not hear of the symptoms of this pestilence, but we should not be surprised by the spreading of illness in a siege camp deprived of food. The Roman cause was only saved by Hiero who came up with ingenious ways of bringing supplies to his allies, although we do not know what these were. Seeing the Roman situation deteriorating, Hanno decided to attack them. He devised a stratagem by which his Numidian cavalry would ride up to the enemy camp and taunt their cavalry, trying to draw them out. Once this was done they retired back towards the rest of the army. When they made contact with the main body, the Numidians and the rest of the Carthaginian host turned on the Roman horsemen, slaughtering many and chasing them back to their camp. Hanno followed up this victory by moving his army's camp closer to that of the Romans, and began a proper siege.[26]

For two months, the armies were locked in a stalemate. Small skirmishes were common, but nothing of consequence was accomplished by either side. Hanno was unwilling to risk an open battle, or to try forcing his way into the Roman camp. Hannibal, however, began relaying to him the situation within Akragas. The population was starving, and the garrison was losing troops deserting to the enemy. This drove Hanno to finally seek battle, one which the Romans willingly accepted on account of their own supply problems. The two sides marched their armies into the no man's land between their camps. What happened next is not precisely clear. We have two different versions of the battle, one preserved by Polybius the other by Zonaras.

Polybius' description of the battle is not extremely detailed. He says that the two armies marched forward and engaged in battle. It was an even contest until the Romans turned the Carthaginian mercenaries, who formed their front line. Hanno had apparently stationed his elephants, and probably additional infantry, as a second line, as the mercenaries collided with 'the elephants and the remaining ranks' once they were routed. Interestingly, we do not hear anything about the Numidian cavalry who had performed so well in the initial clash with the consular force. Hanno's battle plan is not easy to discern from these pieces of information, but it could be that the line of mercenaries was meant to tire out the Roman infantry who would then be run down by the elephants and fresh Punic infantry.[27] The collision of the mercenaries into the line of elephants threw the rest of the army into disorder, probably meaning that the elephants began to run amok. This would have been enough to cause a Punic defeat, let alone a successful Roman push from the front. After the mercenaries and elephants broke, the entire army routed, and was common in ancient battles, the Romans gave chase to the fleeing mob and slaughtered many of them. We do not hear of the formation used by the Romans, but it was undoubtedly the *triplex acies*, the standard formation of their armies at this time.[28]

The version of the battle preserved by Zonaras is much different. In this, the consuls remained inactive while Hanno advanced on their camp. The Carthaginians' front ranks may have then been engaged by Roman skirmishers, keeping them active for quite some time.[29] Late in the day, Hanno ordered a forceful charge against the Roman position, possibly those already fighting outside of the camp's palisade. What he did not know, however, was that a Roman force had infiltrated behind his army and was laying in ambush while fresh Roman troops had mustered secretly behind their fortifications. Also unknown to the Punic general was that his compatriot inside Akragas, Hamilcar, who was supposed to launch an attack on the Roman flank in coordination with the main army, had been held back by the resolute pickets of the Roman camp. Thus, when Hanno's main force reached their Roman adversaries, they found fresh soldiers waiting for them as well as enemies to their rear, launching an assault. The Carthaginian attack was short lived and, like in Polybius' version, the army was routed, resulting in great losses.[30]

Although these narratives provide quite different visions of the battle, both are coherent in depicting a decisive Roman victory. Neither provide figures for the losses on either side, but Diodorus says that Hanno lost 3,000 infantry and 200 cavalry dead, and 4,000 men taken prisoner between the two battles he fought. He also tells us that eight of the elephants were killed, but thirty-three others were disabled by wounds.

Polybius records that the Romans seized most of the elephants, which would be sensible if many were injured in the final battle. The consuls' losses are less clear, Diodorus numbering them at 30,000 infantry and between 450 and 1,500 cavalry, but this is out of a claimed total of 100,000 men. The figures given for the Roman forces, both losses and total number of men, are probably wrong. It is possible that the 100,000 figure included slaves and labourers who had been brought in from the allied settlements on Sicily to help construct the Roman siege camps, though this would mean that around 60,000 men were brought in just for this task. I find this idea suspect. It is more likely that an error in transmission to Diodorus, or perhaps in the preservation of this portion of his text, which is very fragmentary, has occurred. It is clear, however, that the Roman losses were heavy, as Hannibal was able to escape from inside Akragas with his garrison the night of the battle. He and his men were supposedly able to make it through the Roman lines, which must have meant there were not many men left to watch their entirety.[31]

With Hanno's army broken, and Hannibal's garrison having abandoned the city, the consuls were free to seize Akragas. Only a few of the garrison troops, making up a rear guard, were left near the city when the Romans fell upon it, but little more than a small skirmish was fought. They were able to occupy Akragas without resistance from its inhabitants. They looted the town and enslaved the residents. Around 25,000 people became slaves on that day.[32]

The Carthaginians were not happy with this loss. Hanno was stripped of his citizenship, fined 6,000 gold pieces, and relieved of his command. He got off lucky, though, and was not crucified as many Punic commanders were following failure. His dismissal led to the fateful appointment of one of a man named Hamilcar. Although an ancient tradition called him 'son of Barca' and thus father of the infamous Hannibal Barca, this is now thought be incorrect. Hamilcar was sent to Sicily to take over what army was left. Settled into his new command, he began a more offensive strategy against the Romans. Rather than waiting for fresh consular armies to cross the Straights to Sicily, he ordered Hannibal, who was now appointed as an admiral, to take his fleet and raid the coast of Italy.[33] He may have had as many as seventy ships sailing under his command. Hamilcar had hoped that, by having his admiral harass the coasts near Rome itself, he could prevent the Romans from sending another large army to Sicily. This, however, did not work, and the consuls of the following year, Lucius Valerius Flaccus and Titus Otacilius Crassus, came to the island. Rather than keeping the consuls and their legions in Italy, the Romans setup coastal guards to protect against Carthaginian raiders.[34]

The fall of Akragas solidified the Roman objective of driving out the Carthaginians from Sicily. According to Polybius:

> When the news of what had occurred at Agrigentum [Akragas] reached the Roman Senate, in their joy and elation they no longer confined themselves to their original designs and were no longer satisfied with having saved the Mamertines and with what they had gained in the war itself but, hoping that it would be possible to drive the Carthaginians entirely out of the island and that if this were done their own power would be much augmented, they directed their attention to this project and to plans that would serve their purpose.[35]

Oddly, the consuls of 262 BC were not accorded a triumph for their victory at Akragas. Some modern scholars have taken this to mean that the capture of the city was not as significant as others, and Polybius himself, make it out to be.[36] This view is simply wrong. As William Harris wrote in 1979, there is no reason to assume that Polybius was imposing his own views on the history of 262–261 BC.[37] Besides the energy imparted to any victor, there were pragmatic reasons for Rome wanting to expel Carthage from Sicily in the wake of the capture of Akragas. With many other Punic holdouts in the west of Sicily, as well as numerous Greek cities whose allegiance wavered, the victory at Akragas would be in vain if they did not push their current advantage.[38]

As time went on, the war slowed down again, with the capture of Akragas seeming like the climax of a very short story. The consuls of 261 BC did not achieve anything as spectacular as this victory. With the arrival of the new consuls with their armies, and the happenings of the previous year, a number of towns in the centre of the island went over to the Romans. This can probably be interpreted to mean that Valerius and Otacilius were campaigning against inland targets. A story preserved by both Zonaras and Frontinus recounts how Hamilcar used the consuls to remove a mutinous group of Gallic mercenaries from his army. He told the soon-to-be mutineers that one of the cities which had gone over to the Romans would be betrayed to them by a traitor inside upon their approach, and that they could loot it once inside, thus compensating them for wages owed. Meanwhile, Hamilcar sent agents to pretend to be deserters, and informed Otacilius of the coming group of Gauls. Setting an ambush for them, the consul's soldiers slaughtered them to a man, though suffering some losses themselves.[39] This thus achieved two of the Punic commander's goals: get rid of the mercenaries and cause Roman casualties.

When Valerius and Otacilius returned to Italy, Hamilcar's strategy changed. He took command of a fleet and began a seaborne campaign against Roman-allied towns in Sicily, as well as the Italian coast. Some of the cities of Sicily went over to him, more afraid of the Punic fleet than they were of Roman land-armies. The Romans were quick to realize that the war would remain deadlocked so long as the Carthaginians controlled the sea, and they the land. They resolved to construct a navy.[40] The Romans had ships before this, obviously, but they were of no match to those of Carthage. Once they had taken on the challenge of building a strong fleet, the work was carried out seemingly quickly. Within a year of the decision, it was completed. Polybius describes the process of this grand feat, though on a number of points he exaggerates. The Romans had captured a Punic quinquereme in the aftermath of their first crossing to Sicily. The ship had run aground and could not be rescued by its compatriots. Because this type of vessel had never been built in Rome before, they used it as a prototype, modelling their new fleet on its design. This much is believable, but Polybius' claim that 'without this accident, the whole enterprise would have been foiled from the start', is hyperbole.[41] Roman allies, such as Syracuse, had been building powerful warships for generations, and now that they had come into the Roman fold could have lent their expertise in this endeavour.[42]

The new Roman fleet, consisting of 100 quinqueremes and twenty triremes, was completed and trained in time for one of the consuls of 260 BC to take command of it. This was Gnaeus Cornelius Scipio. He had been put in command before the final preparations were made for each ship, but he wanted to begin moving them to what would be their base at Messana. He ordered the captains to sail straight there once their ships and crews were ready, himself taking the first seventeen ships ahead.

Scipio wanted to ensure that all of the fleet's needs would be met at their new home. While in port, however, the consul was made aware that Lipara, that important island-city between Sicily and central Italy, would be betrayed to him if he sailed thither. He did thus, but it turned out to be a poor decision.[43] Hannibal, whose fleet was anchored at Panormus, found out that the consul was making the journey, and sent a squadron of twenty ships, under the command of Boödes, a member of the Council of Elders, to stop the consul. Once the latter had sailed into the harbour at Lipara, Boödes' ships blockaded him in. Seeing that there was no escape, on the next day the Romans beached their ships and the crews fled inland. Scipio, however, surrendered to the Carthaginians, knowing that there was little hope of escape. Undoubtedly elated with the capture of a Roman consul, Boödes sailed back to Panormus, carrying with him both Scipio and the Roman ships.[44]

Hannibal almost let himself get captured in a similar way only days after this. Being aware of the new Roman threat from the sea, the Punic admiral wanted to scout it out and try to assess its strength. Thinking that they would be sailing towards Sicily in a haphazard, unorganized, fashion, he made carelessly for their position. What Hannibal and his ships found, however, was a well-organized, disciplined Roman fleet. A battle ensued in which most of the Carthaginian vessels were lost. Hannibal escaped, but Polybius makes it sound as though he was lucky to do so.[45]

The Roman fleet learned of what happened to Scipio once they reached Sicily. The remaining commanders informed Gaius Duilius, the other consul of the year and current commander of the land forces. He left command of the army to his tribunes and immediately set out for the fleet, where he took charge. Once settled in, Duilius heard that the Carthaginians were raiding the territory around Mylae, a town in north-eastern Sicily, thus not far from the Roman base in Messana. The consul resolved to sail against them, and ordered all of his ships to sea. When they were spotted by the enemy, Hannibal, their admiral, wasted no time in launching his entire fleet of 130 ships. At the head of this force was their leader, sailing in a 'seven' which had been captured from Pyrrhus. The Carthaginians held the Romans in contempt, believing that their inexperience in naval warfare meant they would be easily defeated. Those who survived would regret this conclusion.[46]

Unbeknown to their Punic foes, the Romans had installed an ingenious device on the prows of their ships to level the playing field, if not tip it in their favour. This was known as the *corvus*, or raven. The mechanism consisted of a long pole, at the top of which was a great spike, a gangplank, and a pulley system. It could pivot in place. When an enemy ship came into ramming range, the device would be dropped, with the spike piercing the planks of its deck, holding the two ships together. Roman soldiers, stationed aboard their ships, would then assault the enemy, making it something like a land battle, rather than one of naval skill and manoeuvring, although the latter were still required to some extent.[47]

The Punic fleet recklessly sped towards the Romans, not even keeping formation. Although their crews may have seen the ravens at the fronts of the enemy ships, they were not deterred, probably from not knowing exactly what they were. The lead ships of Hannibal's fleet made attacking runs at the Romans. When they got close enough, however, they found that their ships were now joined to the enemy's, not from a stubbornly stuck ram, but because of the *corvus*. The first thirty Punic ships were seized thusly, with much of their crews slaughtered, though with some surrendering. Amongst these vessels was Hannibal's flagship, the captured 'seven'. The admiral, however, had again escaped capture, this time by means of the great ship's smaller tender boat. The next wave saw what had happened to the lead ships, and attempted to manoeuvre to the sides and aft of the Roman ships, so as to avoid the new weapon. They were no more successful than their predecessors; the Romans simply swung their device to meet the enemy ships whence they attacked. A further twenty Punic ships were lost in this way, after which time their fleet broke off and retreated.[48] Duilius was awarded the first naval triumph in Roman history because of this victory, and was accorded a number of other honours, such as being proceeded by a flute player whenever he returned home from dinner, and being led always by a torch bearer.[49] Two columns were setup in honour of his victory, one in the Forum and one, perhaps, at the Circus Maximus. The column in the Forum was inscribed with a description of Duilius' deeds, and an Augustan-era version of the text survives:

> As consul, he freed the Segestans – allies of the Roman people – from the Carthaginian siege, and all the Carthaginian legions and

(their) highest official, by daylight, openly, after nine days fled from their camp. And the town of Macella he captured in battle. And in the same magistracy he was the first consul to successfully wage war in ships at sea; crews and fleets of warships he was the first to equip and train; and with these ships the Punic fleets and likewise all the might hosts of the Carthaginians, with Hannibal – their dictator – present, he defeated in battle on the high seas. And by force he captured, with their crews, one septireme and thirty quinqueremes and triremes, and he sank thirteen ships.[50]

It has been suggested that the *corvus* was not as revolutionary, nor decisive, a weapon as Polybius makes it out to have been. One contention is that the Romans had recently won a naval battle, that off the southern coast of Italy in which Hannibal was almost captured, without the device. While this is an important point to remember, the lack of details about that battle make it hard to use it as definitive proof that the Romans did not need the *corvus* to better the Carthaginians. We hear that the Punic fleet was not expecting an organized Roman fleet, but rather a steady stream of ships sailing with little structure. This was not the case, and thus may partly explain the Roman victory. We also know nothing of the number of Roman ships involved. Hannibal, only looking to scout out the enemy's strength, had fifty ships with him, while he may have encountered the 100 or so Roman ships currently making their way towards Messana. It is important to remember, though, that boarding was not a new tactic developed by the Romans and only done using the *corvus*. Grappling hooks and more mundane bridges were used by other navies of the period. Nevertheless, the Roman invention itself was new to the scene, and its capabilities compared to traditional methods of grappling, may have been different enough to instil fear in the Carthaginian sailors.[51]

Having come out victorious in their first major naval battle, the Romans turned their attention back to the land-war on Sicily.[52] While Duilius was at sea, Hamilcar had besieged the greater portion of his infantry in Segesta. A relieving force, led by the military tribune Gaius Caecilius, was ambushed on their way to the city, suffering heavy casualties. Making landfall, the consul finally took command of a large force of infantry and marched towards Segesta. Here, he relieved the besieged and drove off Hamilcar, the latter unwilling to risk a battle. On his march back from

Segesta, Duilius stormed and captured the town of Macella.[53] During this time, a Roman force may also have been besieging Mytistratus, though they were unsuccessful and suffered heavy losses.[54] This was the first of two Carthaginian victories of this year. The second came at Thermae. Hamilcar had heard that there was trouble brewing between the Romans and their allies, which centred around who deserved what honours in the battles they had fought. This disagreement led to the allies creating a second camp, separate from that of the Romans. The Carthaginian general, sensing that this was the perfect moment to strike, launched a massive attack at the camp, situated between Paropus and the hot springs near Himera. Hamilcar's army descended upon the enemy camp with tenacity, slaughtering as many as 4,000 soldiers.[55] He then made ready for the winter lull, fortifying Drepanum and demolishing Eryx so that it could not be used against him. He also campaigned further with his army as far as Camarina and Enna.[56]

The expedition to Sardinia was led by Lucius Cornelius Scipio, one of the consuls of 259 BC. He fought successfully against the Sardinians, Corsicans, and the Punic general Hanno.[57] His epitaph read: 'hec cepit Corsica Aleriaque urbe / dedet Tempestatebus aide meretod (he took Corsica and the city of Aleria / he gave a shrine to the Tempestates in just requital).[58] On Sicily, Hamilcar's advance had slowed, perhaps because of the efforts of Caius Aquilius Florus, Lucius Cornelius' colleague, whose command was held through the winter until the arrival of the new consul, Aulus Atilius Caiatinus, and his army. They launched an assault against the territories which Hamilcar had captured in his recent campaign, retaking Camarina and Enna. They attempted to attack Panormus, where the Carthaginian army was wintering, but Hamilcar refused to give battle. The Romans also blockaded Lipara.[59] The reversal of the Punic offensive was enough that Aquilius was awarded a triumph for 258 BC as proconsul. While Atilius was campaigning with the proconsul in Sicily, the other consul, Caius Sulpicius Patercultus, sailed to Sardinia where he was to lead a successful naval war against the Carthaginians. Hannibal, the admiral who failed at Mylae, had sailed for Sardinia as well, somehow escaping punishment for his defeat. Sulpicius defeated him off Sulci, in south-west Sardinia. Hannibal then allowed what was left of his fleet to be blockaded in their port by the Romans, many of their ships captured or destroyed, his sailors had finally had enough and they crucified him.[60]

The following year, 257 BC, saw fewer engagements than the previous, but witnessed even more Roman victories. Campaigning against Sardinia was abandoned, but naval manoeuvres were again the highlights. The consul Gaius Atilius Regulus intended to sail against Lipara, but found the Carthaginian fleet near the Cape of Tyndaris, on northern Sicily. The Romans set a trap for Hamilcar's fleet, in which they separated their ships into two groups. One squadron was sent forward to draw out the Punic ships, bait which they took, thinking that they were up against a relatively small enemy as it consisted only of ten vessels. The Punic ships encircled them, sinking all but Regulus' flagship. As soon as the second Roman squadron caught sight of them, they sailed towards their comrades. This ended in another defeat for Carthage, and Hamilcar was forced back to Lipara. The Romans captured ten ships with their crews, and sank another eight.[61] This naval victory helped open the door to a major change in strategy for the Romans and a much more dangerous war for the Carthaginians.

The Invasion of Africa

Carthaginian raiders had been harassing the Italian coast for much of the war. Perhaps this inspired the Romans' next move, or maybe some historically conscious senator knew of Agathocles' bold action in 310 BC. The motivation could have simply been that little was being accomplished on Sicily now, and the Romans thought that by taking the fight to Africa they would accomplish more against the enemy than they would in any of the islands. In preparation for the invasion of Libya, Rome built a massive transport fleet and recruited a huge army. According to Polybius, it consisted of 140,000 men and 330 quinqueremes. Each ship was crewed by 300 rowers and carried a complement of 120 marines. Dexter Hoyos has made a striking comparison, saying that this force was 'proportionate to population, [larger] than the forces crossing [the English Channel] on D-Day'.[62] Opposing this armada was a Carthaginian fleet numbering 350 ships and containing 150,000 men.[63] Although some scholars have doubted the number of ships which would participate in the invasion and the Battle of Ecnomus, fought before the Romans landed in Africa, there is no substantial evidence to argue this. Based on the ships Rome had before the invasion, they would have only had to build 100–200 new ships. Considering they had built 120 in the first year of maintaining a substantial navy, this was not insurmountable.[64]

With their ships ready, the Roman fleet set sail for Sicily, stopping first at Messana and then moving on to Pintias, near Ecnomus, in southern Sicily. This was where their land-forces were mustering. The Carthaginians sailed to Lilybaeum and then moved their fleet and other armaments to Heraclea Minoa, also in the south of the island. At the head of this was Hamilcar, his defeat at Tyndaris apparently not egregious enough for him to lose command. When the Romans put to sea from their mustering area, there must have been considerable anxiety, as they did not know what the Carthaginian response to their fleet would be, or, indeed, if there would be any response at all. Anticipating that they would face opposition at sea, the consuls, Marcus Atilius Regulus and Lucius Manlius Vulso, arranged their ships in an interesting formation. Each consul was aboard a 'six,' and these two ships were at the vanguard. The rest of their forces were arranged into four different squadrons. The First and Second Squadrons were arrayed to form a wedge shape, with the consular flagships forming the point. This wedge consisted of single, angled, lines of vessels extending back from its head, with a hollow middle. The Third Squadron, whose ships were towing the horse transports, formed as a line connecting the First and Second Squadrons. Thus, together these three groups formed a triangle. Behind this was the Fourth Squadron, arrayed in a straight line, but extending beyond the ends of the wedge in front of them.

Hamilcar's fleet had also launched, and his strategy was to try to stop the Romans from making it to Africa by forcing a battle at sea, just what the consuls had prepared for. After an invigorating pep-talk, the Carthaginians sailed towards their prey. When Hamilcar and the other leaders saw the Roman formation, they devised their own to try and counter it. In a line, one ship deep, they arrayed three-quarters of their fleet at a ninety degree angle from the shore. The first quarter of the line towards the shore, however, were angled outward, forming an obtuse angle to the rest of the fleet. They all faced the enemy straight on, prows pointing towards the Roman wedge. At the rightmost extreme of their line was Hanno, who had been defeated at Akragas, in command of both standard warships as well as a number of exceptionally fast quinqueremes who were to attempt to outflank the enemy. Hamilcar himself was somewhere near the middle of the line, though in command of the entire left wing. With their pieces set, the admirals joined battle.

The Punic strategy was the first to make an impact. As the Romans sailed towards their line of battle, the vanguard was positioned near its middle. As the consuls and their First and Second Squadrons approached, Hamilcar gave a signal from his ship and his middle collapsed, retreating at speed. The Romans, falling into the trap, pursued the fleeing ships rapidly, which caused a gap to form between them and the Third and Fourth Squadrons. When this gap grew large enough, Hamilcar sent another signal to his ships, ordering them to turn on their pursuers. They bore down on the Romans with ferocity, leading to a sharp engagement. Unlike in previous battles, the Carthaginians took full advantage of the extra speed their ships possessed to engage and disengage the Romans. This hit-and-run strategy worked to an extent, but their opponents were still using the *corvus* to great effect. With the Roman wedge now occupied with intense fighting, Hanno took his fast squadron and attacked the Roman's Fourth Squadron. The Carthaginians initially met with success against this line, who were presumably unprepared to face such an effective and quick flanking force. Meanwhile, in the middle of the Punic line, Hamilcar was forced to retreat after suffering considerable losses. Victorious, the consuls and their squadrons began to secure the ships they had captured for tow. Regulus, seeing the deteriorating situation of the Fourth Squadron, ordered his remaining ships to sail to their aid. As soon as the consul's ships reached them, they pounced on Hanno. Seeing their allies joining in with them, the Fourth began to fight with a renewed vigour. The Carthaginians were now fighting to their front and to their rear, a dire situation for any force, let alone one which had been engaged in battle for some time. With their opponents reinforced and re-energized, Hanno's squadron was forced to retreat out to open sea. The Roman Third Squadron had been engaged by the Punic left wing. They cut the horse transports loose, and fought bitterly against their foes. The Carthaginians here had got the upper hand, and the ships of the Third Squadron were pinned against the land. By pushing them so close to shore, however, the Punic ships made an error. This limited potential manoeuvring space, and made the Carthaginian captains afraid of trying to ram their opponents. The chief concern was the *corvus*, which in tight quarters had proved so deadly. Both consuls now rounded on this part of the battlefield, surrounding the Punic ships who had encircled the Roman Third Squadron. Most of these were captured with their crews intact, leading to the loss of an additional fifty ships from Hamilcar's once mighty fleet. Some managed to escape from this group, though few.[65]

This was the end of one of the greatest naval battles in history, and it was a resounding success for the Romans.[66] In total, they sank thirty Carthaginian ships, and captured an additional sixty-four. Conversely, the Punic fleet only lost twenty-four ships sunk. This striking victory was shadowed by the damage done to the Roman ships. Despite not losing many ships, those which survived and were captured had to sail back to Messana for repairs and supplies. Their crews were also given liberty to celebrate the victory 'as they deserved.' They then set sail again for Libya. This time, though, the Romans found no opposition in the seas south of Sicily. This is one of the most interesting 'non-events' in the history of ancient warfare, to use the phrase of Dexter Hoyos.[67] As the Carthaginians were afforded the same amount of time to repair and resupply their fleet as the Romans, it is surprising that they did not again try to stop the Romans from crossing.[68]

An advanced squadron was the first to reach the African coast, rounding Cape Bon. There they waited for the rest of the fleet. Once reunited, all of the Romans ships sailed on and made landfall at Aspis, the same harbour which had been fortified by Agathocles. It was known to the Romans as Clupea. The Romans assaulted the town, whose defenders put up a stiff resistance. Eventually, though, the besiegers were victorious and the Romans were now in possession of a good harbour in North Africa. Meanwhile, the Carthaginian fleet and army arrived in Carthage and made the government aware of the situation. Their initial reaction was to bolster the defences of their city, but as soon as they learned of the siege of Aspis they abandoned their sea defences in favour of those guarding the landward side.[69]

Now that they had established a foothold in Libya, the consuls were unsure of what to do. Their only actions were to raid the nearby countryside and small settlements, capturing a considerable amount of wealth, as well as freeing many of their troops who had been taken prisoner earlier in the war by the Carthaginians. Amongst their plunder were some 20,000 captives. They then sent messengers to Rome to inform the Senate of their victories and to ask for instruction on what to do next. This was an irregular move, as consuls were imbued with *imperium*, giving them the right to command in the field as they saw fit. One thing is clear, there had been no clear plan worked out before they left and reached Africa.[70] It is possible that the consuls were ordered to consult the Senate before proceeding, perhaps because of the enormity of the affair. Alternatively, there may have been a disagreement between the two consuls on what to do, which led them to seek advice from the Senate. The only support for this latter theory is that once word came back to Africa, Manlius was recalled to Rome with part of the army, most of the fleet, and all of the captives. This is still not conclusive, though. This left Regulus in sole command in the theatre with 15,000 infantry, 500 cavalry, and forty ships.[71]

The delay in acting against Carthage itself caused by Roman consternation allowed the defenders to organize a defence. As when Agathocles invaded in 310 BC, the Punic response was to recruit several generals. These were Hasdrubal the son of Hanno and Bostar. Hamilcar was also recalled from Sicily, bringing with him 5,000 infantry and 500 cavalry. He was then appointed as a general. Hamilcar and Hasdrubal quickly decided on a plan of action, and set out to protect Punic possessions in Africa. Their objective was to stop the Romans from running rampant over their lands and continuing to plunder. It is unclear whether Bostar objected to this plan, but Polybius explicitly mentions only those two named above.[72]

With his colleague now gone, Regulus moved out of his base at Aspis and made inroads towards Carthage. He seized numerous unfortified settlements on his march, besieging those which were fortified. The first major siege, however, came when they reached Adys, perhaps Uthina, modern Oudna, which is only 50km south of Carthage.[73] It was here that the Punic triumvirate decided to confront Regulus. They marched their army out, and encamped on a tall ridge once they reached the town. Although it gave them a clear view of the surroundings, the hilltop lacked resources, probably meaning water. As their army was strong in both cavalry and elephants, their choice of camp locations was poorly made.[74] A fear of the Roman infantry in the plains, however, may have influenced their choice.[75] The strategy being employed, however, was similar to that used by Hanno outside of Akragas: camp on a nearby hill and wait until you feel that you have a tactical advantage before attacking.[76] While they sat idle, Regulus decided to make the first move. Polybius attributes this to Roman commanders (a vague term is used) who realized that the terrain the Carthaginians chose to camp upon made their most powerful divisions useless. This sounds very much like hindsight and, without a spy in the Punic camp, it is unclear how Regulus and his war council would have known the exact consistency of their enemies' army. Regardless, the consul decided to attack the Punic camp. He split his forces, ordering one half to march around the hill, allowing him to attack the Carthaginians from both sides. The force coming straight from the Roman camp made contact first, and was confronted by a strong sally from the Punic mercenaries. Their resolve was strong enough to repulse the assault by what Polybius calls the First Legion. Fortuitously for Regulus and his men, the troops he sent around the hill (perhaps the Second Legion?) reached the top of the hill and began attacking the camp and the mercenaries from behind. This resulted in the Carthaginian army routing, with the cavalry and elephants making a break for flat ground and quickly fleeing. The infantry was less fortunate, being pursued by the Roman legionaries for some distance. Eventually, however, the victors broke off their chase and looted the Carthaginian camp.[77]

Now in command of Adys, Regulus was able to overrun much of the surrounding territory. Importantly, he took control of Tunis, that enigmatic city which proved to be such a good base for any hostile army in Carthaginian territory. This positioned the Romans as a threat to Carthage itself, a situation that could not have been ignored within the city. Regulus knocking at their gates was not their only problem, however. Perhaps emboldened by the presence of the Romans, or perhaps a flare up of an existing hostility, groups of Numidians attacked Punic lands, doing more damage to the farmland than the Romans had. These two hostile forces drove many people from the countryside into Carthage, threatening their supplies in case of a siege.[78]

At this point, terms were sought; by whom it is unclear. Polybius says that Regulus was the first to offer negotiations, fearing that his consulship was nearing its end and that his replacement would be able to claim all the glory of the African campaign.[79] Our other sources, however, claim that it was the Carthaginians, due to their dire situation, who sought peace.[80] Both of these are plausible. If Regulus was afraid of not getting credit for his achievements, he would not be the only Roman commander to seek a negotiated peace. This was done by figures such as Tiberius Sempronius Longus in 218 BC and Titus Quinctius Flaminius in 198–197 BC.[81] If this was the case, however, why would he offer such harsh terms that the Carthaginians were not able to accept them? On the other hand, with the Romans in Tunis and the Numidians rebelling, their fleet and army having both suffered defeats, the Carthaginians were likely to be wanting a way out of the war with Rome. The fact that all of our sources agree that the terms were too harsh to be accepted leads me to believe that it was Carthage who sent out peace feelers, though Regulus may have genuinely been open to them, so long as he was able to humiliate his enemy.[82] Even if he was concerned with his replacement being the one to end the war in a victory, a patriotic flame inside of him may have prevented acceptance of less than total surrender of Carthage.[83] It could be that the consul was trying to treat Carthage as if it was 'some small Italian community', rather than the major power that it was.[84] We must also remember that the Carthaginians had been in a similar predicament when Agathocles invaded Libya, and they were unwilling then to seek a peace, so we should not be altogether surprised that whatever terms were offered were disagreeable to them. As had happened during that invasion, a renewed piety took over the city, and sacrifices which had lapsed in their performance were renewed.[85]

Before Regulus had made his way into the Punic heartland, the Carthaginians had sent recruiters to Greece, looking to bolster their army with fresh recruits. Amongst those whom they brought back was Xanthippus, a Spartan commander who brought with him perhaps fifty or 100 troops.[86] How many other Greeks came into Africa we cannot know.[87] What is clear, however, is that Xanthippus was given command of the Punic forces after having vehemently criticized their tactics at Adys. Once in a leadership role, the Spartan began to drill the army, taking care to instruct them as both a complete force as well as in smaller units. His air of professionalism inspired the soldiers now under his command. After they were ready, the Punic generals and Xanthippus led the army out towards Regulus. This force consisted of 12,000 infantry, 4,000 cavalry, and around 100 elephants.[88]

Unlike in the previous engagements of the war, the Carthaginian army stuck to the plains. This frightened the Romans and made them carefully think about their next move. Regulus was still amenable to an offensive strategy. Once aggression was settled upon, the Romans encamped ten stades from the camp of the Carthaginians. Although Regulus was willing to be the aggressor, it was the Punic army who marched out first. This was done at the urging of the soldiers, whose enthusiasm was brimming to the point that they formed into their units even before the orders were given. Xanthippus was at the front of the crowd, urging the Carthaginian generals who seemed to still be in charge of major decisions, to engage the Romans. When they marched out of their camp, Xanthippus ordered them to form into a different formation than they had used in previous battles. At the front was a line of elephants. Behind this in the centre was the phalanx of Carthaginian citizens. A group of mercenaries took up a position on the phalanx's right wing. Protecting both wings of the infantry were the cavalry and the most mobile of the mercenary troops.[89]

Seeing the enemy arraying themselves before him, Regulus was happy to meet their challenge. He decided to alter the usual deployment of the army, with his chief concern being the elephants who would be the first enemies to hit the Roman lines. Polybius tells us that to do this, Regulus stationed his *velites*, or skirmishers, in front of the rest of the army. Their missiles may be enough to disrupt the elephants' advance and possibly even throw them into a panic. The legionary infantry were behind them, arrayed in a deeper formation than usual.[90] The typical Roman army of the period deployed in the *triplex acies*. This was a formation of three lines of smaller units, called maniples. Each line was manned by different types of soldiers. The first being the *hastate*, the youngest soldiers, armed with shield and sword, as well as two *pila*, heavy javelins. The next line, the *principes*, carried similar equipment, but were combat veterans. The final line, the *triarii*, were the most experienced veterans and armed with shields and spears. The idea was that each line would engage the enemy, strategically falling back if they were unable to break them and suffered losses. Once the *triarii* had been engaged, however, it was a desperate fight. The small units called maniples consisted of 120 men. Thus, it is unclear what exactly Polybius or his source envisioned when he wrote that Regulus deployed his infantry 'many maniples deep'. Adrian Goldsworthy has proposed a plausible solution, that the army was formed up in three lines, as usual, but that each maniple was deployed with deeper ranks than usual and that the usual gaps between them were eliminated. This would prevent soldiers in the front ranks from breaking at the sight and impact of the elephants, the primary concern.[91]

Thusly deployed, Regulus' army had a smaller front than usual, but was much deeper. Polybius believed that this was a good formation with which to face elephants. It was, however, in his opinion the wrong formation for combating the Punic cavalry, which outnumbered that of the Romans eight to one. The two armies, now in formation, stared each other down for some time, waiting for the opportune moment to make the first move. Xanthippus gave the first order, which was for his elephants to charge the Roman line and for the cavalry to engage the enemy horse. As they did this, Regulus gave the order to charge forward, the Romans yelling their battle-cries. Quickly, the Carthaginian cavalry overwhelmed their opponents, leaving the flanks of their army exposed. The Roman infantry on the left was finding success against the Carthaginian right, routing the mercenaries who appear to not have had elephant coverage. The centre of Regulus' line, however, was collapsing under the weight of the elephants. All that kept the Roman infantry on the field was the depth of their formation, as the first rank was almost wiped out, with the thrashing elephants crushing countless men beneath their great mass. It was not until the Punic cavalry completed its encirclement that the Roman infantry totally broke down. Attacked in the front by the great grey beasts, and in the rear by skilled horsemen, some of the legionaries forced their way forward. Once making it past the line of elephants, however, they found their doom at the points of the Carthaginian phalanx's spears. The citizen troops were fresh and ready to receive the enemy, whom they cut down readily. A continual rain of javelins from the cavalry, the furious stamping of the elephants, and the deadly iron of the phalanx's weapons broke down Regulus' army like a thresher breaks down wheat.[92]

Only 2,000 men from his army escaped the carnage. These were those who had been victorious on the left wing of the battle and driven the mercenaries from the field. In their pursuit of the enemy they found salvation, a minor victory in what was otherwise a complete disaster for the Romans. Miraculously, they made their way back to Aspis. Regulus and a number of others escaped death, but were taken prisoner. The Carthaginians, however, won one of the greatest victories in the history of their city. Only 800 of their troops were lost, most of them from amongst the mercenaries who routed on the right wing. This mostly intact army stripped the bodies of their slain enemies and took the loot, as well as the prisoners, back to Carthage.[93] With the victory in Africa secured, Xanthippus quickly sailed for home, with Polybius hinting at jealousy developing between the Punic leadership and the Spartan condottiero. As for Regulus, he was to die in captivity, most likely. Later myths about him eventually coalesced into a tale of torture and brutal execution at the hands of the Carthaginians, but as this is absent from Polybius it is almost certainly a fiction.[94] The purpose of the African campaign can never be perfectly known. If it was inspired by that of Agathocles, then it is striking that it ended in almost the same manner. It certainly took attention away from Sicily, though why this would have been necessary is unclear. The idea may have been based in Rome's experiences in conquering the parts of Italy that they had up to this point. In these wars, their armies were threatening the home-cities of their enemies, whether this was Veii or Tarentum, and the Romans had always come out on top in the end. Perhaps someone, or a party, within the leadership thought that taking the fight to Carthage itself would have a similar result. The recall of one of the consular armies, though, cannot be reconciled if the purpose was to force a conclusion to the war on Libyan soil. It is likely that Regulus had been given the power to negotiate a peace, and it was perhaps the Senate's harsh terms which he had relayed to the Carthaginians. Regardless of its original purpose, the African campaign was a failure.

Word of the defeat reached Rome, where it was decided to outfit a new fleet and rescue the survivors who were now under siege in Aspis. Both consuls of the year (255 BC), Servius Fulvius Paetinus Nobilior and Marcus Aemilius Paullus, sailed with the fleet. It consisted of 350 ships, a formidable armada. Although they had originally set out to sail straight for Africa, a storm blew them off course to Cossura, a small island between Sicily and their destination. Evidently it was under Punic control, as the consuls plundered the island and installed a garrison and then went on their way.[95] In Africa, even before this evacuation force reached Libya, the remnants of Regulus' army had beaten back their besiegers and driven them away from their fortress-town. The Carthaginians, either aware of or suspicious of Roman ships sailing towards Africa, began putting together a new fleet of their own. They were only able to launch 200 ships, but they stood watch throughout the seas between Sicily and Libya diligently. Once the Roman fleet had rounded Sicily and made its way to Cape Bon, the enemy had spotted them. What ensued was a bitter naval battle, though we hear of no details. The Carthaginians were again defeated at sea, suffering from 114 of their ships and crews being captured. Although our sources are not explicit, this number of ships being taken sounds as though the *corvus* was again put to good use. Once they were dominant on the waves, the consuls pulled into Aspis and took onboard all of the survivors of Regulus' army.[96]

Haughty pride dominated the minds of Paetinus and Aemilius: they had just won a major victory over the Punic fleet and rescued as many as 2,000 of their countrymen and allies from eventual death in Africa. This drove them to want to gloat over their enemies. Thus, once the fleet crossed safely from Libya to Sicily, rather than sailing straight for Messana, they ordered their ships to turn westward, in order to sail past the many coastal communities who were still loyal to Carthage. Their hope was that by seeing a triumphant Roman fleet, they would be frightened into capitulating. This was done, however, against the warnings of some of the most skilled sailors and pilots the Romans had, who warned that it was a treacherous voyage, especially at this time of year, between the rising of Orion and Sirius (July 4–28). The worst predictions became a reality when, near Camarina, the fleet was tossed violently by a savage storm. Of the 364 ships that were sailing together, all but eighty of them sunk, being smashed into little more than flotsam by the breakers. As many as 100,000 lives may have been lost on that day, not to a skilful enemy, but by the uncaring wrath of nature.[97] Despite this disaster, both consuls were awarded naval triumphs over the Carthaginians, with Dexter Hoyos concluding that 'political influence trumped abominable seamanship.'[98]

A Return to Sicily

The victory led by Xanthippus, as well as the news of the Roman disaster at sea, sent Punic spirits soaring. A renewed determination to fight took over, and led to a new push. Their first move was to send Hasdrubal to Sicily as commander of their forces on the island.[99] On his way, though, he expelled the Roman garrison from Cossura. He made Lilybaeum his base of operations, but to him came the troops remaining at Heraclea Minoa. Spectacularly, he was sent to Sicily with 140 elephants; the success at the so-called Battle of Tunis against Regulus' infantry must have been ascribed, at least in part, to this division there. The other Punic commander on the island, Carthalo, had meanwhile launched a successful campaign against Akragas, taking the city, razing its walls, and burning the rest. Carthage also began rebuilding its fleet, making 200 ships seaworthy. Once all of the armaments had made their way to Lilybaeum, Hasdrubal began drilling his troops in the open, not trying to conceal his intentions for a fresh campaign on the island.[100] It was in this year, as well, that Hamilcar was sent into Numidia to campaign against those who rose against the Carthaginians during Regulus' invasion.[101]

The Romans, upon hearing of the destruction of their fleet, resolved to create a new one with freshly built ships numbering 220. Although surely a large task, these were built in only three months. When they were ready, the consuls of 254 BC, Aulus Atilius Caiatinus (consul also of 258) and Gnaeus Cornelius Scipio Asina (consul of 260 who was captured at Lipara), put to sea. Their first destination was Messana, where they connected with what was left of the old fleet, adding those vessels still seaworthy to theirs, bringing their total number of ships up to 300. They then went on to capture Cephaloedium and executed an aborted siege on Lilybaeum, which was quickly relieved by Carthalo. From here, they sailed to Panormus, one of the most important cities left under Punic control on Sicily. Their objective was to capture the city. They put it under siege, building siege engines and, certainly, blockading it from the sea with their massive fleet. Thanks to their engines, they brought down a large tower on the seaward side of the wall, probably the most prominent defensive position in that part of the fortifications. This hole allowed Roman troops to force their way into the city, and quickly overrun the defenders of the 'New Town'. Not long after, the defenders of 'Old Town' surrendered.[102] When this finally happened, the inhabitants were allowed to ransom themselves from slavery for two minae each; 14,000 people took advantage of this and were allowed to remain free, but 13,000 others were taken as slaves. A Roman garrison was left in the city, and the consuls retired back to Rome. In the wake of this victory, Iaetia expelled its Punic garrison, and Solus, Petra, Enattaros, and Tyndaris came over to the Romans, the people expelling what Carthaginian troops and overseers were in the midst. It is possible that the capture of Panormus and the later capitulation of these towns were due only to the efforts of

Scipio, who was the only one of the two consuls to be awarded a triumph over the Carthaginians for this campaign.[103]

The following year, 253 BC, saw a Roman return to Africa, but not in the form of a large-scale land invasion. Instead, they borrowed a strategy used by the Carthaginians early in the war: they raided their coast. The consuls, Gnaeus Servilius Caepio and Gaius Sempronius Blaesus, took the entire fleet, and presumably their armies, and sailed past Sicily to Libya.[104] They began to prey on the wealth close to the coasts throughout the Lesser Syrtis. Although they made many raids, Polybius did not recount any details of them as he viewed their outcome as 'nothing worth mentioning'. They ran aground on shoals near the island of Menix, thanks in part to an unexpectedly low tide, but surely also unfamiliarity with the area if not poor seamanship. As the tide rose again, their ships were still not floating, so they began to toss overboard much of the heavier cargo they were hauling. After this near-disaster, they sailed back to the now friendly port of Panormus. On their way here, they may have attacked Lilybaeum, but if they did nothing came of it. From here, the Romans sailed, perhaps through bad weather, at a clip back towards Italy. Again, their fleet was caught in a violent storm, this time destroying 150 of their ships. And, as with the consuls who evacuated Libya, Sempronius was given a triumph.[105]

The disasters at sea deterred the Romans from continuing their aggressive naval policy. Polybius, dramatically, says that they were driven 'to abandon their shipbuilding programme' and that all their hope now rode on their land armies. He also claimed that the Carthaginians were now 'undisputed masters of the sea'.[106] This, however, is demonstrably false. During the consulship of Caius Aurelius Cotta and Publius Servilius Geminus, 252 BC, the Romans were able to take Lipara, that important island naval base between Sicily and Italy. It was not an easy victory, with the Roman camp being burned at one point during the siege, and its temporary commander, the military tribune Publius Aurelius Pecuniola, was punished by scourging and being reduced to the rank of a common soldier. Another tribune, Quintus Cassius made the same mistake and was similarly punished.[107] This endeavour would have required naval dominance, otherwise the Carthaginians would have been able to raise the siege, or at least continually relieve the defenders of the city. During this year they also took Thermae on Sicily, but its inhabitants were evacuated to Lilybaeum before the city fell. Aurelius Cotta was awarded a triumph over the Carthaginians and the Sicilians, probably reflecting that Thermae was primarily perceived as a Sicilian city before its capture.[108]

Lucius Caecilius Metellus was the only consul to spend all of 251 BC in Sicily, with his colleague, Caius Furius Pacilus perhaps coming over but returning soon to Italy. Hasdrubal, whose army was prepared, or perhaps just arrived, launched a campaign directed at retaking Panormus. Here, he besieged Metellus, keeping him penned up within the city for a very long time. Although some commentators have frowned upon Metellus staying in Panormus, with Dexter Hoyos describing it as 'an inglorious posture', there may have been good reason for his strategy.[109] Hasdrubal's army supposedly numbered around 30,000 infantry and cavalry, in an unknown proportion, in addition to 130–140 elephants. This meant that his army was about 10,000 men stronger than a typical consular army. Metellus could have had allied contingents making his force larger than normal, but we do not know this for sure. If he knew that his army was smaller than the opponent's, and that the latter had a greater number of elephants than the army which destroyed Regulus, he may well have been right to force them into a siege. Again, as we have no evidence outside of Polybius' hyperbolic statement that the Carthaginians were in control of the sea, meaning that the Roman fleet could have kept him supplied in Panormus. Metellus also achieved an unstated goal: he protected other Roman possessions on Sicily by keeping Hasdrubal's attention on his well-fortified army. Biding his time within the walls of Panormus, the consul slowly formulated a plan by which he hoped to break the Carthaginian army. By waiting in the city, Metellus drew Hasdrubal close to him through a strategy of not defending the crops around Panormus. When the Carthaginian army crossed the river which ran close to the city, Metellus' plan started to unfold. He sent out skirmishers to harass the enemy until they were forced to close their ranks and form up tightly. As this began to happen, he sent fresh mobile troops armed with missiles to the area between the defensive ditch and the walls, these were to throw as many missiles at the elephants as they could. These skirmishers were continually reinforced by troops from inside the city. The consul himself was waiting with the heavy infantry at a gate in the walls which opened up on Hasdrubal's left flank. While he was waiting here, the elephants in the Punic army began breaking ranks and chasing down some of the skirmishers. By the time they reached the defensive ditch, they were under fire from both the skirmishers on the ground as well as archers stationed on the walls. This threw them into a panic and they turned and trampled men in their own army. Metellus had been waiting for this moment, and at seeing the havoc being caused by the crazed pachyderms he ordered his heavy infantry to charge from their hiding place. They crashed into Hasdrubal's line at an angle and easily broke the left wing of his army. This led to an all-out rout. Much of Hasdrubal's army was cut low, perhaps as many as 20,000.[110] The consul, however, offered to grant clemency to any of the enemy who would lay down their arms and help the Romans gain control over the elephants, which had started to run amok. 120 of these he took back to Rome and led in a victory parade. For this victory, Metellus was awarded a triumph. Hasdrubal, though he escaped the battle, was executed upon his return to Carthage.[111]

This was a major reversal of fortunes for Carthage when compared to the defeat of Regulus' army in Africa. Hasdrubal's attack would be remembered as the last land offensive that the Carthaginians launched during the war. It is also a worrying sign of the skills possessed by Punic commanders at this point that Hasdrubal was so easily lured into a trap such as that laid by Metellus. As damaging to Carthage as the loss of soldiers and elephants, this victory invigorated the Romans and gave them a new will to fight, even if their enthusiasm had not sunk quite as low as Polybius would like us to believe. The enthusiasm led to the Romans launching the largest fleet they had in almost three years, consisting of 200 ships. Aboard these vessels were both consuls, Caius Atilius Regulus and Lucius Manlius Vulso, with their armies. Their objective was to take Lilybaeum, probably the most important base on Sicily at this point in the war. According to Polybius, if this city fell the Romans would have been able to again invade Libya, a fact supposedly known to both sides.

Atilius and Manlius landed their armies and camped on opposite sides of Lilybaeum. Between the two camps they dug a trench, built a palisade, and threw up a wall. Their first move was against a tower in the wall which faced towards Libya. Against this they brought a number of siege works: catapults, rams, protective sields, and siege towers.[112] These appear to have been used as a distraction while the real work was being done undermining six different towers near it. All around the rest of the city's fortifications, the Romans brought rams against the walls. Towers were brought down daily, and the consuls were slowly making progress into the city. Undoubtedly, this caused fear to spread through the besieged. Along with the residents, there were 10,000 mercenaries, commanded by a Carthaginian, Himilco.[113] Rather than engaging in a static defence, he was ordering his men to constantly dig counter-mines and rebuild, or construct entirely new walls, in order to slow down the Romans' progress. He also launched sallies daily, in an attempt to burn the siege works which had been brought against the city. Already, the siege was becoming costly for both sides, their losses mounting.

Dissent was growing in the mercenary contingent inside Lilybaeum. A number of their leaders entered into a cabal to betray the city to the Romans. They believed, foolishly in the end, that their subordinates would follow them. The leaders of the conspiracy sneaked out of the city under the cover of darkness and made it into the Roman camp. Their treachery, however, did not go unnoticed amongst their compatriots, and an Achaean Greek by the name of Alexon broke the news to Himilco. Immediately, the Punic general called the remaining mercenary captains to a meeting, in which he pleaded with them not to go over to the enemy, offering them considerable rewards, and reminding them of their oaths. He also took the logical step of putting new men in charge of the different mercenary contingents. In charge of the Celts was now Hannibal, son of the Hannibal who was crucified by his troops on Sardinia earlier in the war. He had fought alongside them before, and was thus in a good position to lead them. Alexon was put in charge of the rest of the mercenaries, whose respect he had, perhaps meaning that they were mostly Greeks. These two men then gathered the troops whom they now commanded and announced the promises of Himilco, swearing that he would fulfil them. This was enough to guarantee the loyalty of the mercenaries. When the would-be traitors approached the walls, bringing terms from the Romans, the defenders would not listen to them, and instead threw rocks and missiles at them, driving them away from the city. The duplicitous rumblings had thus been eliminated.[114]

In Carthage, a relief effort was organized for Lilybaeum. Fifty ships were loaded with supplies and fresh mercenaries. The commander of this expedition was named Adherbal, under him was an admiral named Hannibal, who was the son of the Hamilcar who had commanded at Ecnomus and Adys, and was currently campaigning against the Numidians.[115] They sailed first for the Aegates Islands, which sit between Carthage and Lilybaeum. This was to be their base of operations as they planned how to bring their supplies and reinforcements into the beleaguered city. Besides a storm which forced them to wait a while, the Romans had attempted to block off access to the harbour by scuttling a number of small vessels at its entrance. This was done in haste and, as a strong wind came up as they were trying to sink the vessels, they did not completely block up the harbour. Rather than sailing in himself, Adherbal sent Hannibal. His ships caught a strong wind and raced into the harbour. The Roman ships which were at sea were surprised by this act of daring and were unable to, or purposefully did not, react. Hannibal brought as many as 10,000 additional soldiers into the city, though it may have been as few as 4,000. The arrival of fresh troops, and aid (even if it is denied by Polybius), raised the morale of the defenders.[116]

With new troops and his veterans' morale raised, Himilco decided to attempt a forceful sally against the Roman siege works. At a general meeting of his soldiers, he told them of his plans and gave detailed instructions to each unit. Prizes and rewards were offered for acts of individual bravery which worked them into a fury, and reminded them of the great rewards which they would all share if the city held. After this speech, Himilco dismissed the troops, telling them to rest for now and wait for orders from their officers. These he called into a meeting after speaking to the army as a whole, where he assigned tasks and set the watchword. His instructions were to muster their men at the beginning of the morning watch. They sallied forth at first light, attacking the siege works at a number of places. Expecting to find the Romans unprepared, Himilco was disappointed. Somehow they had known of the coming attack, or perhaps were simply always on guard, but the consuls were prepared to receive the Carthaginian assault. Although as many as 20,000 armed men participated in the sally, they could not overcome the enemy. The fighting was fierce, and unlike a typical pitched battle. The broken ground and countless obstacles, consisting of the siege equipment and the partially destroyed fortifications, forced both armies to fight in small groups. In places the melee resembled a series of single combats. The most intense struggles were happening around the siege engines. Some of the Carthaginian troops who were sent out with torches came close to setting these alight, but to no avail. The Romans were able to defend most of them. As the dead began to pile up, the ground undoubtedly soggy with blood, Himilco sounded the retreat, realizing that he could not lose too many men and still defend the city.[117]

The night after this battle, Hannibal slipped out of the harbour with his ships and sailed to Drepana, where he met Adherbal. They were to now use this well fortified city as their base. Now, however, no news was coming out of Lilybaeum. The Carthaginian leadership back home wanted to know what was happening. A man known as Hannibal the Rhodian, an eminent Carthaginian, volunteered to sail into the harbour and bring back news. The Roman fleet had now closed their blockade tightly, so it was unclear how he planned to do this. Unbeknownst to most, he possessed a well-built ship with an excellent crew, which could outrun most opponents. He sailed from Carthage and, arriving on the coast of Sicily, made a run for the harbour at the fourth hour. The Romans were stunned and were not able to respond in time to stop this single ship. Hannibal spent the night in the city, gathering intelligence on the situation, and decided to leave the next day. The Romans (specifically an unnamed consul) were ready for him to try and leave. They stationed ten of their fastest ships on either side of the harbour's mouth, all of them with their oars deployed in order to stop the blockade runner. The Rhodian, however, proved the quality of his ship and the training of his men by sailing straight past the Roman ships. Having accomplished this feat, he often repeated it in order to keep the Carthaginians informed of what was going on inside Lilybaeum, as well as keep them apprised of the needs of the defenders.[118]

While the fighting around Lilybaeum raged, other Carthaginian forces were striking at the Romans. Cavalry, some of whom had been transferred from the besieged city, ranged out of Drepana in an effort to prevent the Romans from foraging for supplies. They also ran rampant through the territories of the allies. Adherbal, with the fleet, was often raiding the coasts of Sicily that were under Roman control as well as Italy. They seemed to have no counter to these depredations, though the raising of a fleet in the coming year may have been to protect their coastal lands.[119]

Now that Hannibal the Rhodian had set a precedent that the harbour of Lilybaeum was not impregnable, others followed his example. The blockade runners continued to supply the city and keep it connected to the wider Punic world. The Romans again tried to block off the mouth of the harbour, this time by dumping rubble, but to no avail. The water was too deep. They managed to create a small barrier at a shallow spot, though this was still not enough to completely close off the city from the outside. Fortuitously for the Romans, though, a well-built quadrireme ran aground at this spot, allowing them to capture it. They refloated it and manned it with a handpicked crew. Although they were to guard against all blockade runners, their primary target was the Rhodian. On the captured quadrireme's first night on guard, Hannibal happened to be making a run for the harbour. When he made to leave the next morning, the Romans launched their new weapon at the same time as he launched his ship. The smaller ship overtook his, and a strong boarding party sealed his fate. Hannibal the Rhodian and his fast quinquereme were captured. With these two ships now in their possession, the Romans were able to prevent the blockade runners from operating.[120]

Punic hopes were now at the lowest point since the siege began. They were now cut off by both sea and land, though their compatriots on the outside were still trying to harass the Romans. The defenders inside Lilybaeum had stopped making sorties against the siege works, having lost too many men in Himilco's failed attempt to drive the enemy off. One day a strong windstorm developed, blowing from the city towards the besiegers. Some of the Greek mercenaries approached Himilco with a plan to use the wind to their advantage and start an inferno which would destroy the Roman siege equipment. The commander agreed to their plan and provided them with everything that they needed. The mercenaries massed at three points and then launched their assault, using fires and brands. As the engines had been in use for so long, the wood out of which they were built was very dry and susceptible to the attackers' incendiaries. With the wind blowing strongly back into the faces of the Romans, they were unable to protect their siege equipment. Some of those who ran towards the flames were suffocated by the thick smoke bellowing off what was quickly becoming an inferno. In addition to the fire and the smoke it caused, Himilco's troops were raining missiles down upon their enemies, killing many and ensuring that their attack on the engines would be effective. Eventually the Romans were forced to give up their efforts. When the smoke cleared, their towers were burnt down and their rams had been rendered useless. With their fortunes falling, the besiegers abandoned their attempts to breach the city and bolstered their landward defences, in hope of starving out the Carthaginians.[121]

As the siege progressed, the Romans began running low on supplies. The Carthaginian cavalry at Drepana was doing its job well. Disease also began to spread throughout their camp, as was likely to happen during ancient sieges. To their rescue came Hiero, who found ways to bring them grain.[122] The Senate had been kept apprised of what was happening at Lilybaeum and that many of the casualties being suffered were rowers from the fleet who were participating in the siege. They recruited 10,000 men to reinforce the crews and sent them to Sicily with the newly elected consul, Publius Claudius Pulcher. He was forced to march south through Italy to the Straights, cross to Messana, and march across Sicily. This is evidence for the effect that the roving Punic fleet was having and the threat that it posed from its base at Drepana.

Upon his arrival at Lilybaeum, Claudius Pulcher decided on a new strategy. He summoned all of the military tribunes to a meeting and announced his plan. Rather than only concentrating on the siege, he wanted to launch an attack against Drepana; this would relieve some of the pressure on the camps at Lilybaeum by eliminating the Punic cavalry's safe haven. The loss of Drepana would also greatly hinder the Carthaginians' ability to bring reinforcements to the island.

With the tribunes agreeing to his plan, Claudius Pulcher ordered that the crews man the ships. He then handpicked the best soldiers from the besieging army to serve as marines. Many of them accepted this new duty voluntarily, thinking that it would be a quick campaign in which they would be able to plunder considerable booty, because the newly arrived consul had convinced them that Adherbal had neglected his defences and that the city would be easily taken. Claudius Pulcher launched his ships, which numbered around 120, in the middle of the night and sailed in a tight formation.[123] His van reached Drepana as the sun dawned and could be seen by the defenders. After a momentary hesitation, Adherbal collected his men, delivered a speech encourarging them to seek battle rather than allow themselves to be besieged. They then manned the ships, the crews taking up their oars and the mercenaries acting as marines. The Carthaginian commander's ship was the first to depart, the others following. They sailed out of the harbour on the opposite side from which the Romans were entering it.[124]

Seeing that the enemy was leaving the harbour, Claudius Pulcher ordered his ships to turn around and head back towards the mouth of the harbour so as not to be trapped within it.[125] This caused chaos all along his line, as friendly ships ran into one another, snapping oars and making tempers flare. As the Romans were attempting to turn back out towards the open sea, Adherbal was leading his ships out and around them. He took five of his ships past the Roman's new left wing, which had recently been their rear. Turning these ships to point towards the enemy, the rest of his fleet began to arrive and took up similar positions until they were all positioned with their prows pointing towards the Roman fleet. Claudius Pulcher and his men were now in a very precarious position: they were pinned between the Punic fleet and the shore, the latter of which they sat dangerously close to. Once all of his ships were in position, Adherbal gave the signal for attack and battle was joined. The Carthaginians took full advantage of their enemy's poor positioning. When attacking, they were able to force Roman ships to fight as they had no room to manoeuvre to the rear. Some of them were driven into the shallows or driven ashore. If forced to fall back, the Punic captains could flee towards open sea then quickly turn around and engage the enemy from preferable angles, such as from the side or, if they could sail past them, the rear. Polybius also attributes much of the victory to the skill of the Carthaginian crews, compared to the lack thereof amongst the Romans. This is understandable, as many of Claudius Pulcher's crews must have been made up of the 10,000 reinforcements he had just brought into the theatre. As the fighting continued, the consul eventually lost hope and realized that the battle was lost. He was able to beat a quick retreat, with a total of thirty of his ships escaping. The Carthaginians captured the rest, which amounted to ninety-three. Not only were the ships lost, but 20,000 men were either killed or fell into Punic hands as a result of Claudius Pulcher's failed assault.[126]

This was the greatest naval victory Carthage won during the war, and the only major engagement at sea which went their way. Diodorus went so far as to write 'it would not be easy to discover a fierce fight at sea followed by a more glorious victory in this period – no comparable victory, I mean, for anyone, not merely for the Carthaginians.'[127] For the

Romans, this setback was later attributed to Claudius Pulcher's impiety and ignoring the auspices, as it was said that the sacred chickens would not eat, thus meaning that the gods did not give their blessing to the endeavour. Outraged, and determined to launch his attack regardless of the birds' lack of appetite, he threw them into the sea saying 'if they won't eat, let them drink.'[128] It is possible that he had ignored the divine sign, but the elaborate story is certainly a later fabrication.[129] What is more obvious, is that the Romans had abandoned the *corvus* by this battle. It is typically assumed that this was a result of the major losses their fleets experienced in the storms of 255 and 253 BC. The logic is that they made the ships unsteady in turbulent seas, and there is no good reason to reject this. The Battle of Drepana, though, may have made them regret this removal. Adherbal received high praise in Carthage for his victory. He sent to the city those Roman ships which he had captured, as well as the prisoners he had taken. Carthalo then came to join him in Drepana. The former brought with him seventy ships, to which were now added thirty, and he was given a specific assignment. He was to raid the Roman blockade at Lilybaeum and try to destroy or capture as many of their ships as he could.[130] Similarly, Adherbal ordered his admiral, Hannibal, to make a raid upon the Roman supply dump at Panormus. This was successful and he brought much of the grain store back to Drepana.[131]

While Claudius Pulcher was busy in Lilybaeum and losing his fleet at Drepana, his colleague in the consulship, Lucius Junius Pullus, was bringing a supply fleet to help relieve the army at Lilybaeum.[132] Sailing down the Italian coast, he first moored at Messana and added what ships were there to his fleet, which now consisted of 120 warships and 800 transports. Junius then sailed on to Syracuse, where he dropped anchor in anticipation of more grain coming to him from the interior of the island. Here, he gave half of the transports, presumably those already filled with supplies, to the quaestors, as well as a number of warships, and they were to sail directly for the besieging army.[133]

As these ships were making their way towards Lilybaeum, Carthalo was doing the same. He reached the harbour at daybreak and set about trying to take in tow some of the Roman ships, while trying to set fire to others. This was not a quiet endeavour, and his fleet roused the Romans who were nearby in their camp. As a resistance was beginning to form, Himilco was made aware of what was happening and attempted to assist his colleague. He launched attacks out of the city, forcing the Romans to fight on two sides. This allowed Carthalo to carry away a number of their ships, though it was not as resounding a victory as it could have been. The Punic admiral then sailed to the south of Lilybaeum, following the coast. He may have been informed of Junius' supply fleet, as Polybius would have us believe, or he may have simply been in the right place at the right time. Regardless, Carthalo's ships spotted the small fleet commanded by the quaestors and sailed towards it, intending to attack. The Romans, however, knew that they were outnumbered and did not think they had a chance in a battle. Their solution was to anchor just offshore from a friendly town. Here, they brought catapults and ballistae from the battlements down to the shore in order to defend themselves against the Punic ships. Although the Carthaginians tried to force the Romans to abandon their fleet, nothing worked, and Carthalo was only able to tow away a few of the cargo ships. He then sailed to the mouth of a nearby river, waiting for the Romans to again take to the sea.[134]

Junius, unaware of what had happened to his quaestors and their fleet, was sailing towards Lilybaeum when he was spotted by the Punic fleet. Carthalo quickly got his ships back to sea, and raced towards the Romans to force a battle. They had, however, spotted the Carthaginian ships by this point, and the consul, concluding the same thing as his quaestors, decided it would be folly to try to fight the enemy, and instead anchored off a rough coastline, thinking this would deter them from attacking, which it did. A foul wind began to blow, however, and the Carthaginian captains knew what it indicated. They urged their admiral to sail to safety around Cape Pachynus, which he agreed to. They anchored in a sheltered spot. The Romans, being unaware of what the changing weather would bring, did not move, but stayed anchored near the dangerous shores. When the storm hit, their ships were slammed into the cliffs and shallows, destroying almost all of them. According to Diodorus, only two of the warships survived.[135]

Unsurprisingly, Iunius was not satisfied to end his consulship in utter disgrace, and took his two remaining ships, speeding past any Punic vessels which may have remained on the south coast, and raced to Lilybaeum. He and the crews of these two ships made it safely to their destination, probably to the astonishment of those onboard. From here, he led a night attack against Eryx, the hilltop position between Drepana and

Panormus, taking it, and fortified a place called Aegithallus. Carthalo, probably having given chase to the two-ship fleet, found this out and resolved on his own attack. He also marched an army out by night and overwhelmed the 800-man strong garrison which had been installed at Aegithallus. Survivors from the struggle fell back to the main fortress on Eryx, where 3,000 of their countrymen were stationed. Amongst those captured at Aegithallus, according to Zonaras, was Iunius himself.[136]

This was an exceptional year of the war. It saw the only major Punic naval victory, and also the single worst pair of Roman consuls of the twenty-three-year conflict. On the Roman side, the result was the election of a dictator, Aulus Atilius Caiatinus, whose master of horse was Lucius Caecilius Metellus, the hero of Panormus. They took charge of the army in Sicily. This was the first time that a dictator led a Roman army overseas.[137] Nothing of consequence was accomplished under their command, however, and it seemed as though the losses of 249 BC had stalled Roman progress in the war. For the Carthaginians, this was a good but not spectacular year. They had destroyed, or led to the destruction of, two large Roman fleets, both positives, and had clearly established naval dominance over the most efficient sea lane between Sicily and Italy. Despite these gains, they were unable to dislodge the Romans from their siege of Lilybaeum and could not prevent the seizure of Eryx. And while their mastery of the north coast of Sicily, and probably the waters all around Tyrrhenian Italy, was impressive, it did not stop Roman commanders and armies from marching down the peninsula and crossing at the Straits. These were all major problems and indications that the Punic strategy was more centred on small, less daring, hit-and-runs, or raiding, than on full-scale, decisive, battles. Nevertheless, Adherbal, Himilco and Carthalo should be remembered as three of the most competent and effective generals of the war, and possibly even of Punic history.

At this point, Carthage brought in a new commander to Sicily. This was Hamilcar Barca, the father to the infamous Hannibal Barca of the second war with Rome. Another commander, Hanno, referred to as 'the Great' by some of our sources, was continuing the campaigns in Africa against the Numidians, taking the city of Theveste.[138] The investment of military resources in Libya has led numerous modern scholars to criticize Carthaginian judgment. John Lazenby hypothesized a number of alternatives that they could have taken, and Howard Scullard wrote that they had 'missed a splendid opportunity'.[139] Explanations have ranged in credibility over years of debate, with some commentators arguing that Hamilcar and those pushing the war in Sicily belonged to the merchant class while Hanno and those pushing for war in Africa were amongst the landed aristocracy. This is a poor explanation for why Carthage was waging wars on two fronts.[140] Dexter Hoyos implies that the campaigns against the Numidians aimed to increase tax revenues, which had certainly fallen with the loss of most of Sicily, and which were direly needed, as Hamilcar found the mercenaries to be unpaid when he reached the island.[141]

There may have been a more basic reason for Carthage to be fighting both on Sicily and in Africa: a shortage of troops. At first sight this proposal may seem paradoxical, but it only requires a bit of explanation. We know that the city was short on cash and already having problems with mercenaries talking about revolt. They may have been having trouble recruiting at this point, as we do not hear of major reinforcements or the creation of new armies. If this is correct, then a decision had to be made about which enemy was more important to deal with: the Romans in Sicily, who had tried and failed for many years to take Lilybaeum and over whom two major naval victories had recently been won, or the Numidians, who, while not achieving major successes as far as we know, were at the Carthaginians' backdoor. In this case, it seems reasonable to assume that the government would have wanted to deal with the problem closest at hand while they still had an army at their disposal before forcing an end to the war with Rome. They may also have been lulled into a false sense of achievement by holding onto Lilybaeum and Drepana. In past wars, as we have seen, stalemates followed by a treaty were the norm, and it is possible that the Carthaginian leadership thought that this would be the outcome.

No matter the reasons for fighting against two enemies, Carthage continued its struggle against the Romans. Before Hamilcar's arrival, Carthalo was still in Sicily and campaigned against the incoming consuls, Caius Aurelius Cotta and Publius Servilius Ceminus, who had served together in the same role in 252 BC. They maintained the siege of Lilybaeum and attacked Drepana in an effort to counter the pressure that the army there put on their supply lines. At some point during the year, Carthalo decided to take the war to Italy and again raided its coasts, trying to draw the consuls thither, but he accomplished very little.[142] The Romans did not build a new fleet for lack of resources. Instead, they allowed wealthy individuals to restore ships to seaworthiness and act as privateers on behalf of the state. Although they did not seriously injure the Punic cause, they were able to capture Hippou Acra, in Africa, and plunder some wealth, maybe enough to help fund the construction of a new fleet. They may have fought a small naval engagement against the Carthaginian fleet near Panormus, but Zonaras gives us no details.[143]

When Hamilcar finally came to Sicily and took over Carthalo's post, he found an army in shambles. The mercenaries had not been paid and were in various states of rebellion. His predecessor had got rid of some of them, but Hamilcar was forced to kill off some of them while they slept, throwing others into the sea. After securing his position and his army, Hamilcar then began a campaign of raiding against southern Italy. These raids may have been necessitated by the financial situation in his camp, and the plunder would probably have been used to pay the mercenaries. Returning to Sicily, he encamped his army on a hill known as Hercte. It was between Eryx and Panormus and allowed him to protect a good anchorage. On two sides of the hill, near the top, are unscalable cliffs, adding strength to the fortified camp which the Carthaginians built atop it. Although he was now closer to the enemy, Hamilcar found success from this base. He fought them for three years on land, with the Roman camp having been established less than five stades from his. Hercte also proved to be a convenient naval base, and his raids on the Italian coast continued, with his ships hitting targets as far north as Cumae, on the Bay of Naples. These expeditions also targetted Roman allies on Sicily, notably Catana.[144]

For the next three years, no major battles were fought. Polybius describes the period as a struggle between

> a pair of exceptionally brave and skilful boxers fighting it out in a contest for first prize, who pummel each other so incessantly with blow after blow that it is impossible for either the contestants or the spectators to note and anticipate every single attack or punch, though the overall vigour and determination displayed by the two men can be used to gain an adequate impression of their skill and strength and courage.[145]

He was speaking of 'two generals', Hamilcar and a Roman, though numerous consuls circulated through the theatre over this period of time. The last that he mentions, Iunius, had already been taken prisoner by the time Hamilcar had come to Sicily. We learn from Zonaras, however, that in 247 BC, Lucius Caecilius Metellus was in charge of the siege at Lilybaeum and Numerius Fabius Buteo besieged Drepana. While the latter's army was encamped here, the consul decided to attack a small island near the city called Pelias, which had a Carthaginian garrison. The Romans cleared the island of its defenders, but were quickly attacked by Hamilcar. In order to draw the Punic commander away from the recently installed garrison, Fabius launched an assault on Drepana. This strategy worked, and the island remained in Roman hands. In this year, Carthaginian ships continued to raid the coasts of Italy and Sicily. To counter these, a series of colonies were founded on the coast, including Alsium in 247 BC, Fregenae in 245 BC, and Brundisium in 244 BC.[146] A prisoner exchange occurred between the two powers, man for man, with Carthage having to ransom some of theirs as they had had more captives taken than the Romans.[147]

Our sources do not go into detail about the events of the war until 244 BC. This despite Polybius saying that the commanders over this period 'tried everything – traditional ideas, improvised tactics dictated by particular circumstances, and schemes that involved risk and aggressive daring'.[148] Zonaras, writing from a Roman perspective, bluntly pronounced that 'in the period that followed [Metellus' and Fabius' consulship] various persons became consuls, but effected nothing worthy of record.'[149] Starting in 244 BC, however, Hamilcar attacked the Roman forces at Eryx. He took the town at the base of the mountain, killed most of its garrison, and shipped the prisoners to Drepana. Following on this victory, he then besieged the Roman forces at the summit. This would last for two years, during which time a number of stratagems were tried by both sides to break the stalemate, but nothing worked.[150] It was perhaps during this period which saw a lull in Punic raiding, and another dip in their finances, that a group of Celtic mercenaries defected to the Romans.[151] In 243 BC, during the siege of Eryx, a disobedient officer named Bodostor allowed his men to plunder rather than maintain order, which resulted in significant losses. Hamilcar's cavalry covered the failing infantry, though, and saved the situation. The details of this engagement, one of countless, are mostly lost to us.[152]

Whatever Hamilcar was doing, it was enough to prompt the Romans to return to the seas in 242 BC. Although the raiding on their coasts and those of their allies may have helped influence this decision, Polybius tells us that the core mission of this new fleet would be to deny the Punic forces at Eryx supplies and reinforcement. Although this strategy was agreed upon, there were no public funds to make it a reality. Wealthy Romans were sought as an alternative funding source, and individuals, or small groups, invested their own money in constructing new quinqueremes. This was intended as a loan, and they were to be reimbursed upon a successful end of the war. These quinqueremes were modelled on the well-built example captured from Hannibal the Rhodian, at Lilybaeum.[153] To this end, they produced 200 new ships. Command of this fleet was given to one of the newly elected consuls, Gaius Lutatius Catulus. His colleague, Aulus Postumius Albinus, was the *flamen martialis*, the high priest of Mars. The *pontifex maximus* did not allow him to leave the city and abandon his priestly duties, thus Postumius was not given a command during his consulship. In his stead, Quintus Valerius Falto, the *praetor urbanus*, was Lutatius' colleague on campaign.[154]

Leaving Rome, the new fleet sailed for Drepana. Here, they gained control of the harbour and disembarked the land army. They invested the city and fanned out across the countryside to capture the roadsteads at Lilybaeum. Lutatius' forces besieging Drepana began preparing engines for an assault, but the consul's primary concern was to prevent the Carthaginians from bringing supplies and possibly a new army to Sicily. Because of this, he spent much of his time drilling his crews, having them practise the tactics that he expected to use during the coming battle. This is easily understandable in the context of Rome's earlier losses at sea and their difficulty in building this new fleet. As Christa Steinby has put it, 'these thorough preparations are easy to understand: the Romans had to regain their position on the Sicilian coast and they could not afford to lose this fleet.'[155]

When news reached Carthage of the new Roman ships and their attack on Sicily, the Punic fleet was refitted and launched. This consisted of as many as 250 quinqueremes.[156] Hanno was put in command with the primary mission of bringing supplies to the army at Eryx. This would be difficult to do under the eyes of Lutatius, especially as the Punic ships would be slower than usual being loaded with grain and other provisions.

Hanno's plan was to sail to the Aegates Islands, and from there make his run towards Eryx. He would then offload his cargo and take onboard a handpicked group of mercenaries to serve as marines and then seek out and engage the Romans. The fleet left and sailed first to 'The Holy Island', which is the western most of the Aegates chain. From here, he would sail past Aegusa and then straight to Lilybaeum.

Unfortunately for Hanno, Lutatius was informed of his arrival in the Aegates. He immediately loaded his ships with picked soldiers as marines and sailed for Aegusa. There the consul briefed his army and told them to be ready for battle in the morning. At dawn on 10 March 241 BC, the Romans awoke to find a wind blowing into their prows, making conditions for a battle unfavourable. They would have to row through a heavy swell and against the wind to find their targets. Lutatius, however, presumed that the Punic ships would be heavy with cargo and that he might still have an advantage over them if he engaged at this juncture. He formed his ships into a straight line, with their prows pointed towards the Carthaginians. On seeing this, Hanno ordered his ships to drop their masts, let out their oars, and try to fight their way through. None of our sources give us a detailed description of the battle. We do know that it ended in a Roman victory. Punic losses were heavy, with Polybius giving them as fifty sunk and seventy captured, while Diodorus says ninety-seven were sunk and twenty were captured. These are very similar, and it is likely that they lost around 120 ships. Roman losses were probably heavier than they had hoped, with thirty sunk and fifty damaged to the point that they were not viable ships of war. The Romans also took 4,400, 6,000, or 10,000 captives.[157]

The remainder of the Punic fleet fled back to Carthage. Amongst the survivors was Hanno. It was probably unwise for him to return to the city, and his countrymen, overwhelmed with rage, crucified him.[158] The Battle of the Aegates Islands proved to be the breaking point for the Carthaginian will to fight. Although some amongst the leadership were inclined to continue fighting, the general inclination was to seek peace. Polybius says that they left the final decision to Hamilcar Barca, although this may be part of a pro-Barcid tradition which wanted to make him seem like the most level-headed of his fellows. This is hinted at by Polybius' praise in this section of the narrative, saying that 'Hamilcar acted exactly as a good, prudent commander should.'[159] Even if the decision was not left to him, he was granted full authority to negotiate on behalf of Carthage. The Romans, who were almost as war-weary as the Carthaginians, welcomed the peace talks. Although the original draft was rejected when it reached Rome, eventually a treaty was concluded. The terms were as follows: Carthage would evacuate all of Sicily, the Carthaginians were not to make war on Hiero nor Syracuse and its allies, the Carthaginians were to return all of their prisoners taken during the war without ransom, the Carthaginians were to pay an indemnity of 3,200 Euboic talents over ten years, and the Carthaginians were to evacuate all the islands they occupied between Italy and Sicily. It was under these conditions that the longest war in the ancient world came to an end.[160]

Conclusions

What was ultimately an unlooked-for war turned out to be a major disaster for Carthage, and a significant drain on the resources of Rome. The intrepid warriors from Latium, and their allies, had accomplished something that centuries of Greek tyrants and armies could not: they expelled the Carthaginians from Sicily. This was, perhaps, the great loss of the war. The human and financial costs were astronomical, but losing the large cities of the island and its agricultural wonderland were a blow that, at the moment of defeat, was probably viewed as fatal to Punic ambitions as a major Mediterranean power. As Richard Miles has pointed out, however, the situation on Sicily was not much different than it had been before the war, with the Romans supplanting the Carthaginians as the dominant, yet distant, hegemonic power.[161] As well, whatever truth there was to a Carthaginian thalassocracy in the Tyrrhenian Sea was now destroyed, as the Roman fleet was now dominant.

It is difficult to try to make simple conclusions about the reasons for Carthage's defeat in such a complex and long-running war. The most glib answer is that the Punic state was simply not ready for a conflict on this scale, but the same can be said of the Romans. In the end a number of factors may have contributed to the failure.

The first was that this was a type of warfare that Carthage was not used to. Although they had waged wars of conquest in the past, in recent memory they had engaged in a policy of maintaining their position, a generally defensive strategy. They had regularly been willing to accept treaties which re-established existing boundaries even when they may have been able to slowly wear down their enemies, typically Syracuse. The Romans, however, were not going to be beaten slowly, and were dedicated to fighting until the end if the war was to result in a defeat.

The second was that Carthaginian strategy had been conditioned by the wars against the Greeks and Pyrrhus on Sicily. These did not involve major naval engagements, an area in which the Carthaginians were still probably surprised to lose in their war with Rome. But, as we have seen in the preceding chapters, these wars were primarily centred around sieges and the taking of strategic forts. Pitched battles were not common, and when they were fought, Punic defeats were not uncommon. In the war with Rome their commanders' abilities in pitched battle was confirmed as inferior. Their greatest victory, the Battle of Tunis, against Regulus, was organized and led by the Spartan, Xanthippus.

The third was a difference in manpower. Critics of mercenary armies typically point to their lack of patriotic ties to their employers as being a weakness. Although there were some traitors during the war, these were turned because their pay was in arrears, not because they felt their Punic commanders were incompetent. In fact, many mercenaries, such as Alexon, and their units fought valiantly and stuck by their employers through very difficult situations, such as the ten-year siege of Lilybaeum. The problem for the Carthaginians, however, was that by relying on mercenaries they had to take the time to recruit them, while the Romans could levy troops directly from their population and those of their allies. This meant that, although Carthage could raise equally large armies, they could not do so as rapidly and efficiently as the Romans.

Chapter 7

The Truceless War

With the peace treaty of 241 BC came a problematic task for the Carthaginians.¹ They were forced to remove their army from Sicily, which involved transporting 20,000 mercenaries back to Carthage. These were mostly Iberians, Balearic Islanders, Celts, Ligurians, and 'half-breed' Greeks. There were also Libyan conscripts. The Carthaginians owed all of these men one year's salary. Hamilcar Barca, in the wake of the defeat, surrendered his command, leaving the evacuation in the hands of Gisco, the commander of the garrison at Lilybaeum. In sending the mercenaries to Africa, he sensibly did so in waves, not wanting the entire body to arrive in the city at the same time. His superiors in the city, however, thought that they may be able to save having to pay all of the wages owed if they welcomed the mercenaries into the city. Because of this, the mercenaries ended up within the confines of the city all at once. This situation predictably led to an increase of crime, some of it committed in daylight and the mass of unpaid, unemployed mercenaries began to resemble a mob.²

Something had to be done, and the solution settled upon was to send the mercenaries out to a town called Sicca for the time being. Each man was to receive a gold stater to cover his expenses. They would remain in this town until the Carthaginians could pay their full wages owed and until the rest of the mercenaries had crossed over from Sicily. At first the mercenaries were unwilling to take along their wives and children, a condition set by the Carthaginians. After some debate, the issue was resolved, and the entire body of the mercenaries, their families, and their belongings made the trek to Sicca.³

After all the mercenaries were gathered in this place, Hanno, known as 'the great', was charged with dealing with them. He was tasked with the unenviable job of talking the men out of at least some of what they were owed.⁴ He implored them to consider the weight of the indemnity owed to Rome and to the general poverty which characterized Carthage at this moment. His words were not well received, and a wave of mutinous feeling spread throughout the settlement. Because of the polyglot nature of the hoard, as well as cultural differences amongst the mercenaries, dissent was not immediately made physical. This also meant, however, that Hanno was unable to address all of them at once in a general assembly. He was forced to use a number of officers as translators, who misunderstood, or mistranslated, what was being told to them. This created a feeling of uncertainty and distrust amongst the mercenaries. To make the situation worse, the mercenaries did not respect Hanno and questioned why the Carthaginians had sent a man to treat with them who had not witnessed their deeds in Sicily or made promises to them. Order eventually completely disintegrated as even the divisional officers lost their trust. They decided, en masse, to march against Carthage and they made their camp at Tunis, like Agathocles had done just over sixty years before.[5]

There were now 20,000 angry, war-hardened mercenaries at the gates of Carthage. The Punic leadership too late realised that they had made a series of poor decisions and put their city in jeopardy. They attempted to sate the fury of their one-time soldiers by sending them provisions, which were being sold at whatever rate the troops wanted to pay. Politicians were used as ambassadors, continually assuring them that the government was doing everything in its power to meet their demands. These were continually added to, however, making it a difficult task. Eventually Gisco was brought in to arbitrate the payment of the mercenaries' demands, as he was one of the only Punic commanders whom they now trusted, with Hamilcar having given up command.[6]

Taking each ethnic contingent aside individually, Gisco was able to negotiate more successfully than his predecessors had. It was settled that he would personally assure that their arrears were paid in full. Despite this, a dissident faction within the assembly actively campaigned for open conflict with the Carthaginians. This was led by a Libyan named Mathos, a Campanian deserter from the Roman army named Spendius, and the leader of the Celtic contingent, Autaritus.[7] While they were waiting to receive their pay, the leaders of the rebellious movement held public assemblies, continually lambasting the Carthaginians and fanning the flames of dissent. Those who spoke up against this faction, and in favour of de-aligning peacefully with the Carthaginians, were stoned to death as they tried to quell their fellows. This happened so frequently that the only words understood by every member of this group were 'stone him'.[8] When, by force, they had silenced the opposition, the mercenaries elected Mathos and Spendius generals and were thus in a state of open rebellion.[9]

Gisco was still confident that he could win them over and prevent a war. Even though some of the mercenaries had now been paid, peace was not to be. The Libyans were one of the ethnic contingents who were not paid in the first wave. This may have been an element of Punic treachery, as the Carthaginians had a history of dealing with Libyan revolts. Perhaps they thought it was possible to divide the mercenaries along ethnic lines, eventually leaving the Libyans by themselves.[10] If this was the intention, it backfired. Because of this, they were the loudest voice demanding retribution from Carthage. On one occasion, when Gisco was coming to the camp of the rebels, he was approached by a group of Libyans who demanded that they be paid. His reply was that they should ask 'general Mathos' for their money, which drove them into a frenzy. They began to loot the countryside around the city and they took prisoner both Gisco and the citizens who had come along with him. Seeing this as a chance to escalate the conflict, Spendius and Mathos encouraged the actions of the Libyan mob. They arranged for the prisoners to be stripped of their property and to be beaten. They were then shackled and thrown into a prison. With this action, the mercenaries were now in a state of open war with Carthage. The men took pledges to the new generals. Almost all of the Libyan cities came over to the cause of the rebels and began sending them supplies. Mathos, taking command, immediately set in motion sieges at both Utica and Hippou Acra, which had remained loyal to Carthage.[11]

At the outset of the war, the rebels began gathering resources. From the Libyans they received not only foodstuffs, but also money. The households willingly stripped themselves of material wealth, including a large quantity of jewels, and gave them up to the mercenary army's coffers. This, and whatever was already in their camps, was sufficient to pay the arrears of all the troops and still have enough over to prosecute the war.[12]

The Carthaginian reaction was to name Hanno general in command of the war. He had previously put down a rebellion in Hecatontapylus, and was judged suitable for the job at hand.¹³ His first action was to raise an army. Ironically, he sent recruiters out to bring mercenaries into his service. The citizens of military age were given arms, and the citizen cavalrymen were formed into formal units and began drilling. We do not hear details of this force, except that it also contained 100 elephants. As we shall see during the great siege of Carthage known as the Third Punic War, the inhabitants were able to rapidly manufacture arms and armour when needed, and we should not doubt that this could have been accomplished at this point. The 200,000 suits of armour we hear of being handed over to the Romans during that campaign should not be taken as evidence of the strength of their home army. It is probable that the citizen troops raised by Hanno numbered only a couple of thousand, perhaps as many as 8,000–10,000.¹⁴ They could have had combat experience, though, and many of them may have been the soldiers who had earlier served under the general.¹⁵ What was left of the Punic fleet was taken out of dry dock and made seaworthy again, but this consisted only of a few triremes and quinqueremes.¹⁶

While Hanno was organising his army, the rebel army was swelled by troops from the Libyan allies. Supposedly 70,000 soldiers came from these, but that number is too large. It may not be exaggerated if these were not all soldiers proper, but perhaps also serfs or labourers who had left wherever they were to join the insurrection.¹⁷ These were divided between the various army groups which were now scattered throughout the area, with the primary encampment maintained at Tunis as well as the two siege camps at Utica and Hippou Acra. With the rebel army spread out as it was, the Carthaginians were cut off from the interior and whatever African settlements were still loyal to them.¹⁸

With the opening of the campaigning season in 240 BC, Hanno marched his army out of Carthage and tried to relieve Utica. In the first attack, he was able to drive off the rebel army.¹⁹ This victory is credited to his elephants who are said to have overwhelmed the enemy. The rebels were forced to retreat into their camp, opposite which Hanno built his own. From here, his soldiers were able to attack the enemy using the catapults which they had brought with them.²⁰ Using these to keep the enemy from putting up too much of a resistance, he again sent in his elephants. These were able to breakdown the palisade which protected the camp. The rebels were routed as the great beasts began trampling through their encampment, crushing some of them. Those who survived the attack retreated to the top of a nearby hill. This was an easily-defended spot thanks in part to the vegetation being overgrown.[21]

Although he won a small victory, Hanno made a serious strategic error in the aftermath of this battle. He did not pursue those who fled from the camp. Instead, the general returned in triumph to Carthage, looking after his own comfort. He left the army in the field without specific orders. The soldiers, ill-disciplined, began milling about and took no care to maintain their ranks or fortify their position outside of Utica. Polybius tells us that this happened because Hanno was used to fighting against Numidians and Libyans who would withdraw for several days after being driven off. These mercenaries, tempered in the war against Rome, did not behave this way. Instead, they maintained their position on the hill, watching the movements of the Punic army. When they saw that it was in disorder and that the general had returned to the city, they pounced from their hilltop warren and crashed down upon the Carthaginians. They inflicted heavy losses on the unorganized troops and forced them to flee back to Carthage. Besides the casualties they inflicted, the rebels also captured the baggage train and the siege equipment which were brought out by Hanno.[22]

Thanks to Hanno's failure as a field commander, the Carthaginians reinstated Hamilcar Barca as general and assigned him a new army. This consisted of about 10,000 soldiers, including newly recruited mercenaries and deserters from the rebel camp, as well as citizens serving in both the infantry and cavalry, and seventy elephants. With this force, he decided to march through passable shallows at the mouth of the Bagradas river and towards a rebel garrison which guarded one of the most important bridges over the river. Learning of this advance, Spendius ordered 10,000 soldiers from the garrison at the bridge, as well as 15,000 from the camp at Utica, to march into the plain against Hamilcar's army. The Punic general had counted on this and was prepared with a stratagem to deal with being attacked by superior numbers. His marching order was to have elephants in front, followed by the cavalry and the light troops, and finally at the rear was the heavy infantry. As the rebels closed on him, he ordered his army to turn around and make it look as though they were fleeing. The heavy infantry, in serried ranks, stood firm as if to receive the attack of the enemy. The elephants and the cavalry had made a retreat at the double to make it look as though they were leaving the field. Thinking that Hamilcar was in retreat, the rebel army quickly charged, breaking ranks. When they were near the Punic infantry line, Hamilcar's cavalry turned around and charged directly into the disorganised enemy. The army then began to advance as a whole. This reversal forced the Libyans and the rebellious mercenaries into a rout, trying to escape from the trap they had just walked in to. In the end, 6,000 of the rebels were killed and 2,000 were taken prisoner.[23]

Some of those who fled returned to the siege camp at Utica, while others made their way back to the settlement at the bridge over the Bagradas. Hamilcar pursued the latter closely. Catching up to them when they reached the town, he immediately launched an attack against it. The defenders did not put up much resistance and almost immediately fled to the main camp at Tunis when the Carthaginian army pushed their assault. After flushing out these rebels, Hamilcar moved against a number of other towns which had gone over to their side in the region nearby. Most of these he was forced to take by storm, but a few turned coat and were persuaded to realign themselves with Carthage.[24] It also seems that Hamilcar's victory helped to lift the siege at Utica. We find that Spendius was no longer present, and there were good reasons for the rebels to think the position there untenable.[25]

Hamilcar continued his march through the interior. All the while, he was being shadowed by the rebels who were keeping to the hills, rather than risking being caught on the flat plains where the Punic superiority in elephants and cavalry gave them a decisive advantage.[26] The army that was shadowing the Punic general was led by Spendius, who had about 6,000 men with him, drawn from the contingents encamped at Tunis. Autaritus joined him along with 2,000 Celtic troops. They were eventually joined by Numidian and Libyan reinforcements. They waited in the hills, following along with the movements of the Carthaginian army until the time was right to make themselves known. They chose a moment when Hamilcar made camp on a plain surrounded by mountains. The rebels came down from the hills and surrounded the camp. The Libyans entrenched themselves in the front, the Numidians in the rear, and Spendius' original army on the flank. By doing this, they had essentially trapped Hamilcar.[27]

While the armies were staring each other down, the Carthaginians received an unexpected gift. At some point, a group of one hundred Numidians rode up to the Punic camp, amongst whom was Naravas. He was a son of one of the prominent families of his people and had ties of kinship with the Carthaginians, although we do not hear of his precise genealogy.[28] Naravas was an admirer of Hamilcar and respected him as a general. He had ridden to the camp that day in an effort to meet him. After some confusion, he was allowed an audience with the general, at which point he offered his services, as well as that of 2,000 of his men. Delighted, Hamilcar accepted him into the army.[29]

Bolstered by these new arrivals, the general mustered his troops and marched out of his camp to offer battle to Spendius. The latter decided to accept this challenge, and merged his contingents with the Libyan allies and marched into the plain where the Carthaginians were waiting. The battle was hard fought, but Hamilcar was victorious. We do not hear any details about the fight, but Polybius notes that the elephants and Naravas' riders played conspicuous roles in the victory. Both Autaritus and Spendius escaped, but their army suffered considerable damage. We hear that they lost 10,000 dead, with 4,000 being taken prisoner. These numbers are probably inflated, perhaps in the interest of enhancing Hamilcar's reputation.[30] Those who were taken prisoner were granted amnesty, with Hamilcar promising their freedom on the condition that if they were found again to have taken up arms against Carthage they would be punished.

This worried the rebel commanders who feared that it would draw their Libyan allies back to the Carthaginian cause. They were also concerned that many of the mercenaries would also defect. To prevent this, Mathos, Spendius, and Autaritus came up with a plan to prevent this from happening. They called an assembly of their soldiers and slandered Hamilcar's offer of clemency. The leaders claimed that he only did it so that he could win the war, not because he cared if they lived. Also produced at this meeting was a letter, supposedly from the mercenaries on Sardinia who had recently launched an insurrection against the Carthaginians.[31] In this, it was said that Gisco, who was still prisoner in Tunis, needed to be watched closely as elements within their army had begun negotiating with Carthage, looking for an end to the war. These traitors were supposedly set to release the captured Punic commander.

Another letter arrived while the speeches were being delivered, saying the same thing as the letter from Sardinia.[32]

Autaritus and Spendius pushed their compatriots to do horrible things to Gisco and the other Carthaginians in their custody, as well as any future prisoners they may take. They knew that by doing this they would eliminate the offer of clemency and thus ensure that their troops could not abandon them. To draw the full ire of the Carthaginians, they ordered that Gisco and the 700 other Punic prisoners be marched out from the camp at Tunis. Once they reached a suitable spot, they killed them all through a tedious and torturous method. First they cut off their hands, then they broke their legs, and finally tossed them all into a large pit, while they were still alive but in immeasurable pain. They started with Gisco and then worked through the rest of the Carthaginians.[33]

When the people of Carthage learned what had happened, they sent an embassy to the rebel camp, asking for the bodies of the dead so they could be given a proper burial. This was refused, though, and they were sent back to the city with the message that any further envoys would meet the same fate as Gisco. The rebels then passed a resolution, if that is the proper term, that any Punic prisoners they take were to be tortured and killed, while every Carthaginian ally they captured would be returned with their hands cut off. At the same time that this was being told to the Carthaginians, they had sent messengers to both Hamilcar and Hanno, asking that they avenge the murdered citizens. Heeding this call, Hamilcar called for Hanno to join him and they combined their armies.[34]

Unfortunately for the Carthaginians, these two generals did not see eye to eye. They argued continually, and because of this they missed a number of opportunities to attack the rebel army. On a few occasions they even left themselves open to attack, though it never came. More disasters befell Carthage while their best commanders were bickering. A large shipment of supplies which was coming to the city was lost at sea, the impact of which was exacerbated by the earlier loss of Sardinia which regularly supplied the city with food in times of crisis. Worse than all of this, however, was the defection of Hippou Acra and Utica. They sided with the Libyans who themselves were allied with the rebels. In the newly rebellious cities, the Carthaginian garrisons were killed to a man, even their commanders. Requests to bury the dead were denied, a sign of how dedicated Hippou Acra and Utica were to their new cause.[35]

Mathos and Spendius, seeing the dire straits of the Carthaginians, now settled on a bolder plan of action. They resolved to besiege Carthage itself. At the same time, however, a new commander was sent from the city to relieve Hanno of command. This new general's name was Hannibal. Now that the army was under proper leadership, they returned to campaigning against the rebels. Hamilcar, with Naravas, began scouring the Libyan countryside in an effort to interrupt the rebel supply lines. For whatever reason, though, they did not attack the army which was laying siege to the city. This is probably emblematic of the importance of controlling the food supplies from the interior for the rebels.[36]

Despite the armies in the field finding success against the rebel supply lines, Carthage was experiencing food shortages. They needed relief and found this in two sources: Hieron II of Syracuse and Rome. The only complication was that earlier in the war, Carthage had captured 500 merchants from Italy who were trading with the rebels. An exchange of embassies, though, resolved this problem and secured the release of all those who had been imprisoned. The Romans also gave political support, and refused requests by the rebels in Sardinia and Utica to come under their power.[37]

Hamilcar's strategy of depriving the besieging army of supplies began to pay off. Mathos and Spendius were forced to lift the siege when they ran out of food. In the coming campaigning season, 238 BC, however, they assembled a refreshed army of 50,000 troops, including the best of the mercenaries and a contingent of Libyans under Zarzas. The leaders decided to go back to their previous tactic of shadowing the Punic army from the hills, still being forced to avoid flat land because of the elephants and Naravas' cavalry. This began a series of small engagements which went in favour of Hamilcar. His skills as a general, sharpened in the war with Rome, allowed him to cut off small groups of the enemy and slaughter them. A number of pitched battles were also fought, and in these the rebels were often lured into traps. Alternatively, Hamilcar surprised them on a number of occasions, allowing him to kill even more of the enemy. Having given the order to give no quarter, all of those rebels whom they took alive were thrown to the elephants, who were allowed to pulverize them beneath their great weight.[38]

Hamilcar finally caught up to his prey at a place known as The Saw.[39] He found them encamped in terrain which favoured his army, with its powerful cavalry and elephants. Seeing that this was an opportunity to bring the rebels to heel, he besieged them in their camp. He erected a palisade and dug a trench all the way around it. Thanks to this blockade, the rebels quickly found themselves bereft of supplies. Starvation set in so quickly and severely that they resorted to cannibalism to stay alive. Despite these harsh conditions, there is no record of an attempted breakout. This may be due to Hamilcar subjecting those caught trying to do so to horrific tortures, knowing as he did the fate of Gisco.[40] Spendius had sent word to Tunis, requesting a relieving force be sent. This, however, never came. Autaritus, Zarzas, and Spendius were thus forced to negotiate a surrender with Hamilcar. The Celt and the Campanian, accompanied by eight senior officers, acted as ambassadors and met with the general. They negotiated a surrender by which the bulk of their army was allowed to leave peacefully, but the Carthaginians were allowed to choose ten men therefrom as prisoners. Those whom they chose were the ambassadors themselves, thus they captured both Autaritus and Spendius. When news spread that the Carthaginians had seized the commanders, the Libyans took up their arms as if to fight. They were surrounded and slaughtered. 40,000 of them died on that day.[41]

After this victory, Punic spirits were raised. The generals decided to remove the rest of the rebels from Libya, and marched their armies back into the hinterland around Carthage. Here they hunted down those troops in the countryside. They also led a campaign against the Libyan towns. Many of these surrendered in the wake of the defeat of their forces. Once the majority of these settlements were again under the power of Carthage, the generals took the fight to Mathos, who was still camped in Tunis. Hannibal fortified a camp on the Carthage side of the enemy, while Hamilcar built his on the opposite side. After some time in camp, the Carthaginians brought forward Spendius and the other prisoners taken at The Saw. When they were in a position which could be seen from the walls of Tunis, the prisoners were crucified.[42]

Mathos observed, however, that Hannibal was not acting with prudence and was overconfident in his position. He launched an attack on the Punic camp which easily met with success. The rebels were able to breach whatever fortifications as had been built and cut down many of the Carthaginians. They drove them out so quickly that they were able to seize the baggage train. Hannibal was taken alive, which was unfortunate for him. The mutineers hauled him to the place where Spendius was hanging from his cross. Here, they tortured Hannibal mercilessly, leaving him alive for one final indignity. They took down the body of Spendius and on his cross hung the Punic commander. Beside the corpse of Spendius, they slaughtered thirty high-ranking Carthaginians who had also been captured in the sally. When news of this reached Hamilcar, he broke camp and moved his army to the mouth of the Bagradas.[43]

In the wake of this major setback, the Carthaginian government dispatched Hanno, who had previously been relieved of command, to take over Hannibal's forces. Along with him were sent thirty members of the Council of Elders who were to resolve all disputes which might arise between the two generals. They also sent the last of the military-aged citizens to serve in the army. Through the efforts of the councillors, Hanno and Hamilcar were able to settle on a plan of action and worked together in harmony, where in previous times they had quarrelled.[44]

The combined army then went on the hunt, chasing down Mathos near Leptis. They fought a number of small battles, with the rebels coming off worse after each. Mathos' troops must have been getting worn down through attrition, and by the time both armies went into winter quarters both sides were in need of reinforcements. These came to both armies from the garrisons and their allies. The final engagement was set to take place in the campaigning season of 237 BC. Mathos may have had as many as 20,000 troops under his command, while the Carthaginian army could have been as large as 30,000.[45] We do not know any details of the battle, but it is described as a set-piece, pitched battle. Although most of the rebels were killed in the battle, some were taken alive, including Mathos. These were paraded through Carthage, openly beaten and tortured.[46]

Thusly the great mercenary insurrection, the Truceless War, came to an end. While it is fortunate that we have Polybius' account of the war, the lack of details throughout are unfortunate. We learn little about Carthaginian tactics from Polybius, as his focus was on the strategic level as well as the moral implications of the conflict.

Conclusions

We do learn some important details about Carthage's military capabilities through this war. First, they were certainly not the helpless, soldier-less city in the absence of their mercenaries that some authors make them out to be. In the face of an army of hardened veteran mercenaries, their citizen troops and allied contingents were strong enough to hold their ground. Although unnamed mercenaries were sought by the Punic commanders, we cannot say that they formed a significant part of the army. Instead, it was Hamilcar's abilities as a general, the fearsome shock of the elephant corps, and the abilities of Naravas' Numidian cavalry which proved too much for Mathos, Spendius, Autaritus and their soldiers. Perhaps the most significant impact of the war was not in Africa, but rather in the loss of Sardinia. Because they had to dedicate so much of the resources to dealing with the insurrection in Libya, the Carthaginians were unable to send adequate troops to secure their hold on the island. They permanently lost it when the Romans decided to invade. To make sure there was no Punic response, they threatened to declare war on them, a war they could ill afford to fight immediately after dealing with the mutiny in their homeland. Carthage was not, however, down-and-out. Not long after the war they allowed Hamilcar to raise an army and sail to Iberia, where he spent nine years bringing those people under the Punic yoke.[47]

Chapter 8

The Second War with Rome

The Second Punic War, or the Hannibalic War, as it is often called, is probably the most studied ancient conflict. Few struggles even come close to having spurred on the writing of as many books as this one. Many things contribute to this. One of the most important is that it is well documented, more so than most events from the Greek or Roman worlds. We have accounts written by Livy, Polybius, Appian and others which survive and give us a clear picture of what happened, even if they do not always agree with each other. While this plethora of information and secondary research is extremely valuable to us as historians, it poses a problem for a book such as this one. As I laid out in my introduction, the purpose of this work is to give readers a more nuanced view of Carthaginian armies and warfare than is typically presented. This required me to give more space to conflicts that are typically treated in much more summary fashion. It led me to reverse this paradigm in looking at the second war with Rome, by allocating it a relatively equal amount of space compared to the first war. To do this, I have eschewed some aspects of the conflict, although I do not skimp out on any essential information. What has helped me to condense this war into a chapter which fits this volume, has been focusing less on Hannibal than most other authors. In looking at Punic armies and warfare, I am, in the analysis of this war, more concerned with how the state and all the armies worked to fight against Rome. While Hannibal's achievements in Italy are legendary, there are many other places that readers can turn to for a detailed account of them. In this chapter, instead, you will find a discussion of the war which helps us to better understand Carthage's approach to it and how this fit into the deeper history of Punic military endeavours.

Nevertheless, I do not want to diminish the importance of the Second Punic War in any way. As John Lazenby said, it 'was far more than just the second round in the great struggle between Rome and Carthage: the

The Second War with Rome

first war had hardly affected Italy directly and in the third the issue was merely the survival of Carthage – in the second everything was at stake.'[1]

Spain and the Origins of the War

In the aftermath of the Truceless War, Carthage was all but bankrupt. Sicily was lost, thus eliminating considerable income from the Punic treasury. Sardinia was also lost due to the mercenary revolt. Rome took control of it in 238/237, but this was not immediately accepted. Carthage maintained their claim on the island until the Romans threatened war, extorting the former of 1,200 talents to prevent this.[2] Polybius says of this that 'there was no reasonable pretext or justification.'[3] But there was little that Carthage could do about it, and the island was lost.

Interest was then shifted to the Iberian peninsula, essentially modern Spain. Here there had been Phoenician settlements for centuries, and perhaps a Carthaginian presence for some time. In 238/7 BC, Hamilcar Barca, fresh from his victory in the Truceless War, was sent to Spain with the goal of expanding Punic possessions there. I have little doubt that this was an effort to replace the lost income from Sicily and Sardinia. His campaigning against the various native peoples was very successful, and he brought much of the peninsula under his control. The wealth of gold and silver extracted here was enough to reassert Carthage's place as a Mediterranean power. When he was finally killed, whether through self-sacrifice to save his sons or simply in combat, he was succeeded by his son-in-law, Hasdrubal.

As soon as Hasdrubal met up with what was left of Hamilcar's army, he regrouped them all under his command. He was now at the head of an army of 30,000 infantry and 6,000 cavalry, all veterans. After organizing his newly combined force, he marched against the Orissi, the tribe responsible for Hamilcar's death, and captured all of their cities. He was also responsible for founding the city of New Carthage, and after receiving much of the peninsula as allies could field an army of 60,000 infantry, 8,000 cavalry, and 200 elephants. After some time operating as the de facto ruler of Punic Spain, Hasdrubal was killed by a servant.

Power then passed into the hands of Hamilcar Barca's eldest son, Hannibal. Although he was to become the most famous Carthaginian in history, the relatively young man had not been to his home city since he was nine years old. This was when he left with his father for Spain. He continued the conquests of his predecessors, and conquered much of the peninsula. One city in the north remained out of his possession, however: Saguntum. This city had recently entered into an alliance with Rome, almost certainly out of fear of the expansion of Carthaginian possessions in the region. Hannibal's continual provocation of the Saguntines led to Roman embassies being dispatched, both to the city and to him personally. Those that went to see him personally warned that he should not attack a Roman ally and that there would be consequences if he did. Despite these warnings, Hannibal launched an attack on Saguntum that would last eight months, at the end of which the city would be in his hands and war would be declared on his people by Rome. A relief force was not sent in time to stop the city from falling, and it was only after Hannibal began moving towards Italy that a Roman consul came near his army. Although not directly involving the Roman army, this siege was the opening battle of the second war with Rome.[4]

Opening Blows

As we have seen in the previous section, the siege of Saguntum should be seen as the first battle of the Second Punic War, even if no Roman army was present. With the city taken, Hannibal's army probably went into the usual winter hibernation, common in the ancient world. Hannibal himself withdrew to New Carthage. Here, he began his preparations for making war on Rome and Italy. Hasdrubal, Hannibal's brother, was trained in how to administer the Punic holdings in Spain, meaning that the Barcid management of the region was to continue. More importantly, Hannibal saw to the defence of both Iberia and Africa. According to Polybius, he sent 1,200 cavalry, 13,850 infantry, and 870 slingers to Libya. These were mostly from the Iberian Peninsula proper, but the slingers were from the Balearic Islands. He also sent 4,000 infantry to Carthage specially, these men acting both as a supplement to the garrison and as hostages, ensuring the loyalties of the cities of Metagonia. From Africa, Hannibal brought to Spain 2,550 cavalry, 12,650 infantry, and 21 elephants.[5] These numbers are very precise, more so than we usually encounter in ancient texts. This is because, as Polybius himself explains,

'I came across an inscribed bronze plate on which these details had been recorded by Hannibal during his time in Italy.'[6]

The most significant project during the winter, though, was the assembly of an army which would march into Italy. Hannibal brought together 90,000 infantry and 12,000 cavalry, a massive force larger than the Punic armies which took the field in the first war against Rome.[7] Appian includes thirty-seven elephants in this force, though it is worrying that neither Polybius nor Livy mention these beasts. This horde marched out of New Carthage in the spring of 218, crossed the Ebro, and made for the Pyrenees. Between the river and the mountains, Hannibal encountered a number of hostile tribes which had to be subdued before he could continue to Italy. The fighting here was apparently fierce, with Polybius saying that a number of major battles caused 'severe loss of life'. In all, the Carthaginians may have had to supress four different tribes: the Ilourgetes, Bargusii, Aerenosii and Andosini.[8] To ensure that this area was kept under Punic control, Hannibal left a commander named Hanno behind, along with 10,000 infantry and 1,000 cavalry.[9]

What was left of the army then crossed the Pyrenees into what is today France. It was 50,000 infantry and 9,000 cavalry strong. In addition to the troops lost in the fighting north of the Ebro, and those left behind as a garrison, 11,000 Iberian troops were dismissed and allowed to return to their homes. Livy's account claims that 3,000 deserted and that Hannibal then dismissed an additional 7,000 to cover this up, as well as to ensure the loyalty of the population of the peninsula.[10] Whether or not the soldiers that returned to Iberia were released or deserted is unknowable, but it is not farfetched to think that some of them decided their fortunes were brighter back home.[11] If these were relatively untrained levies, it seems likely that the trek through the Pyrenees was enough to demoralise them, especially knowing that there was still a significant march ahead, including the crossing of the Alps. That Polybius says of the army at this point that it consisted of experienced soldiers, it is probable that those who deserted and were sent home were indeed mass levies and not hardened Iberian soldiers.

The next leg of the journey to Italy was up the coast to the Rhone. There appears to have been minor fighting along the way, but no significant engagements are mentioned.[12] When Hannibal reached the river, however, he found his way blocked. On the opposite bank was a mass of warriors from the Gallic Volcae tribe. The Carthaginians began assembling canoes and small boats to make the crossing. To ensure that his army would not be prevented from making a beachhead, Hannibal sent another commander named Hanno (son of Bomilcar the Suffete) upriver with a detachment from the main army, mostly Iberians, and local guides. These men crossed the river 200 stades from their comrades and made camp. They set out the next day back down the river. When they reached the previously agreed spot, they sent up a smoke signal letting Hannibal know that they were in position and that the army could begin crossing the Rhone. As the main army began its struggle against the current towards the left bank, the Gauls assembled for battle. Suddenly, though, Hanno and his troops fell upon their camp and then attacked their rear. With Hannibal's main force crossing the river in numbers, and Hanno attacking from their rear, the Volcae broke, leaving the bank open to the Carthaginian army.[13]

With the banks clear, the army began crossing. It was a bit of a chore, especially getting the elephants to the other side. Nonetheless, the task was accomplished. The time it took gave the troops time to rest and provided Hannibal the opportunity to encourage them. A chieftain of the Gallic Boians, Magilus, and some of his fellows gave speeches to the army encouraging them and promising that they would fight alongside them against the Romans. They also told them about how rich the lands of Italy were, which appealed to the loot-and-plunder approach taken by many soldiers in the ancient world. While this was happening, Publius Cornelius Scipio, the Roman consul assigned to take the war to Iberia, landed at the mouth of the Rhone. Having discovered that Hannibal had already crossed the Pyrenees, he lingered here and sent 300 cavalrymen, along with guides from the allied city of Massalia as well as Gallic auxiliaries, to find the Punic army. These encountered 500 Numidian horsemen that had been sent out to reconnoitre. A fierce engagement ensued between these two bodies in which more than 200 of the Africans were killed while the Romans and their allies lost only about 140. The Numidians hurried back to their camp with their adversaries on their heels. This prompted Hannibal to order camp be struck the next morning, sending his cavalry out to act as a screen against a possible Roman attack while his infantry marched up the river. He waited at the crossing site as his elephants were ferried over.[14]

The northward march of the Punic army is fraught with difficulties from an historical perspective. Our sources do not provide us with enough information to trace the route with absolute certainty. We do know, however, that the march was relatively uneventful. Eventually they made their way towards a pass that ran through the Alps to Italy. Interactions with local Gallic tribes could be violent or more benign, but they did not significantly delay Hannibal's push to get to the other side of the mountain range. Perhaps the most obnoxious obstacle in his path was a massive landslide which impeded his progress down the southern slope. But, once beyond this, the Po Plain was in sight and open to the Carthaginian host.[15] Although the crossing of the Alps is often cited as a sign of Hannibal's genius, it is important to keep in mind that this 'was ordinarily no great task for an army' to do, as Dexter Hoyos has pointed out.[16]

The Romans were not entirely unprepared for this scenario, even if the extent of Hannibal's crossing was not completely known. Publius, having realized that he had missed catching the enemy on the Rhone, sent his brother Gnaeus along with the fleet on to Iberia to establish a foothold. The consul himself went to northern Italy to take command of two legions that had been sent there earlier in the year to deal with Gallic tribes who were resisting the settling of a new Latin colony.

Gnaeus and the Roman fleet first landed at Emporion, an allied Greek city. From here they met with success. The Romans were able to subdue the coast all the way to the Ebro. This was done through making alliances with the local peoples. Some of these were being renewed, others were entirely new. Although Livy makes this sound rather peaceful, the Romans also had to use force to bring some of this area under Gnaeus' control, laying siege to a number of towns according to Polybius. In addition to taking this region out of the hands of the Carthaginians, Gnaeus was able to raise a number of units of auxiliary troops from the tribes. The Punic commander left behind by Hannibal, Hanno, was not willing to sit by idly as his territory was taken from him. He set out with the army left to him and confronted the Roman invaders. They met on the field outside of a town called Cissis. The battle went poorly for Hanno, suffering 6,000 killed and 2,000 captured. He was also taken prisoner, and the heavy baggage left behind by Hannibal was captured.

The value of this booty was vast, as the army that had marched to Italy had left most of their treasure here.

Hearing of the Roman depredations, Hasdrubal, Hannibal's brother, brought his army from New Carthage to counter the threat. He marched 8,000 infantry and 1,000 cavalry across the Ebro, searching for the enemy. Rather than marching for Gnaeus' camp, after hearing of Hanno's defeat Hasdrubal made for the coast, searching for the Roman fleet. He found its sailors and marines scattered throughout the countryside, probably plundering or foraging for food. Throwing his cavalry at them, he killed many and chased the rest back to their ships. After this, the Punic army pulled back beyond the Ebro and went into winter quarters at New Carthage. The Romans may have continued campaigning for some time, but that is unclear. Gnaeus wintered his soldiers at Tarraco.[17]

This year (218 BC) also saw combat in the waters around Sicily, in what could have been the most (or only) coordinated action between Hannibal and leaders in Carthage. Sometime after the declaration of war, the Carthaginians sent twenty quinqueremes and 1,000 marines to raid the Italian coast. Three of these were intercepted by Hiero of Syracuse, a Roman ally. Their crews divulged that another Punic fleet, numbering thirty-five quinqueremes, had been sent to sow dissention amongst the old allies of Carthage on Sicily and to take Lilybaeum. With this advance notice, the Romans were able to prepare for this and prevented the Punic fleet from achieving anything. Seven ships were captured, with only one Roman vessel suffering significant damage. The rest of the Carthaginian squadron fled.[18] Thus, besides Hannibal successfully crossing the Alps, the war was starting well for the Romans. But the campaigning in northern Italy would prove this was not to be a quick and easy war.

Hannibal's Three Early Triumphs

Now that his army was in Italy, Hannibal's tactical skills and the abilities of his army would be tested against the Romans. He probably had with him 12,000 African infantry, 8,000 Iberian infantry, and 6,000 cavalry. These are the figures that Polybius cites as being inscribed by Hannibal himself at Cape Lacinium.[19] Livy preserves other figures, much higher, which should not be considered accurate.[20] This force, relatively small, would first encounter the Romans on the north bank of the River Po near where the tributary called the Ticinus flowed into it. Here, the Carthaginians ran into an army headed by Publius Scipio who had taken command of the forces which had been sent to defend Roman colonists against Gallic attacks in the Po Valley. With both a Punic and Roman army in the area, it was not long before they began feeling each other out. Eventually, they were camped close enough along the Po that their commanders were ready to test the other.

In what can be seen as the opening battle of the Italian campaign, both generals first approached with their cavalry, Scipio also bringing his skirmishers. Whether or not these forces were originally meant to simply reconnoitre the other's army, they came to blows. Hannibal formed the core of his line out of his heavy cavalry. Units of Numidians, lighter and faster horsemen, were stationed on each wing of the army. Scipio formed a front line out of his skirmishers and allied Gallic cavalry, while the rest of his horse followed in a second line. The skirmishers proved to be less-than-useful, as the initial clash came so quickly that they almost immediately retreated behind their allies. Thus, the cavalry of each side rode headlong into each other, resulting in a long and drawn-out skirmish between men on horseback and those who decided, or were forced, to dismount. The impression given by our sources is that the fight was a stalemate until the Numidian cavalry was able to get around the flanks of the Roman line and begin attacking from behind. Sometime during the melee, or as the army was breaking, Scipio himself was wounded and unable to make it out by himself. The Roman and allied cavalry closed in around him and ferried him off towards their main camp in an orderly retreat. However, the skirmishers had broken entirely and were being chased down by the swift cavalry of Hannibal. With the Roman army falling back, the victory clearly went to the Carthaginians.[21]

Although this was a relatively small-scale win, the effects should not be downplayed. It left the Roman commander wounded, as well as the army's pride. But it also secured for Hannibal the support of the Gallic tribes in northern Italy. These had not come over directly to him when he first crossed the mountains – as he had hoped – and had to be swayed. This was accomplished both through the victory at the Ticinus and the razing of the capital settlement of the Taurini.[22] It was supposedly the victory over Scipio which convinced a group of Gallic troops in the

Roman army to desert once they reached the camp at Placentia. Around 2,000 infantry and 200 cavalry defected to the Punic camp one night, killing a number of Romans as they burst out of the encampment in full armour. These were, of course, welcomed into the camp by Hannibal and their actions were a sign of Rome's situation.[23] The troops they murdered on their way out of the camp, as well as 600 Roman soldiers captured whilst trying to destroy the bridge behind Scipio's army, should probably be added to the casualties attributable to the Battle of the Ticinus.

With Scipio camped near Placentia, Hannibal pursued. When he caught up to the enemy, he arrayed his army for battle in full view of the Romans. This did not provoke a response, so he camped around five miles away. It was at this point that the Gallic troops (noted above) deserted. In addition to these, a group of chieftains from the Boii approached the Punic camp offering their friendship, bringing with them three Roman magistrates who had been sent to divide up lands meant for a colony. Hannibal accepted their friendship, but instructed them to keep the hostages and use them in an exchange to get back some of their own people from the Romans. Whether this was made known to Scipio or not, on the same night he ordered that camp be broken and had his army march towards the River Trebia. His attempt to conceal his movements under the cover of darkness was not successful, and Hannibal sent out his cavalry – first the Numidians and then the rest – in pursuit. The first group launched, however, stopped at the now abandoned Roman camp to loot it and set it aflame. This bought the Romans enough time to make it over the Trebia, even their baggage train. Only stragglers were caught up with, and they were either killed or taken prisoner.[24] Once on high ground near the Trebia, Scipio made camp and was determined to wait for his colleague in the consulship, Tiberius Sempronius Longus, to arrive from Sicily.

Around the time that Sempronius Longus arrived and camped near Scipio, Hannibal was handed an unexpected advantage. The garrison commander of the Roman supply depot at Clastidium, a Brundisian named Dasius, betrayed it to the Carthaginians. This could have been in exchange for a considerable sum of gold, as Livy notes.[25] The grain gained here stabilized the otherwise limited Punic supplies and was yet another minor, but important, defeat for the Romans. It also provided Hannibal with the opportunity to show his clemency, as he treated the captives taken there well. This was an important piece of propaganda for a general attempting to capture Italy. However, his position was not entirely secure in the neighborhood of the Trebia. A number of Gallic tribes between there and the Po were supposedly making deals with the Romans, despite giving him their allegiance. Perhaps it was the appearance of Sempronius' army that swayed them? Nevertheless, he sent 2,000 infantry and 1,000 cavalry to conduct raids in their lands. The newly arrived Roman commander sent out his cavalry and 1,000 velites in support of these allies. What emerged was a back-and-forth fight near the Punic camp. Although the units guarding it initially sallied out in support of their fellows, Hannibal took personal command of the fray and ordered an organized retreat back to the camp. Polybius notes that this was an indication of his skill as a general, that he did not believe a decisive battle should be fought haphazardly.[26] The Romans celebrated this as a victory, but it was to be a short-lived feeling of relief.

Hannibal judged his new opponent to be of a spontaneous nature. He believed that now was a perfect opportunity to lure the Romans into a trap from which they would not easily escape. The land between the camps was flat, though a stream flowed through it which had deep banks covered in dense shrubbery. Hannibal believed this would make a perfect shroud for a unit set in ambush. He sent Mago along with 1,000 cavalry and 1,000 infantry there to hide and wait. At first light, the Numidian cavalry was sent towards Sempronius' camp with orders to draw the Romans out. It was a snowy day, and the consul's men were provoked so early that they left without their morning meal. Even then, they pursued their enemy with tenacity, even fording the swollen and surely bitterly cold Trebia to follow them towards their camp. Although he first sent out his cavalry and skirmishers, Sempronius led the entire army across. When they had made it to the other side, Hannibal sent a group of spearmen and Balearic slingers out of camp as a screening force. But these were followed by the entire army.

Eight stades from his camp, Hannibal formed his battle line, stationing his infantry in the centre, flanked by the elephants which made it over the Alps, whose flanks were further guarded by the cavalry. His total strength was about 20,000 infantry and 10,000 cavalry. The Gallic infantry appears to have been stationed in the centre of the line, perhaps because they were untested or Hannibal did not trust them as they were new allies. The Romans numbered about 36,000 infantry in total, 16,000 being Romans and the others allies. Their 4,000 cavalry were formed up on the flanks of an otherwise standard Roman battle line. The Punic infantry was outnumbered by 16,000, but their cavalry outnumbered their opponents by 6,000. As the skirmishers engaged in front of the main lines, it was obvious that the Carthaginians were at an advantage. The Roman velites and cavalry had been chasing the Numidians all morning and had exhausted much of their ammunition; the men were also exhausted.

As the main bodies of infantry marched forwards, the skirmishers retreated through the gaps in their lines. When these came together, the advantage almost immediately went to the Carthaginians. The Roman cavalry was quickly driven off, allowing the Punic horse to attack the flanks of the infantry. At this juncture, the Carthaginian and Numidian infantry were also able to get at their opponents' flanks. There was little movement in the centre of the battle where a vicious melee was developing. As this stagnated, however, Mago and his Numidians, who were laying in ambush, emerged and fell on the Romans from behind. This threw the entire Roman line into confusion. The wings began to buckle first, facing elephants to their front and light troops of all kinds to their sides. Panic surely set in, with only a unit of 10,000 Romans in the centre marshalling themselves into an advantageous position. These fought through the centre of Hannibal's line, cutting down mostly Gauls and some Libyans as they managed to break through. Rather than retreat to their camp, they made straight for Placentia. This group was followed by as many others as could make it out of the fray, but much of the army was cut down on the field or at the river.

Hannibal had achieved a significant victory. Although his infantry was outnumbered, his strength in cavalry and tactical skills showed their value. Through exploiting the personal weakness of Sempronius, he was able to draw the Romans into what was ultimately an unwinnable battle. And not only did he inflict considerable casualties on the enemy, but he earned his soldiers a victory immediately before the long period of inactivity brought on by winter. Of course, the Punic army did pay for this in turn. Many men died from the cold and inhospitable weather, along with horses and all but one of the elephants. This was probably a small price to pay for such a success. When the Romans back home heard of their army's defeat, a panic set in. This was exacerbated, no doubt, by Hannibal's continued campaigning – however small-scale – during the winter. He let his cavalry pillage the land, and attacked a number of Roman depots. But the defeat at the Trebia was just a preview of things to come in June of the next year.[27]

As 218 became 217 BC, the Romans were forced to face the reality that Hannibal and his army had secured a strong foothold in Italy. It was probably obvious to all parties that he could not simply remain near the Po, however, and there were two possible routes for him to take from there south towards Roman territory. One of these was down the Adriatic coast, while the other was over the Apennines and into Etruria. Hannibal settled on the latter, perhaps to the surprise of some.[28] One of the newly elected consuls, Caius Flaminius, had positioned himself at Arretium with his new army to counter any possible move into the region. The consul was unable to stop Hannibal from crossing the mountains, however, and the Punic army pushed on as quickly as possible through marshlands around the River Arno. Cleverly, he stationed the African and Spanish infantry (his veterans) at the front, along with the baggage, and had the Gallic troops following them, who were themselves pushed on by the cavalry under the direct command of his brother Mago. This was a measure to ensure that the Celts did not desert. It was probably a wise decision, as they found the going tough.[29]

Hannibal camped near where he forged the marshes, which seems to have been near to where Flaminius was camped outside of Arretium. Either knowing of the bounty of Etruria, or seeing it firsthand, the Punic general's strategy was not to seek battle with his enemy directly, but to pillage the territory. We are led to believe that he knew the character of Flaminius to be too full of self-confidence and impulsive which would allow him to be drawn into a trap, though the historical tradition surrounding this *novus homo* is so negative that it is hard to tell what is, and what is not, historical truth.[30] Regardless, Hannibal began devastating the territory south of Arretium. This did as he had hoped and provoked the consul into following him. The Roman army was in pursuit of the Punic force, but the latter was still able to wreak havoc wherever they went. But when Flaminius got close enough and Hannibal found the right terrain, the two armies finally caught up to one another.

While continuing through the Etrurian countryside, Hannibal marched his army along the road which led between Arretium and Perugia. This passed by a lake which was to become famous because of the Carthaginian general: Trasimene. It was here that he had a spark of eureka, and yet again displayed his tactical genius. As he was marching his men forward, he noticed that they were passing through a relatively flat valley with hills to one side and the lake to the other. This gave him the idea of setting a vicious trap for his pursuers. On the evening that they marched into the valley, the Carthaginian army conspicuously made camp on hills at its far end. Here stayed the African and Spanish infantry, but the Celts and the cavalry were sent out along the ridge-line of the valley, with the Balearic slingers and spearmen stationed behind the ridge-line to the right of this end of the valley, thus preventing any enemies from fleeing in that direction. These manoeuvres were carried out at night so as to not be detected by Flaminius' men, a feat which is impressive in any age of warfare.

When dawn broke the following day, the consul led his army from the van into the valley. There was apparently a heavy mist that hung about the place, reducing visibility considerably. Between this and their concealed positions, the Carthaginian troops waiting in ambush were never seen. These waited until the Roman army made contact with the Spanish and African infantry at the far end of the valley, at which point Hannibal gave the signal (which would have been passed down the line) and his hidden troops burst over the tops of the hills. Like a great avalanche of men and iron, they came rushing upon their enemies. Many of the Roman units did not even have a chance to break from their marching order into battle formation. As the enemies came together, a savage melee developed. The advantage of surprise swung the battle in favour of Hannibal's army, but the Romans put up a stiff resistance, at least in places. Flamninius himself was said to have ridden around the battlefield encouraging his men and supporting units which were faltering. It was only when his bodyguard was cut down that a Gaul – perhaps named Ducarius – killed the consul.[31] At this, the Romans faltered and their fighting spirit began to leave them. Groups still defended themselves, though others broke and tried to flee in whichever direction they could. Many unfortunate Romans and their allies retreated into the lake, only to drown under the weight of their arms.

The only large body of Roman troops to escape from the battle en masse were 6,000 men at the vanguard of the column. These broke through their enemies, perhaps the Balearic soldiers, and fled to a nearby village. Unfortunately for them, their escape did not go unnoticed, and Hannibal dispatched one of his officers, Maharbal, with a detachment of Iberian infantry to chase them down. By nightfall they were surrounded by this force, and surrendered to them. In all, about 15,000 Romans and their allies were killed at Lake Trasimene, with almost the same number taken prisoner. This was all at the cost of between 1,500 and 2,500 losses on the Carthaginian side (our sources disagree on the figure). Many of these were Celts, against whom the Roman resistance seems to have been the strongest. But perhaps a more significant loss for Hannibal were the thirty officers, likely to be read as Carthaginian citizens. These were afforded special burial, which makes me think that they were of social significance as well as military. But the Punic general was to win one more victory in the wake of this campaign. The other consul, Gnaeus Servilius Geminus, on hearing that his colleague had made contact with Hannibal had sent 4,000 cavalry ahead of his own army to aid Flaminius. Hannibal was made aware of these reinforcements and dispatched Maharbal with a mixed force of cavalry and infantry to intercept them. When the two forces encountered each other they came to blows, with Gaius Cententius, the Roman commander, losing half of his men and the rest being trapped on a hilltop. These were then taken prisoner. Thus, in the course of a couple of days, Rome had lost an entire consular army as well as the whole body of cavalry from another. For Hannibal, this was a great victory.[32]

Defeat at Trasimene led the Romans to elect a dictator, Quintus Fabius Maximus, with Marcus Minucius Rufus serving as his master of horse. This was an understandable reaction, given that one consular army in Italy had just been destroyed, while the other was considerably weakened by the loss of its cavalry. In addition to raising new armies, the newly appointed leaders went about fortifying the landscape around the city of Rome. The city's walls and towers were reinforced, with sentries being placed where appropriate. Interestingly, Livy also notes that they ordered bridges destroyed, though we do not hear any details about which bridges were dismantled at this time.[33] Beyond the other efforts, this may have been one of the more important, if not a little futile given Hannibal's strategy (which would only be known later). But the importance of taking down bridges can be seen by Publius Scipio's efforts to break one down after his defeat at the Ticinus. Although this ended with a body of Roman soldiers being captured, removing easy river crossings slowed enemies down considerably. Fabius was to lead the Romans in a new strategy: one of delay, which kept Hannibal at bay for some time.

The War Outside Italy

As Hannibal's armies won considerable victories over the Romans in Italy, the war continued to rage elsewhere. His brother, Hasdrubal, used the winter to prepare a fleet of forty ships to accompany his land army in a campaign against the enemy in Iberia. After the coming of spring, he assembled his army from the soldiers' winter quarters, and ensured that his fleet was ready to sail. This was left under the command of either a Hamilcar or a Himilco, with Polybius naming the former and Livy the latter.[34] Proceeding from New Carthage, the army and navy stayed together along the coastline all the way to the River Ebro, and here they made camp. Seemingly at the same time, Gnaeus Scipio left his base at Tarraco and sailed towards the enemy. Having heard rumours that the Carthaginian army had been strengthened over the winter, he avoided a land battle and preferred to provoke a fight at sea. In preparation for this, he stocked his thirty-five ships with handpicked infantrymen, hoping that these would be enough to overwhelm his enemies.

After a two day sail, Scipio ordered his fleet to land about ten miles from Hasdrubal's camp, which was pitched at the mouth of the Ebro. From here, the Roman commander hoped to surprise the Carthaginians; knowing that the coastline would afford him some degree of cover, he ordered his ships to make quickly for the enemy. They were spotted, though, by several lookouts, either native Iberians or sentries deployed by Hasdrubal, and thus their approach was made known. This gave the Punic crews some time to man their ships, although Livy portrays them as doing so in a state of panic. It may have been putting to sea in haste and unprepared that led to the ensuing disaster. The Carthaginian ships confronted the Romans, but were quickly broken and sent fleeing back to land. Two ships were sunk outright with all hands, while twenty-five were towed into captivity by Gnaeus' sailors, capitalizing on them being unmanned and beached. Our sources blame the proximity of Hasdrubal's land army to the fleet – thus providing a safe haven – for the hasty retreat, but other factors, such as the Carthaginians' unpreparedness, could have been factors.[35]

Gnaeus Scipio won an important victory by securing the coast for the Romans. This enabled him to launch raids down the Mediteranean seaboard of Spain, hitting the hinterland of New Carthage, going so far as to set alight a number of buildings right against the city's fortifications. They then attacked Longuntica, further south, which was being used as a resource depot by Hasdrubal. Proceeding next to Ibiza, they besieged the island's main city for a short time and then pillaged its lands. Carthaginian fortunes did not fare much better inland. Although a short-lived rebellion by the Ilergetes made Gnaeus refocus his attention on them (though only temporarily), a larger invasion – or more likely a raid – by Celtiberians forced Hasdrubal to defend Punic possessions in Spain. If our source is correct, though, this was a directed attack by Scipio, who had recently received the Celtiberians as allies. Livy records that the Carthaginian losses in this short campaign were heavy, totalling some 15,000 soldiers dead and 4,000 captured, but these figures are probably exaggerated.[36]

This raiding was one part of a wider game of naval predation between the two powers. According to Polybius, Hasdrubal's defeat at the Ebro resulted in Carthage sending out seventy ships which sailed first to Sardinia and then to Pisa, though I believe that the two events were unconnected. These seem to have been sent to conduct raids in the Tyrrhenian Sea, and possibly link up with Hannibal in Italy. According to Livy, they captured some transport ships which had sailed from Ostia destined for Gnaeus Scipio in Spain.[37] At the news of this, the Romans dispatched a fleet of 120 ships under the command of Servilius Geminus, the consul whose imperium lapsed now that Fabius had been made dictator. These apparently gave chase to the Punic squadron but were unable to catch them. The latter made their way back to Carthage. Servilius, however, was not inactive while at sea. He took hostages from Sardinia and Corsica, ostensibly guaranteeing those islands' loyalties. But then the proconsul went on a raiding expedition of his own. He first sailed to the island of Meninx (modern Djerba) which he plundered thoroughly, and then led his fleet to Kerkennah (another island off Tunisia) where the population paid him ten talents of silver to spare their lands. This was a profitable endeavour, until Servilius ordered his men to land on the mainland and wreak further havoc. They were surrounded by locals – though we are not told who these were, and whether Carthaginians were involved – and slaughtered. Roman losses totalled 1,000 men. At this, they retreated back to the stronghold of Lilybaeum on Sicily – capturing the small island of Cossyra – and Servilius passed on command of the fleet as he was to resume command on land with the lapsing of Fabius' dictatorial *imperium*.[38]

Things were thus looking grimmer for Carthage outside of Italy. In the wake of the Ebro defeat, the Romans dispatched Publius Scipio to Spain to join forces with his brother, along with between twenty and thirty ships, 8,000 soldiers and considerable provisions. After his arrival, the brothers decided to cross the Ebro and take advantage of the Celtiberian incursion. They targeted Saguntum, the city at the centre of this war's beginning. Here, a traitor named Abilyx convinced the Punic garrison commander, Bostar, to release the hostages of prominent Iberian peoples back to their parents. These had been taken by Hannibal before leaving Spain in order to secure the loyalties of the different tribes. Rather than simply returning them home, though, Abilyx made a deal with the Scipios to make it seem as though the Romans had brought this on, and that they would treat the Iberian tribes more fairly than the Carthaginians. This gained the Romans more allies on the Peninsula. Gnaeus and Publius were unable to capitalize on this, however, as winter was setting in thus signalling the end of campaigning season. Both their armies and those of Carthage still in Spain demobilized for the season.[39]

Cannae: Hannibal's Greatest Victory

Punic fortunes were threatened in Italy after Trasimene in 217 BC. The new Roman leader, Fabius, devised a different strategy for dealing with Hannibal. The Carthaginian had marched his army over the Appenines and into Picenum following his victory over Flaminius. On their way to the Adriatic coast, the Punic army devastated everything in their path, practising what one could call a precursor to 'total warfare'.[40] Once they reached the sea, Hannibal allowed them to rest, periodically moving camp to keep up with the food-needs of the soldiers and their beasts of burden. He was even able to send a message to Carthage, the first time since his Italian campaign was launched, which was received with jubilance in the city. While there were promises of support issued, there was very little that the leaders in Africa could do to bring him assistance with the Romans having such strength at sea as they did. But his campaign continued on, and the army was marched south along the coast. They were shadowed by Fabius and his army, but the Roman refused to engage in a battle. He was happy to occupy strategic positions, denying them to Hannibal, and to attack the Punic foraging parties. The casualties inflicted were not high, but this strategy did prevent the Carthaginian army from taking possession of the entire countryside.

Fabius followed Hannibal all the way across the Apennines (again) and into Samnium and the plain around Capua. On his way, the Carthaginian even sacked the Roman colony of Beneventum. It was the produce of the Falernan Fields, however, that were the main goal. This region's agricultural output was known throughout the ancient world, and by seizing it Hannibal would be gaining for his army a considerable stock of supplies, and perhaps sway some of Rome's allies to switching sides. But this move trapped the Carthaginian army. With few means of extricating themselves from this region, the decision was made to go back out the same way that they came in. Fabius predicted this and was in a position to prevent it. He made camp on a hill below the pass, stationing 4,000 troops on the pass itself. Hannibal camped his army on flat ground near the bottom of the hills. Here, Fabius may have had the opportunity to attack. Even if this was his intention, though, he was pre-empted by his Carthaginian adversary.

Hannibal saw that his position was disadvantageous and settled on a stratagem to get out of it. He summoned Hasdrubal, the army's quartermaster, and ordered that bundles of combustibles be fastened to the horns of 2,000 cattle that had been captured during the campaign. In the evening, after a meal, he ordered that the army begin to march towards the pass, with the specially equipped cattle in the front. At an arranged signal, the firewood attached to them was lit and they were stampeded up the slopes towards the Romans who were holding the pass. These were frightened by the sight, thinking that they had been surrounded as the flaming cattle began spreading throughout the hills around them, and a general panic set in. Even after the Romans realized that they were not soldiers, fear of being caught in an ambush led them to retreat further.[41] While this was happening, Hannibal led his army through the gorge that formed the pass, with only a unit of light infantry engaging the Romans. These were left behind as the main column pushed through and had to be rescued by a group of Iberian veterans, accustomed to fighting in broken ground amongst large rocks and steep hills. Even though the fighting was relatively minor, the Roman losses numbered about 1,000.

Hannibal was now free to find winter quarters for his army. He settled on Gerunium, in Apulia, as there was said to be considerable grain in its hinterland and because it would make a strong base. He besieged and stormed the town after negotiations for its surrender fell apart, slaughtering the inhabitants. Taking advantage of all the resources at hand, Hannibal ordered that the town's walls be left standing, certainly making the task of fortifying the winter camp less arduous. And indeed, the territory around them was found to be filled with grain, though whether it was still in the field or in granaries (given that it was probably already September) is unknown.[42]

The Carthaginians had been followed by the Roman army, now led by the master of horse, Minucius. Fabius had been recalled to Rome, either to perform certain religious rituals or because the Senate or the people were dissatisfied with his handling of the war. Either way, he left his subordinate with orders not to engage the enemy and to maintain the strategy of shadowing Hannibal as much as possible. Portrayed as a man similar in spirit to Flaminius, Minucius did not obey this order. Tracking the Punic army, he brought his camp nearer to it. This provoked a response, with the Carthaginian general bringing about two-thirds of his army to a forward position, between Minucius and the main base at Gerunium. Of these troops, Hannibal sent 2,000 to hold a smaller hill between the two armies. The master of horse led an assault on these the morning after their occupation of the small summit, routing them with a force of light infantry. He proceeded to relocate the main Roman camp to this hill, and was now in striking distance of the Carthaginian forward camp. From this new position, Minucius launched raids against the enemy foraging parties, ordering that no quarter be given. This was a successful strategy, and he was able to kill a considerable number of them. The Roman was so emboldened that he launched an all-out attack on Hannibal's position when the latter was forced to send out foragers. Screened by the cavalry and light infantry, the Roman heavy infantry assaulted the Punic fort, going so far as to pull down some of the palisade. But a relieving force of 4,000 men under Hasdrubal came from Gerunium and was able to evacuate Hannibal and his men. He was forced to retreat to his main base and to practise a more restrained system of foraging.[43]

But this minor defeat would prove to be advantageous for the Carthaginian cause. It led to the Roman command being split between Fabius and Minucius, each taking half of the army and creating separate camps (and following different strategies).[44] The dictator favoured his previous plan of preventing Hannibal from collecting supplies and waging a war of attrition against his foraging parties. The master of horse, however, was inclined to force a major battle, especially now that he had tasted victory against Hannibal. Division in the Roman camp did not remain a secret, and news of the split was brought to the Punic army by way of deserters, spies, and prisoners. A strategy of targeted provocation was chosen. Hannibal sent a small force to very conspicuously take possession of a small hill between his camp and that of Minucius. This had the desired effect, and the master of horse sent out his light troops to take this strategic point. He then ordered the cavalry to follow them up, and in a third wave would personally lead out the heavy infantry. Hannibal used a similar method of deployment, reinforcing the small unit he had first sent with waves of reinforcements, eventually bringing up the cavalry and the main body of the army. The Punic cavalry drove the first Roman wave back towards their main body, causing dismay amongst the heavy infantry. When the main infantry lines of the two armies came together, Hannibal signalled for the 5,000 infantry and 500 cavalry that he had placed in hiding spots throughout the valley below to attack the flanks and rear of Minucius' line. This wrought chaos amongst the legionaries. Fabius, observing the battle from his camp, ordered his army to march to his colleague's rescue. His arrival was probably all that prevented an all-out disaster for Rome. With the appearance of the second army, Hannibal decided to withdraw from the field, and he emerged again as victor over a Roman army.[45]

As the year was coming to a close, the Romans were forced by their customs to choose new leaders. Two new consuls were elected, Lucius Aemilius Paullus and Gaius Terentius Varro. Their names would live on in history for the disaster which occurred under their auspices in the coming year. But, before that could happen, they recruited fresh soldiers to bring the armies up to their full strengths. While the consuls were otherwise busy, those of the year before, Servilius Geminus and Marcus Atilius Regulus (who was appointed after the death of Flaminius) took command of the armies of the outgoing dictator and master of horse. Their orders were similar to those left by Fabius to Minucius: avoid battle but harry the enemy in small engagements. Eventually, the consuls of 216 BC took command of the refreshed legions and shared command, switching daily who was in charge. They maintained two camps, one nearer to Hannibal than the other. The Carthaginians, rather than being strengthened, were beginning to run out of supplies. Because the peoples of the surrounding territories had taken the harvest into fortified centres, there was little to forage. Shortly after the arrival of Aemilius Paullus and Varro, a large body from the Punic army were searching out food and ended up fighting a small battle with the Romans. In this, Hannibal lost 1,700 men in exchange for only 100 Roman casualties. Or at least this is what Livy would have us believe.[46] Polybius' version of events is that Hannibal broke camp at Gerunium before the arrival of the newly elected consuls, and that Servilius was leading the Roman army in a distant pursuit. The enemy's departure from winter quarters had supposedly spurred the Senate to send out Paullus and Varro.[47] Modern historians typically lean towards Polybius' account, pointing out that Livy's also includes an improbable plan to trick the Romans into a decisive battle almost immediately after leaving camp.[48]

Regardless of when the consuls arrived, it was sometime before Hannibal captured the razed city of Cannae. Though the town was gone, the Romans were using it as a supply depot, taking advantage of its citadel to store grain. Its fall into Hannibal's hands was extremely distressing for the Romans, perhaps what galvanized the Senate into forcing a battle, rather than continuing the Fabian strategy.[49] The current consuls were also in a powerful position to beat Hannibal in the field. Their combined army amounted to about 80,000 infantry and 6,000 cavalry.[50] Hannibal probably had about 40,000 infantry and 10,000 cavalry under his command at this point.[51] Not all of these would actually fight in the coming battle, with the Romans leaving behind around 10,000 soldiers to guard their camp, while Hannibal could have left behind 8,000 of his men to do the same.[52] These men spent a number of days camped near each other just north of Cannae, engaged in a deadly staring game, broken only by skirmishing. Paullus refused battle when Hannibal marched out of his camp on 1 August. The next morning, however, saw command of the combined Roman army shift to Varro who decided that he would lead out the army on that day.

The consul ordered his army to form up in a single line. His right flank was against the River Aufidus and was made up of the Roman citizen cavalry, while the left was composed of the allied cavalry. The heavy infantry was spread between these two units, but was deployed in a rather unorthodox fashion. While the maniples – standard combat-sized unit in a Roman army – typically had space between them, this was reduced considerably. They were also deployed deeper than usual, to the point that the maniples were deeper than they were wide. In front of all of these were the light infantry, supposedly stationed rather far in front of the rest of the army.[53] The exact disposition of the Roman and the allied units is unclear from our sources, though it has been proposed that the line would have consisted, in essence, of four separate armies.[54]

Seeing that the enemy was finally willing to fight a battle, Hannibal led his army out of camp. Using his light infantry as a screen, they crossed the river to meet the Romans. On his left he stationed the Spanish and Celtic cavalry – these would oppose the Roman citizen horse. The Numidian cavalry were on the right, opposed to the Romans' allied cavalry. But the centre was where Hannibal's genius was truly displayed. On the wings of the infantry line, he stationed his African infantry in deep formations. Notably, these had been re-equipped with Roman arms in the wake of the Battle of Lake Trasimene. Between these two detachments were placed the Iberian and Celtic infantry. Rather than being broken up by nationality, as we have generally encountered in the history of Carthaginian warfare, they were divided up into smaller units, perhaps of a few hundred men each, which were deployed alternatively (i.e. Iberian-Celtic-Iberian-Celtic-etc.).[55]

Hannibal led the infantry from the centre, along with his brother Mago. Hasdrubal was in command of the Iberian and Celtic cavalry, while Maharbal led the Numidians. Command in the Roman line was divided between the two consuls and the two proconsuls: Varro led the allied cavalry, Paullus the Roman,[56] while Servilius Geminus and Atilius Regulus were amongst the infantry.

Before the main lines came together, Cannae opened like many other battles from the ancient world, with an exchange of missiles between the skirmishers. The Roman cavalry charged forward only to be countered immediately by the Iberian and Celtic horse. Interestingly, this was not a 'normal' cavalry engagement, with the troopers dismounting and fighting man-to-man rather than manoeuvring and fighting as if a fluid entity, some being forcibly pulled off their mounts by their enemies. The Punic skirmishers may have come to aid their fellows, as Paullus was wounded at the beginning of this engagement by a sling stone.[57] Fierce fighting on this wing eventually led to the Roman horse retreating. By now Hannibal was leading the centre of his infantry forward, having them over-extend the middle of their formation thus forming a crescent shape. These troops engaged the Roman heavy infantry in a vicious fight. Neither side was willing to give. Eventually, though, Hannibal's centre was forced backwards. Energized by what appeared to be success, the Romans pushed forward with vigour. Unbeknown to them, though, the Libyan infantry was waiting for them. As they pressed their advance, Hannibal's reserves dressed their lines and turned to face their enemies, now able to attack them in the flanks and in the rear. They were able to capitalize on the Romans' inability to form a coherent fighting line after they had broken through the Carthaginian centre. Advantages continued to stack up for the Punic army as Hasdrubal directed his cavalry to ride to the assistance of the Numidians on their extreme right who had been fighting indecisively against the Latin cavalry. Even before the reinforcements arrived, Varro and his men fled the field. These were pursued by the Numidians, but Hasdrubal ordered his cavalry to attack the rear of the Roman infantry. Their constant charge-and-retreat manoeuvres further demoralized their enemies and helped the Libyans in cutting down the Romans.

Having fallen into Hannibal's army like fish into a net, the massive Roman army was slowly destroyed. It must have been a relatively slow process to kill their enemies, as the Carthaginian army was still outnumbered. But the killing went on, despite the undoubted exhaustion of all the soldiers involved. Polybius presents it almost as if Hannibal's army was slowly peeling apart an onion made of men; removing the outer layers to reach those of the interior. In total, about 48,200 soldiers from the Roman army were killed, with 19,300 taken prisoner, and 14,550 escaping.[58] Notably, Varro escaped the disaster that he initiated.[59] Hannibal's losses were considerably smaller: 200 cavalry, 1,500 Iberians and Libyans, and 4,000 Celts. Despite the disparity, this was a costly loss. As Louis Rawlings has described it, this victory was 'Pyrrhic in scale'.[60]

The next day was spent cleaning up the battlefield and territory around Cannae. Hannibal's men walked the field, stripping the dead of what they liked as was customary in the Mediterranean world. They also captured what Romans were left standing either in the camps or elsewhere. Rome was now in a very dire position. Their grand army had been utterly destroyed, some of their most experienced leaders and soldiers were dead in a field in Apulia, and they had to reorganize themselves in preparation to defend the city itself from Hannibal. At least, this was expected to be his next move, though it was not. His officers are portrayed as having argued to march on Rome, with Maharbal advocating very strongly for it.[61] Hannibal did not listen to this counsel, and almost certainly for the best.[62] Although Rome had suffered a considerable loss at Cannae, the city itself was not defenceless and would have required a lengthy siege to bring into submission. But, as I have just noted, the Carthaginian losses at Cannae were also significant and the army was in no position to fight a war of attrition outside the walls of Rome.

Rather than opening a window to attacking the city, Hannibal's victory at Cannae gave him a different, probably stronger, advantage. It brought over to his cause a considerable number of cities throughout Italy. Eventually, a good number of the important cities of Italy would side with the Carthaginians. Hannibal would be in Italy until his recall to Carthage in 205 BC, and his ability to stay was largely due to the defection of these peoples. Of course, the Romans did not passively let this happen, and the war in Italy raged.[63] As this is not a book focusing on the Second Punic War, nor the wars against Rome in general, we do not have time for a detailed narrative and discussion of this period.[64] It is important to note, however, that during his time on the peninsula, Hannibal was only reinforced by Carthage once. Whether this was a breakdown in strategic design or because the Punic navy could accomplish little against the Romans is debatable. The lack of a major port for long periods may have prevented this from happening, and there seemed to be an impetus to send aid from Spain rather than over the sea (see below). But for the time being Hannibal continued his campaign against the Romans on their home turf, keeping at least some of their attention focused there. He was also able to form an alliance between Carthage and Philip V of Macedon, which dragged the Romans into a war in Greece, although their involvement was limited.[65]

The War for Spain

The Iberian Peninsula was the focal point for the beginning of this war. It was with the siege of Saguntum that Hannibal provoked the conflict, and it was here that Rome found some of her early successes. When we last left Spain, Hasdrubal had recently lost important hostages held in New Carthage thanks to the incompetence of that city's garrison commander. The brothers Scipio, Publius and Gnaeus, had sent their army into winter quarters and demobilized for the year. With the advent of campaigning season, they took back to the field, with Publius leading the fleet and Gnaeus the army. Hasdrubal, however, was cautious in his manoeuvres. He avoided a direct confrontation with the Romans early in the year, but was bolstered when reinforcements arrived from Carthage to the tune of 4,000 infantry and 500 cavalry. This may have been enough of a boost to convince him to take the offensive against the Romans, but a revolt by the Tartesii, an Iberian tribe, forced him to refocus his efforts. We are led to believe that putting down this rebellion was not an easy task and that it cost the Carthaginians time and troops. Even after Hasdrubal had pacified them, a message was delivered from Carthage which ordered him to march to Italy, rumours of which spread throughout Iberia and caused further uprisings.

An army dispatched from Africa, led by Himilco, was to take Hasdrubal's place in Spain. The newly arrived commander informed his compatriot of the orders from Carthage and was in turn instructed in how to deal with the peninsula. With little that he could do, Hasdrubal extracted resources from the tribes in his area and began marching towards the Ebro with the intention of heading to Italy (probably early in 215 BC). But his movements were countered by the Scipios, who were aware that if he was allowed to reach Italy the Roman cause would be even more imperilled. Eventually the two armies found each other and camped for a number of days just five miles apart. When Hasdrubal and the Scipios decided to offer battle, it was mutual.

Hasdrubal arranged his army in ethnic blocks, as was typical for a Punic army. On the right wing was much of his Numidian cavalry, to the left of which was the Carthaginian citizen infantry. In the middle of his line he stationed his Iberian infantry, with the left wing consisting of the other African infantry and then his 'other' cavalry (perhaps the Moors mentioned later by Livy). The Romans were arrayed in the typical three-line *triplex acies* formation which served them for much of the Republic. When the melee began, the Romans quickly beat back the centre of Hasdrubal's line, his Spanish infantry easily giving way. This caused the Scipios' army to surge through the middle, similar to what had happened to the Romans in the previous year at Cannae. Like that battle, the Punic wings were then able to attack their enemies in the flank, and possibly the rear. But, unlike at Cannae, this does not seem to have been planned, and the Romans were able to reform their battle lines and confront their new attackers.[66] Their superiority in numbers helped them to secure a victory, though a costly one. What is notable about the Battle of Ibera, though, is that we hear of Carthaginian citizen infantry fighting, and fighting well. It is good to remember that despite the comments of some modern commentators, the Punic people were willing to, and did, fight in their own armies.[67]

Gnaeus and Publius had accomplished what they set out to, and prevented Hasdrubal from marching to Italy. Their victory also seems to have had a similar effect as Hannibal's at Cannae: many Iberian tribes defected to the Roman cause. The Punic position in Spain was now tenuous, a far cry from its time providing wealth for a resurgent Carthage. Upon receipt of the news in the assembly in Carthage, Mago Barca was sent to aid his brother against the Scipios, taking with him an army of 12,000 infantry, 1,500 cavalry, and twenty elephants. This force was originally destined for his other brother, Hannibal, in Italy, but the situation in Spain was more dire from the view of the political leaders back home. But what happened next in Iberia is unclear. The narrative we possess is confusing at points, and generally considered faulty by historical standards. A rebellion in Africa led by a Numidian, Syphax, could have been brought about by the Scipios and seems to have drawn some of the military resources out of Spain. Hasdrubal Barca may also have been recalled to lead the fight.[68] It is also clear that in 212 BC the Romans were able to capture Saguntum.[69]

Carthaginian fortunes looked grim until 211 BC. In this year, they were operating three armies in Spain. These were commanded by Hasdrubal Barca, Mago Barca, and Hasdrubal Gisco. The Romans were still led by the Scipios, whose army had been in some ways neglected by their leaders back home. But the brothers had bolstered their strength in the winter by recruiting 20,000 Celtiberians into their ranks. Livy opens his narrative when all of these armies were near one another. Mago and Hasdrubal Gisco had combined forces and were camped some five miles away from the Romans, while Hasdrubal Barca was even closer near the town of Amtorgis. Perhaps it was arrogance developed through a string of victories in years past, but Gnaeus and Publius made the decision to split their army in two. They were convinced that they would emerge victorious regardless of the disposition of their forces, and wanted to engage all three of the Carthaginian armies at once. They were afraid that if they defeated one then the others would flee.

Thus, Publius took two-thirds of the army to attack the combined camp of Hasdrubal Gisco and Mago Barca, while Gnaeus only took one-third to lead the attack on Hasdrubal Barca. Gnaeus found his prey sooner than his brother, and he encamped across a river from him. Unbeknownst to the Roman commander, though, Hasdrubal almost immediately engaged in secret dealings with the chieftains leading his Celtiberian auxiliaries. Through a large bribe, the Carthaginian was able to get them to betray the Romans. As they marched out of camp, Gnaeus realized that his position was now perilous and decided to retreat. His brother, Publius, however, was not afforded this luxury. Masinissa, a Numidian, constantly harassed his column as it was on the move. Encamping did little to save the Romans. When word reached their commander that a force of Iberians was approaching to join the Carthaginian armies, he ordered a night attack to prevent this. Although his men found their prey, they were quickly attacked by the Numidian cavalry while fighting the Spanish reinforcements. The defeat was cemented with the arrival of Hasdrubal Gisco and Mago's armies, who crushed their enemies. Publius Scipio was felled during the battle by a spear which pierced his right side. The remnants of his army fled as best they could, but the cavalry and light infantry of the Carthaginians were too much for them.

News did not reach Gnaeus of his brother's destruction but the approach of the other Punic armies led him to realize what had happened. As his column attempted to make a hasty withdrawal towards territory more firmly in their grasp, they were constantly harassed by the Carthaginian cavalry. This slowed them down so much that there was no hope of escape. Gnaeus ordered his men to the top of a hill, though it afforded only the protection of being higher ground than that around it. It was barren of natural obstacles or impassable cliffs. Here they made their last stand, using packsaddles as makeshift fortifications, and clustering the baggage and cavalry in the middle of an infantry circle. Although confused at first by the objects used to create a palisade, the Carthaginians were easily able to breach the defences and slaughter the Romans. Gnaeus either died on the hilltop, fighting alongside his men, or shortly after having been penned up inside a nearby tower.[70]

Roman success in Spain had finally failed, and it looked as if they were in a position of losing all there that they had gained. Their situation was salvaged thanks to the endeavours of men who survived the disasters brought about by the Scipios. They were able to preserve a small amount of territory under Roman control north of the Ebro. Caius Claudius Nero was sent to Iberia with about 10,000 infantry and 1,000 cavalry to bolster the defences.[71] What he accomplished is unknown, though his efforts were probably concentrated on maintaining a Roman foothold in Spain. At the end of 210 BC, though, a new commander was sent from Rome who would be remembered by history as one of the most significant figures of the war.

This was Publius Cornelius Scipio, later to be called Africanus, son of the Publius Scipio who had just been killed. He brought with him another 11,000 reinforcements, raising the Roman army's strength to 28,000 infantry and 3,000 cavalry.[72] While he wintered at Tarraco, the Carthaginian armies were dispersed throughout the peninsula. Mago was somewhere in the south near the Straits of Gibraltar, while his brother Hasdrubal was near Toledo. Hasdrubal Gisco was in Lusitania near the mouth of the River Tagus.[73] Any of these three armies were probably as large as that now under Scipio's command. Certainly, with the defeat of his father and uncle in mind, the young commander decided against attacking any of the armies in the field, and instead settled on taking one of the key Carthaginian cities: New Carthage. This was similar to the way wars had been waged on Sicily in centuries past, as we have seen in earlier chapters, in which cities were targeted rather than pitched battles sought. He took with him 25,000 infantry and 2,500 cavalry, leaving a garrison behind at the Ebro. In a swift march – though more than the seven days described by our sources – the Roman army made its way towards New Carthage.

The city was fortified by walls and natural barriers. It was connected to the mainland only by a small isthmus, and surrounded on the other sides by the Mediterranean and a lagoon to the north. Inside was Mago, though not Barca, the garrison commander, along with 1,000 soldiers and 2,000 townsfolk levied and armed. Scipio made camp on the high ground at the end of the strip of land which connected to the city. He fortified the rear of his camp, but left the front (towards the city) open. Early the next day, the Romans launched their assault; 2,000 soldiers along with ladder bearers made for the main gate. But they were met by a sally of the town levy. Although these put up a bit of resistance, they were soon routed back into New Carthage. The Roman advance from the mainland was mirrored by an attack by the fleet from the harbour. Ladders were brought against the walls, but they were unable to capture them. Mago's defenders were putting up an admirable fight. With his casualties growing from missile attacks overhead, Scipio sounded the retreat. But it was only to his camp.

Here, the general allowed his men to rest, but had no intention of breaking off his effort. Later in the day, Scipio once again ordered his troops to prepare to attack. They rushed forward as before, with more ladders and probably no less vigour. Even then, though, the defenders were able to repulse them and keep them from mounting the walls. But the Roman commander had already set in motion a plan which would ultimately bring the city down. He had ordered 500 men to march around the lagoon north of the city and wait until the waters receded enough that it could be crossed. The daily flow of this lagoon was a secret Scipio had learned from a number of fishermen early upon his arrival in Spain while he was still stationed at Tarraco.[74] Mago had stationed all of his defenders on the parts of the wall facing what he thought were the only attackers. Thus, when the 500 hand-picked Romans set their ladders against the north wall they easily got control of it and began pushing their way towards the main gate. Driving off the defenders here, they were able to hack through the gate with the assistance of their compatriots on the other side. At about the same time the soldiers in the fleet were able to get on top of the wall from the harbour.

New Carthage was all but taken. The Romans swarmed through the streets like locusts, ordered to kill anyone that they encountered. Importantly, they were not allowed to begin looting yet as there may still have been organized resistance somewhere in the city. There were 500 of the regular soldiers on a hill within the walls, though they were defeated at the first charge. As the slaughter ran on it was apparent that the only place not yet in Roman hands was the citadel. Here, Mago and his soldiers were holding out. Although they may have been in a defensible position, able to survive for days, their commander saw that it was a lost hope. Upon the garrison's surrender, Scipio signalled for his troops to stop killing the population and turn instead to plundering the city. Not only was taking one of the Carthaginian's most important cities in Spain a major boost for the Romans, it also happened to be a supply depot. Amongst the booty and prisoners were a considerable number of projectile-throwing engines, considerable reserves of wheat and barley, and eighteen warships. He also gained a number of important Carthaginian captives, including two members of the Council of Thirty and fifteen members of the Senate. Scipio was also able to release many Iberian hostages being held at New Carthage, bringing even more of the peoples on the peninsula over to the Roman side.[75]

The Romans lingered in their new possession for some time. Scipio ordered his troops to undertake a very strenuous training regimen. This involved both general physical training, such as marching long distances with all of their equipment, and combat drills using dummy weapons. Taking New Carthage was the only accomplishment of this campaigning season, though it was a significant one. Scipio ordered his army back to Tarraco to take up winter quarters, leaving behind a garrison in his new possession. Back across the Ebro, he was able to consolidate his forces, including incorporating the soldiers of the fleet with the land army, and accepted the friendship of numerous Iberian tribes. It was from here in the next spring or summer that he planned to launch a new drive into Punic lands, this time targeting Hasdrubal Barca's army. As the armies were already somewhat near to each other, this was a sensible target. It was also essential for Scipio to engage and defeat this force before the other two Carthaginian armies in Spain were able to link up with it.

The two armies met near the town of Baecula. Hasdrubal took up a defensive position on an easily defended hill. To the rear and in front of his camp was a river, on either side were steep slopes, and in front was a manageable gradient which led down to another flat bit of land, again flanked by steep slopes. Scipio camped nearby and played the usual game of staring down the enemy. It would be the Roman that took the initiative and decided to attack. When the time came, he sent two cohorts out to guard the passages into the valley on either end. These were certainly to prevent Mago Barca or Hasdrubal Gisco from reinforcing Hasdrubal Barca. This is an indication of how ineffective military intelligence was in the ancient world compared to the modern world.

Scipio first sent his light infantry with a handpicked group of heavy infantry against Hasdrubal's skirmishers who were stationed on the flat land below the main camp. A fierce exchange of missiles ensued, with the Romans supposedly throwing stones that they found all around them. Even though they were defending the high ground, the Punic units were having a hard time repelling their enemies. Once the Romans reached the level ground of the plateau and hand-to-hand combat began, Hasdrubal's light infantry fled back to the main battle line, which he had drawn up outside of the camp. Here they found what should have been a safe haven. The army was not small and was led by a capable commander. There may have even been elephants in front of the camp. But it seems that Hasdrubal had not led out his full army before Scipio's attack began. This meant that it was not at full fighting strength when Scipio's second wave reached it. He led this in person from the Roman left, leaving the right to his friend Caius Laelius. These two detachments climbed up the difficult ravines on either side of the hill, taking the Carthaginians by surprise. Falling on Hasdrubal's flanks and rear, this caused panic in his army. Panic turned quickly to defeat. But Hannibal's brother was not willing to make a final stand here.[76]

He may have prepared to leave Spain even before Scipio actually engaged his army, as implied by our sources. Hasdrubal's war chest and elephants were hastily on the move as defeat became obvious, and he marshalled as much of his remaining army as he could up the River Tagus towards the Pyrenees. From here he marched towards Italy. The Gauls did not seem to give him the same amount of trouble as they had Hannibal years before, perhaps because he was able to bribe them. His presence caused a stir in Rome, provoking flashbacks to Hannibal's early years in Italy. Upon descending the Alps, Hasdrubal attacked Placentia, putting it under siege. This was ultimately unsuccessful, as its residents put up a stiff resistance. While here, though, he sent letters to Hannibal which were intercepted. The Romans were now made aware of his plans to meet up with his brother in Umbria and were thus able to predict his movements. Hasdrubal was intercepted by an army near the Metaurus river and his army was destroyed. He was killed in the field.[77]

Iberia saw little action in 207 BC, with Scipio less active than in his first two campaigning seasons in the theatre. The Carthaginians were in the process of rebuilding their forces there. Hasdrubal Gisco had retreated all the way to Gades, in southern Spain on the Atlantic side of the Straits of Gibraltar. Hanno had been sent from Carthage as a replacement commander for Hasdrubal Barca, and joined with Mago. To bolster whatever troops he brought with him from Africa, he set out to recruit more soldiers from the Celtiberian tribes. He seems to have had little trouble in finding men willing to fight for him. But this was not to be a successful venture. Scipio had sent Marcus Silanus with a detachment of 10,000 infantry and 500 cavalry into the Celtiberian lands of the interior. This could have been a direct response to Hanno's recruitment efforts as we hear of Celtiberian deserters guiding the Romans through the countryside. Eventually, Silanus found the Punic camps, one full of the freshly recruited Celtiberians and the other consisting of the Carthaginians. Although the Romans did not take them completely by surprise, there was not enough time to properly form up battle lines. The Celtiberians engaged first, being led by Mago who had just ridden over from his camp. Although they were 4,000 strong with 200 horsemen, the restricted terrain did not allow them to fight in the manner to which they are accustomed – a fluid style of fighting. They were heavily defeated, and an attempted relief column from the Carthaginian camp did nothing to stem the Roman victory. When it was clear that the field was lost, Mago fled along with the cavalry and what elements of the infantry could disengage, but Hanno was captured. The young Barca reached Hasdrubal Gisco at Gades and brought with him around 2,000 infantrymen and supposedly all of the cavalry. The Celtiberian survivors simply slipped away into the countryside, returning to their villages.[78]

Scipio also deprived Hasdrubal Gisco of a Spanish city called Orongis, an otherwise unknown name to us, which he had used as a raiding base. Another 10,000 infantry and 1,000 cavalry were detached from the main army for this duty and led by his brother, Lucius Scipio. When they first arrived, they found the city to be closed to them and protected by walls. It took two assaults to break through the defenders but it was eventually taken. A Punic garrison of unknown strength was captured.

Scipio Africanus was pleased by this success, perhaps indicating that the operations being undertaken from here by Hasdrubal were significant. After this, Lucius Scipio was sent to Rome to report on the Iberian war, taking Hanno as his prisoner. The Romans then went into winter quarters at Tarraco while Hasdrubal remained tucked away out of reach.[79]

Although they had suffered greatly in Spain since the arrival of Scipio Africanus, the Carthaginians were not yet willing to give up the peninsula. In the spring of 206 BC, Hasdrubal Gisco left his winter quarters at Gades and assembled a massive army in an effort to reassert Punic hegemony. Our sources preserve two figures for its size, either 50,000 infantry and 4,500 cavalry, as recorded by Livy, or 70,000 infantry, 4,000 cavalry, and thirty-two elephants as recorded by Polybius. Livy's numbers are generally preferred and they do seem more likely. This army must have consisted of what was left of the troops from earlier campaigns, but both Hasdrubal and Mago spent time levying new soldiers from throughout Spain. Such a widespread effort did not go unnoticed by the enemy and Scipio made the decision to get his army in the field immediately. He marched from his winter quarters in Tarraco and headed towards the Carthaginian position. Along the way he was able to recruit small groups of auxiliaries that had been pledged to him by local tribes, as well as a substantial force from Colichas, an Iberian ruler, of 3,000 infantry and 500 cavalry. This brought his total army up to about 45,000 infantry and 3,000 cavalry.[80]

Hasdrubal and Mago seem to have sat waiting for their Roman adversary to find them, or so our sources make it appear. When Scipio did locate them near Ilipa, he set up his camp nearby, as we have seen was common practice. Mago and Masinissa risked a stratagem to put the Roman off his footing by launching a large cavalry attack while the camp was being settled. Although this does not seem like a terrible idea, Scipio had apparently prepared for it. His entire cavalry arm had been stationed out of sight of the Carthaginian camp and pounced on the attackers as they moved forward out of formation. The surprise this caused was enough to drive off at least some of the Punic horsemen, but the main body stayed and fought on. Eventually Mago and Masinissa's men broke entirely and suffered considerable casualties as they were chased back to their own camp. This attack did little to demoralize or inhibit the Romans, but negatively affected the morale in Hasdrubal and Mago's camp.[81]

Skirmishing went on between the camps for days. This may have been an indication that neither side was entirely confident in victory, or simply that the commanders wanted to develop a fuller understanding of their enemy. But for Scipio it was also an opportunity to deceive Hasdrubal into making an error. Everyday when the armies were marshalled out in front of their camps, the Roman stationed his citizen legions in the centre of his line and the Iberian allies on the wings. Hasdrubal mirrored this by deploying his Libyan infantry in the centre and his Spanish units on the wings. In this way, the Carthaginians' most seasoned troops would meet those of the Romans. Scipio's plan required that the Punic command believe this was going to be his battle order when the day finally came. When the chosen day finally arrived, the Romans ate an early breakfast and prepared to move out at first light. The cavalry and light infantry were sent out first, perhaps even before dawn broke, and provoked Hasdrubal to send out his cavalry and skirmishing infantry in response.

Following this, Hasdrubal marched his main infantry column out from camp, lining them up in the same way that he had done for days, with the infantry arrayed as above, the wings protected by his elephants. In front of him was the Roman army, slowly marching towards the Punic camp. As the skirmishers were engaged in a back-and-forth fight, Scipio's line began to form and reveal to Hasdrubal that they were in a very different formation than on the days before. In the centre were the Iberians, while the wings were made up of the Roman and Italian troops. The Carthaginians had no time to react to this, as reforming the entire battle line would probably have been impossible at this point and would have opened them up to an attack while they were unprepared. Staring each other down as the light infantry and cavalry skirmished, hunger must have been setting in on the Punic side as they had not been able to eat a breakfast before leaving camp. Eventually, the swift troops were recalled, pulling back behind their respective lines. Scipio had these reform on the wings, both the cavalry and the light infantry. As the Romans marched forward, it was also clear that a deeper tactical ploy was unfolding, more complex than merely shifting units' positions. The Spanish troops in the centre were marching far slower than the legions on the wings. At one point, the legionaries wheeled around so that their usual three-line formation was now three columns facing the enemy. In this way they were able to march faster than if they were a dressed battle line, giving them the opportunity to outflank the Iberian troops opposite them. Once they reached a certain point, they wheeled again, now facing towards the enemy but able to attack them both in the front and on the flank. Along with this attack, the light infantry and the cavalry were able to send the elephants into a frenzy. These charged all about the battlefield, as much a menace to the Carthaginians as they were to the Romans.

In the centre, the fighting had not even begun as Hasdrubal's wings were collapsing. The African troops there were unable to wheel about and attack the Roman heavy infantry as this would leave their flanks open to attack from Scipio's Iberian troops still slowly marching towards them. And the Punic general was in no position to do anything. Adrian Goldsworthy has proposed that the Romans' manoeuvre, however daring and perhaps complex, could have taken as little as an hour to execute.[82] Although it was a long and valiant fight, Hasdrubal's army was forced back, retreating calmly at first but then being driven into a route. All that saved them from being utterly slaughtered was a torrential rain which began and signalled the end of the battle.[83]

The next day saw the Carthaginian army attempt to flee. Starting the night of the battle, they had been steadily abandoned by their Iberian troops. Hasdrubal and Mago saw no hope in staying near Scipio, and both fled. Some of the army made an escape as well, but not all of it. Hasdrubal and Masinissa were able to get to the coast and sailed to Africa, while Mago took refuge in Gades, the last major city left under Carthaginian control. Here, though, the failing fortunes of Punic Spain were felt, and a conspiracy was created against them. It was suppressed by Mago, but he did not ingratiate himself to the people of the city. When he was recalled to Africa to prepare for an expedition to Italy, the city quickly surrendered to the Romans. This was the end of Carthaginian control in Spain, aspects of which may have stretched far back into the city's history, though only truly took hold through the actions of Hamilcar Barca. All that was left between the Romans and victory in the war was Africa and Hannibal's army which was still in Italy, though all but cornered in a small part of the south.

Sicily, Africa, and the End of the War

Unlike in the first war against Rome, the island of the Tyrrhenian Sea and Sicily were not major flashpoints. There was an attempt to recover

Sardinia in 215 BC, when Hasdrubal the Bald took an army of about 13,500 troops – and maybe twenty elephants – to the island. While this was meant to support a rebellion led by a native leader called Hampsicora, a storm blew the ships transporting the army all the way to the Balearic Islands, off Spain. Thus, by the time the Carthaginian force arrived, the Sardinian army had been defeated in battle by Titus Manlius Torquatus. In a four-hour long battle, Hasdrubal's army was utterly destroyed, suffering 12,000 dead and 3,700 captured, if our source is to be believed. Committing an entire army to this attempt was a logical choice at the time. Spain was still in Punic hands and Hannibal was still roaming through Italy. But its loss must have been devastating, as this was a field army that could have appeared in almost any other theatre of the war had it survived.[84]

Like Sardinia, Sicily began the war securely in Roman hands. And its importance was not lost on Rome, even from the earliest periods. The year that Hannibal crossed into Italy, an invasion of Africa had been planned and would have launched out of Lilybaeum. With the Carthaginians in northern Italy this was postponed, but the island was used as a launching-off point for raids of North Africa. One such expedition was led by Titus Otacilius who sailed from Lilybaeum to the coast around Utica. With eighty quinqueremes he was able to sail into the city's harbour, disembark his troops, and extensively plunder the hinterland. Amongst his treasure were 130 merchant vessels loaded with both booty and grain.[85] The importance of wresting control of the island from the Romans was not lost on the Carthaginian leadership. But there was little they could do.

This was the situation until the death of Hiero II of Syracuse in 215 BC. He had been a staunch ally of Rome, even supporting them in the wake of Hannibal's initial successes in Italy. With him in control of Syracuse, and the strong Roman garrisons on the island, there was little threat of rebellion. However, when he finally died – being in his 70s at the war's start – chaos erupted. There was a return to factionalism within the city, as we have seen many times before in the earlier chapters of this book. His heir and grandson, Hieronymus had opened up negotiations with Hannibal but was murdered before anything could come of it. Eventually, leadership in Syracuse passed into the hands of Hippocrates and Epicydes, brothers who were descendants of a Syracusan father who had settled in Carthage after being exiled by Agathocles. Their first move was to declare Leontini a free city, garrisoning it with 4,000 soldiers loyal to them, and they began raiding Roman lands on the island. Marcus Claudius Marcellus, one of the Roman consuls of 214 BC, responded in force. He dislodged them, executed all of the deserters from the Roman army that he found in their camp, and began a siege of Syracuse.

This siege was to prove lengthy, as we know from earlier wars fought against Syracuse by Carthage that it was well protected. But its rebellion against Rome lit the fire of independence throughout Sicily, and many other communities did the same. Although these drew away some of the army blockading Syracuse, it was not enough to completely alleviate it. Carthage, however, was happy to support their long-time enemy and sent a relieving force of 25,000 infantry, 3,000 cavalry, and twelve elephants under the command of Himilco. After landing at Heraclea Minoa, he quickly took Akragas and made it his base of operations; once again two of the great cities of Sicily were locked in a war involving the Carthaginians. Marcellus had tried to prevent the fall of Akragas, but was unable to. On his march back to Syracuse, though, he encountered an army led by Hippocrates, perhaps of 10,000 infantry and 500 cavalry, the former of which he defeated, the latter (and their leader, Hippocrates) fleeing towards Himilco. These two rendezvoused at the River Anapus and set up camp. While this was happening, a Punic fleet of fifty-five ships, led by Bomilcar, sailed into the Great Harbour at Syracuse.

Himilco was not inactive. He shadowed Marcellus back to Syracuse, though decided against sitting there idle. He moved inland and captured the Roman supply depot at Morgantina, gaining for his army both booty and provisions. This caused a number of other cities to abandon the Roman cause, some emulating the people of Morgantina and rebelling directly against their Roman garrisons. The town of Henna experienced what could go wrong if an attempt at conspiracy was discovered. All of its inhabitants were slaughtered by the Romans and the town handed over to the soldiers for plunder. After this massacre, Himilco returned to Akragas, perhaps thinking that his presence would not turn any more cities against the Romans. It was here that he was to stay until the closing days of the siege of Syracuse.

Slowly, Marcellus was able to pick apart the city. The outer precincts fell into Roman control one at a time. After he captured the Euryalus, Himilco and Hippocrates finally arrived. They made an initial attack against the Roman positions, but could not quickly produce a decisive engagement. Instead, they encamped near the Great Harbour. Thus, Syracuse was under siege while its besiegers were themselves besieged. It was not long, however, before disaster hit the Carthaginian camp. As had happened in past attempts to capture Syracuse, a vicious plague set in. It was so destructive that the entire Punic army succumbed to it, with both Himilco and Hippocrates dying. The last Carthaginian attempt to help the beleaguered city came in the form of a massive shipment of resources from Africa under the protection of Bomilcar's now enlarged fleet. Despite outnumbering the Romans, he was driven back and the supplies never arrived.[86]

Eventually, the Romans sacked Syracuse and in the wake of their bloodlust killed the great polymath Archimedes. But Akragas was still in Punic hands, and what was left of their army there was now under the command of Hanno. He received from Hannibal's army in Italy a Liby-Phoenician officer named Muttines who would prove his skills in small-scale warfare.[87] Although their campaigning gained some momentum, after a crushing defeat at the River Himera the army was all but broken. They lost an unknown number of men, claimed to be in the thousands, and suffered 6,000 others captured, along with eight elephants. Reinforcements came from Africa, with 8,000 infantry and 3,000 Numidian cavalry. This caused a new wave of defections to the Punic cause. With his newly strengthened cavalry arm, Muttines was able to ravage the countryside throughout the island. But the arrival of one of the consuls of 210 BC, Marcus Valerius Laevinus, signalled the end. He marched directly on Akragas, which Hanno was still using as a base of operations. Muttines had felt betrayed by his commander and made a deal with the Romans. His Numidians let the consul and his men in through one of the gates and with little effort the city was theirs. Hanno and Epicydes fled to Africa, leaving behind a Sicily that quickly fell back under Roman control.[88] While Carthage may not have entirely given up hope of recovering the island, as they were supposedly preparing a large fleet to send there in 210, nothing was accomplished.[89]

With Sicily in Roman hands and Spain falling in 205 BC, there was little left for Rome to do except invade Africa. Perhaps to be seen as a final effort to keep the war raging elsewhere, Mago Barca led a force of 11,000 infantry and 2,000 cavalry to northern Italy where he captured Genoa.

He moved to the Ligurian Alps and entered into a conflict between two local tribes on the side of the Ingauni. This, and probably other factors, drew Celts into his army, as they had done with both of his brothers. Even though Carthage reinforced him with 6,000 infantry, 800 horse, and seven elephants, he would go on to wage an ineffective campaign for two years in Cisalpine Gaul before the Romans finally broke his army.[90] Mago himself was struck in the leg by a javelin during his final battle and died while en route back to Carthage.[91]

Scipio Africanus was to lead the invasion of Africa in 204 BC. Although he was prevented from recruiting new troops, he was in command of the armies in his consular province of Sicily and volunteers were allowed to enlist, of which 7,000 did. In what could be considered an accidental act of retribution, the two legions which fled the field at Cannae were amongst those taken across. Many figures are given for the size of this invasion army, but modern calculations of 25,000 to 30,000 troops in total are acceptable.[92] These landed after three days at sea near Utica and immediately set up camp. They were met by a dispatch of 500 Carthaginian cavalry sent to scout the invasion. A portion of Scipio's cavalry was sent against them and they were driven off. The Punic losses were severe and included the officer in charge, a nobleman named Hanno. The rest of the Roman cavalry was raiding the hinterland. Scipio also took a nearby prosperous town, though we do not know where it was. But he was already able to send back to Sicily 8,000 prisoners and considerable booty. Perhaps the greatest victory at this early juncture, though, was the defection of Masinissa to the Romans.[93]

He brought with him about 2,000 Numidian cavalry who would prove important during Scipio's campaign. Not long after the Romans had moved their camp to within a mile of Utica, the Carthaginians sent a fresh force of 4,000 cavalry against him, again led by a man named Hanno.[94] These were baited into a battle by Masinissa and his skilled riders, who drew them out of the town they had camped in and used feints to get them away from its safety. Scipio then attacked them from the rear with the Roman cavalry. In yet another short period, Carthage lost at least 3,000 more cavalry, including their commander and 200 citizen troopers.[95]

The next week or more was spent pillaging the hinterland and taking as many towns and villages as possible. This was a reasonable strategy which would make Scipio's position more secure. Eventually, he invested the city of Utica directly. After forty days of siege, the Romans were unable to take the city.⁹⁶ They were forced to break off their attempt by the arrival, finally, of a full army from Carthage. It was led by Hasdrubal Gisco and Syphax, a Numidian king. Under the former were 30,000 infantry and 3,000 cavalry, while the latter commanded an army of 50,000 infantry and 10,000 cavalry. It is usually pointed out that the figure for Syphax's army is far too large, but it is the only number we have. Both Polybius and Livy give this number, though it is probable that the latter copied it directly from the former. Hasdrubal and Syphax established two camps some distance from each other, though both within striking distance of the Roman camp. In these all three armies wintered. During the downtime, there was an attempt – spearheaded by Syphax – to negotiate a peace between the two sides. This did not come to fruition, and in the spring Scipio set in motion yet another successful plan.

He feigned that he was going to attack Utica. His preparations went so far as preparing artillery to be mounted on the fleet and sending 2,000 troops to a hill overlooking the city. During the winter, however, Scipio had learned from his emissaries going between the camps during the supposed peace negotiations that the Numidian and the Carthaginian camps were primarily constructed of wood and other combustible materials collected from the countryside. Some of their shelters were even made of reed with thatched roofs. Thus, on the night that his Utica diversion was launched, Scipio ordered that two columns proceed to the enemy camp. One led by Caius Laelius and Masinissa would attack the Numidian camp, while the proconsul himself would lead the assault on Hasdrubal Gisco's. Under the cover of darkness these easily reached their targets without being discovered and were able to put them to the torch; first that of Syphax and then that of the Carthaginians. Owing to the construction materials used, the flames spread with deadly speed. Many soldiers were engulfed in their own quarters, while others were cut down by the attackers whilst trying to flee the inferno. Both the Numidian king and Hasdrubal escaped, along with as many as 2,000 infantry and 500 cavalry, but the rest of their armies were either killed or captured. Among the prisoners were eleven Punic senators. In a show of piety, Scipio dedicated the vast quantity of arms captured to Vulcan and burned them. A pyre to a Roman god to celebrate two still smouldering piles of men.⁹⁷

Hasdrubal retreated to Carthage where he found a city similar to Rome in the wake of Hannibal's victory at Cannae. There was worry that Scipio would march directly on the city following such a crushing victory. A stern resolution was passed by the Punic leadership to continue the war. A levy was begun in the city and its hinterland while 4,000 Celtiberians arrived from Spain. Syphax was also convinced to support his allies, thanks in part – according to our sources – to his wife, the daughter of Hasdrubal. When the two commanders joined together their newly recruited forces, they numbered about 30,000. Word of this reached Scipio who had actually returned to the siege of Utica in the wake of his victory. But he pulled away from this, marching his army to intercept the Carthaginians and Numidians. They would meet at a place known as The Great Plains, in the valley of the Bagradas.

Four days after the armies made camp here, they marched out arrayed for battle. Scipio's battle line was standard for a Roman army, with the *triplex acies* formation for the infantry and the cavalry on the wings. Masinissa and his Numidians were on the left, while the Italian cavalry was on the right. These were opposed by the Numidian cavalry on the Carthaginian side with the Celtiberian infantry stationed in the middle opposite the legionaries. We do not hear of Carthaginian or Numidian infantry, but they must have flanked the Celtiberians. Unlike in other engagements, Scipio did not have to use a stratagem to achieve victory here. His army simply outfought the enemy and routed them. The African units broke after the first charge, but the Celtiberians continued to fight until Scipio had to rotate in his second and third lines to the fight. Eventually, the Romans surrounded them and cut them down. This last stand gave Hasdrubal and Syphax enough time to escape the battle along with many of their soldiers.[98]

Carthage was now even more a city of panic. But a plan was made to send the fleet to relieve Utica, which was still being blockaded, recall Hannibal from Italy, and to prepare the city for a siege. Scipio remained in The Great Plains and proceeded to bring the area entirely under his control. Laelius and Masinissa, however, were sent out with troops to hunt down Syphax. This they accomplished, thanks in part to the Maesulii accepting Masinissa as king. Eventually they were able to take Syphax prisoner and bring him back to Scipio, whence he was further shipped to Rome to be paraded as a war prize. By this time, though, Scipio was already back at Utica, having made a short-lived motion towards Carthage and taken Tunis. His retreat was precipitated by the launching of the Punic fleet and the need of protecting his troops at Utica. But the former took a longer-than-needed time to reach the city, and thus the proconsul was able to organize his ships – burdened with siege equipment – into a more defensible formation. Although the Carthaginians were able to haul off about sixty transport ships, they did very little real damage to the Romans.[99]

Scipio then moved his camp back to Tunis where he received an impressive peace envoy from Carthage. This was spurred on by the capture of Syphax; the Punic leadership seems to have realized that without their Numidian allies they had little chance of defeating the Romans. The Council of Thirty in its entirety went out in an attempt to make terms. Those given were strict, though given the situation may not have been extraordinary. They were given three days to accept, which they took advantage of, perhaps to give Hannibal time to return from Italy. But envoys had also been sent to Rome, so there was probably a genuine desire to make peace. Regardless, peace was yet to come.[100] Both sides used the temporary armistice to shore up their positions. Scipio received supplies from Sardinia, while a convoy from Sicily was broken up by strong winds. Some of the freighters in this fleet were then captured by the Carthaginians, violating the temporary truce in Scipio's eyes. This was exacerbated when the envoys he had sent into the city to announce this were attacked by the Punic fleet as they returned to the camp. The proconsul then ordered for preparations be made to continue the war.

Town after town was taken by force, and the populations sold into slavery. It was through these tactics that Scipio reopened hostilities. John Lazenby rightly described this as 'a campaign of terror and destruction'.[101] But, by this time Hannibal was in Africa, having landed at Leptis Minor. He was severely short on cavalry, though, without which he could not effectively fight the Romans. Many of his horses may have been disposed of in Italy, before even making the crossing.[102] He was supplied with cavalrymen by Tychaios, a relative of Syphax, and someone in a position to lose power – or possibly his life – if the Romans and Masinissa emerged victorious in Africa. The 2,000 riders he brought with him are described as the best cavalry in Africa. Hannibal's base was at Hadrumetum at this point, but Scipio's campaign of terror caused Carthage to send a constant stream of messages asking for him to come to the city's aid.

This he tried to do. Marching out from Hadrumetum, he reached a place called Zama, which was apparently five days west of Carthage. Although this location is remembered in the battle's name, it was fought some distance away.[103] After Scipio moved close, spies that Hannibal had sent out to reconnoitre the enemy were captured. These were shown around the Roman camp and politely returned to their master, perhaps to convince him that Masinissa and his Numidian cavalry had yet to return to the Roman army; this being done with the knowledge that they would arrive the next day.[104] As the story goes, the two commanders even sat down for a chat in the days that their camps were in proximity.[105]

It is unfortunate that we do not have reliable figures for the sizes of either army. Appian assigns 50,000 to Hannibal and 34,500 to the combined army of Scipio and Masinissa, but these are not usually accepted.[106] Judging by Polybius' figures of the Punic casualties, Hannibal could have had around 40,000 troops.[107] Scipio could have had 29,000 infantry and 6,100 cavalry, which would have meant that he was outnumbered in foot by 7,000 but superior in cavalry by 2,100.[108]

Scipio formed his army up in a relatively standard fashion. On the left wing he stationed Laelius and the Roman and Italian cavalry, while on the right was Masinissa and the Numidians. His infantry which made up the core of his line were arrayed in the usual three lines, but there were gaps between the units. In these Scipio put his light infantry. It was on these soldiers that he was relying to break up the attack of Hannibal's elephants which he believed would open the battle. The Carthaginian line was more complex. On the wings he deployed his cavalry, with his own Numidians opposing those of Scipio and the Carthaginian and other horse facing Laelius. His infantry were arrayed in three lines, similar at least in theory to the typical Roman deployment. In front were Ligurians, Celts, Balearic slingers, and Numidians.[109] Behind these were a line of Carthaginian citizens. And in the rear were the veterans from his Italian campaign. But positioned in front of his infantry were eighty elephants. As he made special arrangements to deal with them, these must have given Scipio pause.[110]

The battle opened with the Numidian cavalry skirmishing with one another. But this was followed by Hannibal ordering his elephants forward. Trumpets, shouts, and the other sounds of battle frightened some of the elephants so much that they turned and trampled some of their own troops. Between these beasts running amok and Masinissa's valiant attacks, Hannibal's Numidian cavalry were quickly driven from the field. This left his left flank open to the Romans. But the majority of the elephants were still on course and charging forward. Scipio's light infantry, however, were doing their job and rained missiles down on the animals and their drivers. Although the *velites* suffered considerable casualties, eventually the elephants were either brought down or charged through the gaps in the line. Some were driven off towards the Punic right flank and provided a momentary distraction for the cavalry on that wing. Taking advantage of this, Laelius charged the Carthaginians after the massive animals had passed and sent them fleeing from the field as well. Hannibal was now without horsemen. The infantry combat was fierce, and although the Romans continued marching forward it was not without effort. Their first line of opponents put up a stalwart effort, and may have even incorporated missile troops that could have been inflicting damage on the Romans as they marched forward.[111] Although they felled many of their enemy, they were eventually driven back. When they reached their second line, that composed of Carthaginians and Libyans, they were not permitted to join it or flee backwards through it. Hannibal had expressly ordered this. While it may have caused some conflict between the mostly mercenary troops of the first line and those of the second, it is hard to believe that they inflicted much damage on the Carthaginians whilst trying to get through the line as Polybius implies. When the Romans reached the second line, they found an enemy no less willing to fight. Polybius describes the Punic troops as showing 'frantic and extraordinary courage'. They fought hard enough to throw the Roman first line into a state of confusion, with the officers of the second having to restrain their men from charging forward. Eventually this line of Hannibal's army was also broken and fled backwards. They were again met by the weapons of their allies and forced to retreat to the wings of the line. It is here that we may get a glimpse of why Hannibal ordered his troops to close ranks to their own fleeing comrades. If he could get the broken units to the wings of his army and they could rally, he would be extending his battle line to a point which may have allowed attacks on Scipio's flanks.

Between the remaining lines was a field of gore. Bloody, 'slippery', bodies were heaped about it, and the ground was surely sodden with bodily fluids. As Hannibal had stationed his third line of veterans so far back from the first two, there was a lull in the fighting. This gave Scipio time to reorganize his infantry. He sent his second and third lines, the *principes* and the *triarii* to the wings of the *hastati*, the latter of whom he had had to restrain through trumpet calls from continuing their advance. With Hannibal's veterans almost all equipped with Roman gear from their time in Italy, it must have been a sight to watch the two lines close. What remained of both sides was said to be almost equal in number, and probably in skill and experience. A long and hard-fought melee developed, with neither side making headway. But Hannibal's lack of cavalry proved to be the pivotal element in the battle. After chasing off their opponents, both Masinissa and Laelius returned to the battlefield at this juncture with their squadrons and attacked Hannibal's infantry from behind. They cut many of their opponents down, while others broke and fled. These too they rode down. In all, 1,500 Romans died at Zama, while the Carthaginians lost 20,000 to death and 20,000 more to capture.[112] Appian preserves an alternative tradition, though, in which the Romans lost 2,500 and Masinissa even more, with Hannibal suffering 25,000 dead and 8,500 captured.[113]

Following the Battle of Zama, Hannibal withdrew back to Hadrumetum, but was quickly recalled to Carthage. Here, finally, the leaders agreed that peace should be sought. Before this could happen, though, Syphax's son Vermina rode towards Carthage with a substantial force to give aid to the city. This was intercepted by Scipio's cavalry and a detachment of infantry and was crushed. This happened on the first day of the Saturnalia, placing it on 12 December 202 BC. Although a relatively small battle compared to those fought throughout the war, this would be the last one fought during the conflict.[114] Peace was eventually settled between the two powers, again, with Carthage agreeing to steep terms. All prisoners they had taken were to be handed over, as well as deserters from the Roman cause. Carthage must surrender all of their warships, save ten triremes. Their elephants were to be delivered up to Rome, as well. They were forbidden from making war with any people outside of Africa, and only in Africa with Roman permission. Masinissa was to be restored as king in his lands and all of his property restored to him. The war indemnity to be paid to Rome was 10,000 talents over fifty years, and they were to surrender 100 hostages to Rome. There was a bright spot amongst the treaty's terms, though, and that was the continued hegemony of Carthage over their lands in North Africa.[115]

Conclusions

Thus ended one of the greatest and most brutal wars in human history. It lasted for about seventeen years and cost the lives of countless people. While those who died on the field of battle numbered perhaps in the hundreds of thousands, the losses of civilians in towns slaughtered wholesale and the deaths probably caused by starvation or want of other supplies was certainly staggering.[116] This was a conflict which involved people from the entire western Mediterranean and some of the east, because Macedon was brought into it. What Hannibal and Carthage's goals were when the conflict started are hard to determine. Animosity between the two powers in the wake of the first war had to have played a part, though to what extent we need to believe that the motive lay mostly with the hatred for Rome instilled in Hannibal by his father is questionable. But there is no doubt in my mind that if the war had not started in 219 BC then it would have sooner or later. Rome's expansion in the wake of the first war and Carthage's renewed power thanks to its Iberian possessions created a powder keg in the western Mediterranean. We also must realize that it was not the goal of either belligerent party to destroy the other completely. Hannibal's treaty with Philip V of Macedon – though not discussed in this book – explicitly stated that Rome would still exist as a state in the aftermath of a Punic-Macedonian victory. Likewise, the peace negotiated by Rome at the end of the war preserved Carthage and her hegemony in Libya, even if it stripped away rights inherent to sovereign nations (such as making war).

But the war did show one thing: that the military system of Carthage was not vastly inferior to that of Rome. While it is obvious that they lost, the Carthaginians were, throughout parts of the war, in a superior position. Hannibal's initial invasion of Italy met with resounding success, perhaps because the Romans were not fully mobilized and lacked experienced troops, but he still won a series of significant victories. These were not capitalized on in any significant way. And as Dexter Hoyos has pointed out, the war may have ended very differently if the Carthaginians had sent reinforcements to Hannibal in Italy rather than to Spain or Sicily, to which we might also add Hasdrubal the Bald's force lost on Sardinia.[117] It could have been that their navy was unable to reach Hannibal in Italy, thus he only received one reinforcement.[118] As it stood in 202 BC, though, the western Mediterranean was now in Roman hands.

Chapter 9

Killing a Phoenix: The End of Carthage

The peace with Rome in the wake of the Second War brought on a period of renewed economic prosperity in Carthage. In the year after the war ended, they were already able to send Rome 400,000 bushels of wheat.¹ By 191 BC, the Carthaginians were able to send the Romans 500,000 bushels of wheat, 750,000 bushels of barley, an entire fleet, and, in one payment, the war indemnity that was owed for the previous conflict.² The Romans did not accept the fleet or the lump sum payment for the indemnity, but the offer is still proof of how well the Punic economy was doing. Losing Sardinia and Sicily, the bread baskets of the central Mediterranean, may have encouraged intensified cultivation of the agricultural land in the hinterland of Carthage.³ Developments in the city also attest to the remarkably good conditions after the war. This is most dramatically evidenced by the enhancement of the harbours and their port. Appian preserves Polybius' detailed description:

> The harbours had communication with each other, and a common entrance from the sea seventy feet wide, which could be closed with iron chains. The first port was for merchant vessels, and here were collected all kinds of ships' tackle. Within the second port was an island which, together with the port itself, was enclosed by high embankments. These embankments were full of shipyards which had capacity for 220 vessels. Above them were magazines for their tackle and furniture. Two Ionic columns stood in front of each dock, giving the appearance of a continuous portico to both the harbour and the island. On the island was built the admiral's house, from which the trumpeter gave signals, the herald delivered orders, and the admiral himself overlooked everything. The island lay near the entrance to the harbour and rose to a considerable height, so that the admiral could observe what was going on at sea, while those who were approaching by water could not get any clear view of what took place within. Not even the incoming merchants could see the docks,

for a double wall enclosed them, and there were gates by which merchant ships could pass from the first port to the city without traversing the dockyards. Such was the appearance of Carthage at that time.[4]

Despite this economic prosperity, the Carthaginians were being continually harassed by the neighbouring Numidian king, Masinissa. He was taking advantage of the vacuum created by the destruction of the Punic army in their war with Rome. His cause was helped, indirectly, by the Romans, for whom he fought in the earlier conflict. The Senate, from whom Carthage had to seek permission to raise armies and go to war, continually denied their requests for assistance in dealing with the Numidians. In an interesting twist of fate, Numidian culture had been highly influenced by that of Carthage and they had incorporated many aspects of it into their own. They even began worshipping Punic gods and goddesses.[5] Masinissa had spent part of his childhood in Carthage which probably was the motivation for his efforts to take his countrymen from a nomadic to an agricultural lifestyle.[6]

The End Comes

The Romans decided to cut the throat of their century-old enemy and prepared for an invasion of Africa. They began by assembling an army, raising troops throughout Italy. No one outside of the leadership knew for what purpose the force was being raised. Officially it was to exist in case of an emergency. In Carthage, however, tensions were high and there was a desire to calm down the Romans. To do this, Hasdrubal (who had launched a campaign against Masinissa), Carthalo, and the others responsible for the incident were seized and sentenced to death. Having done this, an embassy was sent to Rome to announce what had happened and to complain about the Numidian depredations. The Romans were not receptive to either point. The senators asked why the Carthaginians only condemned their officers after they failed rather than stopping the operation before it could begin and asked why ambassadors had not been sent before now. They said that the excuses given were not satisfactory. When the Punic mission asked how their people could resolve the situation, they were given one of the most ominous answers in the history of diplomacy: 'you must make it right with the Roman people.' Asking for clarification, they were simply told that they knew what was necessary. After this, they were dismissed.[7]

While the Carthaginians were still trying to come to a peaceful resolution of the discordance between themselves and Rome, closer to home a bloodless disaster foreshadowed the slaughter to come. Utica, the city which had remained loyal to Carthage even during Agathocles' invasion, sent word to Rome that they were willing to submit to their authority.[8] This gave the Romans a foothold in Libya, as well as a fortified position with a good harbour and port for disembarking troops. In the aftermath of this defection, the Roman Senate was emboldened and formally declared war on Carthage. The consuls, Marcus Manilius and Lucius Marcius Censorinus were sent with the army and navy to Utica. Their fleet consisted of fifty quinqueremes and 100 hemiolii. The land army consisted of 80,000 infantry and 4,000 cavalry. According to Appian, the consuls were given secret orders from the rest of the Senate to conduct the war until Carthage was razed.[9]

A messenger was sent to the Carthaginian leaders, announcing the declaration of war and that the fleet and the army were already on their way. They were surprised by this news. There was also a realisation of their situation: they lacked ships, military aged men, allies, and mercenaries. In desperation, they dispatched another embassy to Rome which had the authority to negotiate whatever terms were necessary to secure peace, regardless of how humiliating they were. The Roman Senate offered them a deal, by which 300 high-born children would be given up as hostages and the Carthaginians would have to follow all orders given to them by Rome.[10] Although they were suspicious of this offer, they thought that there was no other option. Importantly, there was no guarantee of safety for the city. They sent the hostages to Sicily, as ordered, anyway. Once they were received there by the consuls, word was sent back to Carthage that further orders would be sent once the expeditionary force reached Utica.[11]

When the consuls arrived, they stationed the fleet in the harbour and pitched camp nearby, on the spot where Scipio's camp had been in the previous war. Envoys were sent from Carthage to the Roman leaders. They were menacingly greeted by the entire army standing at attention in full gear, with their standards raised, the blare of trumpets, and the consuls seated in tall chairs, surrounded by the high-ranking officers. All of this was a show of strength and a blunt statement that the Romans were serious in launching this expedition. They pleaded for compassion and mercy, relating the history of Carthage and its former glory, hoping that its recent change in fortunes would persuade the consuls to restrain the wrath of their people.[12]

> You, Romans, may be moved to moderation and clemency by the example of our sudden change of fortune. The bravest are those who pity the fallen, and they may cherish confidence in their own continued prosperity in proportion as they do nothing to the injury of others. Such a course will be worthy of you, Romans, and of that reverent spirit which you, of all men, most profess. But even if we had met ruthless enemies we have suffered enough. Our leadership on land and sea has been taken from us; we delivered our ships to you, and we have not built others; we have abstained from the hunting and possession of elephants. We have given you, both before and now, our noblest hostages, and we have paid tribute to you regularly, we who had always been accustomed to receive it from others. These things were satisfactory to your fathers, with whom we had been at war. They entered into an agreement with us that we should be friends and allies, and we took the same oath together to observe the agreement. And they, with whom we had been at war, observed the agreement faithfully afterwards. But you, with whom we have never come to blows, what part of the treaty do you accuse us of violating, that you vote for war so suddenly, and march against us without even declaring it? Have we not paid the tribute? Have we any ships, or any hateful elephants? Have we not been faithful to you from that time to this? Are we not to be pitied for the recent loss of 50,000 men by hunger? But we have fought against Masinissa, you say. He was always grabbing our property, and we endured all things on your account. While holding, all the time and contrary to right, the very ground on which he was nurtured and educated, he seized other lands of ours around Emporium, and after taking that he invaded still others, until the peace which we made with you was broken. If this is an excuse for the war, we condemned those who resisted him, and we sent our ambassadors to you to make the

necessary explanations, and afterwards others empowered to make a settlement on any terms you pleased. What need is there of a fleet, an expedition, an army against men who do not acknowledge that they have done wrong, but who, nevertheless, put themselves entirely in your hands? That we are not deceiving you, and that we will submit ungrudgingly to whatever penalty you impose, we demonstrated plainly when we sent, as hostages, the children of our noblest families, demanded by you, as soon as the decree of your Senate ordered us to do so, not even waiting the expiration of the thirty days. It was a part of this decree that if we would deliver the hostages Carthage should remain free under her own laws and in the enjoyment of her possessions.[13]

Censorinus delivered the Roman response. The next condition which they wanted met was for the Carthaginians, who claimed they had no desire for a war, to surrender all of their arms and engines of war. Cornelius Scipio Nasica and Cnaeus Cornelius Hispanus were dispatched back to the city with the ambassadors to receive the surrendered weapons. The Punic armouries were emptied, yielding up 200,000 complete sets of arms and armour, 2,000 catapults, and innumerable numbers of javelins and darts.[14] The train of wagons and carts which hauled these to the Roman camp was an impressive sight. Accompanying them were the Punic ambassadors who received the order, political elites, priests, and other well-known Carthaginian citizens. They hoped that their presence would help preserve their city.

Receiving them into the camp, the Romans led the Carthaginians in front of the consuls. Again, it was Censorinus who spoke, commending them for following the two orders that they had been given thus far so well, surrendering hostages and their arms. He then delivered a new, much harsher, demand. The Carthaginians were to abandon their city and let the Romans raze it to the ground. The population would be allowed to still live in Libya, but would have to settle at least ten Roman miles (c. 15km) away from the sea. Predictably, all of those who had come into the camp reacted poorly. Reproaches were made against the Romans and there was considerable wailing and cursing.[15] There were probably some within the crowd who realised, as modern authors have, that this would be a 'death sentence' for the Carthaginians as a people, and it would prevent the citizens from engaging in what they did so well – maritime trade.[16]

A further moral and emotional appeal by a prominent Punic citizen, named Banno, attempted to persuade the consuls not to make this demand of them and to cage the dogs of war.[17] Censorinus' reply was simple and stern, the Senate 'has issued its decrees and they must be carried out. We have no power to alter the commands already laid upon us.' He went on to explain why they were not to be allowed to stay resident near the sea, because it 'reminds you [the Carthaginians] of the dominion and power you once acquired by means of it. It prompts you to wrongdoing and brings you to grief.'[18] After the delivery of a lengthy speech, the Romans began herding the Carthaginians out of the camp. When they had departed, Censorinus sailed down the coast to Carthage and anchored outside of the city with twenty quinqueremes.[19]

Those who went to the Roman camp returned home to their fellow citizens standing on the city walls, eagerly awaiting them. The atmosphere was tense as they waited to hear the fate. They questioned those who had gone as soon as they arrived. The envoys, however, refused to answer any questions before they reported to the leadership. The news was not well received. A brawl broke out in the government chambers; those who advocated for sending hostages to Rome were torn apart by their colleagues. The envoys who had been sent to the camp were stoned, while others were dragged through the city. Citizens on the rampage, after the news was made known, found resident Italians and beat them and made them suffer 'for the fraud practised' upon the Carthaginians. Some of those who had not lost complete control of themselves made the prudent choice of closing the gates and carrying large stones up to the walls to use in place of catapults and missiles.[20]

After sating their anger with a riot, the Carthaginians collected themselves and resolved to not go down without a fight. The first decision made was to free all the slaves in the city. This was a prudent move which increased the available manpower and, probably, eliminated the possibility of them fomenting dissent. Next, they named Hasdrubal, the general who had been condemned for leading an expedition against Masinissa, as general to lead an army outside of the city. He had already collected 30,000 soldiers. A second general was elected, another Hasdrubal, who was the grandson of Masinissa. A request was also sent to the Romans to allow Carthage to send another embassy to Rome and thus for a thirty day truce. This was again denied. Most impressive of all was the rapid industrialisation, if that is the correct term, of the city's temples and other sacred areas. In these were set up weapons workshops, crewed by both men and women, which were charged with making 100 shields, 300 swords, 1,000 catapult bolts, 500 darts and javelins, and as many catapults as they possibly could. As there was a lack of material to make cord, the women cut off their hair to be used as such.[21]

The Romans hesitated in attacking. We are told that they thought the city would be easy to take as it was unarmed and demoralised. Interestingly, the consuls also alienated Masinissa who retired from the area to observe, rather than participate in, the war. There was also a miscalculation on the part of the Roman commanders, thinking that Carthage would be wanting for supplies. In reality, it was actually their army that was in need. They were being supplied by Hadrumetum, Leptis, Saxo, Utica, and Acholla, which is made to seem inadequate. Hasdrubal, on the other hand, was in command of the rest of Libya and was able to bring supplies into the city. Censorinus and Manilius then decided to march their army against Carthage and laid siege.[22]

They resolved to launch an attack on the walls immediately. Manilius' troops advanced from the mainland and Censorinus launched an attack from the seaward side, mounting scaling ladders from both the land and his ships. Originally thinking that their opponents were unarmed and disheartened, the Romans soon found out that this was not the case. The newly produced weapons were brought to bear against the attackers. The Carthaginians beat back the first Roman assaults. Both consuls ordered their men to break off the attack, and they retreated some distance from the city. Their first objective was to create two fortified camps. Censorinus built his on the lake near the walls, while Manilius built his on the isthmus which connected the city to the mainland. The former, after the completion of his fortifications sent some of his men across the lake to collect wood for siege engines. These were ambushed by a Carthaginian cavalry squadron under the command of Himilco Phameas. The Romans lost 500 men in this skirmish. Enough timber made it back to the camp, however, for an assault to be launched against the walls using unspecified engines and ladders. This, like the first, was quickly beaten back by the defenders. Manilius also sent his men against the walls a second time, meeting with slightly more success. They were able to destroy some of the outer defences but gave up on trying to take the city itself.[23]

Censorinus' next plan was considerably more ambitious. He ordered that a portion of Lake Tunis be filled in order to attack a vulnerable part of the walls. When this was done, he brought up two enormous rams, so large that they were crewed by 6,000 men each. One was manned by infantrymen under the command of a military tribune, the other manned by rowers from the navy, commanded by their captains. These two massive engines were able to bring down a part of the wall and gave the Romans a view into the city. The Carthaginians successfully stopped them from exploiting this breach, driving back any troops who made it into the hole. At night, they sent workers to repair the wall and soldiers to sally out against the attackers. They took torches to burn the rams, but were prevented from entirely destroying them thanks to a well-timed Roman counter attack, but they were made useless for assaulting the walls. Fighting continued at the breach, with the Carthaginians preventing any major incursion into the city. During this fighting, Scipio Aemilianus, who would later destroy the city, was commended for his actions as military tribune.[24]

With the onset of summer, a plague broke out in the camp of Censorinus. It is an interesting twist of fate that an army besieging Carthage would experience an outbreak of disease as her armies had outside of Syracuse. He was forced to move his army to the sea and off the lake. Seeing this, the Carthaginians devised a clever plan to destroy at least some of the Romans' advantage. They sent a number of fireships towards the new camp with the wind. These ran into the fleet which was anchored alongside the land army. Many of the ships were destroyed, but the Roman fleet was not entirely wiped out. About this time, the consul had to return to Rome in order to conduct the elections. While he was away, the Carthaginians sallied against Manilius' camp. They undertook a night attack and were able to make it over the protective ditches of the encampment with planks. The sallying force then started ripping down the enemy palisades. As most of the camp was fighting against the attackers, Scipio rode out the rear gate, which was unmolested, and led a cavalry squadron against the Carthaginians. This took them by surprise and they fled back into the city.[25]

Much of the action of the siege now moved into the hinterland. Himilco Phameas and Scipio Aemilianus engaged in a game of raid and counter raid. The former was trying to prevent the Romans from foraging for supplies. Most of the Roman efforts are presented as incompetent, except for those undertaken by Scipio who is presented as the most capable commander in the army.[26]

Hasdrubal's forces were clearly having an impact on the Romans as Manilius was forced to lead an expedition against him, rather than attack the walls at Carthage. This involved a march to Nepheris, the road to which was narrow and surrounded by heights. Eventually, they caught up to the Punic army. In order to reach them, they had to cross a river with steep sides. Here, Scipio advised his commander to construct a fortification in case the army had to retreat. He realised that this would be a dangerous impediment in such a situation. Manilius and the other officers ignored this suggestion and simply pushed on with their advance. Once the entire army crossed, they encountered Hasdrubal's army. A pitched battle was fought in which both sides suffered considerable losses. The Carthaginians made a tactical retreat back to their stronghold where they were untouchable. Seeing this, the consul decided to retire from his attack. This required that his troops cross back over the river. When the Punic commander saw this, he ordered an attack on the Roman column. Many Romans fell in this move, including three of the military tribunes.[27]

Scipio hastily mounted a counter attack with 300 cavalrymen that were under his command. He split them into two groups and ordered them to make continual attacks against the Carthaginians using darts. They would ride in, launch their weapons, and then retreat. Doing this in smaller groups made it seem as though there was a continual attack and that it was coming from many different angles. This was enough of a distraction to allow many of the Roman troops to cross the river. Four cohorts, however, had been cut off by the Punic attack and were now besieged on top of a hill. Again to the rescue was Scipio, who volunteered to lead a number of cavalry squadrons back to save those who had been separated from the rest of the army. Finding them, and their besiegers, he set up a camp on the neighbouring hill. From here, he was able to launch an attack via a twisting ravine which connected the two hills, and thus positioned himself above the attackers. Seeing that Roman reinforcements had come, and that they were now being attacked from above, the Carthaginian force routed and fled back towards their own lines. Scipio did not pursue them, as their superior numbers would have made a pitched battle dangerous.[28]

This was not the end of disasters for this expedition. On their return march, they were attacked by the roving squadrons of Himilco Phameas, who found a column of demoralised troops who were easily picked off. When they neared their camp, which was just outside of Carthage, a sally came forth from the city which killed a number of the camp followers, if not some of the soldiers as well. Once in their camp they were able to reflect on the great losses which had been endured for no gain. A messenger was sent to Hasdrubal to request the burial of the Roman dead, or at least of the three military tribunes who had been killed. This was granted, and those three men were buried by the Carthaginian troops.[29]

In the following year, 148 BC, the Roman Senate sent a commission to Libya to investigate the conduct of the war. Two important revelations were made. The first was the tactical genius of Scipio, which was good news to the Romans. The second was that Masinissa had died. When envoys had reached his people, they were told that the king had died of old age.[30] This may have been a blessing, in some ways. Gulussa, one of the Numidian king's sons, straight away came over to the Romans and rode alongside Scipio in hunting down Himilco Phameas. They had been trying to counter his raids, when one day Himilco and Scipio found themselves within earshot. In their short conversation, the latter offered safety to the former if he were to defect. Although it could not happen at this moment, it was a good sign for the Roman cause.[31] The opportunity for this to happen, though, was soon at hand, when Manilius launched a second attack on Hasdrubal's army. Although he took precautions as Scipio had earlier advised, he still did nothing of substance against the enemy. On the return march, however, Scipio received word from Himilco that he was ready to defect. When the Punic commander came over, he brought with him 2,200 of his men. This was a significant blow to the Carthaginian cause, as it removed many of their troops as well as one of their most capable commanders from the field. What was left of Himilco's forces were held together by a new commander named Hanno the White.[32]

In the spring, the new Roman commanders, Calpurnius Piso and Lucius Mancinus, arrived in Libya and took command. They decided on a new strategy and neither attacked the city's walls nor Hasdrubal's army. Instead, they marched on a number of towns which were still loyal to Carthage. Their first move was against Aspis, where a combined attack from the land and sea was repulsed. Piso took an unnamed town nearby and razed it. The inhabitants accused him of breaking a treaty, though we know nothing about this. His next target was Hippou Acra, the town which had been fortified and had new docks built by Agathocles. Ships from here had been raiding Roman shipping destined for Utica and were adding to their supply problems. Although this was a problem which clearly needed to be addressed, Piso's siege accomplished nothing. It was maintained throughout the summer but could not breach the fortifications. This was partly due to two forceful sallies made by the inhabitants, aided by the Carthaginians, which destroyed the siege engines of the attackers. The consul was thus forced to return to Utica and settle his army down into winter quarters.[33]

The Carthaginians seemed to be experiencing a number of victories. In addition to repulsing Piso at Hippou Acra, they also received 800 Numidian cavalry who had deserted Gulussa, and their commander, Bithya. Two of Masinissas' sons, Micipsa and Mastanabal, were also playing with the Romans, telling their envoys that they would come to their aid but continually delaying doing this. They also set about fortifying their territory and speaking against the Romans in the town centres. To these two princes, the Carthaginians sent their own embassies, saying that their freedom was under no less threat than that of the city. Punic ambitions had been renewed enough for them to send envoys to Macedonia, urging them to continue their war against Rome, offering money and ships.[34] This positive mood was tempered only by talk of betrayal. Hasdrubal, who commanded the army in the field, accused his compatriot Hasdrubal, who commanded in the city, of plotting to betray Carthage to Gulussa. Those who were in the assembly when this was brought forward pounced on the accused man and beat him to death.[35] The Romans, hearing of the setbacks in Libya, temporarily changed their law to allow Scipio Aemilianus to be elected consul and take over the conduct of the war.[36]

He made preparations and recruited enough soldiers to replace those already lost in Africa. He landed in Utica. While he was en route, Piso had marched into the interior and was besieging an unnamed town.

Mancinus, the other Roman commander in the theatre, had located a neglected section of wall at Carthage and launched an attack against it. His plan was to scale it quietly, without drawing attention to his men before they had mounted the walls. The attack was noticed, however, and the Carthaginians launched a sally through a nearby gate. This was a mistake, as they were routed and the Romans flooded in through the open gate. Mancinus and the rest of his troops, who were currently on ships waiting as reinforcements, rushed to the shore and into the new breach in the Punic defences. The Romans, however, were without supplies. The commander called on Piso and the people of Utica to bring him food and prevent his troops from being forced out of their foothold.[37]

That same evening, Scipio arrived in Utica. Hearing news of the success, but also of its precarious position, he quickly took command of the situation. He ordered riders to leave and urge on Piso and ask him to march as fast as possible. The fleet on which he sailed to Africa was to be made ready and loaded with supplies and men from Utica. These were to sail at the last watch. Scipio ordered Carthaginian prisoners to be released, in order to bring word of his arrival to their countrymen. Speed was important, as Mancinus' troops were attacked at dawn by a large force of Carthaginians. With him he only had 500 armed men, and 3,000 unarmed (presumably rowers from his ships). The former were marshalled in a defensive position around the latter. They were being pressed hard, and almost forced to make a hasty retreat when Scipio arrived. Bolstered by his troops, they gradually forced the Punic sally back further into the city. The Romans then retreated, as there was no way to sustain the attack at this moment. Scipio pulled his troops back about five stades from the walls and constructed his camp. The Carthaginians, shadowing him, built a fortified camp opposite Scipio's where the army of Hasdrubal marched in from the country and was joined by Bithya, the Numidian cavalry commander, who brought with him 6,000 infantry and 1,000 veteran cavalry.[38]

The army that Scipio found was undisciplined, idle, and had found a love of plunder. He openly lambasted them and chastised them for their behaviour. His first action was to expel a crowd of hangers-on, hucksters and booty-hounds, who had no business being in the camp. This, coupled with a supposed awe for their new commander, enlivened the army. With this new-found enthusiasm, Scipio launched a night attack against two different parts of Carthage's fortifications, with the objective of surprising the part of the city known as Megara. This was a large suburban district which was bordered by a part of the city wall. He sent another force around to the opposite side of the walls. He advanced with the main body, however, over a distance of twenty stades. This was done in silence, despite his men carrying axes, ladders, and pry bars. At first they attempted to mount the walls, but were repulsed by the defenders. Scipio decided on a new strategy. There was a tower close to the walls, which was not part of the fortifications. It was, however, of about the same height. He sent a detachment of trusted soldiers to the top of this, whence they used javelins to clear the wall opposite of its defenders. They then used planks to bridge the gap. Roman troops poured over these, seizing the wall and gaining control of one of the gates. Opening this, they let in 4,000 soldiers accompanied by Scipio.[39]

The defenders were frightened and most of them fled to the citadel on the Byrsa. Even Hasdrubal retreated back inside the walls. While this looked like a decisive attack, Scipio was not willing to risk his men in the dead of night. This part of Carthage had been planted with gardens and orchards, all of which were separated by low walls and hedges, and there were irrigation trenches throughout. This would make for a hazardous attack in the daylight, let alone in the dark. Thus, he ordered a retreat and withdrew his men.[40]

In the morning, the effects of the attack were realised. Although the Romans had not made any real progress towards forcing Carthage to surrender, Hasdrubal was enraged that they had penetrated the walls. He ordered that the Roman prisoners in Punic possession be brought to the walls. In sight of their comrades they were tortured to death. He ordered their eyes, tongues, and tendons torn out with iron hooks. For some he ordered the soles of their feet to be cut, for others it was their fingers, which were completely removed. Others were even more unfortunate, and the sadistic Carthaginian ordered them to be flayed alive. This created a terrible situation for his countrymen, as there was now no possibility of peace with the Romans. Perhaps he hoped that this would harden their conviction. Instead, though, it struck them with fear and they hated Hasdrubal for eliminating any possibility of a peaceful resolution to the war. Members of the Council of 104 openly complained. He had them arrested and executed. Through these actions, the general became feared by his own people and is likened to a tyrant by Appian.[41]

Now that he was master of the countryside, Scipio engaged a programme of cutting off the city from all possible aid on land. He first burned Hasdrubal's camp, which sat abandoned. Next, he ordered a massive trench to be dug across the entire length of the isthmus which connected Carthage to the mainland. This was not constructed unopposed, and the Romans were continually fighting off Punic sallies as they worked. Eventually a total of four trenches were dug, and the area around them fortified. Looking towards Carthage, he built a wall twenty-five stades in length, which stood twelve feet high. It included parapets and towers at regular intervals. In the centre of this, he ordered an extremely tall tower to be built, which allowed the Romans to observe what was going on inside the city. These works took twenty days and twenty nights to complete, all while fighting off the enemy.[42]

This fortification cut off Carthage from the interior of Libya. They were now receiving no supplies from the land routes. By doing this, Scipio had begun to starve the city. Foreign traders had stopped coming, thanks to the siege. What little food was still coming into Carthage was brought in by sea, but because of severe weather this was proving unreliable and inadequate. Bithya, the Numidian cavalry commander loyal to Carthage, had been sent out to forage for supplies before Scipio's fort was finished, had managed to collect some but was unable to bring them in by land, even with the force of his horsemen. He was forced to send them a long way via ship. These, and the occasional merchant vessel, were able to run the blockade by setting full sail and out running the Roman ships. This was not enough food for the entire population. To make matters worse, Hasdrubal prioritised the 30,000 soldiers actively participating in the defence, thus making the great mass of inhabitants go hungry.[43] He was also hoarding supplies for those whom he held in favour. For these persons, Hasdrubal was hosting drinking parties and feasts as if during peacetime.[44] Observing this, some of the citizens began to abandon the cause of their city and to desert to the Romans.[45] This was one indicator of Hasdrubal's descent from being a general of the Punic republic to being a tyrant reminiscent of the Syracusans who for so long were the enemies of Carthage.[46] He began wearing a purple cloak and a suit of armour while being escorted by ten swordsmen.[47]

Scipio was able to observe supplies being brought into the city from the sea and endeavoured to solve this problem. Because ancient ships were not well suited for maintaining blockades, especially in the waters off Carthage, he came up with a more daring strategy. He ordered his men to build a giant mole to close off the harbours from all who would try to enter it. As his men were busy doing this, the Carthaginians quickly came up with a plan of their own to prevent this tactic from completely shutting them off. They began digging another channel from the harbour to the sea. From this, they planned to launch a small fleet that they had been constructing using old and discarded materials. It consisted of about fifty ships, including triremes and a number of smaller ships. They first sallied out of the new channel and made a show to the Romans. Unwisely, they refrained from attacking the Roman ships which were at rest near the original entrance to the harbours. When they decided to fight three days later, the Romans were ready for them.[48] The two fleets came to blows for half a day, with the Carthaginians' small boats doing considerable damage by getting close to the larger enemy ships and breaking essential parts off them, such as the oars and the rudders. They also cut holes in their sterns. Because of their smaller size, they were able to do these things and then quickly sail away.

The Punic fleet broke off their attack as evening came, with the intention of renewing the fight the next day. The smaller boats were the first to return to the harbour which caused a problem. There were so many of them that they blocked up the entrance. When the larger ships arrived, they were thus blocked from entering their own safe haven. The captains decided to close up their ranks at a small wharf which was usually used to unload merchant ships. A small parapet had been built here to prevent the landing being used by the enemy. The ships were positioned with their bows pointed outward to better receive any attack the Romans would venture against them. Some of the troops from the fleet manned the decks of their ships, while others positioned themselves on the wharf and on the parapet. Nevertheless, the Romans attacked, finding it easy to ram ships which were not moving. However, they had difficulties backing out of the confined space. To remedy this, they dropped their anchors some distance from the Carthaginians and left the line slack. They would then make their ramming attacks and use the long ropes attached to the anchors to pull themselves straight out of the channel.[49]

Although the naval battle did not end in a Carthaginian victory, it clearly drew Scipio's attention. He endeavoured to deal with this new threat and to not allow further attacks from this small fleet. To do this, he besieged the walls at the point nearest to this wharf. He attacked the parapet with rams and other unnamed siege engines, and was successful in knocking down some of the fortifications. The Carthaginians, seeing that protecting this small footprint in the sea was important, sallied out against Scipio's siege works. They were successful in burning the siege engines but did not drive him off. The next day, he rebuilt his siege works and built a number of static towers on the siege mound. From these, the Romans were able to throw incendiary missiles at the Carthaginians, including a type of ancient grenade. These were enough to drive off the defenders. Scipio's men crossed over the fortifications and were able to seize the wharf. Many of the Punic defenders escaped, however, because the walkways leading out of the area were so covered with blood from the fighting that they were slick and impassable. From the newly captured parapet, the Romans were able to rain missiles down on the defenders who were stationed on the portions of the main wall near them.[50]

As winter set in, Scipio's strategy shifted from the walls to the countryside. He was determined to remove the remaining Carthaginian presence which was still able to send supplies into the city. His first target was Nepheris, Hasdrubal's old stronghold, the garrison of which was now commanded by a man named Diogenes. Scipio decided on a two-pronged attack. He would command troops with which to cross the lake while Gaius Laelius would take an army by the land route. The Romans then built a camp only two stades away from Diogenes' fortress. Gulussa and his quick moving troops were used to continually harass Diogenes and to keep him tied down. While this was happening, Scipio regularly travelled between this camp and those outside of Carthage in order to personally oversee everything that his army was doing. Some time passed and the Romans opened a hole in the walls of the Punic camp which faced their own. The consul attacked this with 3,000 picked troops, while sending a further 1,000 around to the opposite side of the camp. When the first group attacked the breach and raised the battle cry, they drew out defenders from the rest of the fort. Seeing this, the soldiers who had been sent to the rear attacked the palisade and threw the camp into a panic. Thinking that they were completely surrounded and on the precipice of being utterly destroyed, the Carthaginian troops routed. All of those who fled were run down by Gulussa's Numidian cavalry, as well as a number of elephants he had with him. The enormous sum of 70,000 are said to have been killed, but this included non-combatants as well. 10,000 were captured and only 4,000 escaped the carnage. Following on from this victory, Scipio reduced the town of Nepheris by siege, which took twenty-two days. This victory should be seen as the first cut of the mortal wound which would destroy Carthage. By eliminating this army, Scipio took away the last major force which was bringing food into the city, as well as severely demoralised the population who now knew they were completely alone.[51]

The position of Carthage was now hopeless. Even Hasdrubal recognised this. He entered into negotiations with Scipio, using Gulussa as an intermediary. He pleaded that the city be spared, but this was not to happen. Scipio's response highlighted the cruelty with which Roman prisoners were treated at Hasdrubal's command: 'I suppose you were about to make this request, when you treated our prisoners in such an inhuman manner, and now you expect help from the gods after violating even the laws of men.'[52] The consul did offer safety for Hasdrubal and his family, as well as ten other families of his choosing. This the Carthaginian refused, nobly replying that as long as his people were threatened with extinction, he would not seek safety for himself.[53]

In the spring, Scipio again focused on the siege of Carthage. His primary targets were the Byrsa and the harbour. Attacks were launched from the Roman foothold of the wharf captured in the previous effort to breach the city. The harbour was ordered burnt by Hasdrubal, in order to slow the enemy and to make it unusable as fortified quarters for Roman troops once they breached the walls. Laelius, one of Scipio's commanders, however, quickly seized the inner harbour, easily overwhelming the starving and demoralised defenders. From here, he was also able to take the nearby agora. The army stopped here at nightfall. In the morning, 4,000 reinforcements bolstered Scipio's troops. Their next major success was seizing the temple of Apollo, which the soldiers looted despite orders from their officers to refrain from doing so.[54]

From his new base in the agora, Scipio launched his attacks on the citadel of the Byrsa. Three streets went up the hill from his position. Along these were built houses which were densely spaced and tall, noted as being six stories high by Appian. From the roofs of these, the Carthaginians rained missiles down on the Romans as they advanced up the hill. This forced them to try a slower method of attack, which involved going from building to building, clearing out the defenders. Once one was cleared, the legionaries used planks to cross from one roof to the next. As happened in the fighting at Motya during Dionysius' siege, some of the defenders were killed by the weapons of the attackers, while others, perhaps more cruelly, were flung to their deaths from the tall houses. Carthaginian troops were also making a stalwart stand in the streets below. Despite this valiant effort, Scipio's men reached the top of the hill. Once they had cleared the houses of their own men, these were set alight so that they could not be used against them. His troops kept the roads clear, however, to be used as arteries for the army.[55]

The grisly fate of Carthage began to unfold as the inferno spread throughout the city. Soldiers began tearing down the buildings which were not completely consumed by fire, bringing them down all at once into great piles. The sound of this demolition echoed throughout the city, mingled with the sounds of dying people. Some were burning, others were being crushed by the collapsing buildings. Old men, women, and children who had hidden in the deepest rooms of the houses could be heard crying out in agony at the fate of their people. Corpses were torn and crushed in innumerable ways, a gruesome horror as all that constituted them flowed freely into the streets. The Romans who were ordered to keep the streets clear removed debris and humans, or their remains, with impunity. They dug ditches along the roads into which they pitched the bodies, some still living, treated not like people but more like unwanted stumps. Some were run over by horses, unintentionally, crushing their skulls.[56]

Those Carthaginians still holding on the Byrsa were overwhelmed by the sights and sounds of the carnage. They brought forward offerings of peace to Scipio and asked that they be granted safe passage out of the citadel. This was granted, and 50,000 men and women were allowed to leave. Not all were so lucky, though, as the consul had not allowed 900 Roman deserters, or Hasdrubal and his family, passage. They remained on the hill and took up a defensive position in the temple of Eshmoun. They defended this valiantly, until they were finally forced onto the roof of the structure.[57]

Hasdrubal was finally worn down and could no longer maintain his will to fight. He stole himself away from the rest and presented an olive branch to Scipio. Soon after, the Roman deserters set fire to the temple in which they were cloistered and allowed themselves to be consumed by the flames. Hasdrubal, on the other hand, prostrated himself before Scipio, begging for mercy for himself. His wife watched from the temple in shame. She first addressed the consul, and then chastised her husband:

> 'For you, Roman, the gods have no cause of indignation, since you exercise the right of war. Upon this Hasdrubal, betrayer of his country and her temples, of me and his children, may the gods of Carthage take vengeance, and you be their instrument.' Then turning to Hasdrubal, 'Wretch,' she exclaimed, 'traitor, most effeminate of men, this fire will entomb me and my children. Will you, the leader of great Carthage, decorate a Roman triumph? Ah, what punishment will you not receive from him at whose feet you are now sitting.'[58]

She then killed her children, and flung them, along with herself, into the fire burning through the temple of Eshmoun.

From his position on the Byrsa, Scipio was able to see the destruction spreading throughout the great city of Carthage. All of our sources portray him as weeping at the sight, being moved by the sorrowful destruction of such an ancient, and one time powerful, city.[59] Appian has him utter a line from the *Iliad*, either voluntarily or subconsciously, 'a day will come when ancient Ilium falls, when Priam and the folk of Priam perish.'[60] Similarly, Polybius, who was by the consul's side as the city burned, reported him to say 'a glorious moment, Polybius; but I have a dread foreboding that someday the same doom will be pronounced on my own country.'[61] Despite this sentiment, he let loose his troops to plunder as they wished. The silver, gold, and dedications in the temples were reserved for the state. He sent word to Rome of his victory, and envoys to Sicily, announcing the defeat of the perennial enemy of the Greeks of the island. Scipio asked that all who wanted to come and look through what was taken from the temples, and to bring back to their cities whatever had been pillaged by the Carthaginians in earlier wars. Everything else was sold and the captured arms, engines, and useless ships were burned as an offering to Mars and Minerva.[62]

Thus, the great city of Carthage was destroyed, all of her accomplishments undone, and her identity all but wiped from the face of the earth. This final conflict reveals a number of important aspects of Punic military ability. First, and foremost, they were unafraid to fight. Although abandoned by their allies, except for a few Numidian tribes, and completely bereft of mercenaries, they were still able to hold out against the might of Rome for three years. They did not lack good commanders in this conflict. Hasdrubal, for all his later failings, had for a long time held out against the Roman armies and continued to keep some of the countryside under Carthaginian control. This is a feat which should not be disregarded. It is also improper to diminish the role that the population played in defending their city. Serge Lancel wrote that 'Carthage's city wall remained the real hero' of the long siege, but this takes away from the people many of their great accomplishments.[63] They maintained their defences for three years, continually low on supplies and suffering from starvation. They set up arms factories which created weapons at impressive speed. When their harbours were cut off, they dug a new canal linking them to the sea and built an entire fleet from scrap materials. None of these were feats accomplished by the piles of stones which surrounded them, but by the Carthaginians themselves. Their walls, while important, and certainly one aspect of what kept them hanging on for three years, were not the only factor in their glorious struggle for life.

Beyond the End

The destruction of the city and the identity of its people did not mean that they would disappear from world history. The Romans would remember them as a spectre, the forever enemy. But it was the Carthage of Hannibal which formed this image. For many modern historians, Carthage and the Punic people survive as a reminder of how much we have lost from the ancient world. Their literature (whatever it may have been) does not survive in any significant bulk and thus much of their voice has been silenced. But through the ardent work of modern archaeologists and historians who attempt to look beyond the anti-Punic sources with which we are left, they are not truly dead.

Chapter 10

Punic Warfare: Conclusions

We have travelled alongside Carthaginian armies from the emergence of the city as a major player in the central and western Mediterranean through to its ultimate destruction at the hands of the Romans. Her armies we have seen successful, and her armies we have seen destroyed. Just like any civilization, there were ups and downs in the military fortunes of Carthage. But one thing remained true even to the last days with Scipio Aemilianus banging on the gates: Punic citizens fought with determination. In the past, Carthaginians have been described by scholars – both modern and earlier – as not having a taste for war. This is simply untrue. They were not a culture of merchants who wished for nothing but to count their coins and calculate their profits.

Carthaginian Citizens Under Arms

The first issue that I wish to tackle is the idea that Punic citizens did not readily fight in their armies.[1] From the narrative sections of this book, I hope it is obvious to readers that there were indeed citizens present in many of the campaigns waged by Carthage beyond the officers. Supposedly early in the city's history, a figure named Mago first 'organized their military system', or in Justin's original Latin *'ordinata disciplina militari'*.[2] Of course, it is impossible to know what exactly is meant by this, given the faulty nature of our sources for early Carthage. Dexter Hoyos has attractively proposed that this should be interpreted to mean that Mago brought military practice under the regulation of the city's authorities.[3] This could have been in response to the ultimately failed campaigns and coup d'état of Mazeus.[4] But this little snippet is all we hear about domestic Punic military organization until the fourth century. There is, of course, circumstantial evidence to argue that in the early wars Carthaginian citizens readily served. The army that Hamilcar took to Himera in

480 BC contained a large body of Phoenicians from Libya and Carthage, which should probably be interpreted as citizens. And as we noted in the narrative above, the terminology used by Diodorus implies that they were enrolled via a catalogue or something similar.⁵ Supporting the notion that there was a considerable citizen contingent is the scene in Carthage when the few survivors from this campaign made it back. They announced to the city that 'all who crossed over to Sicily have perished' which drove the city into mourning because of the sheer numbers from their own ranks that were killed.⁶ The armies fielded by the other members of the Magonid 'dynasty' – Hamilcar's father Mago and the former's brother, Hasdrubal – may also have contained a significant number of citizens if Hamilcar's forces at Himera were standard practice.⁷

There may still have been a reasonable number of citizens serving in armies through to the end of the fifth century BC. When the Carthaginian siege of Syracuse was clearly broken at the end of the fifth century, Himilco was allowed by Dionysius I to evacuate both himself and the rest of the citizens in the army. Although it could be argued these were mostly officers, he supposedly took forty triremes back to Carthage with him, implying that the contingent coming home was quite large, with perhaps between 5,000 and 10,000 citizens going over at the beginning of the campaign.⁸ The fourth century BC provides us with the only information we have about a named unit of Punic citizens. Twice during this century, we find mention of a group called the Sacred Band (ἱερὸς λόχος), once at the Battle of the Crimisus in 339 and then later at the Battle of White Tunis in 310.⁹ When they first appear, they are described as being 'drawn from the ranks of those citizens who were distinguished for valour and reputation as well as for wealth'. This unit probably numbered about 2,500 soldiers, if Diodorus' numbers are correct.¹⁰ They may have been distinguishable because of their arms, with Plutarch noting that those troops assumed to be citizens at the Crimisus carried white shields and wore ornate armour. The latter was apparently constructed of iron and made them difficult to kill.¹¹

But what do we make of the Sacred Band? To some it may seem like it was a standing unit, perhaps the 'home guard' from Carthage sent out only in special circumstances. Or perhaps they were dedicated to a specific deity, swearing something of a religious oath to fight hard; of course, we have no evidence of this. From what we do know of this unit, though, it sounds as if it was assembled ad hoc whilst on campaign. Diodorus implies that its members were drawn from those who were both wealthy and 'distinguished for valour and reputation'.[12] This clearly implies that they were veterans, though whether we should read this as in previous wars or simply from the present campaign, we cannot say. The supposition that this was an ad hoc unit is supported by their description at the Battle of White Tunis where Diodorus calls them 'picked men' (ἐπίλεκτοι ἄνδρες). Duties assigned to the Sacred Band, or what we can make of them, may indicate this as well. At White Tunis they appear to fight alongside Hanno as a bodyguard, similar to those opposed to them under the direct command of Agathocles. Although the evidence is not as direct, they could have been operating in the same way at the Crimisus.[13] If it was the case that the Sacred Band was a bodyguard unit for Punic generals, then it would stand to reason that they were not necessarily a standing unit but were chosen by each individual commander.

And there was probably no shortage of men to choose from. It was during the fourth century BC that Aristotle wrote of Carthaginian citizens being rewarded with armbands to celebrate each campaign in which they fought.[14] An eagerness to serve, and perhaps reap the social rewards that came with it, may have been what motivated 10,000 citizens to serve in the campaign which ended at the Crimisus (if Plutarch's figure for the citizen contingent is true).[15] And Hasdrubal Gisco's army against Agathocles included at least 2,000 citizens.[16] Later, when Agathocles invaded Africa, the Carthaginians were able to muster 40,000 infantry, 1,000 cavalry, and 2,000 chariots just from those within the city, as they explicitly did not wait for the troops from their hinterland or allied peoples to come.[17] All of this leads to the supposition that military service was not frowned upon in the fourth century (and probably not before this either). There may have been a change in service at this point related to the political upheaval in the Carthaginian state, though this is only conjecture.[18]

Even after the fourth century it is clear that Punic citizens were still willing to take up arms. Although their presence is not well attested during the wars with Rome, when the fighting came to Africa they did serve. The army commanded by Xanthippus included a phalanx of Carthaginian citizens who acquitted themselves well. Hannibal's second line at Zama surely contained citizens, and there were citizens in the cavalry on one of the wings. During the third war, of course, Carthaginians were forced to fight, though the circumstances of this war were unlike those before it. And we should not discount the importance and wide service of citizens as officers during the first two wars. Hannibal's army was full of them, losing around thirty just at Cannae. There must have been a considerable number of Carthaginian officers that made the trek over the Alps with him.

All of this evidence – and other incidents noted in the narrative section of this book – must make us question a famous and influential statement in Polybius. He claimed that the Carthaginians neglected their infantry (meaning that of the citizens) and paid only a little attention to their cavalry, relying instead on mercenaries.[19] Historians for generations have taken this to mean that Punic citizens were averse to serving in their land armies. But, as we have seen above, this was simply not the case. Even for the third century BC it is questionable, and its rhetorical nature – comparing Carthaginian and Roman systems of war – must be acknowledged. That we have seen they served readily in the infantry does not mean that we should reject their interest in cavalry. Again, looking at when Agathocles invaded, the city itself was able to muster 1,000 horse and 2,000 chariots. These may have been a standing force, as riding – and mounted combat especially – are learned skills that require practice. It is difficult if not impossible to simply put a man on a horse and expect him to be an effective cavalryman. When Scipio Africanus invaded Africa at the end of the third century BC, the two cavalry detachments which first confronted him, those led by two young Hannos, may have consisted in part of citizen troopers, with at least 200 dying in the second failed attack.[20] If we are to believe Appian, there may well have been a city garrison of 4,000 cavalry, as he notes that the walls provided stables for that many.[21] Even if this is true, the statement exists in a chronological vacuum and we are unable to say when these may have been added to the city's defences.

There was certainly no shortage of horses for the Carthaginians to conscript into service. When Agathocles invaded, his men supposedly saw the fields of noble estates filled with horses.[22] Perhaps Carthage was a culture which encouraged horsemanship. A sixth century terracotta medallion found in a tomb at Douimès, Carthage, shows an armed rider with a round shield, two javelins(?), and a crested helmet. The interpretation of this artefact is not unanimous, but it appears to me to be a representation of a cavalryman.[23] To others, though, it is a representation of a divinity, with one proposal being that it is Baal Saphon or Ares.[24] The disc is similar to other depictions of armed riders, especially in Phoenician/Punic scarabs. A striking example of these is now published as Carthage no. 604 (Plate II) in the Beazley Gallery. This is the small image which adorns the cover of this book. The absence of a 'sun disc' in the latter depiction means that we do not need to see it as a deity for any reason. There is also the evidence of Punic coinage to consider. Many issues of this include the image of a horse, perhaps a symbol of Carthage. If this is correct, then a deep association between Carthaginians and horses could be considered further evidence for their service as cavalrymen, though this is tenuous. Other activities related to horsemanship are possible, such as hunting or racing.

We must dismiss, then, any notion that Carthaginian citizens did not readily serve in their own armies. While they did indeed engage the services of mercenaries throughout the city's history, this is not a reason to dismiss their own service. It is also not a reason to dismiss the fighting ability of their armies. As Louis Rawlings and I have shown elsewhere, there were many positive forces acting on Punic armies which enabled them to function just as well as their Roman or Greek adversaries.[25]

Imperialism, Strategy, and War-making

The question of what exactly Carthage hoped to accomplish through its various wars is a more difficult issue to address than the service of its citizens. We do not hear that much detail on motives, and we must be careful what we believe. The tinge of Greek patriotism which pervades many of our sources emanates from a tradition which saw the Carthaginians as barbarians, and barbarians as constantly trying to bring down the 'civilized' world of the Hellenes.[26] This was, of course, not true. Greek tyrants on Sicily, especially the Deinomenids, did their best to convince the rest of the Hellenic world that they provided a bulwark against the barbarian hordes, massed at the doorstep of civilization. Trophies set up at Olympia and Delphi, synchronism with events in the eastern Mediterranean, and propaganda-poetry were all used to this end.[27] In spite of this, we know that the Carthaginians worked with Greeks, whether it was Anaxilaos of Rhegium, the Athenians – with whom a formal relationship was created in 406 BC with Hannibal and Himilco, or the Hellenes that served as mercenaries or allies in Punic armies.[28] The friendship with Athens, one of the most interesting if not well-documented relationships from the ancient world, is telling of how willing states were to work with one another against a common enemy. But there is no reason to read into this that Athens only made this alliance because they had to; there is no reason to think that just because the Carthaginians were Phoenicians that they would not be welcome in a diplomatic setting.[29]

But what spurred on their wars probably differed from theatre to theatre. In Africa, the motivation was quite simple: to secure the territory around the city. Whether this was originally done through individual enterprise, only later to be organized by the state, is hard to tell.[30] Mago's structuring of the military may mean that by the end of the sixth century BC African expansion was conducted by the community as a whole. This datapoint is, however, problematic because of its questionable source in our records (Justin). Archaeological evidence supports the theory that Carthage rapidly expanded its hinterland in this period, so perhaps it was done via state (or state-like) mechanisms.[31] If this is true, then there must have been some awareness of the advantages that can be gained through territorial expansion. That there was an awareness of such in Carthage at the end of the sixth century is confirmed by the first treaty with Rome, traditionally dated to 509 BC. In it, the Punic hegemony over parts of Sicily, Sardinia, and parts of North Africa is asserted.[32] Although some modern commentators have doubted that this indicates Carthage had imperial ambitions of some kind, there is no good evidence to support them.[33]

The events in fifth century Sicily may be more complex. Hamilcar's war which led to the disaster at Himera in 480 BC appears to have been motivated by his relationship with Terillus and Anaxilaus. If the Magonid dynasty, of which he was a member, did hold almost absolute power in Carthage at the time, then the war could have been prosecuted out of personal interest though ostensibly on behalf of the state. Regardless, the invasion clearly had wide support at home as citizens and other north Africans were recruited to fight in the expeditionary force. But when we look at the war which began at the end of the century, the motivation is a little less clear. The initial invasion could have again been motivated by ties with a community on the island, this time the Elymians, but the outcome was more significant. About half the island would end up in Carthaginian hands, in what is usually called their *epikrateia*, or governed area.[34] That they would fight to protect this against Greek – often Syracusan – attempts to 'liberate' the western half of Sicily shows that the imperial city-state was dedicated to keeping hold of their overseas possessions. In this way, the motivations for many of the wars fought by Carthage were similar to those of other polities: to protect their territorial possessions.[35] If this was the primary motivation after gaining control of much of Sicily, it makes sense why the Carthaginians never made a concerted effort to take or destroy Syracuse. It was not because their armies or generals were not up to the task, but because this was not their ultimate goal. This was also the case when Hannibal invaded Italy, as shown by the treaty with Philip V of Macedon. His intention was to destroy the alliance system and hegemony of Rome in Italy, but to leave the state itself intact.

Conquests in Spain, though, appear to be much more similar to our traditional thinking about why ancient states went to war. Invasion, combat, and devising means of control over native peoples are all hallmarks of this campaign and of how we usually conceptualize warfare. The management of this new province – or perhaps Barcid possession – again follows patterns we might expect to find in other contexts of invasion and colonization.[36] This shows the capacity for Punic leaders to conceptualize of an imperial-like type of conquest, and thus motive for war. Even if the primary motivation was to seize precious metal mines to enhance Carthage's wealth, how is this different than imperial conquests in other ages and by other civilizations?

If this analysis of Punic war-making is believed, then it runs contrary to traditional thinking, which has admittedly been attacked by many modern scholars. Carthage did not engage in war only when it was convenient or threatened the population's commercial interests. Territorial conquest and wars to protect those gains were readily fought by the Punic people throughout their history. In this way, they were like most of the other peoples of the Mediterranean. As Arthur Eckstein commented over a decade ago, 'the idea that the Punic aristocracy was unwarlike is untrue at any time.'[37] They fought and died to help guide the fortune of their state just as generations of people have for almost every civilization that has existed in the history of humanity.

Finale

So, what do we make of Carthage, its war, and the course of its civilization? It is impossible to stand by the old notion of the Punic peoples being non-warlike and simply concentrated on profits. Although every civilization is unique and cannot be fitted easily into any broad categories, I would describe Carthage as being a typical Mediterranean state at each point in its history. Like Rome, the Hellenistic Kingdoms, and even like Syracuse, Carthage and its inhabitants were involved in events throughout the middle sea and tried to assert themselves in this system in all the ways others did, including through warfare and conquest. The Carthaginians were a major power throughout the reign of their civilization in the central Mediterranean and should never be thought of as a secondary culture compared to the Greeks, Romans, or whomever else one might try to place above them.

Notes

Chapter 1
1. For example, Miles 2010 and Hoyos 2010.
2. The German work in question is Ameling 1993.
3. I will point those readers interested to Goldsworthy 2000, which provides both an accessible narrative and strong analysis. There are countless books on the Punic Wars, however, and I am unable to provide a full accounting in my bibliography here. Readers who want more analysis than narrative should consult Hoyos 2011a, the chapters of which were all written by experts in the field.
4. Diod. Sic. 1.4.3–4.
5. For the life of Diodorus, see Sacks 1990, 161–8.
6. See, for instance, Sacks 1990, Green 2010, and Muntz 2017.
7. On Polybius' friendship with Scipio, see *Suda* s.v. Πολύβιος and Polyb. 31.23–30.
8. Polyb. 3.9.3–5. On Fabius Pictor in general, see now Cornell et al. 2014, 1.160–78. It probably should be noted that we have no reason to think that he was a veteran of the Second Punic War, but he was a commander in a war in Liguaria, probably in the 230s, and was a veteran of the Gallic War in 225 BC.
9. E.g. Eckstein 1995.

Chapter 2
1. Miles 2010, 13.
2. Quinn 2018.
3. Aubet 2001.
4. Lancel 1995, 20–34, Hoyos 2010, 6–12, Miles 2010, 58–62.
5. Just. *Epit.* 18.5.13–14.
6. On the office of *rab*, Hoyos 2010, 33–4, Pilkington 2013, 330–2.
7. Just. *Epit.* 18.7.2, 19.1.3–5, 2.4. Campaigns against *Mauri* based on trading posts: Hoyos 2010, 131–2.
8. Morel 1969.
9. Lipiński 2004, 372–3.
10. Lancel 1995, 262–9, Pilkington 2013, 236–42.
11. For Rome, see Lomas 2017, 262–88.
12. cf. Bradley and Hall 2018 and Terrenato 2019.
13. It was called Gebel Hamed (Mountain of Hamid) during Arab rule and as Monte San Giuliano after the Norman invasion.
14. The date of this comes from Diod. Sic. 5.9.2, who dates the expedition to the 50th Olympiad, which is 580–576 BC. Our two sources for this event, Diodorus and Pausanius, differ on the point of its ethnic make up. Diodorus says that the colonists were both Cnidians and Rhodians, while Pausanius only mentions the Cnidians.

15. Diod. Sic. 5.9.1.
16. Paus. 10.11.3 says that they settled near Cape Pachynos, the extreme south east tip of Sicily. This must be a confusion, as it would make little sense why, in the same account, we hear of them being driven off by the Elymians and the Phoenicians. Some scholars, however, believe that Pentathlus and his companions did found a colony on Cape Pachynos, cf. Krings 1998, 23, with bibliography.
17. Thuc. 6.2.6.
18. Graham 1982, 187.
19. Noted by modern scholars, such as Dunbabin 1948, 326.
20. For instance, Burn 1967, 150, believed that 'the venture must surely have been concerted' with the people of Selinus. We should not read into this incident the kind of extreme dangers that some scholars have assigned to it. For instance, Freeman 1891a, 443, wrote that 'a Greek settlement on Lilybaion [sic] would have been more than threatening to the Phoenician settlement on Motya. In truth it was for all the Phoenicians of Sicily nothing short of a question of life or death to keep all Greek intruders out of that specially reserved possession of Canaan [meaning the west of Sicily].' This is a description which goes beyond the bounds of our evidence.
21. Warmington 1993, 41. Similar opinions have been expressed by other authors, such as Dunbabin 1948, 329, who believed that 'the expedition of Pentathlus' was 'part of a drive to make the west of Sicily entirely Greek'. cf. Krings 1998, 26–32.
22. Diod. Sic. 5.9.2.
23. Paus. 10.11.3. The translation is adapted from that of W. H. S. Jones 1918 Loeb.
24. De Angelis 2016, 148.
25. Diod. Sic. 5.9.3–5; Paus. 10.11.3–4.
26. There is no reason to think that there was any Carthaginian involvement against Pentathlus, Krings 1998, 25 and n. 155.
27. Whitaker 1921, 137–62; Dunbabin 1948, 332; Falsone 1995, 685–6. Malkin 2011, 135, 'Motya's wall, for example, was built only after Pentathlos's [sic] invasion of Lilybaion [sic] (across from Motya) ca. 580.'
28. He is traditionally referred to in modern works as 'Malchus'. This, however, is a corruption originating in the seventeenth century AD and in the mind of Isaac Vossius. He proposed that the real name was related to *mlk*, or king. This is because the manuscripts of Justin and Orosius contain various names: Mazeus, Maceus, and Maleus. The name *Mzl*, quite possibly the true original, means something like 'good fortune' in Punic, Hoyos 2010, 125. cf. Krings 1998, 37–8, 76.
29. Just. *Epit.* 18.7.1; Oros. 4.6.6–7.
30. Just. *Epit.* 18.7.2.
31. Just. *Epit.* 18.7.7.
32. The exile may have had more to do with political enemies than a military failure. As Hoyos 2010, 126, has pointed out, his son's position as a priest of Melqart and the devotion of his army, who accompanies him in exile and agrees to besiege Carthage, may have made him a figure to envy in Punic social and political circles.
33. Just. *Epit.* 18.7.9–18; Oros. 4.6.8–9.
34. Oros. 4.6.9.
35. For a discussion, see Krings 1998, 79–81.
36. e.g. Asheri 1988, 751, and Hoyos 2010, 48. Further discussion in Krings 1998, 82–3.

37. Asheri 1988, 751.
38. Freeman 1891a, 298.
39. e.g. Freeman 1891a, 297–8, and Dunbabin 1948, 333. For Freeman, though, it was not a good enough reason to disbelieve that Mazeus went to war against Phoenicians.
40. On the Roman use of diplomacy and friendship, see Burton 2011. On early Roman expansion in Italy, see Bradley and Hall 2018.
41. Just. *Epit.* 19.1.9. The translation is that of J. S. Watson, 1853.
42. Dunbabin 1948, 350 n. 5 and 411–14, suggested that Justin's text is correct, and that we should not substitute Dorieus for Leonidas, and that the appeal mentioned there came after the events at the end of the sixth century. His hypothesis that this notice actually related to a war led by Gelon against the non-Greek inhabitants of western Sicily is attractive, and discussed below.
43. e.g. Hoyos 2010, 48.
44. Krings 1998, 184–8, quotation at 187.
45. This expedition is often dated to 510 BC as, according to a Sybarite version of their war with Croton, Dorieus aided the latter. This war, and the destruction of Sybaris, is dated to 510/509 BC from a fragment of Diodorus (10.23), which briefly speaks of the war and follows a passage about the fall of Tarquinius Superbus, the last king of Rome who is traditionally said to have been forced from power at this time.
46. Hdt. 5.43. On this 'oracle' and the legend ascribing the land to Herakles, see Malkin 1994, 205–18.
47. Dorieus' Spartan companions, Hdt. 5.46.
48. Hdt. 5.44.
49. Hdt. 5.47.
50. Noted by Krings 1998, 196.
51. Hdt. 5.47.2.
52. Freeman 1891b, 95. Philippos was supposedly an Olympic victor, Hdt. 5.47.1.
53. Diod. Sic. 4.23.3.
54. Asheri 1988, 752–3, is right to call this 'too rhetorical and "ideological"', and may be right in ascribing the version of events we find in Diodorus to the fourth century BC.
55. Hdt. 5.46; Paus. 3.16.5. Though, it is worth noting that Herodotus later (7.158) notes the Segestans as the only party responsible for Dorieus' defeat, in a speech attributed to Gelon.
56. Hoyos 2010, 48–9.
57. Krings 1998, 204–9.
58. Krings 1998, 209.
59. Polyb. 3.22.10.
60. This is essentially Hoyos' 2010, 49, explanation of the incident, which he describes as the 'subtler' possibility, and in it that 'the Carthaginians commissioned their vassals the local Phoenicians and the Segestans to confront Dorieus; to this might be added the extra possibility that it was the Segestan soldiers who actually slew him in battle or claimed to have done so.'
61. Asheri 1988, 753, for instance, believed that this was a 'purely local' affair, and that 'the Punics became involved only secondarily as allies of the Elymians.' As I note in the text, I think that this position does not reconcile well with our

knowledge that Carthage claimed some sort of hegemonic power in western Sicily by this point.
62. Hdt. 5.46.
63. Dunbabin 1948, 334.
64. Tronchetti 1995, 716–18, and Broodbank 2013, 475–77.
65. Tronchetti 1995, 719.
66. Aubet 2001, 238–40.
67. Acquaro 1997, 260.
68. Pisano 1997, esp. 425.
69. Tronchetti 1995, 720–8.
70. Aubet 2001, 236.
71. Tronchetti 1995, 720.
72. Just. *Epit.* 18.7.1.
73. Lancel 1995, 83.
74. Just. *Epit.* 19.1.6–7.
75. Polyb. 1.88.6. On the Roman triumph, generally, see Beard 2007. Examples of other kinds of triumphal parades and ceremonies abound, discussion of numerous can be found in the collected papers of Spalinger and Armstrong 2013.
76. Hoyos 2010, 130.
77. Paus. 10.17.9. Some scholars link this to the information from Justin and see this passage as a reference to the outcome of Hamilcar's campaign(s) on Sardinia, e.g. van Dommelen 1998, 123.
78. Tronchetti 1995, 728–9.
79. van Dommelen 1998, 123–5.
80. Roppa 2014, 259–62.
81. Even in small-scale societies raids can be deadly, especially relative to total population, cf. Keeley 1996, 65–7.
82. Hdt. 1.163.
83. Hdt. 1.163. This story is probably fictitious, although it is possible that the wealth generated by trade with Tartessus funded the construction of a wall in Phocaea. Archaeological excavations have shown that the town was protected by walls constructed, probably, between 590 and 580, cf. Özyiğit 1994.
84. Cf. Domínguez 2004.
85. Suggested, for instance, by Boardman 1999, 162. The foundation story is preserved by Aristotle (frg. 549 Rose) and Justin (43.3.4).
86. Trezigny 1995.
87. Although modern interpretation of the archaeological evidence points to peaceful relations, Justin *Epit.* 43.3.4 knew a tradition by which the early colonists were forced to defend themselves from fierce attacks, and then counterattacked, by the Gallic tribes in the environs of their new city. They had been invited to settle where they did by a chief of the Segobrigii, though, which reveals at least somewhat positive relations (e.g. Arist. frg. 549 Rose; Just. *Epit.* 43.3.8; Plut. Solon 2.7). It could be that he invited the Phocaeans to found a city in his territory as a means to overpower his enemies. We also hear of later conflicts with the Liguarians, as Massalia grew (Just. *Epit.* 43.3.13). It is, perhaps, during this unknown period of conflict that we can ascribe Strabo's 4.1.5 and 14.2.5 notices that 'in earlier times' the Massaliotes had dry docks for a powerful fleet, as well as a well-supplied armoury.

88. Just. *Epit.* 43.3.5. Strabo 4.1.5 wrote that, because of the ruggedness of their land and its poor potential for farming grain, they trusted 'the sea rather than the land, they preferred their natural fitness for a seafaring life', supporting Justin's emphasis on their sea-borne living.
89. Just. *Epit.* 43.3.4. This is a very dubious tale, however, and may well have been invented to link the foundation of Massalia with early Rome. There is a slim possibility that it is based on an actual event, which could have been a river raid by the Phocaeans.
90. Thuc. 1.13.6, cf. Gras 1987, 163. Pausanias 10.8.6–7 describes an offering from the Massaliotes at Delphi commemorating the sea war against Carthage when the city was founded in the wake of Harpagus' attack on their home town in 545.
91. cf. Ameling 1993, 127–30.
92. Just. *Epit.* 43.5.2.
93. Hdt. 1.165. The nature of this foundation is not entirely known, and the archaeological record has been interpreted to show that the Phocaeans established themselves near to the native settlement, or possibly within it; see Domínguez 2004, 434 and n. 14, who provides further bibliography.
94. Hdt. 1.166. It is tempting to see in the early coins of Hyele/Velia, which these Phocaeans would go on to found, an image of how they saw themselves. The earliest coin-type we know of from here, on the obverse, shows a lion devouring a leg of its prey, as shown on an example in the Antikenmuseum Basel und Sammlung Ludwig, in Basel, Switzerland. It was a common image on the coinage of the city. The problem being that the lion was a common symbol in Phocaean coinage more generally, such as that of Massalia. Although my proposition is that they viewed themselves as lions pouncing on sea-borne prey, it is overstretching the evidence to claim it is true with any certainty.
95. The identity of the Etruscan participants is due to Herodotus' description of the division of prisoners after the battle. The 'Agyllans' received the majority of them; Agylla was the Greek name for Caere. While it is possible that other Etruscan cities participated, as implied by Herodotus' text, I think it likely that this was an effort carried on only by the Caeretans and the Carthaginians.
96. Gras 1972, 712–13.
97. I am attracted to the idea of referring to this event as the 'Battle of the Sardinian Sea,' as suggested by Gras 1972, 712, though as in modern parlance this now would refer to the Mediterranean to the west of the island, I fear it would be a bit deceptive to non-specialists.
98. Hdt. 1.166.
99. Hdt. 1.166.3 and 167.3.
100. Gras 1987. Accepted, for instance, by Krings 1998, 93–160.
101. Gras also proposed that we should see Malchus/Mazeus' great defeat as Alalia, which, while possible, I believe is stretching the evidence too far.
102. Krings 1998, 126–9.
103. van Wees 2017.
104. Paus. 10.8.6.
105. Sachs, G., *Phokaia und seine Kolonien im Westen. Handelswege in der Antike* (Hamburg, Verlag Dr. Kovac: 2014), 133 (cited in Wear 2016, 6), wants to also see it as a defeat. I have not had the chance to read his work, however, so I cannot speak to his argument, though it may be right to see the outcome of the battle as such.

106. Krings 1998, 160. The translation is my own: *Ce qui s'impose alors est une Méditerranée «en mouvement», dans laquelle sont amenés à s'illustrer non des blocs bien constitués, mais des groupes d'individus qui agissent en fonction d'intérêts personnels et de circonstances ponctuelles, plutôt que par référence à un intérêt collectif et ands le cadre de grands desseins.*

Chapter 3

1. Brief discussion in Hoyos 2010, 40. Thrige 1828, 192–203, proposed later dates (down to the late fourth century). The story about two brothers from Carthage, both named Philaenus, making a noble sacrifice to put an end to an unending war between their city and Cyrene is entirely anachronistic.
2. For a very pessimistic view of Punic power before the late fifth century BC, see Pilkington 2019.
3. An up-to-date historiography of this phenomenon can be found in Kagan and Viggiano 2013.
4. Snodgrass 1965, Snodgrass 1993.
5. Snodgrass 1986. If this did happen, it could have been a more complex process. For example, the unknown author of the *Ineditum Vaticanum* claims that the Romans learned to fight with bronze-shields in a phalanx from the Etruscans, not the Greeks; von Arnim 1892, 121.
6. The appearance of the supposed hoplite kit can be readily seen, for example, in Etruria and Rome, Stary 1979, 191–198, and Stary 1981, 153–168.
7. Rosenstein 2010, Armstrong 2016, 111–126.
8. van Wees 2004, 52–54.
9. Hanson 1989, 65–71, Schwartz 2013. It is worth noting that the hoplite is named not after his shield, as has often been reported, but actually because of his level of armament, cf. Lazenby and Whitehead 1996.
10. This is strongly supported by studies such as Hanson 1989 and Schwartz 2009.
11. Rawlings 2000.
12. Konijnendijk 2018, 95–106.
13. Except at 16.67.3. Rather he uses more general terms such as στρατιῶται, or 'soldier'.
14. Hdt. 7.158.
15. For instance, BM ANE 127214, originally from Tharros, now in the British Museum, or no. 635 from Carthage.
16. Plut. *Tim.* 27–8; Polyb. 1.33.6.
17. Daly 2002, 87.
18. Hdt. 7.71.
19. Hdt. 7.86.
20. van Wees 2000.
21. Quesada Sanz 2002, 37–42.
22. Cf. Tagliamonte 2002 and Frederiksen 1968.
23. It is possible that they were also present in 409, as proposed by Griffith 1968, 208, although this is purely hypothetical.
24. Diodorus (5.18.3) says that Balearic slingers were especially deadly against the defenders of battlements.
25. Echols 1950, Korfman 1973. For a brief overview, see Elliott 2008.
26. Strabo 3.5.1.

27. Hom. *Il.* 2.362–369.
28. As argued by Hall and Rawlings (forthcoming), though, Carthaginian armies cohered very well because of a number of vertical and horizontal forces.
29. Hdt. 7.165. The concept of *xenia*, typically translated as 'guest-friendship', was a complicated one in Greek culture. In its strongest form it resembled kinship between persons not actually related. Formally, it involved a number of rituals and thus is described by some authors as 'ritualized friendship'. The entry on 'friendship, ritualized' in any edition of the *Oxford Classical Dictionary* will provide the reader with a thorough introduction to the topic. Comments also in Rawlings 2017, 165.
30. Our narrative sources do not give a reason for Theron's action against Terillus, but there is some evidence that it may have been spurred on by a number of prominent families who had been expelled by the latter and had resettled in Akragas. Epigraphic evidence from Ravanusa, within the sphere of Akragantine control, shows a number of Himerans likely moved to the area sometime during the fifth century. A number of modern scholars have taken this as evidence for the motivation behind Theron's ousting of Terillus (see Asheri 1988, 771, who includes earlier bibliography).
31. Diod. Sic. 11.1.4 (cf. Just. Epit. 19.1.10) preserves a tradition that the Carthaginian invasion of Sicily was instigated by Xerxes and was the result of a joint effort to destroy the Greeks. This is almost certainly incorrect, and if there was strong evidence of it one would expect to hear about it from Herodotus, see Krings 1998, 318–319. Dunbabin 1948, 4422–423, suggests that it 'may have been no accident' that the Carthaginians and Persians invaded Sicily and mainland Greece, respectively, in the same campaigning season. If there was some kind of agreement between the two powers it was likely informal and it is dangerous to read too much into this supposed alliance. I doubt that there was any connection.
32. Hdt. 7.154. Herodotus is not specific in who these barbarians were, simply calling them βάρβαρος, a very generic term. It seems likely, though, that they were native Sicilians: Siceli, Sicani, or Elymians. This is fairly safe to assume as the other military engagements mentioned all took place on Sicily.
33. Hdt. 7.155 only tells us that he died at the town of Hybla during a war with the Siceli. It is equally possible that he died of natural causes, an assassination, or an accident. That we hear of his death during a war, though, I believe it is most probable that he died in battle.
34. The dating of Gelon's ascension is explained by Dunbabin 1948, 410–411.
35. The *gamoroi* are one of a number of ruling groups associated with certain aspects of their power amongst the Western Greeks. For a complete discussion see Cordano 1986, 126–7, and Collin Bouffier 1999.
36. For the dating of Gelon's move to Syracuse, see Arist. *Pol.* 1315b.36 and Diod. Sic. 11.38.7.
37. Hdt. 7.156. Transference of population from conquered towns and cities was a common practice in Sicilian Greek warfare. This is a departure from one of the traditionally observed 'rules' of Greek warfare which protected civilians from the ravages of war. This rule, as almost all of those traditionally ascribed to *agonal* 'hoplite warfare', has been successfully argued against by a number of recent scholars, see Krentz 2002, van Wees 2011, and Hall 2018a. On the removal of populations in Sicilian warfare, see Moggi 2006, 77–80.

38. e.g. Warmington 1993, 51.
39. For the development of both Gelon's small empire and Syracuse during his reign, see De Angelis 2016, 101–106.
40. Hdt. 7.157.
41. Hdt. 7.158; Diod. Sic. 10.33.1. Polybius (12.26b) preserves a tradition which held that Gelon sent an embassy to the Greek alliance at Corinth offering his assistance, with the same conditions as we see in Herodotus. It has been suggested that this version was taken from Ephorus and was a resolutely anti-Sicilian version (cf. Dunbabin 1948, 421–422).
42. Herodotus (7.165) preserves a Sicilian tradition that aid was not sent because of the conflict brewing with Terillus and his allies. It is quite possible that this was the reason that aid was not sent to mainland Greece. As noted above with the embassy preserved by Polybius (12.26b), the 'canonical' version of events, that Gelon refused to send help unless he commanded the allied army, may be an element of anti-Syracusan propaganda.
43. Hdt. 7.165; Diod. Sic. 11.20.2.
44. For instance, we are told that Xerxes' army numbered over a million, which as early as Delbrück 1887, 138, was noted as being absurdly large.
45. Warmington 1993, 52, estimated that the army numbered no more than this. Bartoloni 1997, 163–164, estimates that the average Punic army numbered between 28,000 and 30,000 men.
46. Reconstructing the sizes of ancient armies is not an exact science, and different methods can be used, as elaborate by Whatley 1964. Division of troop numbers by ten has been argued for based in the perceived misunderstanding of barbarian numbers by Greek authors; see Green 2006, 46–7, 74.
47. Diod. Sic. 11.20.2.
48. Diod. Sic. 11.21.4.
49. I am entirely unconvinced of the argument that we must dismiss this battle as evidence for an early fifth-century Punic army simply because there were multiple versions of its story in later historians, though some modern scholars do, Pilkington 2013, 54–62, 334–5, idem 2019, 34–37. Just because some Greeks from Sicily conflated its importance to synchronize with the events of the Persian Wars does not mean that it was either insignificant or a complete fabrication.
50. Diod. Sic. 11.1.5.
51. How and Wells 1928, vii.165.
52. Asheri 1988, 772, for example, says that Carthage drew soldiers from 'all the Punic provinces.' Cf. Sartori 1992, 90, Ameling 1993, 25, and Brizzi 1995, 308. Krings 1998, 317, cautions us to not speak about the nature of these soldiers (i.e. subject vs. mercenary) in any concrete way in order to avoid anachronisms. While this is good advice, based on our knowledge of the Punic situation of the time it seems probable to me that the soldiers from Libya, Corsica, and Sardinia were subjects, the Phoenicians citizens, and the others mercenaries. The Phoenicians could have been inhabitants of other cities, such as Motya, though.
53. Diod. Sic. 11.20.3.
54. Diodorus (11.20.5) gives no indication of who these select troops were. It is possible that this was the citizen contingent.
55. Diod. Sic. 11.21.1.
56. Dunbabin 1948, 424, for instance, describes them as 'unreliable'. This is also the view of Asheri 1988, 773, who describes them as exaggerated.

57. Hdt. 7.158.
58. Dunbabin 1948, 419.
59. Diod. Sic. 11.72.3.
60. Diod. Sic. 11.21.5.
61. Hdt. 7.167.
62. Diod. Sic. 11.22.1–2.
63. Diod. Sic. 11.21.4–5.
64. Diod. Sic. 11.22.3.
65. Diod. Sic. 11.22.1.
66. Hdt. 7.166. This is reminiscent of the story of the disappearance of Mardonius' body after the Battle of Plataea, cf. Hdt. 9.84.
67. Hdt. 7.167.
68. Polyaenus *Strat.* 1.27.2.
69. Hdt. 7.167. cf. Krings 1998, 282–284.
70. Diod. Sic. 11.22.4.
71. Diod. Sic. 11.23.2.
72. Diod. Sic. 11.24.2.
73. Diod. Sic. 11.24.3–4.
74. There is no reason to doubt the amount of this indemnity, and it could have reflected Gelon's costs, De Angelis 2016, 104–105.
75. Diod. Sic. 11.26.2–3.
76. Asheri 1988, 776–777.
77. On the Temple of Victory, see De Angelis 2016, 105. Gelon dedicated a trophy of captured linen corselets at Olympia (Paus. 6.19.7) and a gold tripod at Delphi (Diod. Sic. 11.26.7). On the Pan-Hellenic dedications, see Morgan 2015, 30–46.
78. Salamis, Hdt. 7.166; Thermopylae, Diod. Sic. 11.24.1.
79. Arist. *Poet.* 1459a.24–28.
80. For instance, the inclusion of Himera in the first *Pythian Ode* of Pindar (1.71–75), Krings 1998, 261–265, and Miles 2010, 117–121.
81. Miles 2010, 117.
82. Justin *Epit.* 19.2.
83. Dio Chrysostom 25.7.
84. Warmington 1993, 55–82, Lancel 1995, 257–259.
85. Diod. Sic. 5.9; Paus. 10.11.3. cf. Dunbabin 1948, 328. There is likely a reference in Diodorus to a border clash in 454 or 453 (11.86.2). The text, as we have it, names the belligerent states as Segesta and Lilybaeum, but De Angelis 2003, 175, has correctly pointed out that the latter settlement should be Selinus. This was probably part of the process of Segesta establishing itself as a territorial state, see De Angelis 2016, 118, with further bibliography.
86. Diod. Sic. 13.44.3–4.
87. Diod. Sic. 13.59.4–5. Hannibal is the first Magonid we hear of holding power since his grandfather, as his father Gisco, and his brother Hanno, had been exiled to Selinus, Diod. Sic. 13.43.5. This itself could imply familial animosity towards that Greek city.
88. Diod. Sic. 13.44.1–2. The Campanians had been hired by the Athenians to fight against Syracuse in their failed attempt to conquer the city (and thus much of the Greek portion of the island). This attempt is typically referred to as 'The Sicilian Expedition' and is one of the most infamous events of the Peloponnesian War.

In an effort to prevent the Syracusans from giving aid to the Spartan cause in mainland Greece, as well as to conquer Sicily and seize its riches, the Athenians voted to send a large army against Syracuse. Although both sides suffered setbacks and losses throughout the campaign, the Sicilians were eventually victorious, resulting in the almost complete destruction or enslavement of the army from Athens. The ancient version is preserved by Thucydides (6.8–88, 94–105; 7.1–18, 31–87) who describes it as the greatest undertaking of both the war and of Greek history. Good general discussions of the expedition can be found in most modern syntheses of the period, and I would point readers to Rhodes 2010, 139–147, and Hornblower 2011, 168–178. The period after this defeat was one of anger and fear for the Athenians, though its impact on the course of the war was not definite. As Donald Kagan 1987, 23, has suggested, the disaster on Sicily made Athens' situation worse but not necessarily one of utter defeat.

89. Diod. Sic. 13.44.4–5.
90. The total size of the army which campaigned under the Carthaginian banner may have been larger than the force brought over from Libya. Ephorus recorded that the Punic horde numbered around 200,000 infantry and 4,000 cavalry (Diod. Sic. 13.54.5). Timaeus, on the other hand, knew of an army that numbered no more than 100,000 men in total. Neither number is feasible, but the army could have been between 10,000 and 20,000 strong when it came over from Libya. Though an assumption, I base it in Whatley's 'third aid' in interpreting ancient battles; cf. Whatley 1964, 126.
91. Diod. Sic. 13.44.6, 54.1.
92. The verb dictates that they were foreigners being recruited, thus it is unlikely that they would be serving for free. The associated noun, *xenologos*, describes those who hired mercenaries in the Greek world, a position which became very important as these types of forces became more common across Hellenic armies. On these figures in Greek history, see Trundle 2004, 107–111.
93. Diod. Sic. 13.54.1–2.
94. Diod. Sic. 13.54.3.
95. Diod. Sic. 13.58.1.
96. Diod. Sic. 13.54.7.
97. van Wees 2004, 142. As we shall see, the Sicilian Greeks quickly copied the idea of these engines.
98. Diod. Sic. 13.55.4–5. Diodorus implies that by bringing aid to the men defending the town, the women brought shame and immodesty upon themselves. On the participation of women in Greek warfare, see Loman 2004.
99. Diod. Sic. 13.55.8.
100. The siege and sack of Selinus is recorded by Diodorus (13.55–57).
101. Diod. Sic. 13.57.3.
102. On atrocities in Greek siege warfare, see van Wees 2011 and Hall 2018a.
103. Diod. Sic. 13.57.6.
104. This estimate is based on similar figures presented by Hanson, 1989, 203.
105. Examples of excessively bloody battlefields: Plut. *Aem.* 21.3, Polyb. 15.14.1, Thuc. 7.84.5–7.85.1, Xen. *Ages.* 2.14.
106. Diod. Sic. 13.59.4.
107. Diod. Sic. 13.59.6.
108. I have come to this figure assuming that they sailed from Libya with 20,000, brought in the 5,800 strong advanced force, and then adding in the 2,000 native

Sicilian troops. We could possibly add another 1,000 or 2,000 soldiers to the total, assuming that at least one allied settlement sent a comparable sized contingent as did the Siceli and Sicani. Diodorus (13.60.3) implies that there were 80,000 Carthaginian troops on the second day of the siege, but this is, again, probably exaggerated.
109. Diod. Sic. 13.59.8.
110. Diod. Sic. 13.59.9.
111. Diod. Sic. 13.60.5.
112. Diod. Sic. 13.60.6–7.
113. I am still sceptical, though, of this number. It would almost equal the number of troops brought from Akragas and Syracuse.
114. Diod. Sic. 13.61.1–3.
115. Diod. Sic. 13.62.1–2.
116. Diod. Sic. 13.62.2.
117. Diod. Sic. 13.62.3–4.
118. Diod. Sic. 13.79.8.
119. For instance, Miles 2010, 124, says that it 'basically meant 'Carthaginian military administration' and that this inscription is 'surely confirmation that the coins were only for a specific purpose,' paying the mercenaries.
120. Visonà 1995, 170–171, Visonà 1998, 4, Frey-Kupper 2014, 80–81.
121. Diod. Sic. 13.62.6.
122. It has been suggested that the fortress on the acropolis at Selinus should be attributed to his activity there, Holloway 1991, 147.
123. Diod. Sic. 13.63. Caven 1990, 39–41, believes that Hermocrates' actions were based in his belief that Carthage was a threat to Greek freedom. While this may be correct, the emphasis on raiding, and not besieging, towns allied to the Carthaginians points towards his objective being to accumulate wealth.
124. On the colonization of Therma, see Diod. Sic. 13.79.8. On Punic imperialism, see the first and final chapters of this book.
125. We know very little about what this alliance may have looked like. A fragmentary inscription from Athens honours two Carthaginian generals, Hannibal and Himilcon, granting them hospitality (IG I^3 123). The two powers, though, had failed to cooperate in any way during the Athenians' failed expedition to Sicily in 415 (Thuc. 6.34, 88). It has been suggested that the re-foundation of Leontini at the end of the war was an indication that at least one of Athens' goals for Sicily had been achieved and that perhaps this was a result of some sort of agreement with Carthage. Athens had a longstanding alliance with Leontini (cf. Thuc. 3.86, 5.4, 6.8). It is possible, though we have no evidence of what support, if any, the Athenians had given to prosecute the conflict.
126. Diod. Sic. 13.80.2–4. The Campanians from the 409 campaign complained that they had not been compensated enough, claiming that they were primarily responsible for the Punic victories (Diod. Sic. 13.62.5).
127. Diod. Sic. 13.80.5.
128. Diod. Sic. 13.80.6–7.
129. Diododorus does not tell us what 'hills' the first camp was in.
130. Diod. Sic. 13.81.3, 85.3–4. Dexippus is a well known figure from Xenophon's *Anabasis*. Although I have described him as a condottiero, which was the view of Parke 1933, 64–65, it has been suggested that he may have been sent to Sicily

as part of a Spartan strategy, Cartledge 1987, 318–320. On Spartan mercenary service, more generally, including comments on Dexippus, see Millender 2006.
131. Diod. Sic. 13.85.5.
132. Diod. Sic. 13.86.1–3. Diodorus repeats a story that a bolt of lightning struck the tomb of Theron before it was torn down which was interpreted as a divine sign that it was not to be harmed. It was through ignoring this warning that the Carthaginians brought the plague upon themselves. Portents were important to the Greeks, and this story may well be a literary flourish rather than a factual event. On divination and warfare in Greece, see Rawlings 2007, 180–187, and Parker 2016, 127–130.
133. Diod. Sic. 13.86.3. Doubt about this detail has been cast, for example, by Miles 2010, 125, who describes it as a 'questionable detail'. Child sacrifice was almost certainly practised in Carthage, even if some of the ancient literary references to it were meant to slander the Punic people. This is a very complex subject, but to get an idea of the different views, see Aubet 2001, 250–256, Azize 2007, Hoyos 2010, 100–105, and Miles 2010, 68–73.
134. Diod. Sic. 13.86.3.
135. See the entry for μηχανή in *LSJ*.
136. Diod. Sic. 13.86.4–5. These are the numbers given by Diodorus. As can be seen, unlike with the figures provided for Carthaginian armies, these do not seem to be exaggerated.
137. Diod. Sic. 13.87.4–5. Despite Diodorus saying that Menes was put in charge, there is no mention of him after this passage, and Daphnaeus of Syracuse seems to have retained leadership, at least of his own forces.
138. Diod. Sic. 13.88.1–2.
139. Diod. Sic. 13.88.3–5.
140. Diod. Sic. 13.88.6–7.
141. Diod. Sic. 13.89.
142. Diod. Sic. 13.89.2.
143. See the discussion of Walbank 1945.
144. Diod. Sic. 13.90.
145. CIS I 5510. Although the translation has not always been considered to reference Akragas, Schmitz 1994 convincingly argues that the inscription was set up honouring the victory.
146. Diod. Sic. 13.91.1.
147. Diod. Sic. 13.91.2.
148. Diod. Sic. 13.91.3–4.
149. Caven 1990, 50–58. Of note for the present discussion, he had Daphnaeus, the leader of the Syracusan forces at Akragas, put to death.
150. Diod. Sic. 13.94.5–95.1.
151. Diod. Sic. 13.96.5.
152. On the placement of the camp, see Caven 1990, 61.
153. Diod. Sic. 13.108.5–7.
154. Diod. Sic. 13.108.8–9.
155. These are the numbers recorded by Timaeus, but Diodorus also supplies us with a different number, 50,000 total troops, though he doesn't cite his source for this (Diod. Sic. 13.109.2). I am inclined to believe Timaeus' figures. Caven 1990, 62, has suggested that the smaller number did not include the light infantry. He

also argues that Dionysius had more cavalry with him than Diodorus indicates, believing that the number was corrupted at some point in the transmission of the text, and that either 3,000 or 4,000 would make more sense. There is some sense in this, as the army of Daphnaeus, which came to the aid of Akragas, contained 5,000 horse. Caven is likely correct that there were more cavalry in Dionysius' army than we are told, and a range between 3,000 and 5,000 seems reasonable. I am inclined to believe that the infantry likely numbered 30,000 and the cavalry 3,000, a ratio of 10:1 between the two, which is not out of place for Sicilian Greek armies.

156. Diod. Sic. 13.109.3.
157. Diod. Sic. 13.109.4–5.
158. Diod. Sic. 13.110.
159. Diod. Sic. 13.111.1–2.
160. There is no room here to fully discuss the rise of Dionysius. The best account in English is Caven 1990. Champion 2010 provides a readable narrative. On the nature of his power, see Sanders 1991.
161. For instance, Caven 1990, 74. See Diod. Sic. 13.114.1–2.
162. Diod. Sic. 13.114.1.

Chapter 4

1. For a comprehensive account, see Caven 1990, 50–8, 80–8.
2. Prag 2010, 61–2.
3. Diod. Sic. 14.45.3–4.
4. See, for instance, Warmington 1993, 99: 'The chances of Dionysius surviving this humiliating peace must have seemed negligible to many.'
5. Diod. Sic. 14.41.3.
6. Some people have doubted that the quinquereme, or the 'five', was created in Syracuse at this time, partly because we only hear of them in the latter quarter of the fourth century, e.g. Tarn 1930, 130–1. I agree with Caven 1990, 95–6, however, that there is no good reason to doubt what we read in Diodorus. It fits into a pattern which we may refer to as an 'arms race', as the Carthaginians had supposedly invented the quadrireme, or the 'four', before this, Pliny NH 7.207. See also Steinby 2014, 10–11. On how these ships may have been structured, Casson 1971, 100–7.
7. Diod. Sic. 14.42.1. It is controversial whether or not catapults were truly 'invented' at this point or if this was simply a step forward building from older designs, see the discussion in Campbell 2003 and Schellenberg 2006.
8. van Wees 2004, 142
9. Caven 1990, 95, and Rawlings 2007, 139.
10. Diod. Sic. 14.43.2.
11. Diod. Sic. 14.41.4. It is worth pointing out, however, that Diodorus (14.43.4; though see 14.44.1) tells us Dionysius only hired his mercenaries *after* the making of ships and arms was completed. A possible solution is that he had gathered to him a number of mercenary captains representative of different peoples who would later bring the rest of the soldiers to Syracuse. If a scenario similar to this happened, it would explain how Dionysius knew which groups would be fighting for him and thus what types of arms his craftsmen needed to produce. It is interesting that we only hear specifically of him recruiting mercenaries from Greek communities,

listed simply as Greece and from amongst the Lacedaemonians (Diod. Sic. 14.44.2). This is important for the modern understanding of Greek warfare, as this implies that different communities in the very early fourth century used different arms and armour, which runs contrary to the typical idea of uniform armies of hoplites, for instance Hanson 1989. That the Western Greeks may not have adhered to this, see Hall 2021. On Lacedaemonian mercenary service, see Millender 2006.

12. Diod. Sic. 14.47.3.
13. Diod. Sic. 14.54.5.
14. Diod. Sic. 14.46.1.
15. Diod. Sic. 14.46.2 is not specific, but it seems probable that he is only referring to those either under the direct control of Dionysius or those allied to him. In the next line he says that the Greek cities under the control of the Carthaginians did the same, implying open rebellion against their erstwhile overlords. However, the moralizing tone of 14.46.4, in which Diodorus attributes this rebellion to the poor way which the Carthaginians treated their Hellenic subjects, makes me doubt the historicity of this particular episode. Other modern historians, though, are less critical, with, for example, Miles 2010, 127, saying that while expelling the Phoenicians the Greeks engaged in 'an ugly orgy of ethnic cleansing that included atrocities and massacres'.
16. Diod. Sic. 14.47.1–2.
17. For a description and discussion of Motya, see Aubet 2001, 231–4.
18. Bondi 1997, 329.
19. Diod. Sic. 14.47.7.
20. Diod. Sic. 14.48.3.
21. That 40,000 troops were drawn from the rowers and other crew members of the ships may explain why there is no mention of spears in Dionysius' preparations for this campaign, despite the spear being the most common weapon used by Greek armies in this period. Daggers would be much easier for the naval crews to carry with them onboard ship, while spears would have been unwieldy and cumbersome.
22. Similar conclusions were reached by Caven 1990, 100. The numbers are accepted without much question by Roisman 2017, 246, noting that the circumstances for earlier and later wars were different, which may account for the figure of 80,000 infantry. Kern 1999, 178, states without discussion that the army numbered 40,000 infantry and 3,000 cavalry.
23. This could be explained, perhaps, by the levies which came to Dionysius' army on the march, which may have drawn in more men than would have usually come, being thusly drawn to fight because of the cruelty the Carthaginians had shown them (cf. Diod. Sic. 14.46.3).
24. Diod. Sic. 14.48.3.
25. Diod. Sic. 14.48.5. It is probable that Dionysius took with him on this expedition most of the 'regular' infantry, and left behind the naval crews to help finish the mole. This would have left them close to their ships to fend off any Carthaginian force which came to aid Motya.
26. He had earlier sent a smaller squadron of ten ships to the harbour at Syracuse which destroyed the ships left behind by Dionysius (presumably merchant vessels).

This was an attempt to draw the Greeks away from Motya. It was successful in its first goal but failed in the second (Diod. Sic. 14.49.1–2).
27. Diod. Sic. 14.50.1.
28. Diod. Sic. 14.50.2.
29. Diod. Sic. 14.50.4; Polyaenus *Strat.* 5.2.6.
30. Diod. Sic. 14.51.1.
31. Warmington 1993, 101.
32. Diod. Sic. 14.51.2.
33. Diod. Sic. 14.51.3.
34. Diod. Sic. 14.51.5–6.
35. Diod. Sic. 14.51.7.
36. Diod. Sic. 14.52.1–3.
37. Diod. Sic. 14.52.4.
38. Diod. Sic. 14.52.5–7.
39. Diod. Sic. 14.53.1.
40. See, for instance, van Wees 2003. Ducrey 1968, 111, believed that this was an advantage of being a 'civilian' in wartime, although it is lost on me how being enslaved and sold off to a new master somewhere was much more advantageous than simply being killed in battle.
41. Diod. Sic. 13.53.2. Although suppliants are typically considered sacrosanct in studies of Greek warfare, this was not always the case; see Hall 2018a.
42. Diod. Sic. 14.53.3.
43. Diod. Sic. 14.53.4–5.
44. A note must be made about the chronology of their army's assemblage. We first hear of their recruitment efforts at Diod. Sic. 14.47.3, on the eve of Dionysius' campaign against Motya. At 14.54.4–5, however, Diodorus makes it sound as though they only began to collect troops in the wake of the renewed pillaging and siege operations following the sack. I think that it is unlikely they had been sitting idle while Motya was destroyed, and the naval raids sent by Himilco show that they were aware of what was happening. It is probable, as suggested above, that the attack came as such a surprise to the Carthaginians that it was only in its aftermath that they were finally able to assemble their troops at Carthage and sail as a coherent army to Sicily.
45. Diod. Sic. 14.54.5–6.
46. Timaeus's numbers do not breakdown the individual unit types, and it is probable that at least some of the 30,000 additional troops from Sicily were cavalry. For the sake of simplicity, and a lack of other evidence, I have included them en masse to my estimate for the strength of the Carthaginian infantry.
47. Polyb. 1.25.
48. For a defence of fleet numbers in later authors, see Steinby 2014, 55, and 192 n. 5 for a bibliography of discussion.
49. Caven 1990, 107, saw the only 'reasonable' figure in this description of the Punic army as the 600 transports noted by Ephorus. He uses this to calculate that the Carthaginians had a strength of about 50,000 troops total, assuming that 500 of the transports were used to carry 100 men each, and that the other 100 transports were used to convey the horses and chariots (and presumably other supplies?). This is interesting, although entirely arbitrary. It is also problematic that Caven did not take into account the space required to transport the 'engines of war' (siege

engines) which are one of the cargoes actually noted as being conveyed in the transport ships. Roisman 2017, 252, repeats the estimates of Caven, noting a total of about 80,000 troops if we also include the 30,000 Sicilian troops who joined the army after it landed.
50. Diod. Sic. 14.55.1.
51. Polyaenus *Strat.* 5.10.2 knew this manoeuvre as a night-time stratagem. His version also says that Himilco had ordered the ships to cover the fronts of their lamps to conceal themselves further from the Greeks. It is suspicious that we do not hear about this in Diodorus, and what Polyaenus preserves may be an elaboration of the story.
52. Although Caven 1990, 108, rightly questions why this would not have been included in Polyaenus' stratagems attributed to Himilco.
53. Diod. Sic. 14.55.3.
54. Diod. Sic. 14.47.4–48.1. On the ancient foundation legends of Eryx, which were connected to the myths of the Trojan exodus, see Thuc. 6.2.3.
55. Diod. Sic. 14.55.4. We do not hear any details of the treachery involved but it may be that the citizens of Eryx revolted against Dionysius' garrison. Diodorus earlier said that the city had gone over to the Syracusan and his army because they were in awe of his army and because they hated the Carthaginians. It is interesting, though, that they would side with Dionysius as around twenty years earlier Eryx had been part of the coalition which brought the Athenians to Sicily against the Selinus-Syracuse bloc (cf. Thuc. 6.46–7). Their Phoenician neighbours had even helped in a ploy to trick the Athenians into coming to the island. Caven 1990, 100, suggested that some type of 'friction' developed between Motya and Eryx, either from a border dispute or commercial rivalry. This is possible, but the rapidity with which the town went over to Himilco makes me think that Dionysius had taken control by means of his massive army and not because the inhabitants had really turned against the Carthaginians and the Phoenicians of eastern Sicily. It is also telling that Eryx was staunchly in the Punic camp by 368 and Dionysius was then forced to take it by force (Diod. Sic. 15.73.2).
56. Diod. Sic. 14.55.6–7.
57. Caven 1990, 109, noted that 'a readiness to retreat in good time before unacceptable odds is one of the marks of a good general' in the context of Dionysius' eastward manoeuvre, a comment with which I cannot disagree. This action was, perhaps, one of his moments of military brilliance.
58. Diod. Sic. 14.55.4. Likewise, Caven 1990, 109, stated that 'Biton's resistance is unlikely to have been of any long duration.'
59. Diod. Sic. 14.56.1.
60. They frequently fought with Etruscan fleets, evidenced by their dedications at Delphi (Diod. Sic. 5.9.5; Paus. 10.11.3). Dunbabin 1948, 332, thought that the Greeks who settled on Lipara chose to do so because it would provide them with an excellent base for raiding shipping coming and going from Etruria. They may have also asserted themselves as defenders of Hellenism because of the actions they took against barbarians at sea, Scott 2010, 92, Dunbabin 1948, 346–7. Liparians, however, were certainly practitioners of piracy, as well, as shown by their seizure of the Roman ship sent to Delphi in the aftermath of the siege of Veii (Livy 5.28; Diod. Sic. 14.93.3; cf. Plut. *Cam.* 8.8).
61. Diod. Sic. 14.56.2.

62. Diodorus' narrative is problematic on this point. At 14.56.2 he says that the army set out for Messene with the fleet sailing along with them, but at 14.57.1 he implies that the Carthaginian army was in the process of landing and debarking from their ships in the territory of Pelorias. It is difficult to say whether or not the army had embarked on their transports and participated in taking Lipara, and subsequently sailing towards Messene. Authors often write that it had done just this, for instance Champion 2010, location 4416. Roisman 2017, 253, is cautious and described Himilco's army as having 'moved on land and sea along the northern shore'. Caven 1990, 110, observes that Diodorus' sources must have been either divided or ambiguous about this point. We are unaided by the circumstances of Himilco's march on Messene, as making an alliance with Himera implies that his army marched, while subduing the Liparians indicates that the army was transported by sea. The taking of the latter, however, could also have been necessitated if we presume, as I believe we should, that the Punic fleet played an important logistical role in the campaign.
63. Diod. Sic. 14.56.3–4. Not all authors describe them as hostages, for instance Champion 2010, location 4416, says that they were serving with the Syracusan army. Caven 1990, 110, while acknowledging that they are probably to be considered hostages, described this group as 'the Knights' and 'the fighting-men of their [the Messenians] ruling class'. While it is true that we can read ἱππεῖς as a social class, I think that, given the circumstances, it is more likely that Diodorus or his source had intended to imply the actual cavalry, not simply aristocratic soldiers more generally.
64. Diod. Sic. 14.56.5. The translation is that of Oldfather.
65. Diod. Sic. 14.56.6.
66. Diod. Sic. 14.57.1. Diodorus tells us that the Messenians were trying to prevent Himilco's landing near Pelorias. This, again, is a symptom of the confused narratives of marching or sailing that we have noted above. While I have argued that the bulk of the army probably marched up the coast, it is possible that the general had gone with the fleet and what troops were thereupon embarked during the assault on Lipara. If this is correct, then the landing that we hear about in this instance is Himilco rejoining the bulk of his land forces, a reunion that the Messenians would understandably wish to prevent.
67. Diod. Sic. 14.57.2–3.
68. Diod. Sic. 14.57.4–5.
69. Diod. Sic. 14.57.6, 58.3.
70. Diod. Sic. 14.58.1.
71. Caven 1990, 111. Up to thirty per cent of Dionysius' armies may have been mercenaries, which would mean that when groups were dismissed he would have been quite short of troops; De Angelis 2016, 215, with citations.
72. As suggested by Roisman 2017, 253.
73. Diod. Sic. 14.58.1.
74. Diod. Sic. 14.58.2. The notice that few of the ships were triremes may be incorrect, with Caven 1990, 112, positing this or that the text has been corrupted and it should actually read 'few were fivers [quinqueremes].'
75. Diod. Sic. 14.59.1.
76. As was recorded by Diod. Sic. 14.58.2.
77. Diod. Sic. 14.59.3.

78. It is strange, if this is the case, that he had earlier persuaded the Campanians who had settled there to move to the fortified settlement of Aetna, as their numbers could presumably have been added to his army (Diod. Sic. 14.58.2). In the wake of the Sicel defection, Dionysius may have been afraid that the Campanians would do the same, which would explain why he displaced them. This is usually portrayed as Dionysius wishing to protect the Campanians, though, for instance by Caven 1990, 111–12.
79. It is unclear from Diodorus' narrative at 14.59.5–7 when exactly the two fleets arrived off Catane.
80. Diod. Sic. 14.59.7. As with the ship numbers from earlier in this war, 500 may be an exaggeration.
81. Diod. Sic. 14.60.1.
82. Caven 1990, 113, believed that these were the quinqueremes of the fleet, but there is no indication of this given by Diodorus, except that these may have been considered the 'best' ships in the fleet.
83. Diod. Sic. 14.60.2.
84. Diod. Sic. 14.60.3.
85. Diod. Sic. 14.60.4–5.
86. Diod. Sic. 14.60.6.
87. Even Diodorus (14.60.7) noted the inspiring effect that the captured ships had.
88. Diod. Sic. 14.61.1.
89. Diod. Sic. 14.61.2–3.
90. Diod. Sic. 14.61.4–6. According to Diodorus, they would have gone over to the Carthaginians if these hostages had not been in Syracusan hands, but this is almost certainly speculation on the part of his sources.
91. Diod. Sic. 14.62.1.
92. Diod. Sic. 14.62.2–3.
93. Diod. Sic. 14.62.4.
94. This was a similar strategy to that used by Nicias during the Athenian expedition against Syracuse in 415, see Thuc. 6.65–6.
95. Diod. Sic. 14.63.1.
96. Diod. Sic. 14.63.3.
97. Diod. Sic. 14.63.1–2, 70.4. This is not surprising, as events such as plagues were often attributed to 'affronts to the gods', Parker 1996, esp. 273–80. It is worth noting that Diodorus also blames the location of the Punic camp(s) for the outbreak, noting that it was where the Athenians had camped and experienced a similar fate (14.70.5). Five more reasonable (to a modern reader) reasons are given: the camp was in a marsh and a hollow, a cold breeze came in the morning, midday was stifling, and there were too many people gathered into a small area (Diod. Sic. 14.70.5–6).
98. Diod. Sic. 14.77.4–5.
99. Miles 2010, 142–5. Not all modern historians are as sceptical, for instance Lancel 1995, 114, 193, or Hoyos 2010, 96–7.
100. Diod. Sic. 14.63.4.
101. Polyaen. 2.11. Front. *Strat.* 1.4.12, though, says that they captured ten.
102. Diod. Sic. 14.64.1.
103. Diod. Sic. 14.64.3–5.
104. Diod. Sic. 14.65–69.

105. Sanders 1981, 401–8, 1987, 134–9, and Caven 1990, 115–16. Berger 1992, 44, pointed out that while the speech itself is 'of course, not authentic', the contents may reflect the mood in the city at that time.
106. Roisman 2017, 256 n. 42, dismisses all of the problems Caven raised as not being 'critical enough to justify its rejection'.
107. Caven 1990, 116, 'if he *had* departed from Syracuse, would he not have left someone whom he could trust (Pharacidas, or Philistus) in command there.'
108. Diod. Sic. 14.74.1–2.
109. Diod. Sic. 14.70.1–3.
110. Diod. Sic. 14.71.1–2.
111. It could be, as suggested by Lewis 1994, 123, 144 n. 103, that the account of the plague was taken directly from Philistus, by Diodorus, and would thus have been written by a contemporary of the disease. If this is the case, we have no reason to question the details provided.
112. Diod. Sic. 14.71.2.
113. Compare these symptoms with those of the plague in Athens in 430, Thuc. 2.49. Littman 1984, 112–13, helpfully provides a table doing this.
114. Diod. Sic. 14.71.3.
115. The casual reader should note the multitude of identified diseases which may have been responsible for the Athenian plague. I am glad, however, that not all scholars have been as pessimistic about identifying the disease as Caven 1990, 116–17, who wrote that 'it is not possible to identify it [the pathogen] with any certainty.'
116. Littman 1984, 2009. Tyhpoid fever has been assumed in the past, i.e. Warmington 1993, 104. Typhoid fever was suggested by Papagrigorakis et al. 2008 as the epidemic which afflicted Athens in 430.
117. Papagrigorakis et al. 2008.
118. For instance, Caven 1990, 117 and Roisman 2017, 256.
119. Diod. Sic. 14.72.1.
120. Diod. Sic. 14.72.2–3. Roisman 2017, 257, sees this as a 'hostile depiction' and doubts that Dionysius had purposefully sent these men to their deaths. Diodorus' account, however, gives us no reason to feel sympathy for this group and I see no reason to doubt its authenticity.
121. Diod. Sic. 14.72.3.
122. Diod. Sic. 14.72.4–6.
123. Diod. Sic. 14.73.1.
124. Diod. Sic. 14.73.2–5.
125. Diod. Sic. 14.74.4.
126. Roisman 2017, 258.
127. Diod. Sic. 14.74.1–2.
128. Diod. Sic. 14.75.1–2.
129. Caven 1990, 118–21.
130. Diod. Sic. 14.75.3.
131. Roisman 2017, 258.
132. Diod. Sic. 14.75.4–9.
133. This huge figure is perhaps more believable than the large expeditionary armies we find in our sources, simply because during a revolt entire populations could be considered combatants. Even if all of the settlements around Carthage rose up against her, though, this is still a suspiciously large number, as noted by Lancel 1995, 272.

134. Diod. Sic. 14.77.
135. Diod. Sic. 14.76; Justin 19.3. The latter source simply says that he locked himself in his house and committed suicide. I am inclined to believe that he starved himself to death, and that it may have taken place in his own home. Self-starvation was a relatively common method of killing oneself in the ancient world, and has been highlighted as a harsh method preferred by 'Greek sages and Roman dignitaries', van Hooff 1990, 41–7.
136. Diod. Sic. 14.78.5.
137. Diod. Sic. 14.90.2–3.
138. Diod. Sic. 14.90.3.
139. Diod. Sic. 14.90.4–6.
140. The opening line of Diod. Sic. 14.95 makes it sound as though the events of the previous year did not happen. It begins with 'the Carthaginians, after a slow recovery from the disaster they had suffered at Syracuse, resolved to keep their hand in Sicilian affairs.' It is possible that Diodorus has simply copied a line that he found in one of his sources, which was itself ignorant of the smaller expedition of Mago the year before. I see no reason to dismiss the earlier episode.
141. Diod. Sic. 14.95.1.
142. Ray 2012, 29.
143. Caven 1990, 129, is to be credited with describing this as an '"economy" expedition.'
144. Diod. Sic. 14.95.2.
145. Diod. Sic. 14.95.3–7.
146. Diod. Sic. 14.96.1–4.
147. Diodorus tells us that the terms of the treaty with Mago were the same as the previous peace treaty (Diod. Sic. 13.114.1), which is where these particular conditions are given. We may also include the obligation of Selinus, Akragas, Himera, Gela, and Camarina to pay tribute to Carthage, although I am more inclined to believe that the treaty simply reinforced the territorial hegemonies of Carthage and Syracuse. Warmington 1993, 106, believed that Carthage had given up their claims to any Greek cities on the island, which seems reasonable, given their precarious military position.
148. On the empire and Dionysius' strategy, see the extensive discussion in Caven 1990, 124–85.
149. Diod. Sic. 15.14.3–4.
150. Diod. Sic. 15.14.4–15.1–2.
151. The chronology of these events is unclear, but Caven 1990, 196, has proposed that the invasion by Mago occurred in 377 bc. Others, such as Hoyos 2010, 169, suggest 382 or 381 for the conclusion of the war.
152. This is a significant difference from what we have seen earlier in Diodorus. It could point to the historian following a different source for this war than we have seen before, but other differences with the treatment of the West in Book 15 point to more significant challenges. Caven 1990, 186–9, discusses the possibilities, including one in which the text we possess is actually an epitome of Diodorus.
153. Diod. Sic. 15.15.2.
154. Diod. Sic. 15.15.3–4.
155. Diod. Sic. 15.16.
156. Polyaenus *Strat.* 6.16.1.
157. Caven 1990, 197.

158. Stylianou 1990, 204.
159. This was included as *FGrHist* 70 F71 by Jacoby.
160. See Roisman 2017, 269.
161. As suggested by Caven 1990, 198. On recovery of the dead after Greek battles, see van Wees 2004, 136–8, and Rawlings 2007, 193–9, cf. Vaughn 1991.
162. Caven 1990, 198, proposes that a story preserved in Polyaenus *Strat.* 6.16.3 about a Punic fleet defeating one sent by Dionysius, the former destined for Sicily, could have been the reinforcements. While possible, it is certainly not definite. As well, I am dubious of the claim that Mago's son was 'substantially reinforced' as the only evidence for this, however circumstantial, was that they defeated Dionysius outside of Cronium.
163. Diod. Sic. 15.16.2.
164. Polyaenus Strat. 5.10.5 may preserve the memory of this army using a smoke screen to enter the besieged city of Cronium, sneaking past Dionysius' generals. This would mean that Mago's son was named Himilco, otherwise not recorded by Diodorus or in other passages of Polyaenus. Caven 1990, 198, believed that this notice *must* belong to the present war, and noted that it did not fit into the narrative of Himilco son of Hanno. As Hoyos 2010, 134 and 169, has noted, however the other stories in the same section of Polyaenus clearly relate to the earlier Himilco. We are left with Polyaenus either preserving an event from the earlier Himilco's campaign against Dionysius that we do not find in Diodorus or that he has preserved both the name of Mago's son as well as details from the later war against Dionysius that we do not have elsewhere. I am more convinced that the former is correct. It is for this reason that I have not named Mago's son as 'Himilco' in my narrative, as Caven and others do.
165. Diod. Sic. 15.17.1–4.
166. Hoyos 2010, 169.
167. Diod. Sic. 15.17.5.
168. Diod. Sic. 15.24.2–3. Hoyos' 2010, 169, proposition that Libya was subdued before Sardinia is probably correct, although it is possible that the revolts were more serious than he allows for. The deficient quality of Diodorus at this point makes me weary to dismiss these as minor events simply because we do not hear of many details.
169. Diod. Sic. 15.73.1. I do not believe that this was the same rebellion that was noted in the aftermath of the second war, as some do, e.g. Warmington 1993, 107 and Rhodes 2010, 323.
170. Justin 20.5.11. Many scholars share in this view even if it is not explicitly stated, for example Caven 1990, 206, Warmington 1993, 107, Hoyos 2010, 169–70.
171. Diod. Sic. 15.73.2.
172. The largest that we hear of before this was 200 in service of Gelon (Hdt. 7.158), but this was likely an exaggeration, Morakis 2015. Thus, Dionysius' grand fleet was a significant accomplishment if it truly consisted of 300 ships.
173. Diod. Sic. 15.73.2.
174. Diodorus does not state where the land army went after abandoning the siege of Lilybaeum, but Eryx makes the most sense for two reasons. Firstly, the height afforded by being stationed on Mt. Eryx would have given them command of the entire area, augmented by Dionysius' considerable cavalry force. Secondly, the fleet anchored in Drepanum, Eryx's harbour, and it would have been tactically sensible to keep the two near one another.

175. Justin 20.5.11; Polyaenus *Strat.* 5.9.
176. A Punic army may have landed after the death of Dionysius, as Syracuse and Dionysius II felt threatened by the Carthaginians, Plut. *Dion* 6.4.
177. Diod. Sic. 15.73.3.
178. According to Justin 20.5.12, a man named Suniatus, a Latinized version of the Phoenician name Eshmuniaton, had been in treasonous communication with Dionysius and providing him with information regarding Punic military movements and ambitions. I follow Caven 1990, 207, who finds 'attractive the idea that the wily Carthaginians utilized the traitor Suniatus' couriers to convey this' to their enemy. It must be conceded, however, that we have no real evidence for this and it is simply conjecture based in the fact that the Punic fleet was not destroyed in a blaze; there is no reason to think that this episode of information warfare could not have happened. The prohibitions on the Greek language being learned in Carthage after Eshmuniaton, however, are certainly exaggerated by Justin/Trogus's source (20.5.13) and may be entirely fictional, Hoyos 2010, 136.
179. Diod. Sic. 15.73.4.
180. Diod. Sic. 16.5.2.
181. Caven 1990, 208, put it strongly, stating that 'we need have no doubt that the dynast intended to reopen the campaign in the summer of that year.'
182. *RO* 34 = *IG* II² 105 and 523. The text consulted is the translation available at Attic Inscriptions Online (www.atticinscriptions.com/inscription/RO/34) along with a helpful commentary. Additional comments on the treaty and its context can be found in Rhodes and Osborne 2003, 162–8.
183. *RO* 34.12–23.
184. Caven 1990, 209–10.
185. For an overview, see Hornblower 2011, 253–67.
186. Xen. *Hell.* 7.1.37.
187. On the death of Dionysius, see Caven 1990, 211.

Chapter 5

1. Diod. Sic. 16.67–68.
2. Diod. Sic. 16.69.3–6, 70.4–6. Plut. *Tim.* 17 calls the Carthaginian commander Mago and that he had with him 60,000 troops. He also says that these were quartered within the city by Hicetas, but I find this unlikely, if for no other reason than this was a massive army and would not have been easily housed within the walls of a city being shared by three different factions. Unless, of course, the figure has been grossly exaggerated. Plut. *Tim.* 20 also preserves a very romanticized version of the Carthaginian retreat.
3. Diod. Sic. 16.73.1; Plut. *Tim.* 24.4. Diodorus explicitly says that this expedition was made in order to fund the coming war. Plutarch, however, makes it sound as though Timoleon sent these two into Carthaginian territory to weaken their position by encouraging uprisings in the towns loyal to them. The latter is the only of the two sources which names the commanders. There is no reason that both plunder and destabilisation have to be seen as competing goals, and were both probably reasons for the expedition, although some authors only give one explanation. Warmington 1993, 114, for example, notes only that he 'was even driven to the expedient of raiding the Carthaginian territory in the island to obtain plunder to pay his troops'.

4. Diod. Sic. 16.73.2.
5. Diod. Sic. 16.73.3 claims that the Carthaginians believed their generals in Sicily to be feckless, while Plut. *Tim.* 25.1 only records that the leaders were tired of the small campaigns which had been the character of the war up to this point.
6. Diod. Sic. 16.77.4. Plut. *Tim.* 25.3 does not describe the composition of the army, just that it consisted of 70,000 troops. Polyaenus *Strat.* 5.12.3 numbers the Punic army at 50,000.
7. Diod. Sic. 16.73.3.
8. Plut. *Tim.* 25.2.
9. Diod. Sic. 16.78.1.
10. Diod. Sic. 16.79.1; Plut. *Tim.* 25.3. Upon his return to Syracuse, Timoleon dismissed them from his service. They then sailed to Italy and began operating as a pillaging war band. After raiding a coastal town in Bruttian territory, they were slaughtered by a large local army, Diod. Sic. 16.82.1–2; Plut. *Tim.* 30.2–3.
11. Diod. Sic. 16.78.2; Plut. *Tim.* 25.2–3. Diodorus does not break down the number, but Plutarch said there were 3,000 Syracusans and 4,000 mercenaries in the army which marched out of the city, with 1,000 returning in cowardice. Of the remaining army 5,000 were infantry and 1,000 were cavalry.
12. Talbert 1974, 60, postulates that Plutarch's total may not take into account the troops sent by Hicetas or the other allies. If this is correct, it raises questions about Plutarch's sources or may show a misinterpretation on his part of the troop numbers he found in them.
13. Our sources make it sound as though both armies reached their destinations around the same time on the same day, but I find this unlikely. It makes more sense that Timoleon had marched his army to the Crimisus with the intention of ambushing the Carthaginians when they tried to ford the river. This is what the circumstances of the battle support.
14. It was perhaps Timoleon himself that spotted them, or at least climbed the hill to get a view of what he was up against (Plut. *Tim.* 26.1). The story which accompanies this, however, that a number of pack animals came up to him with wild celery/parsley in their mouths, which was taken as a positive omen by the Corinthian, is dubious (also found at Diod. Sic. 16.79.3 and Polyaenus *Strat.* 5.1, though not in the context of Timoleon climbing the hill).
15. Thick fog at Plut. *Tim.* 27.
16. Plut. *Tim.* 27.2.
17. Plut. *Tim.* 27.4. Diodorus's version of the battle does not record this charge, but simply that Timoleon's army immediately crushed the first of the Carthaginians to cross the river, Diod. Sic. 16.79.5. In general, Plutarch's version of the battle is to be preferred.
18. Plut. *Tim.* 27.4.
19. Plut. *Tim.* 27.6.
20. Plut. *Tim.* 28.1.
21. Plut. *Tim.* 28.1.
22. Diod. Sic. 16.80.1.
23. My narrative of the battle is primarily based on the description given by Plut. *Tim.* 28 and Diod. Sic. 16.79.6–80.1–3.
24. Diod. Sic. 16.80.4–5 gives the total dead at 12,500, the Sacred Band plus 10,000 from other elements of the army. Whether we should accept this figure over

that of Plutarch is debatable, as is how accurate we think either number may be. Both Diodorus (16.80.6) and Plutarch (*Tim.* 29.2) note that Timoleon's tent was surrounded by 10,000 captured shields, which makes me want to trust the casualty figures from the latter. Diodorus does say that there were 'more than' 10,000 shields, but that he does not record 'more than 12,500' indicates that his sources listed the former and that when he says that 12,500 in total died, he has made an error that is not true to his source material.

25. Plut. *Tim.* 27.2–3. Modern authors often make this assumption, such as Hoyos 2010, 171.
26. This figure is noted by some modern authors. Warmington 1993, for instance, refers simply to 3,000 Carthaginian citizen casualties, the figure given by Plutarch for the Sacred Band. This number has been taken to be another possible total for the members of the Sacred Band, cf. Ameling 1993, 162–4. We may be able to reconcile the two numbers as well as an interesting line from Plutarch (*Tim.* 28.4) which says that 'at last as the storm still beat upon them [the Carthaginians] and the Greeks had broken their front line of four hundred men, the main body turned and fled.' There is no indication as to who this 'line' was, and this statement does not fit with the rest of the narrative. It is possible that these 400 Carthaginians were either Hasdrubal or Hamilcar's guard unit. This would help us to make sense of why the rest of the army broke after they were killed, as one (or perhaps both) of the generals was either killed or forced off the battlefield. This would also bring total Carthaginian citizens killed to 3,000. Under this assumption, Plutarch's 3,000 would not be an error relating to the size of the Sacred Band, but rather the casualties from that unit along with another group of elite Punic citizens. This is, though, just a hypothesis.
27. Plut. *Tim.* 28.1. Talbert 1974, 61, laments the lack of information on Greek casualties from our sources and suggests that they incurred heavy casualties, especially in the first stage of the battle.
28. Plut. *Tim.* 29.2.
29. Diod. Sic. 16.81.2.
30. That we do not hear of them again, though, leaves open the possibility that they fell at the Crimisus, corroborating my suggestion that the 'front line' 400 may have been their personal guard.
31. Plut. *Tim.* 29.2.
32. SEG 11.126a. See the discussion in Talbert 1974, 76–7.
33. Plut. *Tim.* 29.3.
34. Diod. Sic. 16.81.3.
35. Plut. *Tim.* 30.1.
36. Plut. *Tim.* 30.2–3. The group defeated near Ietae included some of the men who had violated Delphi in the Third Sacred War (355–346 bc). On the outbreak of this conflict, see Ellis 1994, 739–42.
37. Plut. *Tim.* 31.
38. Plut. *Tim.* 34.1.
39. Talbert 1974, 83, believes that 'much of Gisco's force' was killed in this battle. It is possible, though not probable, that the Punic casualties we hear of were Carthaginian citizens. Plutarch describes them as 'ἐπίκουροι Φοίνικες'. I find it unlikely that they would have sent citizens, Carthaginian or otherwise Phoenician, when they had mercenaries at hand.

40. Suggested, for instance, by Westlake 1994, 715. Talbert 1974, 83–4 n. 3, doesn't think that we should place much faith in Diodorus and Plutarch claiming that the Carthaginians were pleading for peace, as our sources are biased in favour of Timoleon. This is an important point to keep in mind, but Plutarch's tying of Punic peace overtures to the defeat at the Arbolus is compelling to me. That the boundary was re-established at the Halycus, however, suggests that either Carthage or the tyrants had made considerable inroads against Timoleon's cause in the east and he was forced to accept a peace which won very little for him.
41. Diod. Sic. 16.82.3; Plut. *Tim.* 34.1.
42. Diod. Sic. 18.19–21; Bosworth 1988, 291–2.
43. Diod. Sic. 19.1.7; cf. Just. *Epit.* 22.1.1, Plut. *Re. et imp. apophth.* 23.1. Meister 1984, 385, rightly notes that the circumstances of Agathocles' life, such as being made an officer and his brother having been a strategos, point to their family being wealthy and not a humble potter's household. Tillyard 1908, 29, thought that the story of Agathocles' family trade was simply 'made up'.
44. Meister 1984, 392, and Huss 1985, 182, both suggest that he besieged Akragas. I am sympathetic to this idea, and think it is probable; the paucity of our sources keeps me from concluding it happened without any doubt.
45. Diod. Sic. 19.102.8.
46. Diod. Sic. 19.103. The fifty ships may have been part of, or all of, the fleet that had sailed into Akragas, as suggested by Tillyard 1908, 68.
47. Diod. Sic. 19.104.1–2.
48. Diod. Sic. 19.104.3–4.
49. His father's name is not mentioned by Diodorus, but is preserved by Just. *Epit.* 22.3.6.
50. Diod. Sic. 19.106.2. The reading of 'horsemen' is a simplification of what we find in Diodorus, which is ζευγίπποι, the only instance of this word. It would mean something like 'pairs of horses/horsemen'. Some scholars have suggested that it is a corruption and should actually read ζευγῖται, meanings 'cars', in this instance probably 'chariots' (Tillyard 1908, 70). While this is possible, as chariots were known in Etruria (though not predominantly from this period), I find that the first reading is more likely correct (cf. Meltzer 1879, 524, and Huss 1985, 184). It is possible that this was a type of unit of which we know very little, perhaps specialized horsemen who operated in pairs. On Etruscan chariots and other wheeled vehicles, see Crouwel 2012 (comprehensive examination) or Emiliozzi 2013 (short overview).
51. Diod. Sic. 19.106.3–5. Unlike in previous wars, there is little reason to doubt the figures given for the Punic expeditionary force in this instance.
52. Diod. Sic. 19.107.2–4.
53. See, respectively, Meister 1984, 393, and Tillyard 1908, 72.
54. Diod. Sic. 19.108.2 preserves a story that a saying from 'earlier times' foretold of many men dying in a battle near the camps. We hear that this made the enemies leery of engaging each other. It is not impossible that there was an oracle which claimed this, but that this was reason enough for Hamilcar and Agathocles to delay their campaigns is suspect. Schubert 1887, 77, could be correct in believing that this was a 'local tradition' which sprung up *after* the battle.
55. Diod. Sic. 19.108.3–4.
56. Diod. Sic. 19.108.5–6.

57. On the sources of Diodorus' narrative, see Tillyard 1908, 96–7.
58. Diodorus notes that they typically used sling stones which weighed one mina, or just under a pound.
59. Diod. Sic. 19.109.1–3. We do not know much about the reinforcements which arrived 'from Carthage'. Scholars have typically accepted that Diodorus' report is correct (e.g. Tillyard 1908, 82–3, Meister 1984, 393). Freeman 1894, 394, postulated that these may have been sent by the government in Carthage upon hearing of the storm which sank a number of the ships sailing to Sicily. It is possible that Hamilcar had been delaying marching out for battle, knowing that they were *en route*. Their timely arrival, at least in the narrative we possess, makes me wonder if they were not actually from a naval camp (which almost certainly existed) nearby on the coast. The main camp of the land army would have been able to easily signal them if in need, thus explaining how they came to their aid at just the right time. This could have been part of Hamilcar's plan, and would mean that he had actually drawn Agathocles into a trap, rather than the latter having surprised the former. Schubert 1887, 79, suggested that Agathocles already knew of the approaching reinforcements and was forced to attack Hamilcar's camp before they arrived, thinking that with the new troops it would be impossible to dislodge the enemy.
60. Diod. Sic. 19.109.4–5. On the saltiness of the Himeras, see Vitr. *De arch.* 8.3.7. Just. *Epit.* 22.3.9 notes the battle (presumably) but does not give any details.
61. Tillyard 1908, 82, cites the low number of Carthaginian losses to argue that the 'defence of the camp cannot have been such a desperate matter as Diodorus believed' (cf. Freeman 1894, 395). I find this unsatisfactory and not enough evidence to throw away the account of the struggle. The disproportionately high losses suffered by Agathocles can be attributed to both his army being the assaulting force and that they broke into an open and undisciplined retreat after being driven out of the Punic fortifications. Hamilcar's losses do not seem suspect to me, even in Diodorus' narrative of a sharp struggle for the camp. The excessive Greek losses can be partly explained when we realise that Agathocles' cavalry had abandoned the fight, and thus did not help ward off the Punic horse (cf. Diod. Sic. 20.4.2 and Schubert 1887, 83).
62. Diod. Sic. 19.110.1–3.
63. Hoyos 2010, 173, described this message of liberation as 'slightly paradoxical', although I am unsure of this, especially in light of Agathocles' treatment of Gela. I think that a message of liberation was probably the best strategy to bring these cities over to the Punic cause.
64. Tillyard 1908, 84–5.
65. Diod. Sic. 19.110.3–5.
66. Diod. Sic. 20.3–4; Just. *Epit.* 22.4. Justin says that he freed all of the slaves of military age (*omnes deinde seruos militaris aetatis libertate*), though I think we should accept the more tempered description we find in Diodorus. It is unlikely that Agathocles would have freed *all* the slaves of military age, as this would have alienated even his allies within the city.
67. Diod. Sic. 20.11.1.
68. Smith 1913, 58.
69. Diod. Sic. 20.5; Just. *Epit.* 22.5.1–2.
70. Meister 1984, 394.

71. This places their date of departure on 14 August 310 BC, as the eclipse occurred on 15 August, see https://eclipse.gsfc.nasa.gov/SEcat5/SE-0399--0300.html. The description in Diodorus (20.5.5) makes it sound as though the ships were in the 'path of totality', meaning that the sun was entirely blocked out. This indicates that their course was to sail around the north of Sicily (https://eclipse.gsfc.nasa.gov/SEsearch/SEsearchmap.php?Ecl=-03090815), probably meant to keep the Punic fleet guessing where he would make landfall. It could have been the course forced on Agathocles, as the grain ships may have been arriving from Gela, thus meaning that the Punic fleet had moved towards the south to intercept. For this, and the calculation of the eclipse, see Airy 1853, 187–191.
72. Just. *Epit.* 22.6.2–3. The translation is that of J. S. Watson 1853. See also Diod. Sic. 20.5 and Frontin. *Str.* 1.12.9.
73. Diod. Sic. 20.6.
74. Diod. Sic. 20.7; Just. *Epit.* 22.6.4; Polyaenus *Strat.* 5.3.5. The latter two sources omit mention of any fear resulting from lack of troops to guard the ships. Some of the more colourful elements of the story, such as the blaring of trumpets sounding for battle and the exuberant war-cry, may have been later additions, Schubert 1887, 98. But, as Gsell 1928, 29, firmly stated, the two reasons given in Diodorus are certainly to be believed.
75. As suggested by Miles 2010, 150.
76. Diod. Sic. 20.8.3–4. On Punic agriculture and rural life, see Lancel 1995, 269–88.
77. Diod. Sic. 20.8.1 and 5.
78. They could have only had ladders, which the army would probably have been able to construct rather quickly. It is unlikely that they would have had any more complex siege equipment.
79. Diod. Sic. 20.8.6.
80. Diod. Sic. 20.9.1–2. The people of the countryside, in fact, sent reports to Carthage, as well, Diod. Sic. 20.9.3.
81. Diod. Sic. 20.8.7.
82. Just. *Epit.* 22.6.5.
83. Diod. Sic. 20.9.3–5.
84. Bomilcar may have been the nephew of the Hamilcar who was accused of treachery and being an ally of Agathocles. Only Justin (*Epit.* 22.7.10) preserves this, and its absence from Diodorus causes us a problem, as he seems to have known quite a bit about Bomilcar. Certainly, the actions of this man show that he did not fully support the government in power at Carthage, as Hamilcar did not, so it is possible that he was at least part of the same political faction.
85. Diod. Sic. 20.10.1–2.
86. Diod. Sic. 20.10.5. Although I do find this number to be quite high, I am reticent to completely reject it as does Champion 2012, who believed that 'even allowing that the Carthaginians conscripted every able-bodied man, regardless of social class and age, they could not have raised over 40,000 troops from the city alone.' One point alone makes his conclusion less likely, which is that he does not account for the refugees from the countryside who had fled there in the wake of Agathocles' path of destruction. As well, I do not see it as fruitful in this case to try to engage with population estimates for Carthage in order to determine how many soldiers they could have raised from the population. These estimates are problematic and,

as we are not presented with an absurd figure, such as 300,000 troops, I think we should accept this number. The figures, and narrative, of Just. *Epit.* 22.6.5–8 are so different from what we find in Diodorus that they are probably corrupted or based on an inaccurate source used by Trogus.
87. Diod. Sic. 20.10.6–11.1.
88. Diod. Sic. 20.11.2.
89. Tillyard 1908, 113.
90. Schubert 1887, 109–12.
91. Diod. Sic. 20.11.3–4. Owls were considered sacred to Athena.
92. The basis of the trick was to make his soldiers think that they had a divine blessing, thus, the majority of the troops could not have known about them beforehand or the narrative would be unravelled. This is, amongst all the other problems, a good reason to disbelieve this story.
93. Tillyard 1908, 113.
94. Diod. Sic. 20.12.3 says that he died of exhaustion, which is possible, though it is more probable that he was at least mortally wounded by an enemy soldier.
95. Diod. Sic. 20.12.1–4.
96. Diod. Sic. 20.12.6–8.
97. Diod. Sic. 20.13.1 says that not more than 1,000 Carthaginians were killed, 'but as some have written, upwards of 6,000'. Just. *Epit.* 22.6.6 says that 2,000 Sicilians and 3,000 Carthaginians were killed, and Orosius 4.6.25 gives 2,000 Punic dead. I am inclined to believe Diodorus' figures more so than those of Justin or Orosius, whose versions of this battle are significantly different. Justin's entire narrative at this point is either corrupt or may have been based on faulty sources used by Trogus. The first difference is that he gives Hanno as the only general appointed before the battle, and that he advanced on Agathocles' position with 30,000 troops, rather than the more detailed description of the army that we find in Diodorus. As well, the text of Justin as we have it reads *obuius ei fuit cum XXX milibus paganorum Hanno*, or 'Hanno advanced to meet them with 30,000 men from the countryside' (*Epit.* 22.6.5). The *paganorum* is almost certainly an error and should be read as *poenorum* (Phoenicians), as is preserved by Orosius 4.6.25 and as is suggested by Tillyard 1908, 111. Champion 2012 suggested a combination of the two narratives, in which Hanno had been sent to collect troops from the countryside and Bomilcar had been left in the city to enrol the citizen soldiers. This is possible, and the presence of non-Carthaginians in the army may explain the 'Libyans' of Diod. Sic. 20.12.7, who were the first of the Punic army to flee *en masse* rather than in a steady retreat. The very fluid use of Λίβυς as an adjective, which could have also been used to describe Carthaginians, may mean, though, that there was not actually an ethnic distinction being made. As well, this proposed version makes the rest of the narrative, about internal struggles in Carthage, seem much less important, as the generals were separated from one another. I am inclined to believe the version that we find in Diodorus, but we do have to keep in mind the possibility that it is not the entire truth.
98. Diod. Sic. 20.14.1–5. Miles 2010, 151, suggests that this may be the time when new temples were built for the goddesses Tanit and Astarte. This is based on *CIS* 1.3914, an inscription that I will admit that I have not been able to read myself, but Miles' suggestion is sound and corroborates the religious scare that we hear about in Diodorus.

Notes 281

99. Tillyard 1908, 120, opined that 'it is not easy to believe that the whole tale of sixty ships'-beaks was ever brought to Sicily.' His suggestion that 'one beak may perhaps have been sent' is sensible. I doubt that all of the prows were sent, although perhaps more than one made their way to Hamilcar's camp. As well, his conclusion that this was 'not to confirm the burning of the fleet... but merely as a kind of symbol such as the Semites love' is unnecessary.
100. Diod. Sic. 20.15.1–2.
101. Diod. Sic. 20.15.3–6.
102. Diod. Sic. 20.16.1 gives a description of Antander as being 'unmanly' and 'of a disposition the direct opposite of the boldness and energy of his brother [Agathocles]'. There is almost certainly an intentional play on words between his name and the Greek word for 'unmanliness' (more classically defined as 'wanting in manhood, cowardly, or doing things unworthy of a man') which is ἄνανδρος, thus 'Antandros' and 'anandros', obviously very similar sounding. It is unclear whether or not Antander actually considered surrendering the city, and I am inclined to think that this description of him as being 'wanting in manhood' was a later addition to the tradition.
103. *P. Oxy.* 2399, col. II-IV for the debate and Diod. Sic. 20.16.1 for the involvement of Erymnon. For a summary of what can be found in the papyrus, see Huß 1980, 68–71 and Meister 1984, 400–1.
104. Diod. Sic. 20.16.2 says that Hamilcar began building siege engines after he received word from Antander that he was not going to surrender the city. It is unlikely that these had not already been built, or at least started, before this point; this was the conclusion reached, for example, by Tillyard 1908, 121. We need not entirely dismiss this notice in Diodorus, however, and as I have included in my main narrative it is possible that Hamilcar paraded his siege engines in front of the Syracusans while waiting for their reply as a further incentive to surrender without a fight.
105. Diod. Sic. 20.16.3–6.
106. Diod. Sic. 20.16.7–9.
107. Diod. Sic. 20.17.1–2.
108. Diod. Sic. 20.17.3–5.
109. Grote 1857, 420–1 n. 1. He concluded this despite believing that Diodorus 'had good authorities before him in the history of Agathokles' and that the narrative was, in fact, 'quite distinct and intelligible'.
110. Tillyard 1908, 124.
111. Champion 2012. Freeman 1894, 420, resigned that 'it is for Alpine climbers to say where among the mountains... the point, if there be any, best suited to such a purpose may be found.' As far as I know, nobody has made suggestions as to the specific point or points at which the fires may have been lit.
112. Schubert 1887, 127 and Tillyard 1908, 124.
113. Schubert wrote 'Dass die Adrumetiner würden getäuscht werden können, hätte sich nicht annehmen lassen, da dieselben ein ankommendes Heer zunächst wohl für ein karthagisches gehalten hatten und sich ausserdem auch mit der Ergebung wohl wenigstens so lange wurden Zeit genommen haben, bin das vermeintlich ankommende Heer auch wirklich vor der Stadt erschienen war.'
114. See Just. *Epit.* 22.6.9–10.

115. It must be admitted that Tillyard's 1908, 124, alternative version is more plausible, though much less spectacular and innovative: 'all that can be believed is that Agathocles in marching to the relief of Tunis surprised the Carthaginian camp: the men fled in a panic, and left all their artillery behind. Then Agathocles came back to Hadrumetum, which at once made terms.' The only thing that I find problematic is that the Greek army would have been able to completely depart Hadrumetum and then return, suddenly, and force a surrender. Also, according to the author of *P. Oxy.* 2399, col. 1.3–26, and Diodorus 20.18.1, Agathocles' army was still split in two parts when the Carthaginians began to actively deal with the threat with armies in the field.
116. Diod. Sic. 20.17.6. His position also must have appeared to be the better of the two at this point.
117. cf. Huß 1980, 64–6.
118. *P. Oxy.* 2399, col. 1.11–19.
119. Diod. Sic. 20.18.1–2.
120. Diod. Sic. 20.18.3.
121. Diod. Sic. 20.29.5. This could be an indication that many, or perhaps most, of the 5,000 soldiers sent to Carthage from the army in Sicily were citizens, as a Greek was appointed to this position. Hamilcar could have simply been out of good Punic leaders by this point, though. Meister 1984, 401, puts Deinocrates as the leader of the refugees and allies, as he had been during the Greek resistance to Agathocles, which could very well have been the case. If he was acting as the liaison between the Greek soldiers and the Punic command then his role at the head of the cavalry may have been symbolic of that position's status in Carthaginian armies. On the other hand, Freeman 1894, 424, suggested that the 5,000 cavalry were mostly, if not all, Greeks, and this was the reason that Deinocrates was appointed as their commander.
122. Diod. Sic. 20.30.1.
123. Meltzer 1879, 383–4, cautions us to not hastily dismiss the figures, implying that the massive army may be attributed to Deinocrates bringing a great number of Greeks with him.
124. If the Greek allies did provide a considerable portion of the soldiers for the army, however, this could be one of the reasons that Deinocrates was appointed to lead the cavalry. See note above.
125. Diod. Sic. 19.106.5. Huss 1985, 191 n. 104, refers his readers back to this figure after describing those given as 'überhöht', exaggerated. I think that he is correct in citing this as a reference, and Hamilcar's army in 309 was probably around that size. Surprisingly, the often critical Tillyard 1908, 132, accepted the larger figure and wrote that 'with this great host he won over the remaining towns or strongholds in the island, and then resolved to make an assault on Syracuse.'
126. Diod. Sic. 20.29.2 says that Hamilcar had intended to take the city by storm from the outset, but then notes the efforts to deprive it of food. The narrative here is illogical.
127. This entire episode is bizarre, cf. Tillyard's 1908, 135, comments. Diodorus' narrative makes out the assault on the Euryalus to have been made rashly, based on a soothsayer's interpretation of a sacrifice, but as the Syracusans were able to respond it could not have been all that impulsive. Although there is little evidence to support it, I believe that a more complex strategy was at play. The Epipolae

hill was an important position for anyone who wanted to be master of the city. Hamilcar undoubtedly knew that the last two major campaigns against Syracuse which failed to capture Syracuse involved camps only at the Olympieum, without possession of the Epipolae. His resolve to take the hill, then, was likely quite earnest. Unlike his predecessors, however, he had an army of Greeks, including exiled Syracusans, with him. Some, if not most, of these exiles would have still had friends or family inside of the city. This attack on the fortress may have been coordinated with a traitor inside. The paranoia which we find in the work of Aeneas Tacticus is reflective of treachery being common in war time. If this mere hypothesis is accepted, then it appears that the traitor and the plot were found out. This would explain why the Syracusans knew to station extra troops on the hill and why they so easily defeated the assault. Regardless of whether or not there was a plot to betray the fortress, Diodorus 20.29.4 tells us that the city's inhabitants found out about Hamilcar's planned march.
128. Diodorus suggested that there was some brawling within the army over minor disagreements, but a variant tradition of the fall of Hamilcar said that the Carthaginians and Greeks within his army became openly hostile to one another, Cic. *Div.* 1.50, Val. Max. 1.7ext.8, cf. Tillyard 1908, 135–6 n. 1.
129. Diod. Sic. 20.29.2–10. It is possible that Antander led the Syracusan army in person, cf. Just. *Epit.* 22.7.2. For other descriptions of these events, see Freeman 1894, 425–8, and Tillyard 1908, 132–5.
130. Diod. Sic. 20.29.11.
131. Diod. Sic. 20.30.2. Not all commentators believe that the head was sent to Africa, e.g. Tillyard 1908, 136–7, who believed that it would have 'been a tiresome business' and 'such a savage act does not suit what is known of the Greek character.' This is an unnecessarily critical stance, and there is no reason to think that Hamilcar's head was not sent to Agathocles. Champion 2012 rightly calls Tillyard's conclusion 'a product of its time and reflects the general pro-Greek bias of the Edwardian gentleman and scholar'. Freeman 1894, 429, rightly juxtaposed the sending of the head with the sending of the prows to Sicily by the Carthaginians in the previous year.
132. Diod. Sic. 20.31.1–2. Freeman 1894, 431, suggests that the source of the friction between the Carthaginians and the Greek allies was because the latter elected Deinocrates as general of the entire army, which was 'clearly in the teeth of all Carthaginian discipline. Its effect was that the remnant of the army of Hamilcar parted asunder.' This could be, but there is no more weight to this theory than that which Diodorus presents us: without Hamilcar's leadership the army simply fell apart. Relations were already strained between the two groups during the night march to the Olympieum.
133. Diod. Sic. 20.31.4–5–32.1–2. For example, Tillyard 1908, 137, refers to it as 'The Acragantine League.'
134. Freeman 1894, 436–8.
135. Diod. Sic. 20.32.3–5.
136. Tillyard 1908, 140. He is also probably correct that the grain ships made it to the city safely, though Diodorus does not explicitly tell us this.
137. The chronology is unclear, and I follow the order in which Diodorus' narrative flows, thus placing it immediately after the naval battle over the Syracusan grain ships.

138. Diod. Sic. 20.33.3–8.
139. Diod. Sic. 20.34.1–7. Cf. Tillyard 1908, 130–1.
140. It is unclear if these chariots were captured and crewed by Greeks or if they were manned by locals. It is even possible that the riders were traitorous Carthaginians.
141. Diod. Sic. 20.38.1–2.
142. Diod. Sic. 20.38.3–6.
143. Diod. Sic. 20.39. The 200 soldiers who had earlier deserted Agathocles' army may have been amongst those slaughtered, and perhaps were the reason for the massacre, cf. Tillyard 1908, 142–3.
144. As with other parts of Diodorus' narrative, the chronology here is likely confused. Tillyard 1908, 144–5, suggested that Orthon, Agathocles' envoy, reached Ophellas in 309 BC. Thus, the narrative that I have provided may be slightly deceptive.
145. On Ophellas' ties to Athens, see Tillyard 1908, 145–6.
146. Diod. Sic. 20.40.
147. Diod. Sic. 20.41.1–2.
148. Diod. Sic. 20.42.1–2. Tillyard 1908, 147, regards the description of their challenges as 'right in all its details'.
149. Diod. Sic. 20.42.3–5.
150. Justin *Epit.* 22.7.5 uses the verb *interficio*, which is rather vague, but does not sound the same as Diodorus' story in which Agathocles used his entire army to bring down his opponent.
151. Polyaenus *Strat.* 5.3.4.
152. Tillyard 1908, 149, following the suggestions of Schubert 1887, 145.
153. Diod. Sic. 20.44.7.
154. Meister 1984, 397, argued that we should not think that Agathocles was plotting against Ophellas from the beginning, and that attacking his camp in full view of the Carthaginians was an act 'taken only out of dire necessity'. The origin of the conflict may have been in a disagreement of some kind between the two leaders, as suggested above.
155. Tillyard 1908, 149–51, provides a number of hypotheses relevant to this discussion.
156. It was perhaps this action which helped to bring Ophellas' army fully into the camp of Agathocles.
157. The only source for this battle is Just. *Epit.* 22.7.6. Because of this, not all modern commentators believe that a battle occurred. Grote 1857, 435, for instance, says that in the wake of Ophellas' murder, 'it would have fared ill with Agathokles, had the Carthaginians been at hand, and ready to attack him in the confusion'. Others, such as Warmington 1993, 124, completely ignore it. Tillyard 1908, 152, though was firm in his belief that 'the truth of the account cannot reasonably be doubted.' In this I believe that Tillyard is correct. Champion 2012 also follows Tillyard.
158. I do not follow the chronology given at Diod. Sic. 20.43.3–6. As I have stated in the narrative, the battle found in Justin should not be discounted and thus provides the timing for the attempted rebellion. Diodorus' explanation of why Bomilcar didn't defect to Agathocles, or Ophellas to the Carthaginians, is most likely a later invention. Meister 1984, 398, rightly states that any assumption that Bomilcar actively sought 'treasonous relations with Agathocles... on the authority of Justin, is certainly not true'.

159. Diod. Sic. 20.44.1–6. I have reproduced the English translation of C. B. Wells from the Loeb Classical Library series. This is one of the only passages that I have reproduced entirely throughout this book, as I do not think that there could be any improvement on Diodorus' words. I have, however, changed the original's 'Bormilcar' to the more standard 'Bomilcar'. Scholars tend to regard Diodorus' source for the attempted coup as reliable, e.g. Warmington 1993, 124. On the topography of Carthage and the location of the 'New City', see Lancel 1995, 141–2.
160. Just. *Epit.* 22.7.9–10. Tillyard 1908, 154 n. 2, believes the death speech to be 'pure rhetoric' which could be true, noting that it would have probably appealed to Trogus' readers, thus attributing its creation to Justin's source.
161. Diod. Sic. 20.54.2 says that Utica had, at one point, gone over to Agathocles but had now deserted him, and this was why he targeted the city. Polybius 1.82.8, however, knew of Utica, and Hippou Acra, as never betraying Carthage during Agathocles' reign. I am inclined to believe Polybius that Utica had not previously defected to the tyrant.
162. Diod. Sic. 20.54.2–7. The account is more graphic than I have reproduced.
163. On asylum in temples during Greek sieges, see Hall 2018a.
164. Diod. Sic. 20.55.1–3.
165. As stated by Meister 1984, 398.
166. Diod. Sic. 20.55.3.
167. App. *Pun.* 110.
168. Diod. Sic. 20.55.5.
169. Diod. Sic. 20.56.1–3.
170. For the geography of this campaign, see Tillyard 1908, 162–3.
171. Diod. Sic. 20.57.4–6. He may have been forced to allow his troops to loot the last city on their campaign if their salaries were in arrears. Diod. Sic. 20.58.1 notes that he returned to Hippou Acra 'after sating his army with booty'. It may have simply been bad luck that this settlement was looted, and not because of any special characteristics of it or of its people.
172. Diod. Sic. 20.58.1–2.
173. Diod. Sic. 20.58.3–6.
174. Diod. Sic. 20.59.
175. Diod. Sic. 20.60.
176. Tillyard 1908, 166, is probably right in suggesting that Archagathus also recalled all the 'outlying guards', meaning the garrisons of the smaller centres.
177. Diod. Sic. 20.61.1–4.
178. Diod. Sic. 20.61.5–8.
179. Diod. Sic. 20.62.1.
180. Just. Epit. 22.8.4–5. This is not mentioned in Diodorus. Freeman 1894, 440–1 n.1, connected this with the mutiny in Agathocles' army in 309, which Tillyard 1908, 174, dismisses. The latter's view is probably correct, and we should not discount it. There were probably good reasons that the soldiers had not been paid, despite Justin saying that the pay had been withheld by Archagathus until his father returned from Sicily. The expedition of Eumachus to the south was probably meant to gather enough plunder to pay the army, but it never made it back to the main camp, and we hear that the Carthaginian army captured considerable loot from its baggage train.

181. Diod. Sic. 20.64. At this point all of the Carthaginian armies may have been combined, as suggested by Tillyard 1908, 174.
182. Diod. Sic. 20.65–66.
183. Diod. Sic. 20.67. Tillyard 1908, 176–7, believed that the stated losses were too high, but there is no evidence to make us reject what we find in Diodorus.
184. Diod. Sic. 20.68–69.1–3; Just. *Epit.* 22.8.9–12.
185. Diod. Sic. 20.69.3–5; Just. *Epit.* 22.8.13–15. Those garrisons which held out may have been Syracusan citizens, as they were supposedly hopeful for Agathocles to return. The foreign mercenaries would probably not have had such loyalty to a commander who had not been paying them and also abandoned them in hostile territory.
186. Diod. Sic. 20.71–72.
187. On this, see Tillyard 1908, 191–4, Meister 1984, 400–5, and Champion 2012.
188. The amount of bullion to be paid was also stated as 150 by Timaeus. This has been rationalised by modern historians as a discrepancy in which measure of a talent was being used. The 300 talents represents the indemnity in Punic talents, which would equal 150 Greek talents, cf. Tillyard 1908, 195 n.2.
189. Diod. Sic. 20.79.5.
190. Just. *Epit.* 22.8.15 says that after the conclusion of the African war, the Carthaginians sent new commanders to Sicily and that they terminated what remained of the conflict there. This does not seem like a proper campaign, and may have just been the ambassadors who had already been negotiating peace with Agathocles.
191. For a narrative, see Tillyard 1908, 203–221, and Meister 1984, 405–9.
192. Diod. Sic. 21.16.
193. Diod. Sic. 21.18.
194. As usual, our sources for this particular bit of Punic history are not great; cf. Lévêque 1957, 451–2.
195. See Bradley and Hall 2018.
196. Diod. Sic. 22.2.1.
197. Dion. Hal. Ant. Rom. 20.8.1 makes it sound as though they held power as an allied unit, saying that 'Sosistratus, the ruler of the city…, and Thoenon, the commander of the garrison…' Our evidence elsewhere suggests that it was not a harmonious relationship.
198. Diod. Sic. 22.7.6 says that they had 10,000 men, though later (22.8.4) claims that Sosistratus had more than 10,000 troops just under his command. It is likely that many of these were stationed in Akragas and the other towns under his rule.
199. Diod. Sic. 22.8.1.
200. Plut. *Pyrrh.* 22.1–2.
201. Diod. Sic. 22.8.2.
202. Franke 1989, 477, proposed that Pyrrhus' motivation for going to Sicily was to prevent Syracuse from falling into the hands of Carthage, which would 'virtually mean the collapse of his whole policy so far, which had advertised the liberation of the Greeks from the barbarian threat' and that this would negatively affect his reputation. This is possible.
203. Just. *Epit.* 18.2; Val. Max. 3.7.10. We do not know for sure that this was when the treaty was struck, as a proud Roman version of the story says that the Senate said 'thanks but no thanks' to the Punic offer of aid. But this seems like the perfect time for the treaty to have been made, cf. Scullard 1989, 536–7.

204. Polyb. 3.25.
205. Franke 1989, 476–7.
206. Diod. Sic. 22.7.4.
207. Diod. Sic. 22.7.5. All of this information comes to us in a chronologically nebulous state. The siege of Syracuse by Carthage, the calling for help to Pyrrhus, and the alliances all happened sometime between 280 and 278, but we cannot assign exact dates. It could be that some of the events happened in a different order than I have presented them.
208. App. *Sam.* 28 says that he sailed across with 8,000 cavalry plus his elephants, but it is usually assumed that we should read this as 8,000 soldiers in total (e.g. Lévêque 1957, 455–6). Pyrrhus bringing Tyndarion into alliance, Diod. Sic. 22.8.3; the tyrant's friendliness towards the Epirate is probably confirmed by his coinage: Lévêque 1957, 470.
209. Diod. Sic. 22.8.3.
210. Lévêque 1957, 458–9.
211. Champion 2009, 98.
212. Though, Dion. Hal. *Ant. Rom.* 20.8.1 says that he was given 200 warships. This may have been a confusion with the total size of Pyrrhus' fleet after the Syracusan ships were added; Lévêque 1957, 459–60 n. 6.
213. Diod. Sic. 22.8.4–5.
214. Diod. Sic. 22.10.1–2 gives us 1,500 cavalry, while Plutarch (*Pyrr.* 22.4) gives 2 500. There is no way to know which is to be believed.
215. Diod. Sic. 22.10.2.
216. Just. *Epit.* 23.3.4. The word Justin uses, *proelium*, usually implies a pitched battle or naval battle, not a siege, but given the nature of the source it would be unwise to argue that Pyrrhus and the Carthaginians engaged in a number of major pitched battles; cf. Champion 2009, 98–9.
217. See above.
218. Plut. *Pyrr.* 22.5.
219. Diod. Sic. 22.10.3; Plut. *Pyrr.* 22.5–6.
220. Polyb. 1.56.3.
221. Champion 2009, 100.
222. Diod. Sic. 22.10.4–5.
223. Diod. Sic. 22.10.5–7; Plut. *Pyrr.* 23.2.
224. Plut. *Pyrr.* 23.3–6; Dion. Hal. *Ant. Rom.* 20.7.
225. Zonar. 10.6.

Chapter 6

1. Polyb. 1.7–8; Diod. Sic. 21.18. On both events, but mostly covering the events in Rhegium, see Diod. Sic. 22.1–3 and Dion. Hal. *Ant. Rom.* 20.4.
2. On the events and chronology of Hiero II's reign, see Hoyos 1985b. The history of his reign can be found in Champion 2012.
3. It is possible that the defeat was orchestrated by Hiero. According to Polybius, he only ordered his mercenaries to engage the enemy, holding back the Syracusan citizen infantry and cavalry in a feigned attack position from the Mamertines' flank. This was done in order to kill off the mercenaries who were causing social and political problems in Syracuse, Polyb. 1.9.3–6. It is tempting to believe this, but it seems more reasonable that Hiero lost the battle and his mercenaries bore

the brunt of the losses. It is not inconceivable that Polybius' version is truthful, but one wonders why Hiero would risk open war with the Mamertines when his objective was simply to kill off some mercenaries. It is possible that the mercenaries were abandoned by the rest of the army due to circumstances unknown to us, cf. Walbank 1957, 56.
4. This brief note ignores the extremely complex discussion about the date of this battle. None of our sources date it specifically to 264 BC, and are rather vague in their details. Scholarly arguments have placed it as far back as 269 BC. I am, however, convinced that it should probably be placed early in 264 BC. Detailed analysis and discussion can be found in Hoyos 1998, 33–40, idem 2011b, 137–8.
5. The most detailed narrative of this campaign is to be found in Diod. Sic. 22.13; briefer accounts are provided by Polyb. 1.9.7–8 and Zonar. 8.8.
6. Diod. Sic. 22.13.7–8; Polyb. 1.11.4; Zonar. 8.8.
7. Extensive discussion in Hoyos 1998, 33–99.
8. 20,000 men would be about the usual size of a consular army. Though how many were brought over in the first crossing is unknown.
9. Wells 1949, 433. This may be seen as an exaggeration when looking back upon the Second World War.
10. Goldsworthy 2000, 73.
11. Polyb. 1.11.7–15–12.1–3. The account preserved by Zonaras is more detailed than that of Polybius, portraying the Romans as initially losing the battle but wheeling around on the Carthaginians during an unregulated pursuit, killing many of them and driving them from the field, Zonar. 8.9. Goldsworthy 2000, 73, suggested that these battles were nothing 'more than a large skirmish', which is plausible given the difficulty the Romans had in crossing the straits. It is probable that none of these three armies was very large. Champion 2012 presumes that Claudius had brought across his entire army, which would have numbered around 20,000 men. While this is possible, I find it improbable.
12. Goldsworthy 2000, 74. Hoyos 2015, 36–7, portrays the siege in a more traditional way, but describing it as a 'fiasco' and comparing it to the Athenian's siege during the Peloponnesian War, citing the strength of the city's fortifications.
13. Polyb. 1.12.4; Zonar. 8.9.
14. In general, I follow the conclusions of Hoyos 2015, 35–6, on this point.
15. Livy *Per.* 16.
16. According to Diod. Sic. 23.4.2 this 'Hadranon' was a village, and thus differentiated it from the Hadranum said to have been taken by force.
17. Hoyos 1998, 108–10. Hoyos' conclusion is based on two pieces of evidence. The first is that in 262 Valerius celebrated a triumph alone (according to the *fasti triumphales* it was for his victories over the Carthaginians and 'Hiero king of the Sicilians'). The second is a couplet from Naevius' now lost epic, *Bellum Punicum*, which reads 'Manius Valerius the consul led part of the army/ on an expedition' (frg. 35 Baehrens; translation belongs to Hoyos).
18. The most detailed version of the campaign can be found in Diod. Sic. 23.4–5; cf. Polyb. 1.16 and Zonar. 8.9. According to Diod. Sic. 23.4.1 the indemnity owed by Hiero was 150,000 drachmas, which would only equal twenty-five silver talents, as opposed to the 100 talents found in Polyb. 1.16.9. Francis Walton's note in his 1957 Loeb edition of Diodorus' text suggests that the figure found therein was the first payment of the indemnity, which is a plausible explanation for the

discrepancy between it and Polybius, and this idea is supported by recent authors such as Hoyos 2015, 37–8.
19. As proposed by Hoyos 2015, 37.
20. Diod. Sic. 23.4.1.
21. It is unclear if these were sent to Akragas or were part of Hanno's later army. The placement of their recruitment in Polybius' narrative makes it seem as though they were brought to the city, and this is accepted by some modern authors, for instance Rankov 2011, 151. Others are not so sure, a scepticism which dates back at least to Meltzer 1896, 270, who thought that these new recruits were still in camp when hostilities broke out at Akragas. It does appear that Hannibal had a small garrison, though some of the newly recruited mercenaries could have already made their way to the city.
22. Polyb. 1.17; Diod. Sic. 23.7.
23. We are not told which consul commanded from which camp.
24. Diod. Sic. 23.8.1 provides the size and makeup of the expeditionary force. Hoyos 2015, 39, writes of these figures speculatively, saying that Hanno 'supposedly' had an army of this consistency. Diodorus explicitly cites Philinus of Akragas as his source for this information, and as he was a contemporary of the events it seems that it could be a reliable description. As he was a pro-Carthaginian writer, it seems like it would have been folly to inflate the numbers of an army which was destined to be defeated by the Romans. I am sceptical of the notice in Orosius which states Hanno had 1,500 cavalry, 30,000 infantry, and thirty elephants (4.7.5). That it is the number of Philinus but halved is suspicious; as well, it would make the army smaller than the combined consular armies. Polyb. 1.19.2 says that Hanno had about fifty elephants. Diodorus/Philinus' figures are typically accepted, e.g. Scullard 1989, 547, and Goldsworthy 2000, 79.
25. Polyb. 1.18.8–9, Herbessus taken by surprise; Diod. Sic. 23.8.1, Herbessus betrayed; Zonar. 8.10.
26. Polyb. 1.19.1–5.
27. Similar to Goldsworthy's 2000, 80, suggestion. Scullard 1989, 547, described the positioning of the elephants as 'curious'.
28. Polyb. 1.19.8–11.
29. Frontin. *Str.* 2.1.4.
30. Zonar. 8.10.
31. Polyb. 1.19.12–13; Zonar. 8.10 says that only Hannibal escaped, but that his men were 'recognized and killed' by the Romans and some of the angry inhabitants of Akragas.
32. Polyb. 1.19.14–15; Diod. Sic. 23.9.1; Zonar. 8.10.
33. This is probably the same Hannibal who was the garrison commander at Akragas and had prevented Massana from falling to Hiero in 264; Walbank 1957, 71, and Hoyos 2010, 183.
34. Zonar. 8.10; Oros. 4.7.7. We, unfortunately, do not hear any details about how the Romans protected their coast.
35. Polyb. 1.20.1–2; translation is that of W. R. Paton's 1922 Loeb.
36. Walbank 1957, 73, and Lazenby 1996, 59.
37. Harris 1979, 111.
38. Hoyos 1998, 112–13.
39. Zonar. 8.10; Frontin. *Strat.* 3.16.3.

40. The *Ineditum Vaticanum* 4 states that Valerius Messala, who was consul in 263, spearheaded the idea of building a strong fleet. This is absent from Polybius and our other sources, and may have been an attempt by his family to enhance their own history and glory.
41. Polyb. 1.20.16; translation is that of R. Waterfield's 2010 Oxford World's Classics.
42. Steinby 2014, 64. Walbank 1957, 75–6, rightly argued against earlier scholarship that we should not discount the story of the captured Punic ship. Although it was an established trope of Roman historiography that their success was due in part to copying and improving their enemies' weapons and ways of war, this does not mean that the stories, in particular this one, are necessarily false.
43. It is unclear whether this was a trap set up by the Carthaginians or what transpired was a stroke of luck and quick thinking.
44. Polyb. 1.21.5–8.
45. Polyb. 1.21.9–11.
46. Polyb. 1.23.1–3.
47. The description of the device is given in Polyb. 1.22.
48. Polyb. 1.23.4–10; Zonar. 8.11.
49. Livy *Per.* 17; Pliny *HN* 34.11; *Fasti Triumphales* p.100.
50. CIL 1^2.25 = ILS 65 = Inscr. Ital. 13:3 no. 69 p. 46. The translation is adapted from Steinby 2014, 71; I have not preserved the lines as they appear in the inscription, simply the text.
51. I am arguing primarily against Steinby 2014, 68–9, on the importance of the *corvus*. Many other scholars have doubted its importance, and for a bibliography of the earlier debates, see Walbank 1957, 77–8. On the device itself, and its use, see Wallinga 1956.
52. The chronology of the land campaign and the Battle of Mylae are unclear. Some sources portray the engagements on land as preceding the sea-battle. I have presented them fairly simply because it is not worth getting bogged down in this detail. For discussion, see Walbank 1957, 79–80.
53. Polyb. 1.24.1–2; Zonar. 8.11.
54. Diod. Sic. 23.9.3. The chronology is unclear.
55. Polyb. 1.24.3–4; Diod. Sic. 23.9.4. The fragments of Diodorus at this point claim that this was a defeat of the Romans, though Polybius probably preserves the correct version, that it was the allied camp which was attacked.
56. Zonar. 8.11. I see no reason to think that his notice that 'if Gaius Florus, who was wintering there, had not restrained him, he would have subjugated the whole of Sicily' has much meaning to it, except that the consul was held in Sicily until the arrival of a new army.
57. Livy *Per.* 17. For this he was awarded a triumph 'over the Carthaginians, Sardinia, and Corsica', according to the *Fasti Triumphales*.
58. *CIL* 1^2.2.8 and 9 = *ILS* 2 and 3. Translation is that of Scullard 1989, 553.
59. On the land-campaigns, see Polyb. 1.24.3–4 and Zonar. 8.10–11.
60. Polyb. 1.24.5–6; Livy *Per.* 17; Zonar. 8.11–12. Diod. Sic. 23.10 (cf. Val. Max. 7.3(ext.).7; Dio. Cass. 43.18) preserves a fanciful story of Hannibal sending a single ship back to Carthage aboard which was one of his friends. This man asked the government if Hannibal should engage a Roman fleet of 120 ships with his fleet of 200 ships; they all cheered and agreed, after which the man announced that this had already happened, Hannibal was defeated, and was now absolved of

punishment because they had agreed to the attack. While this is interesting, and perhaps shows a bit of Punic political intrigue, I find it dubious; cf. Walbank 1957, 80–1.
61. Polyb. 1.25.1–4; Zonar. 8.12.
62. Hoyos 2015, 45..
63. Polyb. 1.25.7–9, 26.7–8.
64. Steinby 2014, 75–6.
65. The events around the Battle of Ecnomus are narrated in Polyb. 1.26–28. The details of the battle and the manoeuvres of the fleets are generally believed, with retired US Navy Rear Admiral William L. Rodgers 1937, 279, writing that 'the account in Polybius clearly describes the strategic objectives of the campaign and the tactical story is so good that when an attempt is made to plot the movements on a chart, the result is consistent in all its parts.'
66. It is usually referred to as the Battle of Ecnomus (as I have done above). This has derived from the vagueness of Polybius' narrative of where the battle took place. Zonar. 8.12, following a different source, notes that it took place off Heraclea Minoa, where the Punic fleet had been based. This location is more probable than off Ecnomus, as it would mean that the Carthaginians were reacting to the sighting of the Roman fleet moving, not simply floating off the coast waiting for them; cf. Rankov 2011, 156. Regardless, I follow the typical nomenclature of referring to it as the Battle of Ecnomus.
67. Hoyos 2015, 47.
68. Polyb. 1.29.1.
69. Polyb. 1.29.2–5. Zonar. 8.12 says that the Romans took the city without a struggle, though this is unlikely. The fortifications built by Agathocles certainly made the defenders feel as though they could hold out against the invaders, perhaps thinking that reinforcements would come from Carthage.
70. Hoyos 1998, 117, believes that 'evidently they [the consuls] had brought no exhaustive guidelines for warring and negotiating.' He echoed his belief that this was a strange occurrence in Hoyos 2015, 48.
71. Polyb. 1.29.6–10; Zonar. 8.12.
72. Polyb. 1.30.1–3.
73. On the location, see Lazenby 1996, 100.
74. We do not know the size or make up of the Punic army, but Polybius claims they had strong cavalry and elephant divisions.
75. Walbank 1957, 89, with references.
76. A comparison also made by Goldsworthy 2000, 85.
77. Polyb. 1.30.4–14. Zonar. 8.13 says that the attack on the Punic camp came at night, rather than at dawn, and that many of the Carthaginians were slain in their beds. This is dubious, though Goldsworthy 2000, 86, proposed that a night attack may have preceded the main assault. This is possible.
78. Polyb. 1.30.15–31.3.
79. Polyb. 1.31.4–5.
80. Dio. Cass. 11.43.22; Zonar. 8.13.
81. See, respectively, Polyb. 3.70.7 and 18.11–12. These examples are taken from Goldsworthy 2000, 87 and 374 n. 20.
82. I follow other scholars in this judgment, such as Lancel 1995, 367, and Hoyos 2010, 185.

83. That the terms were too harsh to be accepted: Polyb. 1.31.5–7; Diod. Sic. 23.12; Dio. Cass. 11.43.22–3; Zonar. 8.13. Dio preserves the supposed terms of the peace, though they are often doubted. Hoyos 2010, 185–6 suggests that the demands were to surrender Sicily, set free all the Roman and allied prisoners of war, ransom the Punic prisoners, and pay an indemnity. He adds to this list in his 2015, 49, volume that the surrender of Sardinia was also plausible.
84. Warmington 1993, 177.
85. Diod. Sic. 23.13.
86. Diod. Sic. 23.16 says that he came over either alone, with fifty others, or with 100 others.
87. Diodorus does not mention further troops than those who may have come with Xanthippus. Polyb. 1.32.1 says that the recruiters brought back with them 'a considerable number of soldiers', but gives no definite figure.
88. Polyb. 1.32.2–8.
89. Polyb. 1.33.1–7.
90. Polyb. 1.33.8–9.
91. Goldsworthy 2000, 89.
92. Polyb. 1.34.1–8; Zonar. 8.13. For a more technical reconstruction, see Sabin 2009, 174–7, where it is referred to as the Battle of Bagradas, 255 bc.
93. Polyb. 1.34.9–12.
94. Polyb. 1.36.1–3 on Xanthippus. For the dramatic version of Regulus' death, a supposedly harrowing experience of having his eyelids sliced off and then being trampled by a crazed elephant, see Diod. Sic. 23.16; Zonar. 8.13; Val. Max. 9.6; Sil. *Pun.* 6.682; App. *Pun.* 1.4. A good dismissal of these stories is to be found in Lancel 1995, 369. Further legends grew up around Regulus and the expedition to Africa, most notably the slaying of the so-called Bagradas Serpent or Dragon. During their march towards Carthage, the Romans supposedly encountered a serpent or dragon of unnatural size at a river (the Bagradas). In their battle with it, the beast slew many of them but in the end the Romans were victorious. This is obviously fantasy, however the longest version of the story we possess is quite an interesting read, see Sil. *Pun.* 6.140–293. Unfortunately, I have no space to include a translation, but a good version can be found in Ogden 2013, 142–5, with discussion; analysis of the incident, see Bassett 1955, Stothers 2004, and Hall 2018b.
95. Preserved in Zonar. 8.14, but not in Polybius. Although this would usually make the notice suspect, both consuls were to receive triumphs in 254/3 for victories over the Cossurenses, according to the *Fasti Triumphales*.
96. Polyb. 1.36.5–12; Diod. Sic. 23.18.1; Zonar. 8.14.
97. Polyb. 1.37.1–6; Diod. Sic. 23.18.1; Zonar. 8.14; Oros. 4.9.8; Eutr. 2.22. Lazenby 1996, 102–12.
98. Hoyos 2015, 52.
99. There is doubt whether Hasdrubal came to Sicily in 254 or 251, as is evidenced by Oros. 4.9.14 and Eutr. 2.24, and accepted by many; for earlier bibliography see Walbank 1957, 97–8. I am unconvinced that his inaction against the Roman attack on Panormus is good evidence for his absence from the island. It may be that Polybius actually misrepresents the nature of the forces under his command. Hasdrubal may not have had an entire army with him, but rather was the vehicle for transporting a new, large, elephant corps to Sicily in preparations for a later

campaign. This would make sense why Carthalo, the Carthaginian general already on the island, was campaigning against Akragas without Hasdrubal or his contingent. Hoyos 2015, 52, accepts that the elephants were sent over in 255 BC.
100. Polyb. 1.38.1–5; Diod. Sic. 13.18.2–3; Zonar. 8.14.
101. Oros. 4.9.9.
102. Walbank 1957, 98–9, on the identification of these different parts of Panormus. Zonar. 8.14 may refer to the 'Old Town' as the citadel, although I am not sure of this identification.
103. Polyb. 1.38.5–10; Diod. Sic. 23.18.4–5; Zonar. 8.14.
104. Only Sempronius is credited with a triumph for this year over the Carthaginians, and it may be that he was the one to lead the raids, with his colleague operating in Sicily. Cf. Walbank 1957, 99.
105. Polyb. 1.39.1–6; Diod. Sic. 23.19; Zonar. 8.14.
106. Translation is that of R. Waterfield's Oxford World's Classics.
107. Val. Max. 2.7.4; Frontin. *Str.* 4.1.31; Zonar. 8.14.
108. Polyb. 1.39.7–14; Diod. Sic. 23.20; Zonar. 8.14.
109. Hoyos 2015, 54–5.
110. The casualty figures may have been inflated, and authors such as Goldsworthy 2000, 94, find them implausible. 20,000 out of a total of 30,000 is a high proportion, at two-thirds, though Regulus' losses in Africa amounted to about eighty-seven per cent of his army, an even higher proportion. Regardless, this was a significant defeat.
111. Polyb. 1.40; Diod. Sic. 23.21; Zonar. 8.14; Oros. 4.9.14; Eutr. 2.24; Pliny *HN* 7.139. I discount the statement in Diodorus that the drunkenness of Hasdrubal's Celtic mercenaries helped lead to the defeat.
112. These are only mentioned by Diod. Sic. 24.1.1.
113. These are figures given by Polyb. 1.42.11. Diod. Sic. 24.1.1 gives 7,000 infantry and 700 cavalry. I am inclined towards Polybius' larger number, but there is no way to be certain. Walbank 1957, 107, though hypothesized that Polybius had simply rounded down the total of 11,700 mercenaries (4,000 were shipped in after the siege began).
114. The narrative of the siege of Lilybaeum up to this point can be found in Polyb. 1.41–43; Diod. Sic. 24.1.1; Zonar. 8.15; Oros. 4.10.2.
115. Walbank 1957, 108–9.
116. Polyb. 1.44; Diod. Sic. 24.1.2.
117. Polyb. 1.45.
118. Polyb. 1.46. The ultimate source of this narrative, whether Philinus or an informant of his, may have been an eyewitness, as suggested by a number of scholars, cf. Walbank 1957, 110. On Hannibal the Rhodian, see Ameling 1993, 134–6.
119. Zonar. 8.15.
120. Polyb. 1.47; Zonar. 8.15, who calls him Hanno. The latter also says that the Romans used his captured ship as a prototype for new vessels they were building.
121. Polyb. 1.48; Diod. Sic. 24.1.3. Walbank 1957, 111–12.
122. Diod. Sic. 24.1.4.
123. The total number of Roman ships is not as clear as I make it out in the narrative, and could have been between 120 and the 220 which is found in Eutr. 2.26; 210 appears in Diod. Sic. 24.1.5. On the calculations of various scholars, see Walbank

1957, 114–15, comments in Lazenby 1996, 133. Steinby 2014, 93, prefers Polybius' figure which equals 123, calculated based on the recorded losses (30 fled, 93 captured). This is also the number preferred by Rodgers 1937, 298.
124. Polyb. 1.49; Diod. Sic. 24.1.5.
125. He supposedly was at the back of his fleet, so how it was the consul who gave this order is unclear. Signals were used between ships, but his position seems like this would have been difficult. Perhaps it was a delay to, or interruption of, his signals being transmitted all the way up the line which caused the chaotic turn about. Alternatively, the captains of the ships in the vanguard may have taken it upon themselves to get turned around so as not to be trapped. Rodgers 1937, 297, points out the poor choice of the consul carrying up the rear.
126. Polyb. 1.50–51; Diod. Sic. 24.1.5; Oros. 4.10.4–5; Eutr. 2.26.
127. Diod. Sic. 24.1.5. The translation is that of F. R. Walton's 1957 Loeb.
128. Cic. *Nat.* D. 2.7; *Div.* 2.20; Livy *Per.* 19; Livy 22.42.9; Val. Max. 1.4.3; Suet. *Tib.* 2.2; Flor. 1.8.19; Eutr. 2.26.
129. Hoyos 2015, 57.
130. Polyb. 1.53.1–3.
131. Diod. Sic. 24.1.6.
132. On the problems of determining the chronology of his travels, see Walbank 1957, 115–16.
133. Polyb. 1.52.5–8. Junius was not newly elected for 248 BC, as implied by Polybius, but was a colleague of Claudius Pulcher, see Walbank 1957, 115.
134. Polyb. 1.53; Diod. Sic. 24.1.7. The version preserved by Diodorus records that the Carthaginians sank seventeen warships, captured fifty cargo ships, and disabled a further thirteen of the warships.
135. Polyb. 1.54; Diod. Sic. 24.1.8–9. Walbank 1957, 117–8.
136. Polyb. 1.55.5–10; Diod. Sic. 24.1.10–11; Zonar. 8.15.
137. Livy *Per.* 19; Suet. *Tib.* 2.2; Zonar. 8.15.
138. The chronology is in dispute, and our evidence is paltry. I follow Hoyos 2010, 188–9, in dating this campaign around 247 BC. Others have proposed dates ranging from 247 to 241 BC.
139. Lazenby 1996, 143, and Scullard 1989, 563.
140. Dismissed, for instance, by Scullard 1989, 563.
141. Hoyos 2010, 189.
142. Zonar. 8.16.
143. Zonar. 8.16.
144. Polyb. 1.56; Diod. Sic. 24.6; Zonar. 8.16.
145. Polyb. 1.57.1–2. The translation is that of R. Waterfield's Oxford World's Classics.
146. Patterson 2006, 192.
147. Zonar. 8.16.
148. Polyb. 1.57.5.
149. Zonar. 8.16.
150. Polyb. 1.58; Diod. Sic. 24.8.
151. Zonar. 8.16.
152. Diod. Sic. 24.9 preserves the only mention of it, and even this is brief.
153. Some commentators don't believe that this ship was used as a model for the new fleet, but I see no reason to reject it. For an opposing view and bibliography, see Steinby 2014, 100–1.

154. Polyb. 1.59.1–8; Zonar. 8.17. Diod. Sic. 24.11.1 numbers Lutatius' fleet at 300 quinqueremes and 700 transports, while Oros. 4.10.5 and Eutr. 2.27 both only list the 300 warships. Walbank 1957, 124, proposes that Polybius' figure can be attributed to Fabius Pictor, and I am inclined to believe that the Roman fleet probably numbered 200 quinqueremes.
155. Steinby 2014, 101. Polyb. 1.59.9–12.
156. Diod. Sic. 24.11.1 is the only source to give a number for the Punic fleet.
157. Polyb. 1.60–61; Diod. Sic. 24.11.1.
158. This is only preserved by Zonar. 8.17. Hoyos 2010, 189, points out the irony that this was the same fate of the first Hanno who failed at Messana at the beginning of the war.
159. Polyb. 1.62.3; Walbank 1957, 126.
160. Polyb. 1.62; Diod. Sic. 24.13; Zonar. 8.17; Oros. 4.11.1–3; Eutr. 2.27.
161. Miles 2010, 198–9.

Chapter 7

1. This war took place over the course of three years and four months, 240–237 BC. While I have provided a complete narrative of events, I have not indulged in considerable speculation regarding the events of this conflict. On a number of occasions I have inserted my thoughts, or those of scholars with whom I agree. The limited sources, and my lack of first-hand experience in the terrain of North Africa, leads me to yield to more knowledgeable scholars. In this, I recommend any of my readers who find this war interesting to seek out a copy of Dexter Hoyos' 2007 study on the topic. It is full of many theories fleshing out the events described in this chapter, many of which are based in complex arguments which are interesting, though not always conclusive.
2. Polyb. 1.66.1–6; Diod. Sic. 25.2.
3. Polyb. 1.66.6–12.
4. We do not hear of an amount owed, but Hoyos 2007, 27–9, calculated estimates, noting that one years' service may have ran up a Punic debt of 1,530 talents.
5. Polyb. 1.67.
6. Polyb. 1.68.
7. Spendius may have actually been named Spedis or Spedius, cf. Walbank 1957, 135. Griffith 1935, 220, suggested that he served in the fleet.
8. In what language this was being uttered is unknown.
9. Polyb. 1.69.
10. Walbank 1957, 135–6. This may be corroborated by their mistreatment of the Libyan subjects during the first war with Rome, cf. Polyb. 1.72.1–3.
11. Polyb. 1.70.
12. Polyb. 1.72.5–6.
13. Diod. Sic. 24.10.2; Polyb. 1.73.1.
14. Hoyos 2007, 92.
15. As suggested by Hoyos 2007, 33.
16. Polyb. 1.73.1–2.
17. cf. Hoyos 2007, 84 n. 10.
18. Polyb. 1.73.3–6.
19. There could have been as many as 10,000 rebel troops at Utica, cf. Hoyos 2007, 93.

20. These either came from Carthage or Utica. They are often assumed to have come from the former, but Hoyos 2007, 97–8, makes a compelling argument that they came from Utica.
21. Polyb. 1.74.1–6.
22. Polyb. 1.74.7–12. Hanno is credited with other failures as well, including missing four chances at engaging the enemy at a town called Gorza, Polyb. 1.74.13–14.
23. Polyb. 1.75–76. The narrative of this battle is complex, and the version I have provided reflects how I believe it unfolded. I see both rebel contingents connecting and forming a single line of battle, which was attacking Hamilcar's army head on. When he saw this, he ordered his army to feign a retreat and for his heavy infantry to open their ranks. He then had these stop and turn to face the enemy, allowing the contingents which used to be in the vanguard to pass through. As the enemy approached at a run, having broken ranks, the cavalry then passed back through the open ranks of the infantry, and together these received the attack and simultaneously struck back. There are a number of interpretations of Polybius' narrative, discussed in detail by Hoyos 2007, 116–24; cf. Walbank 1957, 142–3.
24. Polyb. 1.76.10–11.
25. Hoyos 2007, 130.
26. Hoyos 2007, 132, hypothesized that Hamilcar had received cavalry or elephant reinforcements from either Carthage or one of the allied cities. This is possible and would explain the rebels' concerns.
27. Polyb. 1.77.
28. He is probably mentioned in an inscription dated to around 128 BC which lists the genealogy of a Numidian governor, Hoyos 2007, 148.
29. Polyb. 1.78.1–9.
30. Walbank 1957, 143–4. Hoyos 2007, 151, is more forgiving and rightly points out that whatever the number of casualties, the army seems to have disintegrated. This does support a rather high number.
31. I have doubts that this or the other letter genuinely came from Sardinia, although that is a judgment made without evidence. Hoyos 2007, 165, believes that as the letter from Sardinia advised them to guard Gisco, rather than what actually happened, that it is genuine. I have less confidence in his conclusion that if they were forgeries the letters would not have been so timid in the actions they encouraged. Rather, it seems likely that by coming up with the torture and murder scheme themselves, the leaders would have cemented their place at the top of the mutiny. All of this, though, is simply opinion.
32. Polyb. 1.79. The mercenaries on Sardinia rebelled against their commanders and killed them, including the overall garrison commander, Bostar. A Hanno was sent to relieve the Punic forces on the island, but the mercenaries under him rebelled when they reached Sardinia and he was crucified. They then rampaged across the island, torturing and murdering all the Carthaginians they came across. On this, see Hoyos 2007, 154–9.
33. Polyb. 1.80.
34. Polyb. 1.81–82.2.
35. Polyb. 1.82.3–10; Diod. Sic. 25.3.
36. Polyb. 1.82.11–14.
37. Polyb. 1.83.
38. Polyb. 1.84.1–8.

Notes 297

39. This location is unsettled. See the discussion in Hoyos 2007, 206–9.
40. Hoyos 2007, 212–13.
41. Polyb. 1.84.9–12–85.
42. Polyb. 1.86.1–4.
43. Polyb. 1.86.5–9.
44. Polyb. 1.87.1–6.
45. As suggested by Hoyos 2007, 240.
46. Polyb. 1.87.7–10–88.
47. Polyb. 2.1.5–7.

Chapter 8
1. Lazenby 1998, 1.
2. Polyb. 1.88.
3. Polyb. 3.28.
4. An extensive and up-to-date discussion of Barcid Spain and the lead up to the Second Punic War can be found in Miles 2010, 218–34.
5. Polyb. 3.33; cf. Livy 21.21–22.
6. Tr. Waterfield.
7. Our sources agree on the figure: Polyb. 3.35.1; Livy 21.23.2; App. *Hann.* 1 The troop numbers may not be reliable, here, though; cf. Lazenby 1998, 33–4.
8. Polyb. 3.35.1–3. The tribes defeated are given by Livy (21.23.2) as the Ilergetes, Bargusii, and Ausetani. The former is to be preferred.
9. There is no reason to think that this was his brother, also named Hanno; Lazenby 1998, 34.
10. Polyb. 3.35.6; Livy 21.23.4–6.
11. Some authors, such as Goldsworthy 2000, 159, accept without discussion that some of them deserted.
12. There is a discrepancy in troop numbers between when the army left the Pyrenees and when it left the Rhone amounting to 12,000 infantry and 1,000 cavalry. As we are not presented with any plausible reason for losses of this magnitude, it may be right to think that these were left behind as they marched forward as garrisons, in order to maintain communication between Hannibal and Iberia; Lazenby 1998, 34. Hoyos 2015, 104, rejects this and proposes that there were mass desertions, which were then covered up by 'tactful accounts' of the march. Given that the sources did know about the rather high losses on the other side of the Pyrenees, I do not find this entirely convincing. In the end, though, I think we must concede that Polybius' silence here causes significant problems.
13. Polyb. 3.42–43; Livy 21.27–28.
14. Polyb. 3.44–47; Livy 21.28–30. Livy's chronology places Hannibal and Maligo's speeches after the return of the Numidian scouts, but I follow here Polybius; cf. Lazenby 1998, 36–7.
15. Hannibal's crossing of the Alps is a famous piece of military history, but has been retold countless times. Lazenby 1998, 37–48, provides a good account.
16. For a brief but refreshingly calm reflection on this 'feat', see Hoyos 2003, 111–13. I reject as anachronism the stories that the army almost had to resort to cannibalism, as discussed in Rawlings 2007/9.
17. Polyb. 3.76; Livy 21. 60–61. Livy includes additional campaigning by the Romans, which is not attested elsewhere. Lazenby 1998, 126, doubted it though I do not think it should be dismissed out of hand.

18. Livy 21.49–50.
19. Polyb. 3.56.4.
20. Livy 21.38. Polybius' numbers are generally accepted by modern commentators: e.g. Lazenby 1998, 48, and Goldsworthy 2000, 167. Discussion in Walbank 1957, 366.
21. Polyb. 3.65; Livy 21.46.
22. Polyb. 3.60.
23. Polyb. 3.67; Livy 21.48.1–3.
24. Polyb. 3.68; Livy 21.48.5–6.
25. Livy 21.48.9.
26. Polyb. 3.69; Livy 21.52.8–11.
27. On the Trebia campaign: Polyb. 3.69–75; Livy 21.52–57.
28. Though Lazenby 1998, 60, points out that in Etruria, Hannibal would have still been able to communicate with his new Celtic allies to the north, with Spain, and perhaps sway the Etruscans – some of whom were friendly with Carthage centuries before (see above) – to come over to his side. He had perhaps also intended to meet a Punic fleet which sailed near Pisa this year (Polyb. 3.96.9).
29. Polyb. 3.78.8–79; Livy 22.2.
30. Goldsworthy 2000, 185–6, provides a good argument against Flaminius' behaviour being any different than we would expect to see from other commanders of the period.
31. Livy 22.5.1–2 and Plut. *Fab.* 3.3 both portray Flaminius as keeping his cool and trying to salvage the situation, while Polyb. 3.84.6 claims he was killed whilst in a state of despair. In this case, the version in Livy seems to match better with the situation, as the Roman army did put up a considerable resistance, probably meaning their leader was active throughout most of the battle.
32. The narrative of the Trasimene campaign can be found in Polyb. 3.81–86 and Livy 22.3–6.
33. Livy 22.8.6–7.
34. cf. Walbank 1957, 431.
35. Polyb. 3.95–96.1–6; Livy 22.19–20.1–3.
36. Though repeated at face value by some, e.g. Edwell 2011, 321. Livy 22.20–21.
37. Livy 22.11.6.
38. Polyb. 3.96.8–14; Livy 22.31.1–7.
39. Polyb. 3.98–99; Livy 22.22.
40. This term comes with problems when applied to the ancient world, though, as by its definition it requires the existence of persons and resources viewed as 'civilian'. Whether or not these existed in the ancient world is up for debate.
41. I follow here the more colourful narrative of Livy 22.16.6–17.7 than that of Polyb. 3.93–94.
42. On this point see Walbank 1957, 433.
43. Polyb. 3.101–102; Livy 22.24. The latter reports 5,000 Romans and 6,000 Carthaginians killed in this fight.
44. The equalization of imperium between a dictator and master of horse was unprecedented in Roman history.
45. Polyb. 3.104–105; Livy 22.28–30.
46. Livy 22.32–41.3.
47. Polyb. 3.107.1–7.
48. e.g. Lazenby 1998, 76.

49. Daly 2002, 16–17.
50. The strength of the Roman army is different in our sources and has been a source of scholarly debate for a long time. Daly 2002, 25–29, provides a good discussion and convincing argument in support of the figures given in Polyb. 3.113.5.
51. Daly 2002, 29–32, on the problems with the Punic army figures.
52. Daly 2002, 29 and 211 n. 56.
53. Polyb. 3.113; Livy 22.45.6–7.
54. Lazenby 1998, 80.
55. Size of the units: Goldsworthy 2000, 207.
56. Though App. *Hann.* 19 believed that Paullus was in command of the centre.
57. Livy 22.49.1.
58. Daly 2002, 202, makes a convincing (if brief) case for accepting Livy's figures over Polybius' 70,000 dead.
59. Doubt has been cast over who should be blamed for Cannae, and which of the consuls was in command; cf. Daly 2002, 119–21.
60. Rawlings 2011a, 303. Though this was noted as early as App. *Hann.* 26.
61. Livy 22.51.1–4.
62. This is generally the opinion of modern commentators, in contrast to Livy 22.51.4 who believed that this delay was all that saved Rome. Hannibal's objective was likely never to destroy Rome itself, cf. Fronda 2010, 34–7, and 2011, 249–54.
63. Consequences of this 'social war': Rawlings 2011a, 308–10.
64. For a brilliant examination of Hannibal, see now Eve MacDonald's 2015 volume. Rawlings 2011, 301–2, provides a helpful table listing the engagements fought against Hannibal during these years and the primary sources for them. An abbreviated narrative can be found in Goldsworthy 2000, 222–44.
65. The 'First Macedonian War', see Goldsworthy 2000, 253–60, and Hoyos 2015, 155–7.
66. Goldsworthy 2000, 250, cautions us, rightly, not to think that the deployment was meant to emulate Hannibal's at Cannae. He attractively suggests that it may have been more similar to the deployment at the Trebia, where Hannibal's best infantry were stationed flanking the weaker centre of the line.
67. Livy 23.29.
68. Livy 24.48; App. *Hisp.* 15; Lazenby 1998, 129.
69. Livy 24.42.9; Lazenby 1998, 129, for the date.
70. Livy 25.32–36.
71. Lazenby 1998, 131–2.
72. Total figures based on Polyb. 10.6.7 and 10.9.6.
73. These are the locations given in Polyb. 10.7, which are more believable than those found in Livy 26.20.6; cf. Lazenby 1998, 134.
74. Lazenby 1998, 136–7.
75. Polyb. 10.8–19; Livy 26.42–51; cf. the problematic account in App. *Hisp.* 20–23.
76. Polyb. 10.38.7–39.6; Livy 27.18.
77. Livy 27.43–49; Polyb. 11.1; App. *Hann.* 52. Full narrative in Goldsworthy 2000, 238–43.
78. Livy 28.1–2.
79. Livy 28.3–4.4.
80. Polyb. 11.20.2–8; Livy 28.12.13–13.5. Discussion of both army sizes in Walbank 1967, 296–7.

81. Polyb. 11.20–21; Livy 28.13.6–10.
82. Goldsworthy 2000, 283.
83. Polyb. 11.21.7–24; Livy 28.13.6–15.11.
84. Livy 23.32.7–12, 40.
85. Livy 25.31.13–15.
86. Livy 24.25–39, 25.23–31; Polyb. 8.3–7, 37, Plut. *Marc.* 14–20. Cf. Goldsworthy 2000, 260–8.
87. Rawlings 2016.
88. Livy 24.40–41, 26.40.
89. Livy 27.5.11–13; Steinby 2014, 151–5.
90. Though Lazenby 1998, 200–1.
91. Livy 28.46.7–16, 29.5.2, 30.18–19.6.
92. Goldsworthy 2000, 287–8.
93. Livy 29.28–29.4.
94. There is no reason, as has been the case in the past, to dismiss this and the earlier cavalry engagement simply because the commanders of the Carthaginian force shared the same name. As we have seen through the course of this book, Hanno was a common name.
95. Livy 29.34.
96. App. *Pun.* 3.16.
97. Polyb. 14.1–6; Livy 30.3–6; App. *Pun.* 4.21–23.
98. Polyb. 14.8; Livy 30.8; to be read along with Lazenby 1998, 209–10.
99. Lazenby 1998, 211–12.
100. Peace may have been agreed to and then broken by the Romans, though this is inconclusive, Lazenby 1998, 213–14, Hoyos 2001.
101. Lazenby 1998, 217.
102. App. *Hann.* 59.
103. Lazenby 1998, 218.
104. Goldsworthy 2000, 300–1.
105. MacDonald 2015, 214.
106. App. *Pun.* 7.41.
107. Polyb. 15.14.9, cf. 15.11.1; Lazenby 1998, 220–1, and accepted (to an extent) by other authors such as MacDonald 2015, 214.
108. Lazenby 1998, 221.
109. This line was probably composed mostly of the remnants of Mago's army from northern Italy.
110. Polyb. 15.9–11; Livy 30.32–33.11.
111. Lazenby 1998, 222–3.
112. Polyb. 15.12–14; Livy 30.32–35.
113. Lazenby 1998, 225, preferred Appian's numbers.
114. Livy 30.36.8.
115. Polyb. 15.18.
116. App. *Pun.* 20.134 claims that Hannibal killed 300,000 Romans in battle and destroyed 400 towns in Italy. Though we must be cautious with these numbers, they indicate the scale of bloodshed.
117. Hoyos 2010, 205–6.
118. cf. Steinby 2014.

Chapter 9

1. Livy 31.19.2.
2. Livy 36.4.5–7.
3. As suggested by Miles 2010, 324, with further citations.
4. App. *Pun.* 14.96. The translation is that of Horace White, 1899. Further discussion in Miles 2010, 325–8.
5. Miles 2010, 328–9.
6. cf. Walsh 1965.
7. App. *Pun.* 11.74; Diod. Sic. 32.3. The names of the Punic ambassadors are preserved in Polyb. 36.8. as Gisco Strytanus, Hamilcar, Misdes, Gillimas, and Mago. Misdes and Gillimas may be Libyan names, suggested by Hoyos 2015, 255.
8. There is no reason to believe Appian's statement that the Uticans held an 'ancient animosity' towards the Carthaginians. Clearly there were differences between the two cities now, in the middle of the second century BC.
9. App. *Pun.* 11.75.
10. App. *Pun.* 11.76; Diod. Sic. 32.6.1–2; Polyb. 36.4.6.
11. App. *Pun.* 11.77.
12. App. *Pun.* 11.78. The version we have from Polyb. 36.6.4–6 is much less spectacular.
13. App. *Pun.* 11.78–79. The translation is that of Horace White, 1899.
14. App. *Pun.* 11.80; Diod. Sic. 32.6.2; Polyb. 36.6.7. Hoyos 2010, 217, and 2015, 256, astutely calls the slow revelation of Roman demands as a 'cat-and-mouse game'.
15. App. *Pun.* 12.81. The more dramatic elements of the story may be fictious, such as the image of Carthaginians throwing themselves on the ground and throwing tantrums like children. Smith 1901, 246, though preserves these elements in his narrative.
16. Poignantly put by Lancel 1995, 413. Miles 2010, 340, believes that the 'angry and grief-stricken' response of the Carthaginians was proof that 'they understood [the demand's] full implications.'
17. It is too long to reproduce here, see App. Pun. 12.83–85.
18. App. *Pun.* 12.86.
19. App. *Pun.* 13.90.
20. App. *Pun.* 13.91–92; Polyb. 36.7.3–5.
21. App. *Pun.* 13.93.
22. App. *Pun.* 13.94.
23. App. *Pun.* 14.97. Called Hamilcar Phameas by Polyb. 36.8.1.
24. App. *Pun.* 14.98.
25. App. *Pun.* 14.99.
26. App. *Pun.* 14.100–15.101. The praise of Scipio throughout Appian's narrative cannot be trusted at face value and should be seen as a type of partisan reporting, e.g. Hoyos 2015, 258.
27. App. *Pun.* 15.102.
28. App. *Pun.* 15.103.
29. App. *Pun.* 15.104; Diod. Sic. 32.8.
30. App. *Pun.* 16.105.
31. App. *Pun.* 16.107.

32. App. *Pun.* 16.108. Diod. Sic. 32.17.1 says that he only brought 1,200 cavalry over to the Romans.
33. App. *Pun.* 16.110.
34. Hoyos 2015, 261, describes this as not more 'than a gesture of defiance' which is probably correct. It seems unlikely that the Carthaginians would have been able to give significant aid, especially in ships, to the Macedonians. Goldsworthy 2000, 346, more positively says that 'The Carthaginian mood was ebullient, sending a delegation to Macedonia to form an alliance.' I think that this characterisation is too much, and at most the Punic envoys probably expressed their people's admiration of another enemy of Rome.
35. App. *Pun.* 16.111.
36. App. *Pun.* 17.112; Diod. Sic. 32.9a.3. On this election, see Develin 1978. On Scipio Aemilianus generally, see Astin 1967 or, for a briefer account, Goldsworthy 2003, 109–26.
37. App. *Pun.* 17.113.
38. App. *Pun.* 17.114.
39. App. *Pun.* 17.115–18.117. That the Carthaginians would have left such a tower standing has been doubted, e.g. Lancel 1995, 422, and it is a good question as to why it was allowed to remain upright.
40. App. *Pun.* 17.117. Lancel 1995, 422, describes it as 'merely a reconnaissance', which could have been the purpose from the outset.
41. App. *Pun.* 18.118.
42. App. *Pun.* 18.119.
43. App. *Pun.* 18.120.
44. Polyb. 38.8.11; Diod. Sic. 32.22.
45. Polyb. 38.8.12.
46. A comparison made by Miles 2010, 346.
47. Polyb. 38.7.2. Cf. Diod. Sic. 32.22.
48. Goldsworthy 2006, 350, suggests that the three days were used to train the crews of the new ships. This could be the case, rather than a tactical miscalculation, although there may have been room to train in the harbour as soon as the individual ships were built.
49. App. *Pun.* 18.121–123; Livy Per. 51.2.
50. App. *Pun.* 18.124–125.
51. App. *Pun.* 18.126.
52. Polyb. 38.8.1.
53. The negotiations are described in detail in Polyb. 38.7–8 and briefly in Diod. Sic. 32.22.
54. App. *Pun.* 19.127.
55. App. *Pun.* 19.128.
56. App. *Pun.* 19.129.
57. App. *Pun.* 19.130.
58. App. *Pun.* 19.131. The translation is that of Horace White, 1899. Cf. Polyb. 38.20.7–10; Diod. Sic. 32.23.
59. Weeping can be found in App. *Pun.* 19.132, Polyb. 38.22.1, and Diod. Sic. 32..24.
60. Hom. Il. 6.448–449. The translation is that of Robert Fitzgerald, 1974.
61. Polyb. 38.21.1. Diodorus' 32.24 version is slightly different, though it delivers the same message.

62. App. *Pun.* 20.133.
63. Lancel 1995, 421.

Chapter 10
1. cf. Ameling 1993, 190–4, and Quesada Sanz 2009, 161–9.
2. Just. *Epit.* 19.1.1.
3. Hoyos 2010, 129.
4. Just. *Epit.* 18.7.
5. Diod. Sic. 11.1.5.
6. Diod. Sic. 11.24.2–4.
7. We know little about them, but all three waged wars in the central Mediterranean, with both Hamilcar and Hasdrubal dying in battle; Just. *Epit.* 19.1–2.6.
8. Diod. Sic. 14.75.1–2, 4. It is *possible* that the citizens were simply the crews of the ships, though I am convinced that there was a sizable number of them in the land army. Hoyos 2010, 154, calculated that between 8,000 and 9,000 men could have come back on the ships, including the sailors. He postulates based on this, and the losses incurred in the campaign, that the original citizen component of the army was between 5,000 and 10,000.
9. Diod. Sic. 16.80.4, 20.10.16; Plut. *Tim.* 27–28. The latter does not explicitly name the unit, but it is clear that he is talking about the same group as found in Diodorus, Ameling 1993, 163.
10. Plut. *Tim.* 28.10–11 records 3,000 Carthaginians of high birth dead at the Crimisus, which is not far off from Diodorus' 2,500, and may include cavalrymen or those from other citizen units.
11. Plut. *Tim.* 28.1.
12. Diod. Sic. 16.80.4.
13. Hall and Rawlings, forthcoming.
14. Arist. *Pol.* 7.2.10 = 1324b.
15. Plut. *Tim.* 27.2–3.
16. Diod. Sic. 19.106.2.
17. Diod. Sic. 20.10.5, Hoyos 2010, 154–5.
18. On this, see Hoyos 2010, 132–8.
19. Polyb. 6.52.
20. Livy 29.34.
21. App. *Pun.* 14.95.
22. Diod. Sic. 20.8.4.
23. Fantar 1993, 108.
24. Picard 1954, 196; though cf. Bieber 1957, 414.
25. Hall and Rawlings, forthcoming.
26. See for instance Prag 2010.
27. Trophies: Paus. 6.19.7, Diod. Sic. 11.26.7. Synchronism: Hdt. 7.166, Diod. Sic. 11.24.1, though Arist. *Poet.* 1459a.24–8. Poetry: Pind. *Pyth.* 1.71–80. Discussions in Prag 2010 and Whitley 2011.
28. Anaxilaus and Terillus: Hdt. 7.165. Relations with Athens: IG I³ 123. Greeks in Punic armies, e.g.: Clinon and his cavalry (Diod. Sic. 20.38.6) or Alexon in the first war against Rome (Polyb. 1.43).
29. Unlike Caven 1990, 45, who wrote that this alliance happened in spite of 'Athens' vaunted Hellenism' which 'was not strong enough to permit her at this juncture to

throw away the opportunity of putting difficulties in the way of the Syracusans'. The tone of this presentation is misguided.
30. Roman expansion in Italy has been argued to have mostly been spurred on by individuals, Terrenato 2019, so it is not inconceivable that a similar process happened in Libya.
31. Miles 2010, 76–81, Pilkington 2013, 182–249.
32. Polyb. 3.22.
33. In particular Whittaker 1978. He is widely rebuked, e.g. Eckstein 2006, 160, and Serrati 2006, 114 n. 2.
34. I have avoided using this term throughout this book as I believe its vagueness makes its usefulness minimal.
35. This may also be supported by the Carthaginian fortification of the Sicilian landscape, Miles 2010, 135.
36. It is always worth noting the contentious status of this conquest as either private or public in nature; Miles 2010, 218–28.
37. Eckstein 2006, 163.

Bibliography

With my target audience in mind, I have endeavoured to cite relevant literature in English. Much of the scholarly discussion on ancient Carthage, however, has occurred in other modern European languages. I apologize to my readers who cannot readily access these works.

Translations of primary sources can be found readily. Penguin Classics and Oxford World's Classics provide some of the best and most widely available English versions. The Loeb Classical Library editions have both English translations and the original text, side-by-side, and should be of great interest to the average reader with a background in Greek or Latin. The latter are generally the versions of the texts cited in this book.

Abbreviations
AJN = American Journal of Numismatics
CPh = Classical Philology
CQ = Classical Quarterly
CR = The Classical Review
CW = The Classical Weekly
CAH² = Cambridge Ancient History, Second Edition
DHA = Dialogues d'histoire ancienne
G&R = Greece & Rome
Historia = Historia: Zeitschrift für Alte Geschichte
JHS = Journal of Hellenic Studies
JNES = Journal of Near Eastern Studies
JRS = Journal of Roman Studies
Latomus = Latomus: Revue et collection d'études latines
Méditeranée = Méditeranée: revue géographique des pays méditerranéens
PPS = Proceedings of the Prehistoric Society

Acquaro, E., 'Phoenicians and Etruscans,' in S. Moscati (ed.), *The Phoenicians* (London, I. B. Tauris: 1997), 611–17.
Airy, G. B., 'On the Eclipses of Agathocles, Thales, and Xerxes,' in *Philosophical Transactions of the Royal Society of London* 143 (1853), 179–200.
Ameling, W., *Karthago: Studien zu Militär, Staat und Gesellschaft* (Munich, Beck: 1993).
Armstrong, J., (2016a) *War and Society in Early Rome: From Warlords to Generals* (Cambridge, Cambridge University Press: 2016).
Armstrong, J., (2016b) *Early Roman Warfare: From the Regal Period to the 1st Punic War* (Barnsley, Pen & Sword: 2016).
Asheri, D., 'Carthaginians and Greeks,' in *CAH² IV* (1988), 739–80.
Astin, A., *Scipio Aemilianus* (Oxford, Oxford University Press: 1967).
Aubet, M. E., *The Phoenicians and the West: Politics, Colonies, and Trade* (Second Edition) (Cambridge, Cambridge University Press: 2001).

Azize, J. J., 'Was There Regular Child Sacrifice in Phoenicia and Carthage?' in J. Azize and N. Weeks (eds.), *Gilgameš and the World of Assyria: Proceedings of the Conference held at Mandelbaum House, the University of Sydney, 21–23 July 2004* (Leuven, Peeters: 2007), 185–206.
Barcceló, P., 'Punic Politics, Economy, and Alliances, 218–201,' in D. Hoyos 2011a, 357–75.
Baronowski, D. W., 'Roman Treaties with Communities of Citizens,' in CQ 38.1 (1988), 172–78.
Bartoloni, P., 'Army, Navy and Warfare,' in S. Moscati (ed.), *The Phoenicians* (London, I. B. Tauris: 1997), 160–6.
Bassett, E. L., 'Regulus and the Serpent in the Punica,' in CPh 50.1 (1955), 1–20.
Beard, M., *The Roman Triumph* (Cambridge, MA, Harvard University Press: 2007).
Beck, H., 'The Reasons for the War,' in D. Hoyos 2011a, 225–41.
Berger, S., *Revolution and Society in Greek Sicily and Southern Italy* (Stuttgart, Franz Steiner: 1992).
Bieber, M., review of 'Catalogue du Musée Alaoui. Nouvelle Série (Collections Puniques), Vol. 1, by C. Gilbert Picard,' in *American Journal of Archaeology* 61.4 (1957), 412–14.
Boardman, J., *The Greeks Overseas: Their Early Colonies and Trade* (Fourth Edition) (London, Thames & Hudson: 1999).
Bondi, S. F., 'City Planning and Architecture,' in S. Moscati (ed.), *The Phoenicians* (London, I. B. Tauris: 1997), 311–48.
Bosworth, A. B., *Conquest and Empire: The Reign of Alexander the Great* (Cambridge, Cambridge University Press: 1988).
Botto, M., 'The Phoenicians in the central-west Mediterranean and Atlantic between 'precolonization' and the 'first colonization',' in L. Donnellan, V. Nizzo, and G.-J. Burgers (eds.), *Contexts of Early Colonization*. Papers of the Royal Netherlands Institute in Rome – Volume 64 (Rome, Palombi Editori: 2016), 289–309.
Bradley, G., and Hall, J. R., 'The Roman Conquest of Italy,' in G. Farney and G. Bradley (eds.), *The Peoples of Ancient Italy* (Berlin, De Gruyter: 2018), 191–214.
Brizzi, G., 'L'armée et la guerre,' in V. Krings (ed.), *La civilisation phénicienne et punique. Manuel de recherche* (Leiden, Brill: 1995), 303–15.
Broodbank, C., *The Making of the Middle Sea: A History of the Mediterranean from the Beginning to the Emergence of the Classical World* (London, Thames & Hudson: 2013).
Burn, A. R., *The Lyric Age of Greece* (New York, Minerva Press: 1967).
Burton, P., *Friendship and Empire: Roman Diplomacy and Imperialism in the Middle Republic (353–146 BC)* (Cambridge, Cambridge University Press: 2011).
Campbell, D. B., *Greek and Roman Artillery: 399 BC–AD 363* (Oxford, Osprey: 2003).
Cartledge, P., *Agesilaos and the Crisis of Sparta* (London, Duckworth: 1987).
Cary, M., 'A Forgotten Treaty between Rome and Carthage,' in *JRS* 9 (1919), 67–77.
Casson, L., *Ships and Seamanship in the Ancient World* (Princeton, Princeton University Press: 1971).
Caven, B., *Dionysius I: War-Lord of Sicily* (New Haven, Yale University Press: 1990).
Champion, J., *Pyrrhus of Epirus* (Barnsley, Pen & Sword: 2009).
Champion, J., *The Tyrants of Syracuse: War in Ancient Sicily. Volume I: 480–367 BC* (Barnsley, Pen & Sword: 2010).
Champion, J., *The Tyrants of Syracuse: War in Ancient Sicily. Volume II: 367–211 BC* (Barnsley, Pen & Sword: 2012).

Chaplin, J. D., *Livy's Exemplary History* (Oxford, Oxford University Press: 2000).
Collin Bouffier, S., 'Les elites urbaines en Sicile grecque du VIIe au Ve siècle av. J.-C. ou la reproduction d'un modèle homerique,' in C. Petitfrère (ed.), *Construction, reproduction et representation des patriciats urbains de l'Antiquité au XXe siècle: Actes du colloque des 7, 8, 9 septembre 1998 tenu à Tours* (Tours, Presses universitaires François-Rabelais : 1999), 363–73.
Connolly, P., *Greece and Rome at War* (London, Greenhill Books: 1998).
Cordano, F., *Antiche fondazioni greche: Sicilia e Italia meridionale* (Palermo, Sellerio Editore: 1986).
Cornell, T. J., *The Beginnings of Rome: Italy and Rome from the Bronze Age to the Punic Wars (c. 1000–264 BC)* (London, Routledge: 1995).
Cornell, T. J., et al., *The Fragments of the Roman Historians* (Oxford, Oxford University Press: 2014).
Cowan, R., *Roman Conquests: Italy* (Barnsley, Pen & Sword: 2009).
Crawley Quinn, J., and Vella, N. C. (eds.), *The Punic Mediterranean: Identities and Identification from Phoenician Settlement to Roman Rule* (Cambridge, Cambridge University Press: 2014).
Crouwel, J. H., *Chariots and Other Wheeled Vehicles in Italy before the Roman Empire* (Oxford, Oxbow: 2012).
Cusumano, N., 'Gérer la haine, fabriquer l'ennemi. Grecs et Carthaginois en Sicile entre les Ve et IVe siècles av. J.-C.' in *Diodore d'Agyrion et l'histoire de la Sicile, Dialogue d'histoire ancienne, supplément* 6 (2011), 113–35.
Daly, G., *Cannae: The Experience of Battle in the Second Punic War* (London, Routledge: 2002).
David, J.-M., *The Roman Conquest of Italy* (Oxford, Blackwell: 1996).
De Angelis, F., *Megara Hyblaia and Selinous: The Development of Two Greek City-states in Archaic Sicily* (Oxford, Oxford University Press: 2003).
De Angelis, F., *Archaic and Classical Greek Sicily: A Social and Economic History* (Oxford, Oxford University Press: 2016).
Develin, R., 'Scipio Aemilianus and the Consular Elections of 148 B.C.' in *Latomus* 37.2 (1978), 484–8.
Domínguez, A. J., 'Greek Identity in the Phocaean Colonies,' in K. Lomas (ed.), *Greek Identity in the Western Mediterranean: Papers in Honour of Brian Shefton* (Leiden, Brill: 2004), 429–456.
Domínguez Monedero, A. J., 'Los Mercenarios Baleáricos,' in B. Costa and J. H. Fernández (eds.), *Guerra y ejército en el mundo fenicio-púnico*. XIX Jornadas de Arqueología Fenicio-Púnica (Ibiza, Govern de Les Illes Balears – Conselleria d'Educació i Cultura: 2005), 163–89.
Domínguez Monedero, A. J., 'Los contactos «precoloniales» de Griegos y Fenicios en Sicilia,' in S. Celestino, N. Rafel, and X.-L. Armada (eds.), *Contacto cultural entre el Mediterráneo y el Atlántico (siglos XII-VIII ane). La precolonización a debate* (Madrid, Escuela Española de Historia y Arqueología en Roma: 2008), 149–59.
Ducrey, P., *Le traitement de prisonniers de guerre dans la Grèce antique* (Paris, De Boccard: 1968).
Dunbabin, T. J., *The Western Greeks: The History of Sicily and South Italy from the Foundation of the Greek Colonies to 480 B.C.* (Oxford, Oxford University Press: 1948).
Echols, E. C., 'The Ancient Slinger,' in CW 43 (1950), 227–230.

Eckstein, A. M., *Moral Vision in the Histories of Polybius* (Berkeley, University of California Press: 1995).
Eckstein, A. M., *Mediterranean Anarchy, Interstate War, and the Rise of Rome* (Berkeley, University of California Press: 2006).
Eckstein, A. M., "The Treaty of Philinus', and Roman Accusations Against Carthage,' in *CQ* 60.2 (2010), 406–26.
Edwell, P., 'War Abroad: Spain, Sicily, Macedon, Africa,' in D. Hoyos 2011a, 320–38.
Elliott, P., 'Humble and Deadly: The ancient slinger,' in *Ancient Warfare* 2.1 (2008), 24–27.
Ellis, J. R., 'Macedon and North-West Greece,' in *CAH² VI* (1994), 723–59.
Emiliozzi, A., 'Princely Chariots and Carts,' in J. M. Turfa (ed.), *The Etruscan World* (London, Routledge: 2013), 778–97.
Falsone, G., 'Sicile,' in V. Krings (ed.), *La civilisation phénicienne et punique: Manuel de recherche* (Leiden, Brill: 1995), 674–97.
Fantar, M. H., *Carthage: Approche d'une civlisation, Tome 2* (Tunis, Alif: 1993).
Fields, N., *Carthaginian Warrior 264–146 BC* (Oxford, Osprey: 2010).
Forsythe, G., *A Critical History of Early Rome: From Prehistory to the First Punic War* (Berkeley, University of California Press: 2005).
Frank, T., 'Mercantilism and Rome's Foreign Policy,' in *AHR* 18.2 (1913), 233–52.
Franke, P. R., 'Pyrrhus,' in *CAH² VII.2* (1989), 456–85.
Frederiksen, M. W., 'The Campanian Cavalry: a question of origins,' in *Dialoghi di Archeologia* 2 (1968), 3–31.
Freeman, E. A., (1891a) *The History of Sicily from the Earliest Times, vol. 1 the native nations: the Phoenician and Greek settlements* (Oxford, Clarendon Press: 1891).
Freeman, E. A., (1891b) *The History of Sicily from the Earliest Times, vol. 2 from the beginning of Greek settlement to the beginning of Athenian intervention* (Oxford, Clarendon Press: 1891).
Freeman, E. A., *The History of Sicily from the Earliest Times, vol. 4 from the tyranny of Dionysios to the death of Agathoklēs* (Oxford, Clarendon Press: 1894).
Frey-Kupper, S., 'Coins and their use in the Punic Mediterranean: case studies from Carthage to Italy from the fourth to the first century BCE,' in J. Crawley Quinn and N. C. Vella (eds.), *The Punic Mediterranean: Identities and Identification from Phoenician Settlement to Roman Rule* (Cambridge, Cambridge University Press: 2014), 76–110.
Fronda, M. P., *Between Rome and Carthage: Southern Italy during the Second Punic War* (Cambridge, Cambridge University Press: 2010).
Fronda, M. P., 'Hannibal: Tactics, Strategy, and Geostrategy,' in D. Hoyos 2011a, 242–59.
Fulminante, F., *The Urbanisation of Rome and Latium Vetus: From the Bronze Age to the Archaic Era* (Cambridge, Cambridge University Press: 2014).
Goldsworthy, A., *The Fall of Carthage* (London, Phoenix: 2000).
Goldsworthy, A., *In the Name of Rome* (London, Phoenix: 2003).
Gras, M., 'A propos de la «bataille d'Alalia»,' in *Latomus* 31.3 (1972), 698–716.
Gras, M., 'Marseille, la bataille d'Alalia et Delphes,' in DHA 13 (1987), 161–181.
Green, P., *Diodorus Siculus: The Persian Wars to the Fall of Athens. Books 11–14.34 (480 – 401 BCE)* (Austin, University of Texas Press: 2010).
Griffith, G. T., *The Mercenaries of the Hellenistic World* (Groningen, Bouma's Boekhuis N. V.: 1968).
Grote, G., *History of Greece. Vol. XII* (New York, Harper & Brothers: 1857).

Gsell, S., *Histoire ancienne de l'Afrique du nord. Tome III. Histoire militaire de Carthage* (Paris, Librairie Hachette: 1928).
Hall, J. R., 'The Tyrrhenian Way of War: warfare, social power, and the state in Central Italy (c. 900 – 343 BC),' PhD Thesis (Cardiff, Cardiff University: 2016).
Hall, J. R., (2018a) 'As They Were Ripped from the Altars: Civilians, Sacrilege and Classical Greek Siege Warfare,' in A. Dowdall and J. Horne (eds.), *Civilians Under Siege from Sarajevo to Troy* (London, Palgrave-Macmillan: 2018), 185–206.
Hall, J. R., (2018b) 'Regulus and the Bagradas Dragon,' in *Ancient World Magazine*, 1 June 2018, https://www.ancientworldmagazine.com/articles/regulus-bagradas-dragon/.
Hall, J. R., 'The Western Greeks and the 'Greek Warfare' narrative,' in R. Konijnindijk, C. Kucewicz, and M. Lloyd (eds), *Brill's Companion to Greek Land Warfare Beyond the Phalanx* (Leiden, Brill: 2021).
Hall, J. R., and Rawlings, L., 'Unit Cohesion in the Multi-Ethnic Armies of Carthage,' in J. R. Hall, G. Lee, and L. Rawlings (eds.), *Unit Cohesion and Warfare in the Ancient World* (London, Routledge: Forthcoming).
Hanson, V. D., *The Western Way of War: Infantry Battle in Classical Greece* (Second Edition) (Berkeley, University of California Press: 1989).
Holloway, R. R., *The Archaeology of Ancient Sicily* (London, Routledge: 1991).
Hornblower, S., *The Greek World 479–323 BC* (Fourth Edition) (London, Routledge: 2011).
Hoyos, B. D., 'The Roman-Punic Pact of 279 B.C.: Its Problems and Its Purpose,' in *Historia* 33.4 (1984), 402–39.
Hoyos, B. D., (1985a) 'Treaties True and False: The Error of Philinus of Agrigentum,' in CQ 35.1 (1985), 92–109.
Hoyos, B. D., (1985b) 'The Rise of Hiero II: Chronology and Campaigns 275–264 B.C.' in *Antichthon* 19 (1985), 32–56.
Hoyos, B. D., *Unplanned Wars: The Origins of the First and Second Punic Wars* (Berlin, De Gruyter: 1998).
Hoyos, D., 'Polybius and the Papyrus: The Persuasiveness of "P. Rylands" III 491,' in *Zeitschrift für Papyrologie und Epigraphik* 134 (2001), 71–9.
Hoyos, D., *Hannibal's Dynasty: Power and politics in the western Mediterranean, 247–183 BC* (London, Routledge: 2003).
Hoyos, D., *Truceless War: Carthage's Fight for Survival, 241 to 237 BC* (Leiden, Brill: 2007).
Hoyos, D., *The Carthaginians* (London, Routledge: 2010).
Hoyos, D. (ed.), *A Companion to the Punic Wars* (Oxford, Blackwell: 2011a).
Hoyos, D., (2011b) 'The Outbreak of war,' in D. Hoyos 2011a, 131–48.
Hoyos, D., (2011c) 'Carthage in Africa and Spain, 241–218,' in D. Hoyos 2011a, 204–22.
Hoyos, D. (ed.), *A Companion to Roman Imperialism* (Leiden, Brill: 2013).
Hoyos, D., *Mastering the West: Rome and Carthage at War* (Oxford, Oxford University Press: 2015).
Huß, W., 'Neues zur Zeit des Agathokles: Einige Bemerkungen zu P. Oxy. XXIV 2399,' in *Zeitschrift für Papyrologie und Epigraphik* 39 (1980), 63–71.
Huss, W., *Geschichte der Karthager* (Munich, Beck: 1985).
Kagan, D., *The Fall of the Athenian Empire* (Ithaca, Cornell University Press: 1987).
Kagan, D., and Viggiano, G. F., 'The Hoplite Debate,' in D. Kagan and G. F. Viggiano (eds.), *Men of Bronze: Hoplite Warfare in Ancient Greece* (Princeton, Princeton University Press: 2013), 1–56.

Keeley, L., *War Before Civilization: The Myth of the Peaceful Savage* (Oxford, Oxford University Press: 1996).
Kern, P. B., *Ancient Siege Warfare* (Bloomington and Indianapolis, Indiana University Press: 1999).
Konijnendijk, R., *Classical Greek Tactics: A Cultural History* (Leiden, Brill: 2018).
Koon, S., 'Phalanx and Legion: the "Face" of Punic War Battle,' in D. Hoyos 2011a, 77–94.
Korfmann, M., 'The sling as a weapon,' in *Scientific American* 229 (1973), 34–42.
Krentz, P., 'Fighting by the Rules: The Invention of the Hoplite Agôn,' in *Hesperia* 71 (2002), 23–39.
Krings, V., *Carthage et les Grecs c. 580–480 av. J.-C.* (Leiden, Brill: 1998).
Kunze, C., 'Carthage and Numidia, 201–149,' in D. Hoyos 2011a, 395–411.
Lancel, S., *Carthage: A History* (Oxford, Blackwell: 1995). Translated by Antonia Nevill.
Lazenby, J. F., *The First Punic War: A military history* (London, Routledge: 1996).
Lazenby, J. F., *Hannibals War: A Military History of the Second Punic War* (Norman, University of Oklahoma Press: 1998).
Lazenby, J. F., and Whitehead, D., 'The Myth of the Hoplite's Hoplon,' in *CQ* 46.1 (1996), 27–33.
Le Bohec, Y., 'The "Third Punic War": The Siege of Carthage (148–146 BC),' in D. Hoyos 2011a, 430–46.
Leigh, M., 'Early Roman Epic and the Maritime Moment,' in *CP* 105.3 (2010), 265–80.
Leighton, R., *Sicily Before History: An Archaeological Survey from the Palaeolithic to the Iron Age* (Ithaca, Cornell University Press: 1999).
Lendon, J. E., *Soldiers and Ghosts: A History of Battle in Classical Antiquity* (New Haven, Yale University Press: 2005).
Lévêque, P., *Pyrrhos* (Paris, De Boccard: 1957).
Lewis, D. M., 'Sicily, 413–368 B.C.' in *CAH² VI* (1994), 120–55.
Littman, R. J., 'The Plague at Syracuse: 396 B.C.' in *Mnemosyne* 37.1/2 (1984), 110–16.
Littman, R. J., 'The plague of Athens: epidemiology and paleopathology,' in *Mt. Sinai J Med* 76 (2009), 456–67.
Loman, P., 'No Woman No War: Women's Participation in Ancient Greek Warfare,' in *G&R* 51.1 (2004), 34–54.
Lomas, K., *Rome and the Western Greeks 350 BC–AD 200: Conquest and Acculturation in Southern Italy* (London, Routledge: 1993).
Lomas, K., *The Rise of Rome: From the Iron Age to the Punic Wars* (Cambridge, MA, Harvard University Press: 2017).
MacDonald, E., *Hannibal: A Hellenistic Life* (New Haven, Yale University Press: 2015).
Malkin, I., *Myth and territory in the Spartan Mediterranean* (Cambridge, Cambridge University Press: 1994).
Malkin, I., *A Small Greek World: Networks in the Ancient Mediterranean* (Oxford, Oxford University Press: 2011).
Manfredi, L.-I., *La politica amministrativa di Cartagine in Africa* (Rome, Accademia Nazionale dei Lincei: 2003).
Meister, K., 'Agathocles,' in *CAH² VII.1* (1984), 384–411.
Meltzer, O., *Geschichte der Karthager. Erster Band* (Berlin, Weidmannsche Buchhandlung: 1879).
Meltzer, O., *Geschichte der Karthager. Zweiter Band* (Berlin, Weidmannsche Buchhandlung: 1896).

Miles, R., *Carthage Must be Destroyed: The Rise and Fall of an Ancient Mediterranean Civilization* (London, Allen Lane: 2010).
Millender, E., 'The Politics of Spartan Mercenary Service,' in S. Hodkinson and A. Powell (eds.), *Sparta & War* (Swansea, Classical Press of Wales: 2006), 235–66.
Mitchell, R. E., 'Roman-Carthaginian Treaties: 306 and 279/8 B.C.' in *Historia* 20.5/6 (1971), 633–55.
Moggi, M., 'Peculiarità della Guerra in Sicilia?' in M. A. Vaggioli (ed.), *Guerra e pace in Sicilia e nel Mediterraneo antico (VIII-III sec. a.C.). Arte, prassi e teoria della pace e della Guerra*, vol. I (Pisa, Edizioni Della Normale, Scuola Normale Superiore: 2006), 67–89.
Morakis, A., 'The Fleet of Syracuse (480–413 BCE),' in *HISTORIKA: Studi di storia greca e romana V. Great is the power of the sea: The power of the sea and sea power in the Greek world of the archaic and classical period* (2015), 263–76.
Morgan, K. A., *Pindar & the Construction of Syracusan Monarchy in the Fifth Century B.C.* (Oxford, Oxford University Press: 2015).
Moscati, S., *The World of the Phoenicians* (London, Phoenix: 1968). Translated by Alastair Hamilton.
Moscati, S. (ed.), *The Phoenicians* (London, I. B. Tauris: 2001).
Muntz, C. E., *Diodorus Siculus and the World of the Late Roman Republic* (Oxford, Oxford University Press: 2017).
Ogden, D., *Dragons, Serpents, and Slayers in the Classical and Early Christian Worlds. A Source Book* (Oxford, Oxford University Press: 2013).
Özyiğit, Ö., 'The City Walls of Phokaia,' in *REA* 96.1 (1994), 77–109.
Palmer, R. E. A., *Rome and Carthage at Peace* (Stuttgart, Franz Steiner: 1997).
Papagrigorakis, M. J., Yapijakis, C., and Synodinos, P. N., 'Typhoid Fever Epidemic in Ancient Athens,' in D. Raoult and M. Drancourt (eds.), *Paleomicrobiology: Past Human Infections* (Berlin, Springer: 2008), 161–73.
Parke, H. W., *Greek Mercenary Soldiers: From the Earliest Times to the Battle of Ipsus* (Oxford, Oxford University Press: 1933).
Parker, R., *Miasma: Pollution and Purification in early Greek Religion* (Oxford, Oxford University Press: 1996).
Parker, R., 'War and Religion in Ancient Greece,' in K. Ulanowski (ed.), *The Religious Aspects of War in the Ancient Near East, Greece, and Rome* (Leiden, Brill: 2016), 123–132.
Patterson, J. R., 'Colonization and Historiography: The Roman Republic,' in G. Bradley and J.-P. Wilson (eds.), *Greek and Roman Colonization: Origins, Ideologies and Interactions* (Swansea, The Classical Press of Wales: 2006), 189–218.
Picard, C. G., *Catalogue du Musée Alaoui. Nouvelle Série (Collections Puniques), vol. 1* (Tunis, La Rapide: 1954).
Pilkington, N., 'An Archaeological History of Carthaginian Imperialism,' PhD Thesis (New York, Columbia University: 2013).
Pilkington, N., *The Carthaginian Empire: 550–202 BCE* (Lanham, Lexington Books: 2019).
Pisano, G., 'Jewellery,' in S. Moscati (ed.), *The Phoenicians* (London, I. B. Tauris: 1997), 418–44.
Prag, J., 'Tyrannizing Sicily: The Despots who Cried 'Carthage!',' in A. Turner, K. O. Chong-Gossard, and F. Vervaet (eds.), *Private and Public Lies: The Discourse of Despotism and Deceit in the Graeco-Roman World* (Leiden, Brill: 2010), 51–71.
Prag, J., 'Sicily and Sardinia-Corsica: The First Provinces,' in D. Hoyos 2013, 53–65.

Quesada Sanz, F., 'La evolución de la panoplia. Modos de combate y tácticas de los iberos,' in P. Moret and F. Quesada Sanz (eds.), *La guerra en el mundo ibérico y celtibérico (ss. VI-II a. de C.)* (Madrid, Casa de Velázquez: 2002), 35–64.

Quesada Sanz, F., 'De guerreros a soldados. El ejército de Aníbal como un ejército cartaginés atípico,' in B. Costa and J. Fernández (eds.), *Guerra y ejército en el mundo fenicio-púnico*. XIX Jornadas de Arqueología Fenicio-Púnica (Ibiza, Govern de Les Illes Balears – Conselleria d'Educació i Cultura: 2005), 129–61.

Quesada Sanz, F., 'En torno a las instituciones militares cartaginesas,' in B. Costa and J. H. Fernández (eds.), *Instituciones, demos y ejército en Cartago*. XXIII Jornadas de Arqueología Fenicio-Púnica (Ibiza, Govern de Les Illes Balears – Conselleria d'Educació i Cultura: 2009), 143–72.

Quinn, J., *In Search of the Phoenicians* (Princeton, Princeton University Press: 2018).

Rankov, B., 'A War of Phases: Strategies and Stalemates 264–241,' in D. Hoyos 2011a, 149–66.

Rawlings, L., 'Celts, Spaniards, and Samnites: Warriors in a Soldiers' War,' in T. Cornell (ed.), *The Second Punic War: A Reappraisal* (London, Institute of Classical Studies: 1996), 81–95.

Rawlings, L., 'Alternative agonies: hoplite martial and combat experiences beyond the phalanx,' in H. van Wees (ed.), *War and Violence in Ancient Greece* (Swansea, Classical Press of Wales: 2000), 233–259.

Rawlings, L., *The Ancient Greeks at War* (Manchester, Manchester University Press: 2007).

Rawlings, L., 'Hannibal the cannibal? Polybius on Barcid atrocities,' in *Cardiff Historical Papers* (2007/9), 1–30.

Rawlings, L., 'The Carthaginian Navy: Questions and Assumptions,' in G. Fagan and M. Trundle (eds.), *New Perspectives on Ancient Warfare* (Leiden, Brill: 2010), 253–87.

Rawlings, L., 'The War in Italy, 218–203,' in D. Hoyos 2011a, 299–319.

Rawlings, L., 'The Significance of Insignificant Engagements: Irregular Warfare during the Punic Wars,' in J. Armstrong (ed.), *Circum Mare: Themes in Ancient Warfare* (Leiden, Brill: 2016), 204–34.

Ray, F. E. Jr., *Greek and Macedonian Land Battles of the 4th Century B.C.: A History and Analysis of 187 Engagements* (Jefferson NC, McFarland & Company: 2012).

Rhodes, P. J., *A History of the Classical Greek World 478–323 BC* (Second Edition) (Oxford, Wiley-Blackwell: 2010).

Rhodes, P. J., and Osborne, R., *Greek Historical Inscriptions 404–323 BC* (Oxford, Oxford University Press: 2003).

Riera Vargas, R., 'Relaciones militares y diplomáticas de Cartago en el Mediterráneo Occidental (410–221 a.n.e.)' PhD Thesis (Barcelona, Universitat Autònoma de Barcelona: 2015).

Rodgers, W. L., *Greek and Roman Naval Warfare: A Study of Strategy, Tactics, and Ship Design from Salamis (480 B.C.) to Actium (31 B.C.)* (Annapolis, Naval Institute Press: 1937).

Roisman, J., *The Classical Art of Command: Eight Greek Generals Who Shaped the History of Warfare* (Oxford, Oxford University Press: 2017).

Roppa, A., 'Identifying Punic Sardinia: local communities and cultural identities,' in J. Crawley Quinn and N. C. Vella (eds.), *The Punic Mediterranean: Identities and Identification from Phoenician Settlement to Roman Rule* (Cambridge, Cambridge University Press: 2014), 257–81.

Rosenstein, N., 'Phalanges in Rome?' in G. G. Fagan and M. Trundle (eds.), *New Perspectives on Ancient Warfare* (Leiden, Brill: 2010), 289–303.
Sabin, P., *Lost Battles: Reconstructing the Great Clashes of the Ancient World* (London, Continuum: 2009).
Sacks, K. S., *Diodorus Siculus and the First Century* (Princeton, Princeton University Press: 1990).
Salimbeti, A., and D'Amato, R., *The Carthaginians 6th-2nd Century BC* (Oxford, Osprey: 2010).
Sanders, L. J., 'Diodorus Siculus and Dionysius I of Syracuse,' in *Historia* 30.4 (1981), 294–411.
Sanders, L. J., *Dionysius I of Syracuse and Greek Tyranny* (London, Croom Helm: 1987).
Sanders, L. J., 'Dionysius I of Syracuse and the Origins of the Ruler Cult in the Greek World,' in *Historia* 40.3 (1991), 275–287.
Scardigli, B., 'Early Relations between Rome and Carthage,' in D. Hoyos 2011a, 28–38.
Schellenberg, H. M., 'Diodor von Sizilien 14,42,1 und die Erfindung der Artillerie im Mittelmeerraum,' in *Frankfurter elektronische Rundschau zur Altertumskunde* 3 (2006), 14–23.
Schmitz, P. C., 'The Name "Agrigentum" in a Punic Inscription (CIS I 5510.10),' in *JNES* 53.1 (1994), 1–13.
Schubert, R., *Geschichte des Agathokles. Neu untersucht und nach den Quellen dargestellt* (Breslau/Wrocław, von Wilhelm Koebner: 1887).
Schwartz, A., *Reinstating the Hoplite: Arms, Armour and Phalanx Fighting in archaic and Classical Greece* (Stuttgart, Franz Steiner Verlag: 2009).
Schwartz, A., 'Large Weapons, Small Greeks: The Practical Limitations of Hoplite Weapons and Equipment,' in D. Kagan and G. F. Viggiano (eds.), *Men of Bronze: Hoplite Warfare in Ancient Greece* (Princeton, Princeton University Press: 2013), 157–175.
Scullard, H. H., 'Carthage and Rome,' in *CAH² VII.2* (1989), 486–569.
Serrati, J., 'Neptune's Altars: The Treaties Between Rome and Carthage (509–226 B.C.),' in *CQ* 56.1 (2006), 113–34.
Smith, R. B., *Rome and Carthage: The Punic Wars* (New York, Scribner's Sons: 1901).
Smith, R. B., *Carthage and the Carthaginians* (London, Longmans, Green and Co.: 1913).
Snodgrass, A., 'The Hoplite Reform and History,' in *JHS* 85 (1965), 110–122.
Snodgrass, A., 'Interaction by design: the Greek city state,' in C. Renfrew and J. F. Cherry (eds.), *Peer polity interaction and socio-political change* (Cambridge, Cambridge University Press: 1986), 47–58.
Snodgrass, A., 'The "hoplite reform" revisited,' in *DHA* 19 (1993), 47–61.
Spalinger, A., and Armstrong, J., (eds.) *Rituals of Triumph in the Mediterranean World* (Leiden, Brill: 2013).
Stary, P. F., 'Foreign Elements in Etruscan Arms and Armour: 8th to 3rd centuries B.C.' in *PPS* 45 (1979), 179–206.
Stary, P. F., *Zur Eisenzeitlichen Bewaffnung und Kampfesweise in Mittelitalien (ca. 9. bis 6. Jh. v. Chr.)* (Mainz, Philipp von Zabern: 1981).
Steinby, C., *The Roman Republican Navy: From the sixth century to 167 B.C.* (Helsinki, Societas Scientiarum Fennica: 2007).
Steinby, C., *Rome versus Carthage: The War at Sea* (Barnsley, Pen & Sword: 2014).

Stothers, R. B., 'Ancient scientific basis of the "Great Serpent" from historical evidence,' in *Isis* 95 (2004), 220–38.
Stylianou, P. J., *A Historical Commentary on Diodorus Siculus, Book 15* (Oxford, Oxford University Press: 1990).
Talbert, R. J. A., *Timoleon and the Revival of Greek Sicily 344–317 B.C.* (Cambridge, Cambridge University Press: 1974).
Terrenato, N., *The Early Roman Expansion into Italy: Elite Negotiation and Family Agendas* (Cambridge, Cambridge University Press: 2019).
Thorne, J., 'Rivals for Empire: Carthage, Macedon, the Seleucids,' in D. Hoyos 2013, 113–25.
Thrige, J. P., *Res Cyrenensium: a primordiis inde civitatis usqve ad ætatem, qva in provinciæ formam a romanis est redacta* (Copenhagen, Gyldendalske: 1828).
Tillyard, H. J. W., *Agathocles* (Cambridge, Cambridge University Press: 1908).
Trezigny, H., 'La topographie de Marseille antique de sa fondation (600 av. J.-C.) à l'époque romaine,' in *Méditerranée* 82.3 (1995), 41–52.
Tronchetti, C., 'Sardaigne,' in V. Krings (ed.), *La civilisation phénicienne et punique. Manuel de recherce* (Leiden, Brill: 1995), 712–42.
van Dommelen, P., *On colonial grounds. A Comparative study of colonialism and rural settlement in first millennium BC west central Sardinia* (Leiden, Faculty of Archaeology, Leiden University: 1998).
van Hooff, A. J. L., *From Autothanasia to Suicide: Self-killing in Classical Antiquity* (London, Routledge: 1990).
van Wees, H., 'The Development of the Hoplite Phalanx: Iconography and reality in the seventh century,' in H. van Wees (ed.), *War and Violence in Ancient Greece* (Swansea, Classical Press of Wales: 2000), 125–166.
van Wees, H., 'Conquerors and serfs: wars of conquest and forced labour in archaic Greece,' in N. Luraghi and S. E. Alcock (eds.), *Helots and Their Masters in Laconia and Messenia: Histories, Ideologies, Structures* (Washington D.C., Center for Hellenic Studies: 2003), 33–80.
van Wees, H., *Greek Warfare: Myths and Realities* (London, Bristol Classical Press: 2004).
van Wees, H., 'Defeat and destruction: the ethics of ancient Greek warfare,' in M. Linder and S. Tausend (eds.), *Boser Krieg: exzessive Gewalt in der Antiken Kriegsfuhrung und Strategien zu deren Vermeidung* (Graz, Grazer Universitatsverlag: 2011), 69–110.
Vaughn, P., 'The Identification and Retrieval of the Hoplite Battle-dead,' in V. D. Hanson (ed.), *Hoplites: The Classical Greek Battle Experience* (London, Routledge: 1991), 38–62.
Visonà, P., 'La numismatique – *partim* Occident,' in V. Krings (ed.), *La civilisation phénicienne et punique. Manuel de recherche* (Leiden, Brill: 1995), 166–181.
Visonà, P., 'Carthaginian coinage in perspective,' in *AJN* 10 (1998), 1–27.
von Arnim, H., 'Ineditum Vaticanum,' in *Hermes* 27.1 (1892), 118–130.
Walbank, F. W., 'Phalaris' Bull in Timaeus (Diod. Sic. xiii. 90. 4–7),' in *CR* 59.2 (1945), 39–42.
Walbank, F. W., *A Historical Commentary on Polybius*, vol. 1 (Oxford, Oxford University Press: 1957).
Walbank, F. W., *A Historical Commentary on Polybius*, vol. 2 (Oxford, Oxford University Press: 1967).

Wallinga, H. T., *The Boarding-Bridge of the Romans. Its Construction and its Function in the Naval Tactics of the First Punic War* (Groningue-Djakarta, J. B. Wolters: 1956).
Walsh, P. G., 'Massinissa,' in *JRS* 55.1/2 (1965), 149–60.
Warmington, B. H., *Carthage: A History* (New York, Barnes & Noble: 1993).
Wells, H. G., *The Outline of History: Being a Plain History of Life and Mankind. Revised and Brought up to the end of the Second World War by Raymond Postgate* (Garden City, Garden City Books: 1949).
Whatley, N., 'Reconstructing Marathon and Other Ancient Battles,' in *JHS* 84 (1964), 119–39.
Whitaker, J. I. S., *Motya: A Phoenician Colony in Sicily* (London, G. Bell and Sons: 1921).
Whitley, J., '*Hybris* and *Nike*: agency, victory and commemoration in Panhellenic sanctuaries,' in S. D. Lambert (ed.), *Sociable Man: Essays on Ancient Greek social behavior, in honour of Nick Fisher* (Swansea, Classical Press of Wales: 2011), 161–91.
Whittaker, C. R., 'Carthaginian Imperialism in the Fifth and Fourth Centuries,' in P. D. A. Garnsey and C. R. Whittaker (eds.), *Imperialism in the Ancient World* (Cambridge, Cambridge University Press: 1978), 59–90.

Index

Abilyx (traitor in the First War with Rome), 194
Adherbal (commander in the First War with Rome), 150–8
Adranum, 76
Adys, 139, 140, 141, 151
Aegates Islands, 151, 163
Aegean Greeks, 28, 32, 80
Aegean Sea, 27, 41–2, 74
Aelymas, 95, 97
Aemilius Paullus, Lucius, 197–200
Aemilius Paullus, Marcus, 144
Aeneas, 8
Aeneas Tacticus, 56
Aeschrion, 108
Aetna (mountain), 59
Aetna (settlement), 60, 113
Agathocles, 75, 82–97, 99–107, 109–13, 114, 115, 135, 138, 139, 141, 144, 167, 213, 227, 235, 247–8
Agriculture, 164, 195, 225, 226
Agyris, 68
Agyrium, 4, 68, 71
Akragas (Agrigentum), 3, 31–3, 36, 40–7, 49, 52, 55, 72, 82, 99, 107, 114–17, 124–9, 136, 139, 146, 214–15
Alalia, 7, 23–5
Alexander the Great, 69, 93, 104
Alexon (loyal mercenary), 150, 165
Alps, 181, 183, 184, 187, 208, 216, 248
Anapus (river), 98, 214
Anaxilaus, 31, 250
Antander (brother of Agathocles), 93–4, 112
Apes, 107
Apollo (temple of), 241
Appian (ancient historian), 6, 178, 181, 220, 222, 225, 227, 238, 242, 243, 248

Apulia, 196, 201
Archagathus (son of Agathocles), 91, 100, 106–109, 111, 113
Archimedes, 215
Aristocrats, aristocracy, 73, 77, 82, 83, 85, 92, 159, 251
Aristotle, 247
Asheri, David, 13
Aspis (settlement), 138, 139, 143, 144, 145, 235
Assorus (settlement), 58
Asylum, 106
Atarbas, 109
Athena, 91
Athens, Athenians, 42, 64, 74, 83, 102, 250
Atlantic Ocean, 1, 7, 209
Aufidus (river), 199
Aulus Atilius Caiatinus, 134, 146, 158
Aulus Postumius Albinus, 162
Autaritus, 167, 171–3, 175, 177

Baal Saphon, 249
Bagradas (river), 170, 171, 176, 218
Balearic Islands (and slingers), 7, 30, 42, 83, 85, 166, 180, 187, 190, 191, 213, 220
Boii, 186
Bomilcar (general against Agathocles), 90, 92, 104–105, 107
Bomilcar (admiral in the Second War with Rome), 214–15
Booty, plunder, 13, 14, 20, 21, 39, 42, 46, 77, 80, 82, 86, 89, 98, 102, 123, 138, 139, 144, 154, 160, 161, 182, 184, 193, 207, 213, 214, 216, 236, 243
Bostar (garrison commander at Saguntum), 194

Bostar (general in the First War with Rome), 139
Bruttium, Bruttians, 112
Byrsa, 21, 237, 241, 242, 243

Cabala (battle of), 70
Caere, 23, 69
Callipolis (settlement), 31
Calpurnius Piso, 234
Camarina, 31, 44, 45–9, 52, 86, 99, 134, 145
Campania, Campanians, 29, 30, 37, 38, 42, 43, 44, 45, 48, 59, 60, 76, 120, 121, 167, 175
Cannae, 6, 194, 198, 199, 201, 203, 216, 218, 248
Cape Bon (peninsula), 9, 10, 88, 89, 138, 145
Cape Lacinium, 184
Cape Pachynus, 157
Cape Pelorias, 57–8
Cape Tyndaris *see* Tyndaris
Captives, 36, 39, 49, 66, 79, 105, 138–9, 161, 163, 187, 207
see also Prisoners
Carthage, Carthaginians, *passim*
Carthalo (son of Mazeus), 13
Carthalo (commander in the First War with Rome), 146, 156–60
Casmene, 31
Catana, 76, 81, 86, 116, 160
Catapults, 53, 106, 118, 149, 157, 169, 229, 230, 231
Caven, Brian, 63, 70
Celtiberians, 193, 204, 209, 218
Celts, 77, 91, 109, 124, 150, 161, 166, 167, 171, 175, 189, 190, 191, 199, 200, 216, 220
see also Gauls
Censorinus, Lucius Marcius, 227, 229–32
Centuripa, 124
Cephaloedium, 57, 146
Chariots, 32, 55, 56, 76, 77, 78, 79, 90, 92, 101, 102, 110, 247, 248
Child sacrifice, 92
Cineas (Pyrrhus' deputy), 115

Cinyps (river), 15
Cisalpine Gaul, 216
Clastidium, 186
Claudius Pulcher, Publius, 154–6
Cnidus, Cnidians, 11–12
Coins (coinage), 41, 249
Corinth, Corinthians, 61, 62, 66, 75, 76, 77, 80
Cornelius Nepos, 75
Corsica, 11, 23, 24, 25, 33, 134, 193
Corvus, 132–3, 137, 145, 156
Council of 104, 237
Council of Elders, 131, 176, 207, 219
Crassus, Manius Otacilius, 123
Crassus, Titus Otacilius, 129
Crimisus (battle and river), 77–81, 246–7
Cronium (battle), 71
Crucifixion, 55, 105, 112, 128, 134, 150, 163, 175
Cumae, 160
Cyamosorus (battle), 120
Cyme, 5
Cyrene, 27, 81–2, 102–103

Daly, Gregory, 29
Daphnaeus, 44–5, 47
Deinarchus, 77
Deinocrates (Syracusan rebel), 83, 97, 99, 109, 112
Delphi, 15, 24, 25, 249
Demaretus, 77, 78
Demeter, 61, 66, 88
Demophilus, 83, 106
Deserters (desertion), 45, 48, 60, 64, 100, 111, 126, 130, 167, 170, 181, 186, 189, 197, 209, 214, 222, 235, 238, 242, 243
Dexippus, 43, 45
Dido (Elissa), 8
Diodorus Siculus, 4–5, 11, 12, 17, 28, 32–4, 35, 37–40, 42, 44, 49, 51, 57, 61, 63, 65–6, 68, 70–3, 77, 80, 82, 84, 85, 95–7, 103, 111, 114, 126–8, 155, 157, 163, 246–7
Diognetus, 94
Dion, 75

Dionysius I (Syracusan tyrant), 28, 46–9, 50–74, 81, 242, 246
Dionysius II (Syracusan tyrant), 73, 75–6
Disease *see* Plague
Docks (dockyards), 106, 169, 225–6, 235
Dorieus, 7, 9, 15–18, 117
Drepana, 11, 152, 154, 156–7, 159, 161–2
Duilius, Gaius, 131–4

Ebro (river), 181, 183–4, 192–4, 202, 205, 207
Echetla, 99
Eckstein, Arthur, 251
Eclipse (solar), 87
Ecnomus (battle and mountain), 83–4, 135–6, 151
Elephants, 117, 125–8, 139–43, 145, 148–9, 169–72, 174–5, 177, 179–82, 187–8, 203, 208, 210–16, 220–2, 228, 241
Elymians, 7, 11–12, 17–18, 36, 38, 49, 56, 69, 250
Engyum, 76
Enna, 99, 116, 134, 193, 214
Entella, 52, 55, 73, 76–7
Ephorus, 5, 55, 70
Epicydes, 213, 215
Epipolae, 98
Erymnon (Aetolian mercenary), 94
Eryx (city and mountain), 11, 15, 17, 56–7, 73, 117–18, 134, 157–8, 160–3
Eshmun (temple), 21
Eshmuniaton (Punic spy), 73
Etruria, Etruscans, 19, 23–5, 69, 83, 91, 109–10, 189–90
Eumachus, 107–108
Euryalus, 98, 214

Fabius Buteo, Numerius, 161
Fabius Maximus, Quintus, 191–8
Fabius Pictor, 5
Flaccus, Lucius Valerius, 129
Flaminius, Caius, 189–91, 194
Flaminius, Titus Quinctius, 141
Fleets, 23–6, 33, 38, 43–5, 47, 53, 56–7, 59–61, 63–5, 70–1, 73, 76, 80, 82–5, 87–90, 93–4, 98, 109, 111, 114–16, 118–19, 121–4, 128, 130–6, 138–9, 141, 144–9, 152, 154–8, 160, 162–4, 169, 183–4, 192–4, 202, 206–207, 214–15, 217–19, 225, 227, 229, 232, 236, 239–40, 244
Fortifications, 12, 19, 39–40, 43–4, 47–9, 57–8, 64, 94–5, 105–106, 118, 127, 146, 150–1, 175, 193, 205, 231, 233, 235, 237–8, 240
France, 22, 181
Freeman, E. A., 14, 16
Fulvius Paetinus Nobilior, Servius, 144

Gades, 209–10, 212
Gauls, 33, 129–30, 182–3, 185–9, 208 *see also* Celts
Gela (Geloans), 28, 31, 44, 46–9, 50, 52, 64, 68, 83–6, 99
Gelon (Syracusan tyrant), 18, 28, 31–6, 41, 46, 61
Geminus, Gnaeus Servilius, 191, 193, 198
Geminus, Publius Servilius, 147
Gerunium, 196–8
Gisco (son of Hanno the Great), 80–1
Gisco (third-century general), 166–8, 172–3, 175
Gold, 19, 35, 55, 67, 116, 128, 166, 179, 186, 243
Goldsworthy, Adrian, 122, 142, 212
Great Harbour (Syracuse), 61, 76, 83, 214–15
Greece, 1, 28, 32, 50, 62, 102, 103, 115, 141, 201
Greeks, 'half-breed', 166
Gulussa, 234–5, 240–1

Hadrumetum, 95–6, 219–20, 222, 231
Halaesa, 124
Halicyae, 52, 57, 117
Halycus (river), 81, 112
Hamilcar (general in 341–340), 77–80
Hamilcar (general in 261–255), 127–30, 133–9, 146, 150
Hamilcar ('son of Gisco'), 83–6, 90, 93–4, 96–9

Hamilcar Barca, 128, 158–63, 166–7, 170–7, 179, 212
Hamilcar the 'Magonid', 9, 20–1, 30–7, 41, 49, 245–6, 250
Hampsicora, 213
Hannibal (admiral under Adherbal), 150–3, 156
Hannibal (commander in the First War with Rome), 121, 124–6, 128, 131–4
Hannibal (general in 410–405), 29, 37–8, 40–4, 46, 250
Hannibal (general in the Truceless War), 174–6
Hannibal ('the Rhodian'), 153, 162
Hannibal Barca, 178–203, 208, 212–13, 215, 218–24, 244, 247–8, 251
Hanno (general against Aeschrion), 108
Hanno (general against Agathocles), 90–2
Hanno (general against Timoleon), 76
Hanno (son of Hamilcar the 'Magonid'), 36
Hanno the Great, 73, 80
Harbours, 51, 53, 58, 59, 60, 61, 62, 66, 76, 81, 82, 83, 87, 94, 99, 106, 109, 116, 122, 131, 138, 151–3, 155, 156, 162, 206, 213, 214, 215, 225, 227, 239, 241, 244
Hasdrubal (brother of Hannibal Barca), 180, 184, 192–3, 202–205, 207–209
Hasdrubal (general against Agathocles), 139
Hasdrubal (general in the First War with Rome), 145, 146, 148–9
Hasdrubal (general in the Third War with Rome), 226, 230, 231, 233, 234, 235, 236, 237, 238, 240, 241, 242–3, 244
Hasdrubal (general against Timoleon), 77–80
Hasdrubal (Hannibal Barca's quartermaster), 195, 197, 199–200
Hasdrubal (Magonid leader), 9, 14, 20–1
Hasdrubal (son-in-law of Hamilcar Barca), 179

Hasdrubal Gisco, 203–204, 205, 208, 209–12, 217–18
Hasdrubal the Bald, 213, 224
Hecatontapylus, 168
Heraclea Minoa, 107, 117, 125, 136, 145, 214
Heracleides (son of Agathocles), 103, 111
Heracleides (tyrant of Leontini), 116
Herbessus, 125–6
Hermocrates, 42, 46, 55
Herodotus, 7, 16–17, 22, 23, 24, 25, 30, 31, 32, 33, 34, 35
Hicetas (tyrant of Leontini), 76, 80
Hicetas (tyrant of Syracuse), 113, 114
Hiero (Deinomenid tyrant of Syracuse), 31, 36
Hiero II (king of Syracuse), 120–4, 126, 154, 164, 174, 184, 213
Himera, 9, 17, 30–6, 37, 40–2, 44, 49, 57, 59, 134, 245–6, 250
Himeras (river), 84, 85, 86, 215
Himilco (fifth-century general), 29, 42, 43, 44, 45, 46, 48, 49, 52, 53, 56–68, 246, 250
Himilco (general in the First War with Rome), 150–3, 156, 158
Himilco (general in the Second War with Rome), 202, 214–15
Himilco (third-century general), 108–109
Himilco Phameas, 231, 233–4
Hippocrates (Syracusan leader), 213–15
Hippocrates (tyrant of Gela), 31
Hipponium, 71–2
Hippou Acra, 106, 107, 160, 168, 169, 173, 235
Hoyos, Dexter, 17, 20, 135, 138, 145, 148, 159, 183, 223, 245
Hunger, 45, 126, 211, 228

Iberia, 22, 42, 51, 177, 179, 180, 182, 183, 192, 202, 203, 205, 209, 210, 223
see also Spain
Iberians, 21, 29, 30, 33, 37, 38, 39, 41, 42, 44, 48, 51, 66, 68, 77, 124, 166, 181, 182, 184, 191, 192, 194, 196, 199, 200, 202, 203, 204, 207, 210–12

Ibiza, 193
Ietae, 80
Ilergetes, 193
Ilipa, 210
Indemnity, 70, 72, 118, 164, 166, 223, 225
Inscriptions, 41, 46, 74
Italy, *passim*

Jewellery, 19
Justin (epitomizer of Pompeius Trogus), 6, 10, 13, 14, 15, 18, 19, 20, 22, 23, 24, 25, 26, 73, 87, 103, 105, 117, 245, 250

Kerkouane, 10
Kore (goddess), 61, 66, 88
Krings, Véronique, 15, 17, 25

Lancel, Serge, 20, 244
Latomiae, 88
Leonidas, 14–15
Leontini, 31, 49, 59, 76, 86, 99, 116, 214
Leptis, 176, 219, 231
Leptines (general under Agathocles), 106
Leptines (general under Dionysius), 55, 56, 59–60, 62, 64, 71, 76
Leuktra, Battle of, 74
Libya, Libyans, *passim*
Ligurians, 33, 77, 124, 166, 220
Lilybaeum, 11, 12, 38, 73, 77, 79, 80, 117–19, 125, 136, 145–54, 156, 157, 158, 159, 161, 162, 163, 165, 166, 184, 194, 213
Lipara, 12, 121, 131, 134, 135, 146, 147
Livy, 6, 23, 123, 178, 181, 183, 184, 186, 191, 192, 193, 198, 203, 204, 210, 217
Locri, 67
Longanus (river), 121
Longus, Tiberius Sempronius, 141, 186
Lutatius Catulus, Gaius, 162–3

Macae, 7
Mago (admiral in 279 BC), 115
Mago (general against Dionysius), 59, 60, 67–70
    Mago's son, 70–1
Mago (Magonid dynasty namesake), 7, 9, 14, 15, 20, 245, 246, 250
Mago Barca (brother of Hannibal), 187–9, 199, 203–10, 212, 215–16
Mamertines, 115, 120–1, 123, 129
Manlius Torquatus, Titus, 213
Manlius Vulso, Lucius, 136, 139, 149
Mantinea, Battle of, 74
Marcellus, M. Claudius, 214
Masinissa, 204, 210, 212, 216–22, 226, 228, 230–1, 234, 235
Massalia, 22–5, 182
Mathos, 167–8, 172, 174–7
Mazarus (river), 38
Megalepolis, 88–9
Megara (district of Carthage), 237
Megara Hyblaea, 99
Melqart, 13–14, 93
Menon (murder of Agathocles), 113
Mercenaries, 21, 29, 33, 37–9, 41–3, 45, 47, 48, 51, 55, 58–9, 61, 64, 66, 68–9, 76, 77, 78, 80–1, 83, 91, 101, 104, 109, 110, 113, 116, 120, 124, 126–7, 129–30, 140, 142, 143, 150, 153, 154, 159, 160–1, 163, 165, 166–77, 227, 244, 248, 249–50
Merchant ships, 51, 59, 65, 83, 87, 213, 225, 238, 239
Merchants, 159, 174, 245
Messana, 76, 115, 120–3, 125, 130, 131, 133, 136, 138, 145, 146, 154, 156
Metellus, Lucius Caecilius, 148–9, 158, 161
Miles, Richard, 7, 164
Minucius Rufus, Marcus, 191, 196–8
Motya, 4, 11–12, 14, 27, 33, 42, 45, 52–7, 59, 73, 74, 242
Mylae, 131, 134

Naravas, 172, 174, 177
Navy, 32, 44, 52, 56, 59, 73, 130, 136, 192, 201, 224, 227, 232
Naxos, 31
Neapolis (Nabeul), 95–7
Nepheris, 233, 240–1
New Carthage (Cartagena), 179, 180, 181, 184, 192–3, 202, 205–207

Nomands, North African, 101, 106, 226
  see also Zouphones
Numidia, Numidians, 9, 10, 126–7,
  140–1, 146, 151, 158–9, 170–2, 177

Olympieum (at Akragas), 36
Olympieum (at Syracuse), 98
Ophellas, 82, 102–104
Orissi, 179
Orosius, 13
Ortygia, 61, 66, 76, 114

Panormus, 27, 42, 45, 52, 56, 71, 117–18, 131, 134, 146–8, 156, 158, 160
Pasiphilus, 83
Paullus *see* Aemilius Paullus
Pausanias, 12, 17, 24, 25
Pay (for soldiers), 100, 112, 115, 160, 165, 166, 167, 168
Pentathlus, 11–13
Penteconters, 106
Persia, Persians, 1, 22, 23, 29, 33, 69, 74
Phalaris, 46
Phalarium, 84
Pharacidas, 62–4, 74
Philistus of Syracuse, 5
Phintias, 114
Phocaea, Phocaeans, 7, 22–5
Phoenicia, Phoenicians, 3, 7–8, 11–15, 17–21, 23, 25, 27, 29, 33, 35, 38, 42, 49, 51–5, 61–2, 67, 69, 72, 74, 82, 123, 179, 215, 246, 249, 250
Placentia, 186, 188, 208
Plague, disease, 44, 49, 50, 51, 61, 63, 64, 72, 126, 154, 215, 232
Plunder *see* Booty
Plutarch, 75, 77, 79, 80, 81, 117, 246, 247
Po (plain and river), 183, 185, 187, 189
Polyaenus, 34–5, 71, 73, 103
Polybius, 5–6, 118, 122, 125–31, 133, 135, 139–40, 142–4, 147–9, 151, 155, 157, 160–3, 170, 172, 176, 178, 179, 180–1, 183, 184, 187, 192–3, 198, 200, 210, 217, 220, 221, 225, 243, 248
Polyxenus, 61
Pompeius Trogus, 6, 15, 19, 20

Priests, 34, 162, 229
Prisoners, 41, 64, 79, 101, 105–106, 108, 110, 127, 138, 143–4, 156, 161, 164, 168, 171, 172, 173, 175, 183, 186, 191, 197, 200, 207, 210, 216, 217, 218, 222, 236, 237, 241
  see also Captives
Ptolemy I, 82
Ptolemy Ceraunus, 115
Pygmalion, 8
Pyrenees, 181–2, 208
Pyrgi, 69
Pyrrhus, 75, 114–19, 120, 131, 165

Quadriremes, 50, 113, 153
Qart-Hadasht, 8, 41
Quinqueremes, 50, 130, 133, 135–6, 162, 169, 184, 213, 227, 230

rab (Punic title), 9
Ramming (naval warfare), 53, 60, 65, 109, 132, 137, 239
Rams (battering), 38, 47, 53, 149–50, 154, 232, 240
Rams (warships), 24, 59, 132
Rebellions, revolts, 10, 14, 58–9, 61, 66–7, 68, 69, 72, 100, 159, 160, 168, 179, 193, 202, 203, 213, 214
Regulus, Gaius Atilius, 135
Regulus, Marcus Atilius (general in the First War with Rome), 136–7, 139–46, 148, 149, 165
Regulus, Marcus Atilius (general in the Second War with Rome), 198–9
Rhegium, 24, 31, 67, 115, 120, 249
Rhodes, 11
Rhone, 181–3
Rome, Romans, *passim*

Sacred Band, 77, 78, 79, 83, 85, 90–2, 246–7
Saguntum, 180, 194, 202, 203
Salamis, Battle of, 36
Samnium, Samnites, 91, 109, 195
Sardinia, Sardinians, 11, 13, 14, 19–22, 23, 24, 25, 29, 33, 67, 68, 72, 113,

134–5, 150, 172–4, 177, 179, 193, 213, 219, 224, 225, 250
Saw, The, 174–5
Scarabs, 29, 249
Scipio, Lucius Cornelius, 134
Scipio, Publius Cornelius (Africanus' father), 182, 185–6, 192, 194, 202–203, 204, 205
Scipio Aemilianus, 232–44
Scipio Africanus, Publius Cornelius, 5, 205–12, 216–22, 227
Scipio Asina, Gnaeus Cornelius, 130–1, 146–7
Scipio Calvus, Gnaeus Cornelius, 192–3, 194, 202–203, 205
Scipio Nasica, 229
Segesta, Segestans, 11, 12, 16–17, 30, 36–8, 52, 55, 112, 117, 124, 132, 133–4
Selinus, Selinuntes, 11, 12, 13, 18, 29–30, 32, 34, 37–8, 39–40, 41–2, 47, 49, 52, 72, 73, 107, 117
Senate, Roman, 129, 138–9, 144, 154, 196, 198, 226, 227, 230, 234
Ships *see* Merchant Ships, Navy, Pentecouters, Quadriremes, Quinqueremes
Sicani, Sicans, 40, 49, 56–7, 69, 77
Sicca, 166
Siceli, Sicels, 31, 40, 49, 55, 58–9, 66, 67, 68–9, 77
Sicily, Sicilians, *passim*
Siege towers, 38, 43–4, 52, 53–4, 105–106, 149, 153, 240
Silver, 19, 35, 55, 65, 66, 124, 179, 193, 243
Slaves, slavery, 31, 54, 58, 87, 93, 107, 112, 128, 146, 219, 230
Smallpox, 64
Solus, Soluntum, 14, 27, 52, 112, 146
Sosistratus, 114, 116–17
Spain, 2, 27, 179–80, 193–4, 201–12, 213, 215, 218, 224, 251
Sparta, Spartans, 7, 14–16, 18, 41, 43, 81, 141, 144, 165
Spendius, 167–8, 170–7

Steinby, Christa, 162
Storms, 32, 35, 78, 83, 118, 144, 145, 147, 151, 153, 156, 157, 213
Strabo, 30
Syracuse, Syracusans, *passim*
Syrtis Major, 9
Syrtis Minor, 9, 147

Tagus (river), 205, 208
Tarentum, 114, 144
Tarraco, 184, 192, 205, 206, 207, 210
Tartessus, 22
Tauromenium, 5, 59, 69, 86, 114, 116
Tax, 159
Temples, 11, 21, 35, 36, 39, 46, 55, 61, 67, 83, 87, 106, 231, 241, 242–3
Tarias (river), 114
Terillus, 30–2, 250
Thapsus, 96
Tharros, 19
Theodorus, 62–3
Thermae, 134, 147–8
Theron, 31, 33, 36
Theveste, 158
Thoenon, 114, 116
Thucydides, 23–5
Thurii, 54
Ticinus, Battle of, 185–6, 192
Tillyard, H. J. W., 86, 91, 95, 96, 100, 103
Timaeus of Tauromenium, 5, 55, 62
Timoleon, 75–81
Tin, 22
Tocae, 107
Torture, 41, 99, 105, 112, 144, 173, 175, 176, 237
Trade, traders, 1, 8, 11, 12, 18, 22, 230, 238
Trasimene, Battle of, 190–1, 194, 199
Trebia, Battle of, 186–7, 189
Tribute, 9, 10, 20, 49, 72, 228
Triremes, 41, 42, 43, 52, 53, 59, 66, 73, 76, 83, 99, 130, 133, 169, 222, 239, 246
Truceless War, 20, 166–77, 179

Tunis, 66, 89, 91–7, 108–109, 140–1, 145, 165, 167, 169, 171–3, 175, 193, 219, 232, 246–7
Tyndarion, 114, 116
Tyndaris, 135, 136, 146
Tyre, 8, 13, 14, 20, 93

Uthina, 139
Utica, 105–106, 168–71, 173–4, 213, 216–19, 227, 231, 235–6

Valerius Maximus, Manius, 123–4
Veii, 144
Volcae, 182
Vulso, Lucius Manlius, 136, 149

War indemnity *see* Indemnity
Water, lack of, 70, 102, 108, 139
Weapons, development of, 50, 53–4
Women, 24, 38, 39, 41, 47, 54, 58, 231, 242

Xanthippus, 141–5, 165, 247
Xenodicus, 99, 106
Xerxes, 32

Zama, Battle of, 220–2, 247
Zancle, 31
Zarzas, 174–5
Zonaras, 122, 126–7, 129, 158, 160–1
Zouphones, 101–102